C.A.P.E.S. / Agrégation
ANGLAIS

Le Crime organisé à la ville et à l'écran
(États-Unis, 1929-1951)

ouvrage dirigé par
Pierre Lagayette et Dominique Sipière

Gregory D. Black
Director of American Studies at the University of Missouri-Kansas

Jean-Eric Branaa
Maître de conférences à l'université René Descartes (Paris V)

Françoise Clary
Agrégée d'Anglais, Docteur en Littérature américaine, Professeur à l'université de Rouen

John Dean
Maître de conférences à l'université de Versailles, spécialiste de civilisation américaine contemporaine

Pierre Floquet
Responsable du département de langues, ENSEIRB, université de Bordeaux I

Divina Frau-Meigs
Docteur ès Lettres et Professeur en études américaines à l'université d'Orléans, spécialiste en sociologie des médias

Matthew Guillen
Maître de conférences à l'université de Nantes, Juris Doctor – Faculté de droit, Columbia University, admis au barreau de l'Etat de New York

Armand Hage
Professeur à l'université de la Nouvelle-Calédonie

Reynold Humphries
Agrégé d'anglais et Professeur d'Etudes Cinématographiques à l'université Charles de Gaulle-Lille III

Pierre Lagayette
Professeur à l'Université de Paris IV-Sorbonne, Directeur du Centre de recherches sur « L'Ouest américain et l'Asie/Pacifique anglophone »

Gilles Menegaldo
Agrégé d'anglais et Docteur ès Lettres, Professeur à l'université de Poitiers, vice-président de la SERCIA

Marie-Christine Michaud
Maître de conférences à l'université Bretagne-Sud de Lorient, spécialiste de la communauté italo-américaine

Eithne O'Neill
Enseignante à l'université de Paris XIII

Daniel Peltzman
Maître de conférences à l'université Paris X-Nanterre

Zeenat Saleh
Maître de conférences d'anglais à l'université de Franche-Comté Besançon

Dominique Sipière
Agrégé d'anglais et Docteur ès Lettres HDR, Professeur des Universités (Université du Littoral) et Président de la SERCIA (Société d'études et de recherche sur le cinéma anglophone)

Ruth Vasey
Lecturer in Screen Studies at Flinders Université, South Australia

ISBN 2-7298-0750-0

© Ellipses Édition Marketing S.A., 2001
32, rue Bargue 75740 Paris cedex 15

Le Code de la propriété intellectuelle n'autorisant, aux termes de l'article L.122-5.2° et 3°a), d'une part, que les «copies ou reproductions strictement réservées à l'usage privé du copiste et non destinées à une utilisation collective», et d'autre part, que les analyses et les courtes citations dans un but d'exemple et d'illustration, « toute représentation ou reproduction intégrale ou partielle faite sans le consentement de l'auteur ou de ses ayants droit ou ayants cause est illicite » (Art. L.122-4).
Cette représentation ou reproduction, par quelque procédé que ce soit constituerait une contrefaçon sanctionnée par les articles L. 335-2 et suivants du Code de la propriété intellectuelle.

www.editions-ellipses.com

Table des matières

Pierre Lagayette et Dominique Sipière	Avant-propos	4

1re partie : Civilisation

Pierre Lagayette	A propos du crime organisé	6
Armand Hage	Prologue: Organized Crime During Prohibition	15
Gregory D. Black	Mirror of Violence: the Social Dimension of Gangster Movies	29
Marie-Christine Michaud	De la mafia, ou d'un business à l'américaine	35
Jean-Eric Branaa	The regulation of morals in the United States – a study of State and federal controls of organized crime	45
Ruth Vasey	Well-educated, well-dressed and polite? The changing face of the Hollywood gangster in the 1930s	61
Daniel Peltzman	Le gangstérisme des années trente et la censure à Hollywood	69
Matthew Guillen	Juvenile Crime and the Kefauver Hearings	76
Françoise Clary	Le crime organisé dans le ghetto afro-américain (1920-1940)	88

2e partie : Cinéma

Dominique Sipière	Introduction	98
John Dean	American Gangsters in Fact and on Film : the Social Construction of an American Popular Hero	115
Dominique Sipière	The Classic Three, *Little Caesar, Public Enemy* et *Scarface*	138
Matthew Guillen	"Sanitizing" *Little Caesar* & Co	153
Divina Frau-Meigs	Cultivating Crime and Criminalizing Culture: Screening Violence From the Depression to the Cold War	164
Eithne O'Neill	Clans in *Scarface* and *The Maltese Falcon*. Screening the female	180
Pierre Floquet	*The Enforcer, La Femme à abattre* : un film, des regards	191
Gilles Menegaldo	*Key Largo* : le gangster au miroir du cinéma, réflexivité et mélange des genres	201
Reynold Humphries	"Investigators, undercover men and the F.B.I.: from gangsterism to Communism and back again"	212
Zeenat Saleh	Sergio Leone's *Once Upon a Time in America* looks back at the roaring twenties	225

Bibliographie sur le crime à l'écran ... 237

Les auteurs ... 239

Avant-propos

Par Pierre Lagayette et Dominique Sipière

Comme beaucoup de questions qui mêlent l'art à son objet, celle-ci sur « Le crime organisé à la ville et à l'écran » peut paraître hybride et inconsistante. L'historien n'y trouvera peut-être pas son compte parce qu'il s'agit d'un phénomène limité dans le temps et qui, par nature, a gardé un côté malsain ou ancillaire. L'érudit du cinéma, à l'inverse du spectateur moyen, regrettera sans doute que l'on se penche principalement sur le personnage emblématique du gangster en abandonnant, faute de moyens, l'analyse filmique, la problématique du genre, les qualités esthétiques et autres aspects séduisants de l'art cinématographique. La frustration, toutefois, n'empêche nullement la fascination.

Car cette question a l'immense privilège de détourner les regards convenus. Elle s'attache à l'envers des choses de la vie américaine : l'envers de la prospérité et du *business* des années vingt, l'envers de la Grande crise de 1929, l'envers du New Deal et celui de l'après-guerre de Truman ou d'Eisenhower. Avec le crime organisé, on effectue une visite guidée de l'« autre Amérique », celle que les Américains eux-mêmes, à force de vouloir l'ignorer, ont failli laisser ronger la République idéale. La fausse noblesse de la Prohibition, les fausses vertus des commissions sénatoriales, représentent une tentative désespérée de redonner quelque lustre, en le retournant, à un vêtement dont on ne voyait plus que la doublure lépreuse et déchirée. Caricature du pouvoir absolu, de l'ordre absolu et de la liberté absolue, le gangstérisme présentait aux citoyens américains, et présente à l'observateur d'aujourd'hui l'image d'une pathologie létale, d'un poison dont il fallait absolument découvrir l'antidote.

L'art, comme toujours le meilleur des antidotes, a réussi là où les bulldozers de l'idéologie démocratique avaient échoué : emprisonner les nuisibles dans une histoire, les écraser implacablement sur une toile d'argent minuscule, où leurs gesticulations ne menacent plus personne. Après tout, si le crime organisé fut un échec social et politique, sa vision cinématographique n'en fut-elle pas le plus grand succès ?

Les films examinés ici, qui couvrent plus de vingt ans, sont doublement remarquables : à la fois parce qu'ils permettent d'aborder la société américaine de l'intérieur (Warshow insiste : « Il n'y a pour ainsi dire rien que nous comprenions mieux ou à quoi nous réagis-sions plus spontanément ou plus intelligemment ») et parce qu'ils constituent, à côté du western et des *musicals*, une création artistique originale dans un pays et dans une époque. Ils naissent de la rencontre de la technologie du parlant avec l'intensité et la rapidité des images du cinéma et avec la réalité du crime, déjà diffractée par la presse de l'époque. Dans cet univers, tout paraît suivre une logique binaire associée au noir et blanc des Bons et des Méchants. Pourtant, ces lignes fermement tracées sont sans cesse franchies dans des jeux de symétries et de miroirs à l'intérieur comme à l'extérieur des films. On en trouvera un exemple dans cet ouvrage : certains auteurs insistent sur la noirceur, le désespoir et la cruauté, là où d'autres expriment une sorte de jubilation devant la vitalité exacerbée des gangsters. Bref, si cet univers est manichéen, on se gardera de le croire sim-pliste, car il ne faut pas confondre la « psychologie » dessinée au fusil-mitrailleur des Rico, Tom et Tony Camonte avec la complexité des *effets* qu'ils produisent sur les spectateurs.

James Cagney – dans son duo en *noir et blanc* avec Bogart sur la couverture – résume assez bien les ambiguïtés entre un personnage et la persona de l'acteur, entre la violence inexcusable (avec les femmes...) et la séduction sur le public de l'époque. Les pistes de travail sont alors très nombreuses : histoire du cinéma, des studios et des genres ; dynamique – ou jeu du chat avec la souris ? – des rapports entre la censure et les cinéastes ; évolution des représentations du crime et de son image dans le public ; contrepoint techniciste et urbain ancré dans le présent, face aux mythes américains originels ; irruption du point de vue des groupes ethniques dans la production de masse, évidemment liée aux possibilités du cinéma parlant, etc. Mais il conviendra de se souvenir que ce groupe compact de films, clairement identifiables, inclut aussi quelques chefs-d'œuvre individuels conçus parfois à contre-courant, parfois comme des variations ou des commentaires sur des genres dominants.

1re partie
Civilisation

À propos du crime organisé
Par Pierre Lagayette

Le phénomène

En abordant la question du « crime organisé » aux Etats-Unis, quelle que soit la période d'observation, il est conseillé de s'arrêter un instant aux deux notions évidentes de criminalité et d'organisation, dont les ramifications ouvrent des perspectives vertigineuses dans la société et la culture américaines.

La criminalité, entendue comme rupture de légalité (ou « l'égalité ») et comme désordre engendrant les peurs sociales les plus radicales, n'est pas une innovation de l'entre-deux-guerres, même si un déferlement visible de violences inhabituelles (hors la guerre outre-mer) marque les années 1930-1950. Si l'on ne retient que les chiffres bruts des homicides volontaires, on s'aperçoit d'une envolée saisissante à partir de 1930[1] qui atteint plus d'un quart du total de la précédente décennie. Comme on pouvait s'y attendre, la guerre permettra d'infléchir la tendance, même si une recrudescence se fait jour après 1946. Mais la guerre marque un désordre social de telle ampleur qu'il en occulte tous les autres. Une autre caractéristique prévisible, que confirment les statistiques des arrestations et des condamnations entre 1930 et 1950, est la prédominance d'une criminalité blanche, ce qui, bien entendu, bouscule les modèles conventionnels de stigmatisation raciste et contraint la majorité des citoyens à rechercher la cause du mal parmi eux, à une sorte d'auto incrimination qui confine à la castration idéologique. La « reprise en mains » dogmatique des années cinquante, accomplie par le biais des vertueuses « commissions » Fulbright, Kefauver ou McCarthy, n'est rien moins que la tentative de restitution à l'Amérique, militairement triomphante, de sa virilité démocratique.

D'autant que la flambée de criminalité entre les guerres pose avec acuité le problème de l'ennemi intérieur, un ennemi dont la visibilité insuffisante (pas de marquage ethnique probant) exige de reconsidérer les moyens de défense d'une société majoritairement WASP. La chasse au coupable n'est donc pas seulement une œuvre de justice, elle est aussi une entreprise de ravalement socio-politique. On ne sera donc pas surpris de retrouver, à la base de l'argumentation sécuritaire des gouvernants, entre la crise de 1929 et celle de Corée, l'obsession du complot, de la conspiration et de leur valet, la corruption. Le vrai danger est celui d'une subversion organisée et subreptice de l'appareil démocratique et de la paix sociale. La vraie solution, empruntée à une médecine communautaire d'un autre âge, est de séparer l'ivraie du bon grain, de restaurer la morale collective en désignant clairement ceux qui ont entrepris de la saper en pervertissant certains de ses principes.

---

1. 1920-1929 : 81 451 homicides volontaires ; 1930-1939 : 103 917 homicides volontaires (+27,6%) ; 1940-1949 : 79 620 homicides volontaires (mais seulement 28 935 durant les années de guerre mondiale 1941-1945). Source : *Historical Statistics of the United States*, Part 1 (Washington, D.C. : US Department of Commerce, 1975), Series H 971-986.

Car, et ce n'est pas le moindre des paradoxes du « crime organisé » aux Etats-Unis, il s'agit d'un phénomène presque entièrement endogène, un détournement inattendu des évangiles de richesse auxquels la nation devait ses triomphes économiques (aussi bien, soyons justes, que ses tourments sociaux) au XIXe siècle. La liberté, le succès, la fortune, l'autodidactisme, la promesse du bonheur, l'individualisme, le laissez-faire, le progrès personnel, le « rêve » américain – quel que soit l'ordre dans lequel on feuillette le lexique de la république idéale, on retrouve des idées, érigées en règles dont on peut, si l'occasion se présente ou si on la provoque, dénaturer l'essence. Il en faut peu pour dérégler l'ordre démocratique justement parce qu'il refuse de soumettre l'individu à une règle absolue, ou autocratique. Tocqueville avait noté que l'égalité isolait l'individu et l'affaiblissait par la solitude : à cet écueil il ne voyait qu'une solution associative : « I think that private citizens, by combining together, may constitute bodies of great wealth, influence, and strength, corresponding to the persons of an aristocracy » (Tocqueville, 308). Un demi-siècle plus tard, les grands industriels américains reconstituaient, selon ce modèle, une sorte d'aristocratie économique, rendue possible par les libertés inscrites dans la doctrine démocratique. Un demi-siècle après les industriels, les alliances idéalisées par Tocqueville étaient devenues des associations de malfaiteurs.

La philosophie du succès autorise, aux Etats-Unis, des logiques contradictoires, dont deux des aspects les plus évidents sont la mobilité sociale et la responsabilité morale. On y retrouve, sans trop creuser, les deux pôles de la pensée politique américaine : l'élitisme et l'égalitarisme. Déjà les aphorismes de Franklin, du *Poor Richard's Almanac*, où un Richard appelé « pauvre » (il y a pourtant « rich » dans Richard) tentait de convaincre le peuple que le bonheur passait par un bon sens terrien sans failles, suggéraient qu'il y avait écart entre les ambitions personnelles et leur réalisation que seule la Raison pouvait combler, avec le secours du travail, de la frugalité, de la tempérance et de l'honnêteté. Richard détestait la pauvreté parce qu'elle était avilissante (« 'Tis hard for an empty Bag to stand upright ») mais suggérait aussi, en creux, que l'enrichissement redonnait à l'homme une sorte de noblesse naturelle. Cette conception d'une vie vertueuse et gratifiante (fortement influencée par la morale protestante en dépit de son caractère séculier) se retrouve dans la vision politique et sociale, proposée par Jefferson, d'une néo-aristocratie américaine fondée non sur l'hérédité mais sur le mérite. Et la révolution industrielle suscite une nouvelle philosophie de la richesse et du succès, toujours fondée sur les traditionnelles qualités de l'Américain – travail, intégrité, frugalité, tempérance – mais sur laquelle viennent se greffer de nouveaux facteurs tels que concurrence, efficacité, pouvoir, supériorité, bien-être matériel. La rhétorique du succès continue de se vêtir, pour un temps, de probité : Andrew Carnegie prêche la respectabilité auprès des élèves d'une école de commerce de Pittsburgh en 1885 : « You all know that there is no genuine, praiseworthy success in life if you are not honest, truthful, fair-dealing » (Cawelti, 170). Mais il s'attache aussi, par ailleurs, à rappeler l'existence d'une élite sociale, dont le pouvoir économique – et bientôt politique – est issu du libre exercice de l'individualisme le plus sauvage. Les magnats du rail, du pétrole ou de la finance avaient conscience d'avoir fait plus pour la nation en produisant des biens matériels que tous les prédicateurs ou philosophes réunis, dans l'ordre spirituel. La criminalité ? C'est bien sûr la pauvreté qui l'alimentait et seul l'accroissement général des richesses pourrait en venir à bout. En réalité, les grands industriels de l'époque créèrent un nouveau type de criminalité qui n'avait plus rien à voir avec la pauvreté ; de cette élite de détrousseurs richissimes (les fameux « Robber Barons ») est issu un système qui « organise » l'accès aux richesses dans des conditions de concurrence absolue, mais qui n'« organise » absolument pas la mobilité sociale. La société américaine demeure irrémédiablement stratifiée ; pire, on voit se rétablir une espèce de féodalité économique et politique, où les rôles sont prédéfinis, et les chances d'ascension de plus en plus aléatoires. Trente ans plus tard, les choses ont si peu évolué que le sociologue P. Sorokin écrit, dans son ouvrage *Social Mobility* (1927) :

> In theory, in the United States of America, every citizen may become the President of the United States. In fact, 99.9 per cent of the citizens have as little chance of doing it as 99.9 per cent of the subjects of a monarchy have of becoming a monarch. (Sorokin, 154)

Le crime d'organisation

Une telle rigidité s'explique, en grande partie, par la mise en place de structures, à la fois très complexes et très résistantes, dans tous les compartiments de la vie publique. Vers la fin du XIXe siècle, le parti politique acquiert, avec une influence grandissante, un pouvoir d'organisation sans précédent. Chez les Républicains, en particulier, sous la houlette des « bosses » locaux, la hiérarchisation et la répartition des tâches paraissent singer l'univers industriel : « We are told the Republican party is a machine, » s'exclame un jour Roscoe Conkling, l'équivalent Républicain du Démocrate « Boss » Tweed à New York, « Yes. A government is a machine ; a church is a machine ; an army is a machine... the common school system of the State of New York is a machine ; a political party is a machine. » (Cité dans Hofstadter, 224). A cette liste, il aurait pu ajouter l'entreprise et le gang sans écarteler le sens du mot « machine ». L'analogie mécanique démontre, certes, un besoin d'organiser l'activité, qu'elle soit économique ou politique, licite ou illicite, pour le bien individuel ou collectif, mais elle suggère surtout la présence d'un moteur, c'est-à-dire d'une autorité indispensable à laquelle sont soumis les mouvements du mécanisme. En exigeant une instance de décision et de pouvoir, l'« organisation » – l'entreprise capitaliste, aussi bien que le parti politique ou l'association de criminels (les mauvaises langues dénient toute distinction entre les trois) – est fondamentalement inégalitaire. L'ordre démocratique lui-même, en Occident, a été et demeure générateur d'élites ou d'oligarchies. La nécessité d'organisation ouvre donc à l'industriel, à l'homme politique, et au gangster, un espace de rencontre, voire de collusion, où l'enchevêtrement des intérêts et des initiatives tend à effacer les différences de comportement et à aiguiser l'appétit de pouvoir.

A cet égard, le gangstérisme de l'entre-deux-guerres emprunte assez clairement aux structures et aux pratiques de l'industrie ou de la politique. Il y a là davantage qu'une inspiration ; c'est un véritable plagiat. Le vocabulaire du crime offre un éventail de termes dont la référentialité est elle-même corrompue, société, corporation, cartel, syndicat, ou des désignations spécifiques comme « Murder Inc. ». De même la structuration des diverses « familles » siciliennes ou italiennes au début des années trente rappelle le système féodal et la tentative de les rassembler peut se concevoir comme un exercice de « confédération », où l'expérience politique ou diplomatique des chefs (notamment Lucky Luciano) joue un rôle primordial. Quelle que soit la façon dont on aborde la question de la criminalité à cette époque, il faut tenir compte du caractère extrêmement structuré, et complexe, des organisations criminelles, dont la puissance est précisément fondée sur un respect sans faille de la hiérarchie et de modes de fonctionnement bien définis[1]. Donald R. Cressey, dans son excellent ouvrage *Theft of the Nation, The Structure and Operations of Organized Crime in America*, signale la difference cruciale entre crime ordinaire et crime organisé, le second offrant « a specialized set of positions rationally developed with an eye to efficiency and continuing operations. » (Cressey, 31). Cette description pourrait aisément s'appliquer aux activités d'une société manufacturière ou commerciale. Comme pourraient s'appliquer sans mal les lois du marché, la concurrence sauvage et la monopolisation.

Dans ces conditions, on comprend que toute entreprise de production d'alcool durant la Prohibition ait répondu à deux exigences, celle d'obéir aux lois de l'économie et celle de désobéir aux lois de la nation. Pour ce qui est des nécessités économiques, l'accroissement de la demande d'alcool tout au long des années 1920 imposa aux malfaiteurs de pratiquer l'intégration verticale bien connue du capitaliste, et de sécuriser leurs activités :

> *A successful bootlegging enterprise requires sources of supply, a means of collection – ships, offloading boats, landing sites, truck, drivers, guards, warehouses – and bars, clubs, restaurants, speakeasies, and other means of distribution. In addition, bribes have to be paid, lawyers must be on call, dummy corporations established to launder funds, and accountants and bookkeepers hired to maintain accounts and disbursements* (Lupsha, 47)

Quant au non-respect des lois, il est vrai que le fonctionnement des institutions, malgré les efforts des réformistes, n'avait pas empêché la corruption d'envahir les partis politiques ou les gouvernements locaux. Déjà en 1903, dans son implacable étude du fonctionnement des grandes villes du pays, *The Shame of the Cities*, Lincoln Steffens avait noté la dégénérescence du monde politique américain : « The great truth I tried to make plain », affirmait-il, « was... that bribery is no ordinary felony, but

---

1. Nathan Rosenberg et L.E. Birdzell relèvent l'omniprésence de l'« organisation » dans les procédures économiques des pays industrialisés, y compris les marchés : "In economics, it has become orthodox to hold that all economic activity is organized. Thus people who buy and sell in markets are collectively choosing goals, dividing the work of attaining them among large numbers of people and rewarding those who help. Even an apparently simple economic task like supplying eggs to the consumer's breakfast table involves a network of thousands of individuals scattered through many countries... The task could not be performed as reliably as it is in capitalist economies were not markets a powerful organizing force, capable of inducing large numbers of people to form shared goals, dividing the work of achieving the goals among many specialists, and supplying the rewards and incentives needed to get the work done." (*How the West Grew Rich*, ix)

treason, that the corruption which breaks out here and there and now and then is not an occasional offense, but a common practice, and that the effect of it is literally to change the form of our government from one that is representative of the people to an oligarchy, representative of special interests. » (Steffens, 17)

Les années passent sans que la situation change radicalement. L'après-guerre voit le retour non seulement de la « normale » chère à Warren Harding, mais à une prospérité qui ranime les aspirations matérielles du peuple et à des valeurs individualistes qui s'interprètent sans mal comme une nouvelle permissivité. Celle-ci s'exprime aussi bien à travers un relâchement des mœurs qu'à travers la course au profit qui mènera promptement les Etats-Unis à la ruine économique. Dans un environnement où la richesse nationale ne cesse de s'accroître (le PNB des Etats-Unis augmente de 40% entre 1920 et 1929), où l'on exalte l'individu et l'on affiche, comme le fait Hoover, une volonté d'alléger le contrôle de l'Etat sur l'activité économique, chacun se prend à rêver de fortune et cherche à créer les conditions de sa propre ascension.

La réalité sociale, cependant, est tout autre : les frustrations montent en proportion des espoirs déçus ou des opportunités disparues. La stratification sociale est inoxydable et le culte du succès offre une dissonance parfaite avec la condition ouvrière, la vie urbaine, et même la réalité quotidienne d'une classe moyenne qui s'accroît sans vraiment s'enrichir. Theodore Dreiser en fait une peinture au vitriol, en plein cœur de la décennie, dans *An American Tragedy* (1925), tragédie ordinaire d'un fils de pasteur qui glisse vers le crime parce qu'il a cru un instant à la rhétorique du succès et à l'accomplissement du « rêve américain ». Avec le naufrage de Clyde Griffith, c'est une certaine vision de l'Amérique sublime qui s'abîme irrémédiablement.

Contextualiser l'histoire des gangsters américains au point d'en faire le produit des circonstances ou d'un conditionnement social particulier serait exagéré. Néanmoins le lien entre la politique, les affaires et le crime saute aux yeux et ce dernier offre la caricature d'un système où la mobilité sociale et l'accès aux richesses ne peuvent s'accomplir que par la violence. Capone, Schultz, Luciano, Lansky, Siegel et les autres se voient, et se présentent comme des *businessmen*, organisateurs méticuleux et fins stratèges qui font fortune comme naguère les maîtres des grands trusts et, comme eux, tentent de contourner les lois. Le mimétisme est saisissant : l'uniforme du gangster puissant est celui des grands barons d'industrie. Avant d'être un signe d'aisance, il est un indice de respectabilité et de pouvoir. Pourtant, dans leurs pratiques, les gangs forcent les traits les plus noirs de l'entreprise capitaliste : leur interprétation de ses principes est d'une littéralité funeste. Les pots-de-vin et la subornation règlent les problèmes de capital ou de réglementation, l'assassinat ceux de la concurrence. Le monopole est à ce prix. Il n'est donc pas incongru de concevoir le crime organisé comme un paroxysme du capitalisme sauvage. Et l'on observera avec intérêt que le même Estes Kefauver qui fait adopter, en janvier 1950 la résolution 202 au Sénat pour organiser l'enquête sur les paris et le racket prépare en même temps la loi anti-trust la plus vigoureuse jamais votée depuis le Clayton Act de 1914, promulguée en décembre 1950 sous le nom de Celler-Kefauver Act[1].

Le territoire du crime

Pour s'organiser, le crime a besoin d'espace et toute explication du gangstérisme passe aussi par une attention particulière à la « géographie » du phénomène. Dès la fin de la guerre, une première observation s'impose : l'Amérique rurale a vécu, l'Amérique urbaine a vaincu. Pour la première fois, au recensement de 1920, la population des villes dépasse celle des campagnes et en 1950 il y a aux Etats-Unis deux fois plus de citadins que de ruraux. Le territoire du crime recouvre donc essentiellement les zones traditionnelles de forte activité économique, sociale ou politique, New York, Philadelphie, Chicago, Detroit ou Cleveland. La Prohibition n'est pas étrangère, bien sûr, à ce déploiement géographique : dès 1916 le Michigan avait mis l'alcool hors la loi et l'artisanat criminel local s'était empressé de fournir les classes laborieuses en tord-boyaux et bières de toutes sortes, jusqu'à ce que des bandes mieux organisées (notamment des immigrants siciliens, les Licavoli, Bommarito, Lucido et autres Zerilli) viennent mettre bon ordre dans cet amateurisme lucratif. Le fameux « Purple Gang » de Detroit, en particulier, élargit les activités du *bootlegging* au Canada, faisant de la contrebande internationale un des piliers de sa réussite[2]. Capone fera de même pour son propre compte, aussi bien que Dion O'Banion et Georges « Bugs » Moran à la tête des Irlandais de Chicago. Le caractère emblématique de la criminalité dans cette dernière ville, la focalisation sur la guerre des gangs ou la forte personnalité de certains *mobsters* comme Al Capone, fait souvent oublier la présence du crime organisé dans d'autres régions des Etats-Unis, Missouri, Georgie, Louisiane, Californie, Arizona, Nevada, ou d'autres villes, Buffalo, Washington, D.C., New Orleans, St Louis, Tampa, Kansas City, Denver, Los Angeles, pour ne citer que les plus célèbres.

L'exemple de ces villes ne sert qu'à souligner le caractère local du développement de la criminalité dans un pays où précisément le contrôle de légalité ne s'exerce pas suffisamment au plan national. Le FBI, créé en 1908, ne peut, même sous l'autorité de l'implacable J. Edgar Hoover, se substituer à une législation fédérale déficiente. Or, et c'est un aspect significatif de la « géographie du crime organisé », les autorités régionales et locales sont, depuis longtemps, exposées à la corruption et leur vénalité avérée assure l'impunité aux malfaiteurs de tout poil. La structure fédérale elle-même, en assurant l'autonomie législative et policière des Etats, favorise la tâche des corrupteurs, d'autant que le pouvoir politique décentralisé subordonne la loi et l'ordre à des préoccupations électoralistes. Les seules armes fédérales efficaces sont le contrôle du commerce inter-étatique et la législation fiscale : et l'on sait que ce sont les agents du Trésor, et non les policiers, qui feront « tomber » Capone en octobre 1931.

---

1. Cette loi était particulièrement attentive aux problèmes de monopole et de concurrence déloyale !
2. Durant la période de Prohibition, 80 % du whisky produit au Canada fut exporté (plutôt illégalement) vers les Etats-Unis.

Parmi les exemples de gangstérisme local, le cas de Kansas City est révélateur : longtemps plaque tournante ferroviaire, marché de bétail florissant et porte des Plaines, axée sur la spéculation foncière, Kansas City évolua rapidement du petit banditisme de la Frontière à une forme de criminalité urbaine digne des grandes cités de l'Est. Alors que, déjà en 1860, Horace Greeley se plaignait des deux « malédictions » du Kansas, « land speculation... and one-horse politicians[1] », la concentration d'entrepreneurs et de politiciens ambitieux établit à Kansas City un système de gouvernement local corrompu dominé par les frères Pendergast, James d'abord, puis Tom. Ces deux « bosses », avec l'aide explicite des autorités municipales (en particulier le bras droit du maire, Tom McElroy) et de gangsters notoires tels que Johnny Lazia et Jake « Cutcherheadoff » Weissman, parvinrent, dans les années vingt et trente, à transformer la ville en capitale du vice et en cité d'accueil pour criminels en cavale. La pègre de Kansas City, par un trait typique rappelant les traditions de la Frontière, marquait sa différence avec les autres villes en pratiquant une criminalité de dandy, bonnes manières et tenues vestimentaires impeccables exigées. Lazia confiait les « corvées » salissantes à un bataillon de sbires, dont le zèle finit par mener ce beau monde à sa perte : le fameux *Union Station Massacre* de 1933 (une évasion ratée et sanglante) sonna le glas de la machine Pendergast. Lazia, condamné pour fraude fiscale, ne vit jamais sa prison, criblé de balles sur un trottoir en 1934. Et Pendergast, convaincu de fraude électorale en 1936 et condamné par le fisc en 1939, dut abandonner tous ses pouvoirs. Kansas City n'en était pas pour autant débarrassée du gangstérisme. Lorsque la fin de la Prohibition força les gangs à la reconversion, l'expérience accumulée au fil des années dans le domaine du trafic de drogue permit de transformer la ville en plaque tournante des narcotiques, assurant l'approvisionnement des Rocheuses et de la côte Ouest. Ce trafic nous ramène à des considérations géographiques puisque, non seulement il ne se développa qu'à la faveur d'une étonnante dispersion de petits gangs sur l'ensemble du territoire – difficiles à démanteler – mais il confirma la place importante que devaient jouer, jusqu'à la fin des années cinquante, la Floride et surtout Cuba dans l'univers du jeu, du racket, des nightclubs et des courses.

L'ignorance prononcée où était le peuple d'un espace du crime sans marges rigides et durables n'a pas cessé d'alimenter les stéréotypes et les a priori. Si l'on veut bien cesser de croire que tout gangster est italien et sévit à Chicago ou New York, alors il faut se pencher sur le détail de l'immigration, sur les phases de l'intégration des étrangers aux Etats-Unis, sur la question des origines. Comment comprendre, sinon, les guerres, en apparence fratricides, entre ceux qu'on désignait, par amalgame péjoratif, comme des « wops ». Que Siciliens et Napolitains s'entretuent n'avait aucun sens, pour qui ne voulait pas connaître ces contrées lointaines, sinon comme lutte de pouvoir aisément explicable par l'idéologie dominante de l'individualisme et de la réussite impérative. La réaction nativiste est aussi un échec de la conscience géographique, c'est-à-dire de l'aménagement de l'espace social en fonction d'une certaine conception du monde. Tous les

---

1. Horace Greeley, *An Overland Journey*, p. 36.

« dagoes » de la terre alimentaient une vision quasi-ptoléméenne de l'Amérique, géocentrique et séparatiste. Le monde obscur des criminels (« underworld ») était aussi celui des étrangers, boucs-émissaires parfaits des maux de la société américaine. « When such a scapegoat can be found, the culture is not only relieved of sin but can indulge itself in an orgy of righteous indignation[1] ».

Mais la réaction moralisante des églises (notamment Catholique) et des défenseurs de la tradition se fonde sur une perception individualiste de la vertu. Dès qu'il est question de groupe ou d'organisation, le problème culturel de la criminalité devient difficilement gérable pour les Américains. Il verse rapidement dans l'hystérie du complot et de la subversion organisée. L'obsession de la conspiration, attisée par le mystère et le silence (penser à la règle de l'*omertà*), rejoint ici l'anticommunisme et la peur des Martiens. On réfléchira utilement d'une part à la quasi-concomitance des travaux des commissions Kefauver et McCarthy, et d'autre part à la perception qu'avait la frange dévote de l'Amérique bien-pensante d'une perversion fondamentale des valeurs familiales traditionnelles par les Italiens immigrés (ou leurs descendants), pour qui la notion de « famille » servait essentiellement à repérer les cibles à abattre.

Pourtant, on l'aura compris, il y a bien un certain air de famille entre tous ces hors-la-loi en guêtres et chapeau-feutre et les décideurs qui contrôlent les grandes organisations nationales ou internationales. La géopolitique du crime a des exigences voisines de celles qui règlent les rapports de force dans toute une société, et les relations diplomatiques, économiques ou militaires entre nations. Rappelons, par exemple, que pour la presse Frank Costello, alias Francesco Castiglia, spécialiste de la corruption politique, qui avait, comme on dit, dans sa poche le leader de Tammany Hall Michael Kennedy (élu en 1942) et l'un des juges les plus influents de la Cour suprême de l'Etat de New York, Thomas Aurelio, était devenu en 1947 « The Prime Minister of Crime ». Rappelons que le monde parallèle (et occulte) de la grande criminalité avait ses guerres et ses paix, et ses « sommets » où l'on retraçait les frontières du vice, où l'on redistribuait les zones d'influence et de rapport. Les « rencontres » de Cleveland en 1928, d'Atlantic City en 1929, de New York (Franconia Hotel) en 1933, de Kansas City en 1934, et même celle d'Appalachin (New York) en 1957 sont restées mémorables pour les effets qu'elles ont eu sur les stratégies de gang, les alliances ou les reprises d'hostilités. A tel point qu'on peut, sans mal, admettre que le tournant le plus important dans l'histoire du crime organisé fut un renversement d'alliances, un « coup » politique sans précédent de Lucky Luciano qui, à l'issue de la guerre *Castellamarese*, et au mépris de toutes les traditions mafieuses, accepta une alliance Italo-juive avec le gang Lansky-Siegel. Le mouvement fit tache d'huile : à Chicago apparut une coalition Moe Annenberg – Frank Nitti ; à Cleveland, Moe Dalitz se ligua avec James Licavoli ; à Detroit, Abe Bernstein se retrouva associé à Joseph Zerilli ; et au New Jersey, c'est Abner Zwillman qui s'allia à Willie Moretti. Si l'on ajoute quelques outsiders ni juifs ni italiens, comme Frank Erickson à New York ou Jake Guzik à Chicago, ne voit-on pas surgir une communauté

---

1. Cité dans Cressey, 16.

multiculturelle, paraphrase obscène d'une société bien-pensante qui censure le cinéma mais tolère les bakchich, les casinos et la drogue ?

Empire contre empire : l'empire du crime contre les Etats-Unis triomphants, plus efficaces contre le nazisme que contre Cosa Nostra. Luciano avait rêvé, et presque réalisé, l'union parfaite des *businesses* malpropres. Sa National Crime Commission, constituée en 1934, voulait fédérer 24 familles de la pègre pour une meilleure répartition territoriale de leurs affaires. Sa condamnation en 1937 mit un terme au projet. Mais les réseaux se reformèrent dès la guerre achevée. En fait, le conflit extérieur permit au crime organisé de reconstituer ses structures et de consolider ses appuis à l'intérieur des Etats-Unis comme à l'étranger. Aux lieux « classiques » du gangstérisme il fallut ajouter la Californie et, ô ironie, Hollywood dont certains studios (la Fox, en particulier) furent victimes d'un nouveau type de « racket syndical » orchestré par Bugsy Siegel et Mickey Cohen (transfuge d'un gang de Cleveland). Les résultats de l'enquête Kefauver glacèrent le sang des Américains : la vénalité des responsables politiques, à tous les niveaux, la terrifiante collusion entre les différentes branches de la pègre et l'extraordinaire complémentarité de leurs activités, n'était pas de nature à rassurer le citoyen. Une nouvelle « pieuvre », bien pire que le cartel du rail dénoncé par Frank Norris au tournant du XXe siècle, semblait reléguer l'action sporadique du gouvernement et les gesticulations historiques d'un Thomas Dewey ou d'un Fiorello La Guardia au rang de rodomontades dérisoires. On s'interrogera donc sur les finalités et les conséquences d'une investigation comme celle de la commission Kefauver. On pourra se demander, entre autres, si aux mains de ce cinquième pouvoir, le crime organisé, les Etats-Unis ne pourraient pas bien connaître la décadence où sombra l'orgueilleuse Rome des Césars, ruinée par l'appétit de pouvoir et l'obsession du lucre.

Bibliographie

Cawelti, John G. *Apostles of the Self-Made Man, Changing Concepts of Success in America* (Chicago : The University of Chicago Press, 1965).
Cressey, Donald R. *Theft of the Nation, The Structure and Operations of Organized Crime in America* (New York : Harper & Row, 1969).
Greeley, Horace. *An Overland Journey, from New York to San Francisco in the Summer of 1859* (New York : Barker, Saxton & Co., 1860).
Hofstadter, Richard. *The American Political Tradition* (New York : Random House, Vintage Books, 1974).
Lupsha, Peter A. « Organized Crime in the United States », in Robert J. Kelly ed., *Organized Crime, A Global Perspective* (Lanham, Md : Rowman & Littlefield Publishers, 1986).
Rosenberg, Nathan & L.E. Birdzell. *How the West Grew Rich, The Economic Transformation of the Industrial World* (New York : Basic Books, 1986).
Sorokin, Pitirim A. *Social and Cultural Mobility* (Glencoe, Ill. : The Free Press, 1959).
Steffens, Lincoln. *The Shame of the Cities* (New York : Hill & Wang, American Century Series, 1957).
Tocqueville, Alexis de. *Democracy in America* (New York : The New American Library, Mentor Books, 1956).

Prologue: Organized Crime During Prohibition
By Armand Hage

"Organized crime", just like "crime", an abstract word, has a broad range of meanings. In the nineteenth and early twentieth centuries it consisted in organizations or individuals whose activities were in many ways illegal. The first group representing one variety was Tammany Hall, originally a friendly society; in the 1860s and 1870s, it drifted into graft, corruption, and machine politics; in other words, organized crime was in the hands of some politicians, called bosses.

After the Civil War, the rise of big business in turn gave rise to a group of industrialists known as the « Robber Barons ». On the one hand, they built up the American economy, but on the other hand they practiced a form of organized crime. Admittedly, they did not kill with guns, or smuggle prohibited liquor, or set up gambling businesses, but they bought politicians with their ill-gotten money, and the politicians passed laws that greatly helped them in their doings.

Organized crime in the modern sense started at the turn of the twentieth century with Sicilian mafiosi arriving in the United States. They and other criminal groups practiced racketeering, preying on other immigrants. "The Black Hand" was the most feared organization. It is interesting to note that most organized crime operatives were immigrants or descendants of first generation immigrants that did not belong to the WASP category. Being rejected by WASPs, they had to find a way of sharing in the "American Dream."

No single individual can be credited for setting up organized crime as it is conceived of today, but a few figures emerge in the first two decades of the twentieth century. Johnny Torrio brought major and pioneering innovations to the gangster business in New York City. He was a sort of Dr. Jekyll-and-Mr. Hyde figure, a respectable man conducting a numbers racket and running whorehouses. Torrio's genius lay in the idea that illegal activities should be conducted as in any other corporation, i.e., they needed efficient organization and administration, and at the same time they should expand. His importance and influence would be reflected in the top two mobsters of the Prohibition era, Al Capone and Lucky Luciano. Another major figure was Arnold Rothstein, who had a gambling empire. Bucket shops, loan sharking, bookmaking[1] and gambling were the main staples of organized crime, as were bail bond and labor racketeering.

Ironically, Prohibition was one of the major causes of organized crime on a large scale. This article will analyze the history of prohibition, the major figures of organized crime that it spawned, and the attempts at law enforcement that were made during that period.

Prohibition's Historical Background

The Bible credits Noah with discovering vinification; *Genesis* reports his unwitting and embarrassing drunkenness that had dire consequences for

---

1. The term started to be in common use in the first decade of the twentieth century.

the Canaanites. For centuries, alcohol production was conducted on a relatively limited scale, but the Industrial Revolution in England witnessed a huge development in the output of alcoholic beverages, especially gin, and this development meant drinking not wine but "hard liquor."

By the 1840s, the hard working conditions in industry caused more drinking. At the same time, Western expansion meant the emergence of saloons. Lincoln compared alcohol to the angel of death in *Exodus*. East and West were thus confronted with drunkenness, associated with violent and criminal conduct and with the breakup of family life. Women were the first to suffer from it; they started a number of actions whose purpose was to limit or suppress liquor. These Temperance Movements were often closely associated with demands for more rights for women. Their efforts bore fruit as early as 1851, when Maine enacted the first state prohibition law. A law was thought necessary because persuasion did not seem to work and the churches were inefficient. In 1855, 13 states out of 31 had prohibition statutes on their books; the restrictions seemed to bring consumption down to about 8 liters.

Unfortunately, with the Civil War and the subsequent start of the Gilded Age, the momentum was lost; the atmosphere of the 1860s was not conducive to abstemiousness. Women were frustrated; a prohibition party was set up, and in 1869 it made prohibition a national issue. In the 1870s women marched to express their wish to see saloons – whose numbers had ballooned – closed. The drinking problem seemed so serious in the 1880s that a Protestant minister introduced Coca-Cola as the "temperance drink."

The turn of the 20th century saw the emergence of the Anti-Saloon League of America, whose purpose was to protect the family. The organization was efficient in selecting candidates on the basis of their stance regarding saloons and it required referendums on these establishments. Proponents of prohibition supported their demands by practical and scientific arguments. Doctors and social researchers purported to show that alcohol was both addictive and harmful. Temperance movements contended that the huge number of saloons meant competition for men's money and led to an increase in crime and corruption. It is a fact that saloons were so numerous and competition so fierce that to attract patrons, especially young ones, owners had to add extra activities besides drinking, such as gambling and prostitution.

The women's activism gradually paid off. In 1916, more than 20 states out of 48 had banned alcohol or passed laws closing down saloons. At the same time, W. Wilson, during his reelection campaign, promised he would grant the franchise to women, which would mean national prohibition, seen by many as the only efficient way to curb alcohol consumption. But before the female vote was enacted into the Constitution, national prohibition could come about because the Anti-Saloon League had helped elect a Congress with more than a two-thirds majority in favor of banning alcohol. Ratification of the Eighteenth Amendment was completed on January 29, 1919. It was fast and, more than the vote in Congress, it showed how powerful the prohibition movement was; not only did 46 state legislatures out of 48 ratify, the overall approval percentage was about 80%.

The Eighteenth Amendment looks straightforward and clear; it provides that one year after its ratification the manufacture, sale, transportation or exportation of intoxicating liquors "for beverage purposes" would be prohibited, but drinking *per se* is not.

The Volstead Act was passed in October 1919 to implement the Amendment. It is interesting to note that Wilson vetoed the act but Congress overrode the veto. The Volstead Act is presented as a statute in continuation of the "War Prohibition Act", which had restricted the production of alcohol. It may seem somewhat surprising to see wartime restrictions continued after hostilities have ended, but the apparent near unanimity in favor of prohibition will be analyzed and explained below. At this point it can be said that the ASL talked Congress into holding the firm belief that victory over the "German Hun" in the war was due to abstinence by soldiers – quite the opposite of the French *poilus* – and by the population at large. Forswearing liquor, the ASL contended, would keep Americans stronger both physically and mentally.

The Volstead Act defines intoxicating liquors such as beer, wine, gin, whiskey and others as beverages containing "one-half of 1 per centum or more of alcohol by volume." To the Amendment wording it adds that what is prohibited is not only manufacture, sale, transportation, importation and exportation, but also bartering, delivering, furnishing or possessing intoxicating liquors, apart from exemptions for medicinal or sacramental purposes. Section 18 furnishes an additional list of prohibitions, in this instance regarding the items needed to make alcohol – it is "unlawful to advertise, manufacture, sell, or possess for sale any utensil, contrivance, machine, preparation, compound, tablet, substance, formula direction, recipe advertised, designed, or intended for use in the unlawful manufacture of intoxicating liquor."

Section 21 provides that "any room, house, building, boat, vehicle, structure, or place where intoxicating liquor is manufactured, sold, kept or bartered" in violation of the law is a "common nuisance," and maintaining it is punishable by a fine not exceeding 1,000 dollars and/or by imprisonment for not more than a year. The punishment for manufacturing, selling, etc., for a first offense is a fine not exceeding 1,000 dollars; for a second offense fines range from 200 to 2,000 dollars and imprisonment for one month to five years.

What the Volstead Act did authorize was possession of liquor in the home where the person resided provided it was "for use only for... personal consumption" by the owner, his family and his guests. The burden of proof was on the possessor, that is, he had to prove that the liquor was lawfully "acquired, possessed and used." The Eighteenth Amendment and the Volstead Act were called by their proponents "The Noble Experiment."

Major Figures of Organized Crime

Before Prohibition, organized crime as described above was conducted on a relatively small scale in the activities mentioned above. Prohibition provided the major opportunity by far to the practice. Not only was a new crime added, but it also reinforced the previous forms.

Before national prohibition became the law of the land, among the dry states was Michigan. Detroit smugglers, led by the Purple Gang, universally known like their future colleagues all over the nation as bootleggers[1], were many steps ahead of New York's and Chicago's. Henry Ford was annoyed because although "booze" was no longer legally available in his state, it was overabundant in Canada, just across the border. Ohio was also a good watering place since it had no prohibition law. All means of smuggling were employed; in automobiles false floorboards, second gas tanks and hidden compartments were used. Smugglers also utilized false bottomed shopping baskets and suitcases. Whiskey and other hard drinks were even carried in camouflaged flasks or hot water bottles. Bootleggers' activity in Michigan came to an abrupt stop a few months before the Eighteenth Amendment, when the state prohibition act was ruled... unconstitutional. With the Volstead Act taking effect, Detroit bootleggers were ready.

It came as no surprise when organized crime switched to bootlegging, seeing there a new opportunity. The man who is believed to be the major initiator of the communication between the Sicilian Mafia and the United States Mafia was Vito Ferro. Ferro had come to New York from Sicily in 1900 and he was active in the "Black Hand." Because he was wanted for murder, he had to return to Sicily; the killer status earned him a high rank in the Sicilian Mafia. From his native country he could send his henchmen to the United States.

Prohibition was, to be sure, a great opportunity, but making money from bootlegging was no easy task. It took considerable ingenuity and teamwork – the very definition of organized crime and organized business – to supply the huge amounts of illegal alcoholic beverages. Transportation of beer, for example, required trucks in great numbers. In other words, the criminals who had not been able to achieve the American Dream through legal activities built their illegal operations in the spirit of American entrepreneurship and capitalism. Criminals owned not only trucks but also ships. Their communication was made easy thanks to radio communication, with a network that was equivalent to an army's.

In the early 1920s Canada repealed dry laws, and the flow soared. Boats were equipped to tow liquor underwater; a cable delivery system was set up thanks to sunken houseboats; tunnels, and even a pipeline, were built. The bootleg business employed about 50,000 people in the Border States, and there were 25,000 speakeasies, or blind pigs, as the illegal saloons were called. "Productivity" seemed to be much higher than at Ford's plant, since Ford's sales, with 100,000 employees, barely exceeded the 215 million dollar figure recorded, or estimated, by mob operatives. In Chicago, Al Capone alone owned and used more than 700 trucks.

The Mafia boss in New York was Giuseppe Masseria. Masseria had come to America in 1903 because in his native Sicily he was wanted for murder as a Mafia enforcer. In New York he joined existing gangs, developed bootlegging, and gradually squeezed out other members. He was feared and often hated by his own men, but no real challenge came until about

---

1. The term was commonly known by 1900, but its first use occurred during the Civil War, when traffickers hid prohibited alcohol in their cowhide boots to sell it to Union soldiers.

1927. One of Masseria's characteristics was his rejection of non-Sicilian mobsters. The challenge came in the person of Salvatore Maranzano, a fellow Sicilian. Maranzano was a rarity among Mafiosi in Sicily because as a former seminarian he was well educated. In 1927 Ferro dispatched Maranzano with a clear mission – prepare for a complete takeover of the Mafia by Ferro himself. Mussolini who was waging an all-out war against the mob, however, imprisoned Ferro, for life. Maranzano saw an opportunity to make him the leader of the mob. His action took the form of hijacking Masseria's vehicles[1]; but to Masseria it was a *casus belli*.

Maranzano's aggression led to what is known as the Castellamarese Wars – named after Maranzano's hometown in Sicily – that lasted until 1931. The outcome depended mainly on Salvatore Lucania, aka Charles "Lucky" Luciano, born in Sicily in 1896 or 1897. Young Salvatore resorted to shoplifting, and when he was ten he was arrested and imprisoned. Upon his release he started offering his protection to Jewish boys younger than he was so they could avoid being beaten up. The boys did not always need Sal's protection, but he decided they had to pay just the same, thereby setting up a racket. Later, as a teenager, he became a narcotics dealer. This time he was jailed for six months[2]. His résumé may have impressed his fellow gangsters; before he turned 20 he was one of the leaders of one of the most vicious gangs, the Five Points gang, where he met other future bosses, including Al Capone. Luciano's reputation meant that police had a tendency to suspect him of most crimes in New York City.

Luciano, besides racketeering, ran a bootlegging empire set up on the theory of vertical integration as it had been practiced by the « Robber Barons », i.e., he mastered the whole process by taking care of the manufacture, storage, transportation, importation and sale of alcohol. In his biography, Luciano states that they had a bigger company than Ford and they had more than what corporations needed; his business had "lawyers by the carload," and these were on call 24 hours a day.

Luciano learned the importance of using a legal front – as narcotics dealer, he hid the heroin among the hats he was delivering. He was also excited by the thrill he could get from illegal activities and not only by the "fast buck" approach. When asked why he did not choose to run a legitimate company which could have been profitable thanks to his business acumen, he answered that he would not have enjoyed it as much as bootlegging and racketeering.

Masseria coveted Luciano's lucrative business. Luciano and his friends, aware that they were still young and less powerful than Masseria, thought that they eventually would have to join him, but they wanted to wait until they acquired more strength so they could be more influential in the organization. By the mid twenties Luciano became Masseria's chief aide; but the alliance was doomed from its inception because of the irreconcilable differences between the two men.

---

1. The word "hijack" began to be used around 1923.
2. After his release he changed his first name to Charlie because he believed that "Sal" sounded like a girl's name, that is, it did not sound tough.

Masseria's rejection of non-Sicilians caused the organization to lose quite a few opportunities. By contrast, many of Luciano's friends were Jews, and his idea was to give a greater scope to the business. The disagreements were still part of the Masseria-Luciano relationship when the Castellamarese Wars started to rage on. Masseria, being aware of Luciano's ambitions, felt Luciano was a threat to him. Maranzano, for his part, knew that to overcome Masseria he needed Luciano. He approached him, but Luciano was far from willing to cooperate. One reason was that Maranzano too belonged to the old school; he and Masseria were known as "Mustache Petes." Luciano also hated what he called the "fatherly" approach, as Maranzano kept calling him "son"; Maranzano had an inflated ego and he saw himself as the Julius Caesar of the mob, so he called Luciano "Young Caesar" and started to quote the Roman leader in Latin – Maranzano's view of himself was one of the inspirations for the title of the movie *Little Caesar*.

After Luciano turned down Maranzano's offer to kill Masseria, he found himself exposed because he had two enemies. That is the reason why it is hard to know for certain who is responsible for the next episode, in which Luciano was taken for a ride[1]. One day, he was whisked into the back of a limousine, beaten up and left for dead on a beach. During the beating he had his face cut by a knife. Luciano miraculously survived, and this earned him the nickname "Lucky" because no one was ever known to have survived a ride. He managed to reach a police station and said he needed a taxi. Instead officers took him to hospital and in the process started asking questions. But Luciano followed the Omerta rule and told them he had no enemies and that he would take care of the matter himself.

When Luciano recovered, he contacted Maranzano and offered to kill Masseria. His idea was to join one boss, kill the other, bump off the first one and become the real boss. Luciano thought that the Castellamarese Wars were a disaster for the mob and a total loss in business. People were killed to no purpose because with bootlegging and other illegal activities there was enough to go around and everybody could have a piece of the pie. In the spring of 1931, Luciano invited Masseria to a restaurant and had his gunmen shoot him while he, Luciano, was in the bathroom. After the gunsels left and police came, he could "honestly" say that he did not see anything.

Now that Masseria was gone, Maranzano wasted no time proclaiming himself the "boss of all bosses" in New York – *capo di tutti capi* – the head of the five crime "families" led by five Italians, including Luciano, and thus they were all answerable to him. Maranzano-Caesar also planned to become the boss of all bosses all over the United States. He planned to kill off those that could constitute a threat to him, like Luciano and Capone. Luciano got wind of the whole scheme and gave Maranzano a dose of his own medicine. He sent killers disguised as government agents Maranzano was expecting, and they killed Maranzano. Subsequently, Lucky became the only boss of all bosses, but his organization, the "Commission", or "The Syndicate," was set up more like a corporate board with heads of families acting like

---

1. At the time the phrase was used in the underworld to mean "rub out," i.e., kill an enemy after literally taking him for a ride in a car to an isolated place.

directors; in other words, his attitude was less authoritarian and hegemonic; it was based on cooperation.

Other major organized crime figures are Arnold Rothstein and Meyer Lansky. Rothstein inspired the character of Meyer Wolfsheim in Fitzgerald's *The Great Gatsby*. His reputation was so great that he was credited with fixing the 1919 World Series although he appears not to have played any part in the scheme. The advent of Prohibition confirmed Rothstein as one of the founders of organized, or more appropriately, well-organized crime. Just as Luciano had a genius for running bootlegging and other illegal activities like corporations, Rothstein's organizing genius showed itself in bankrolling operations, buying and arranging protection from politicians and police, and getting lawyers. He was one of the first rumrunners, but eventually he mostly provided money to bootleggers and financed speakeasies. Moreover, he cast the parts, telling each what turf he would play on. Rothstein also suggested what covers should be used for rumrunning operations.

Meyer Lansky is interesting because he was the brain behind the mob and Luciano's most faithful friend and adviser. The two met as Lucky was racketeering Jewish boys. Lansky would not accept to be shaken down although Luciano was older than he. "F– off," was his retort. A fight ensued, and the endgame was the lifelong friendship. It was Lansky who induced Luciano to double cross the Mustache Petes. He provided the gunmen that shot Masseria and Maranzano because he thought Masseria organized Luciano's ride. The two friends were partners in bootlegging rackets; Lansky also impressed on Luciano how important it was to buy police protection. He also contributed to the idea of forming a crime syndicate. His main characteristics were toughness, vision – he could anticipate events within the underworld – and unobtrusiveness. Lansky was so "invisible" that the Kefauver Commission in 1950-1951 never realized how important he had been and did not think it necessary to call him to the witness stand. His unobtrusiveness allowed him to live until 1983.

The most representative mobster of the time, Al Capone, and the one whose name became almost synonymous with organized crime and bootlegging, did come from New York, but his career boomed in Chicago. Capone was born in Brooklyn in 1899 and, like Luciano, found himself in a multi-ethnic neighborhood as opposed to Little Italy. Associating with Irish, German, Chinese and Jewish children broadened his scope. Capone's early childhood was typical of the ghetto experience. Immigrant and minority children were expected to leave school early so they could work. Capone left in sixth grade after a fight with a female teacher. Thereafter, he met Torrio, but he did not use violence – Torrio was a "gentleman mobster."

Capone's violence was probably more the result of life experience and nurture than nature because it bloomed after he associated with a Calabrian named Francesco Uale, aka Frankie Yale, a friend of Torrio's. Yale was aggressive and violent. Advised by Torrio, he employed Capone, then a teenager, as a bartender and bouncer, and occasionally as a waiter. One day Al told a customer, an Italian girl who was having a drink with her brother, that she had a "nice ass", adding that he meant it as a compliment. The brother then started a fight during which Capone got the scar that became his trademark. In addition, the brother complained to Luciano; Luciano and Yale told Capone to apologize. After his first baby was born Capone left his job and became a bookkeeper in Baltimore, leading the life of a good husband and a good father. His father's death in 1920 caused him to make up his mind to accept the offer made by Torrio in Chicago. Torrio was an influential member of 'Big Jim' Colosimo's mob, Colosimo being the Windy City's big boss. His business was expanding into bootlegging, a "growth industry" while at the same time retaining other traditional activities such as racketeering and pimping. Colosimo was killed by Yale in May 1921, but Yale's plan to take over the empire failed and Torrio held on.

Capone did not mind the gambling houses and the speakeasies but he was somehow reluctant to run whorehouses. The qualms soon vanished, however; his success made Torrio promote him from employee to full partner. As from Torrio he learned how important it was to keep a facade of respectability, he tried to pass off as a second-hand furniture dealer. This psychological need for a respectable front could be interpreted as one way for Capone to convince himself that the original good boy he had been was not dead and that he was not as bad as his public image showed.

The first years in Chicago were relatively uneventful for Capone; business was humming and there were no serious turf wars, each gang having an assigned section, Torrio-Capone "owning" the South Side and an Irish gang the North Side. But the election of a reform mayor in 1924 meant Capone and Torrio had to move out to suburban Cicero. The quiet period came to an end when a small-time mobster called Capone a "dago pimp." Capone shot the offender; he was not convicted, but now he knew that he was in the limelight and his life could be threatened, especially because gang wars were starting.

The peace-loving Torrio tried to prevent conflicts; he called a conference, suggesting a division of business among the different gangs. The leader of the Irish gang, Dion O'Banion, rejected the offer because it involved paying Torrio some tribute. Not only did he try to sell liquor to his rivals' clients in their area, he also hijacked their trucks. Retaliation and escalation were inevitable, and things were made worse by personal animus caused by differences in national origin, the Irishman looking down upon Italians. They were all the more damnable to him because they operated whorehouses, which are "against the teaching of our mother, the Church."

O'Banion was the first to go; his partner, George "Bugs" Moran, vowed revenge. He and his henchmen tried to assassinate Torrio; Torrio was hit but not dead. Moran pulled the trigger once more against his temple but now there were no bullets left. Eventually, Torrio, tired and rich enough to live on his earnings, made over his Chicago assets to Capone and retired. Now Capone was the real king of gangland in Chicago. The following years saw many other gangland wars in which he was involved, not only in Chicago but also in New York. Capone did away with many enemies and competitors. The number of assassinations in the area was believed to stand at around 400 every year. Business dealings with New York expanded as liquor was transported all the way from New York to Chicago. Capone was so powerful that newspapers said Chicago was the "imperial city" of the gang world, and New York a "remote provincial place." Capone was regarded as the greatest gang leader in history.

Al kept posing as an honorable citizen and a benefactor, since his business employed thousands of poor people, especially Italian immigrants, and this facade of respectability made him popular. His power could expand further because after the 1927 mayoral election in Chicago he could go back to the city he had to leave a few years earlier. It was estimated that in 1927 alone he took in 105 million dollars. However, with Moran and others still hunting for him, he felt more and more at risk. For this reason and for other personal reasons he eventually bought a house in Miami, but the cycle of killings and retribution went on; some gangs hijacked his trucks or tried to sell booze to his regular customers.

Things came to a head in February 1929. Capone decided to kill Moran and ruin his business. His men set a trap – they would make an enticing offer to sell good whiskey at a very low price. The merchandise was to be delivered at a North Side garage that was used by Moran. The killers were to be disguised as policemen with a stolen police car and pretend to raid the garage. When execution time came the killers saw a man who looked like Moran. They moved in, lined up the seven men who were inside and mowed them down with the new Tommy guns and other weapons. The scene, known as the Saint Valentine's Day Massacre, was immortalized in Billy Wilder's *Some Like It Hot*. Although everybody knew Capone was behind the operation, Capone could not even be arrested because he had an airtight alibi – he was lolling on a Miami beach. Likewise, the top organizer of the operation had checked into a hotel with his mistress and soon married her so she could not testify against him. The massacre did ruin Moran's business but there was a twist. What the killers did not know was that Moran was not among the casualties. It was a case of mistaken identity that made things more complicated for Capone. The Massacre was the climax of his power, and the only way he could go now was down, as will be seen below.

Law enforcement and the difficulties it involved

The emergence and boom in organized crime in the twenties as a result of Prohibition could not go unchecked. Enforcement, however, was no easy task and in many instances futile for many reasons most of which are easy to understand. They relate to the way Prohibition, with its legal defects, was perceived, to lack of enforcement means and corruption. One reason was that Prohibition was unpopular. This attitude, although well known and well documented, may sound surprising in view of the fact that the Eighteenth Amendment was passed with a large majority. A closer look shows otherwise and leads to the motives behind Prohibition. Simply stated, the situation pitted the old Anglo-Saxon stock against the products of immigration. WASPs realized that their predominance was starting to be threatened by "wops", "micks," Jews, Germans, and other "ethnics." Prohibition can be seen as a desperate attempt at holding on to their privileges. As usual, they viewed the situation in terms of good and evil just as the Puritan forebears had done – most Prohibitionists were Baptists, the heirs of the Puritans. They were the "good guys" and the "immigrant scum" made up the "bad guys." Prohibition was a way to have the Federal government step in and shove WASP values down other people's throats.

It so happened that the rising group within the population was made up of Catholics, and among these were people – the Irish – to whom drinking was a way of life and a habit that had nothing immoral, let alone criminal. Combined to the ghetto mindset, this challenge lined up an increasing number of people against what was seen as the sanctimoniousness of the old WASPs. The word "Puritan" as applied to them and their behavior took on a derogative connotation. The biggest gadfly at the time, H.L. Mencken, defined Puritanism as the haunting idea that somebody, somewhere, might be happy.

Of course, in terms of sheer numbers, the WASP population was greater than that of the "newcomers," but the great majority that brought Prohibition did not reflect the real numbers. It was the result of gerrymandering, the practice of dividing the nation into districts designed to favor WASPs, in other words a practice that runs counter to the "one man, one vote" principle. WASPs were often rural, and at the turn of the 20th century the United States had become an urban society; but the weight of the urban districts was reduced. Besides, many immigrants were not yet citizens, and those who were did not always bother to vote.

Another motive behind Prohibition was the hostility of WASPs toward Germans. During and after World War I Germans in the United States had a rough time, to put it mildly, although most of them had been loyal to the host country. Their case was made worse by the fact that Germans dominated the brewing industry.

Because the law was unpopular, and although saloons were shut down, demand for all kinds of alcohol remained strong. This attitude accounts at least partly for the popularity of organized crime figures because they provided a product that was in demand. A huge part of the public was happy to accept the idea that the law should not be enforced; indeed, judges were lenient. Besides being unpopular, the law had another serious defect linked to hypocrisy. The fact that consumption was not prohibited led to a loophole meaning that WASPs could drink legally – although secretly – while proclaiming that drinking was the devil's work. If they did not always patronize speakeasies they could still drink thanks to bathtubs turned into gin machines and purchased products that could be fermented. It can be added that the penalties provided by the Volstead Act were not really harsh, so people, and especially gangsters, could take chances at breaking the law. Capone was arrested and jailed in the twenties not for violating Prohibition law, but for carrying concealed guns.

Yet the law was ostensibly meant to be tough. The Amendment gave concurrent power to the Federal government and to state governments in terms of enforcement. The Supreme Court itself came to the rescue as early as 1920. Opponents of Prohibition were so much infuriated that they challenged not only the constitutionality of the Volstead Act, but also the validity of the Amendment itself, an unheard of initiative since by definition a constitutional amendment *is* constitutional. Seven cases came before the Court; they were all turned down. In addition, the Court made a series of decisions designed to make prosecution and conviction easier. In 1922,

United States v. Lanza upheld the concurrent enforcement powers of states and the Federal government. The ruling meant that an offender could be charged and tried by both authorities and this double procedure is not double jeopardy. Likewise, *Carroll v. United States* (1925) upheld warrantless automobile searches; *Lambert v. Yellowly* (1926) set restrictions on medicinal liquor prescriptions and *Olmstead v. United States* (1928) upheld wiretap telephone surveillance. As can be noticed, these decisions were a blow to individual liberties.

One problem in terms of enforcement was that jurisdiction to enforce Prohibition was given to the Treasury Department, and that Department was not at all equipped both legally and in terms of manpower to deal with the "octopus" that was organized crime. Treasury created the Prohibition Bureau, but it had no chance of prevailing against bootleggers, the less so as it had to fight individual violations as well, that is, it was supposed to check in every house. As a result, the law was flagrantly flouted and broken; liquor was smuggled not only from Canada and the Caribbean but also from Saint-Pierre et Miquelon. The number of speakeasies was staggering; it surpassed that of the saloons that had been closed; thus it was an insuperable task for authorities. More demand meant more speakeasies, more competition, and more organized crime to share the wealth produced.

The labor force that was available for enforcement was hopelessly insufficient. The Canadian and Mexican borders are several thousand miles long and the coastline more than 18,000 miles long and thus they were undermanned and could not be policed effectively. It can be estimated that only an insignificant fraction – some say 5% – of smuggled alcohol could be seized. To all this must be added the surveillance and tracking of thousands of trucks. Domestic production was collected by thousands of organized crime employees, who were virtually certain they would not be caught.

Another, and major, aspect of the difficulty of law enforcement relates to the corruption and intimidation of authorities and buying protection from them. This phenomenon is an integral part of the history of organized crime during Prohibition. Organized crime had it easy because objectively speaking, it was a step ahead of the sheriff, but things became still easier with corruption. A friend of Luciano's and Lansky's, Frank Costello[1], was in charge of making contacts in political circles. If the group became the most powerful force in organized crime while its members were in their twenties, it is thanks to these contacts with police, judges, mayors, and even governors. In this way they could have a free hand to conduct their operations in New York, and later from coast to coast. The pipeline between the underworld and Tammany Hall was Rothstein; he was ready to provide bail and legal defense. Besides, the mayor of New York for most of the twenties, J. Walker, was the mob's man.

In Chicago, corruption went hand in hand with election fraud. The Irish gang used diverse methods, including corruption and intimidation to determine the outcome of elections. The situation of officials was an uncomfortable one: if they could stand up to one gang they were eventually

---

1. Costello was eventually the man who gave some of the most damaging testimonies before the Kefauver Commission.

bound to give in to the others. With payoffs or threats, they looked the other way. After all, they were the mob's clients. Mobsters usually went to polling stations and they both forced voters to vote their way and stuffed the ballot boxes.

O'Banion was never afraid to proclaim that he held a sway over authorities and representatives of public opinion. He stated publicly that sales of beer alone stood at 30 million dollars every month, and one million was distributed among police, politicians and federal agents "to keep it flowing." When O'Banion was assassinated, his body lay in state for about a week. Thousands of Chicago residents paid tribute. Even journalists often showed no hostility. They loved him because of his humor and because he was always – just like other mobsters – good press and kept material flowing and sales booming. Reporters also loved Moran because he kept hurling insults at his arch enemy, Capone, calling him "the Behemoth", or "the Beast." People and journalists had sympathy for Moran because in his fight with Goliath Capone he played the part of David, which shows that for many years public opinion was not taking Prohibition and its enforcement seriously. The fight was like a serial with endless episodes.

Of course, Capone and his gang were very active in election fraud. Oftentimes in Cicero police were not allowed to enter polling stations, and they did not protest, even when judges and poll watchers were kidnapped. Whenever a politician showed hostility, his house could be bombed or torched. Voters were intimidated; the few who resisted were abducted and taken for a ride. Torrio had a knack for dealing with people in authority. When, in 1923, reform mayor W. Dever in Chicago defeated the corrupt "Big Bill Thompson" and Torrio and his men relocated to Cicero it was because City Hall had already shown that it was "on the take," so they could buy the whole municipal government, including the police department. The only time the mayor disagreed with Capone, Capone threw him down the steps of City Hall; Capone placed one of his brothers on the Cicero city government.

Although Colosimo was universally known as the ultimate whorehouse boss, police captains, judges, a Congressman, two assistant state attorneys, and nine aldermen attended his funeral. Corruption was so rampant and Capone's stranglehold on Illinois' law enforcement agencies and politicians so strong and his reputation so high that in late 1928 a mind-staggering incident took place. To secure an honest election, the Crime Commission, given the fact that all elected officials in office from mayors to the governor were corrupt, asked Capone for help, and when Capone obliged, Cook County had the first honest election that the state had witnessed in a very long time.

Corruption was widespread not only among local authorities; it was also very common in federal agencies and within the whole Harding Administration. Fiorello La Guardia testified to Prohibition's failure before the Senate Judiciary Committee in 1926, contending it was impossible to tell whether Prohibition was a good thing or a bad thing because it was never enforced. La Guardia added that such an enormous traffic could not be carried on without the knowledge, if not the connivance of the officials entrusted with the enforcement of the law. La Guardia asserted that at least a million dollars a day was paid in graft and corruption to Federal, state and local officers. Law enforcement on the whole got a boost in 1924 with the advent of Hoover at the head of the FBI. J. Edgar Hoover realized how important it was to earn the support of the population, but the FBI had no real jurisdiction in Prohibition matters.

The Saint Valentine's Day Massacre gave law enforcement the break it needed. While some of the publicity around the incident was positive and added to Capone's glamour, a good deal was negative; there was a kind of outcry for retribution because of the heinous and cruel character of the crime, although the targets were gangsters. In 1929 Herbert Hoover, as soon as he took the oath of office[1], directed the Secretary of the Treasury to set up and coordinate operations to bring Capone down. This decision eventually led to Al being named Public Enemy No. 1 – later, in the movie *Scarface*, the subtitle was *The Shame of the Nation*, both as a bona fide description and in deference to the Hays Code.

The man in charge of the operation was a young agent named Eliot Ness, one of the few honest agents, and the approach was two-fold: one part dealt with Prohibition violations and the other with tax evasion; once evidence was gathered, the IRS would work with the Justice Department to bring charges. The tax evasion part was made easy thanks to a recent court decision establishing that money earned through criminal and illegal activities was subject to income tax. Capone's brother had been prosecuted for tax evasion, but Al thought that he himself could get away because he signed no checks and had nothing officially to his name, except the lavish house in Florida. The house was to lead to his undoing – the prosecutor stated that having such a lavish dwelling was impossible if there had been no income.

Meanwhile, Ness and his men, while tapping phones and sending a man to infiltrate Capone's organization, were after Prohibition violations that could be used as backup in case tax evasion did not lead to conviction. They conducted a series of raids on speakeasies, breweries and distilleries. After a while the damage inflicted was very serious. Capone, thinking that every man had his price, tried to bribe Ness, but Ness informed the newspapers; articles were published all over the nation, further damaging Capone's reputation although he conducted publicity campaigns of his own and opened free soup kitchens and other establishments to help the poor and alleviate the sufferings of the victims of the Depression. One paper reporting on the honesty of Ness and his men called them "Untouchables", and the name stuck. Ness's operation initiated a vicious circle for Capone: as his finances deteriorated, he was no longer able to bribe and corrupt as he used to. This deficiency meant law enforcement officers would now be after him, especially when they saw the tide was turning.

In the spring of 1931 a grand jury indicted Capone on 22 counts of tax evasion, claiming 200,000 dollars[2]. The indictment was soon followed by

---

1. At the time the President took office in March.
2. As a matter of fact, Capone's conviction should be considered legally invalid. Because the mobster tried to bribe or intimidate the jurors, when the trial started, the judge sprang a surprise by calling another jury. To make sure the new panel would not be tampered with, he

another one charging Capone and his men with 5,000 violations of Prohibition law. From a legal standpoint, the first indictment took precedence over the second. Still, Capone was able to strike a deal because the government was afraid the charges would not stick. The U.S. attorney agreed to a 2-to-5-year sentence instead of the 34 years that the defendant was liable to. The deal and the prosecutor got a scathing attack from the press. At the same time, Capone was making his case worse with the press and the public as he was parading and telling about a movie of his life being planned. Eventually, the sentencing judge said he was not bound by the plea-bargaining; so Al had to be tried in October 1931. He was convicted for tax evasion and sentenced to 11 years. In 1934 he was transferred to Alcatraz, where he was cut off from the rest of the world. In November 1939 he was released, and he died in 1947 – the same year as Volstead, who lived to be 87 – partly as a result of syphilis. One final irony in the Capone family is that his eldest brother, James, who had left home in 1908, changed his name, settled in the West and became a... Prohibition enforcement officer. The only time he met Al again was in 1946.

It could be said for Al Capone and other mobsters that they helped faltering law enforcement by liquidating one another and that their crimes against Prohibition were not the most serious crimes because they were committed in violation of a law that had no serious or honest legal or moral justification. Moreover, the mob relatively seldom killed innocent people. Prohibition's attendant irony lies in the fact that it was meant to do away with crime. Not only did it boost it, but it also helped glamorize organized crime and lawbreaking; glamorizing was the easier because the mob was keeping the government from collecting excise taxes. Organized crime could also look good because it was challenging the federal government, to which Prohibition had given too much power over citizens' lives and made it oppressive, an argument that invariably works in a federal nation founded by people who questioned what seemed illegitimate authority. When Prohibition ended, organized crime did not stop; mobsters had to revert to old ways and find new niches, but with the huge opportunities it afforded, Prohibition was an apt prologue to organized crime in the thirties and forties.

Bibliography

Behr, Edward, *Prohibition: Thirteen Years That Changed America* (New York: Arcade, 1996).
Gage, Nicholas, *Mafia, USA* (New York: Dell, 1972).
Kobler, John, *Capone* (New York: G.P. Putnam's Sons, 1971).
Messick, Hank and Burt Goldblatt, *The Mobs and the Mafia* (New York: Crowell, 1972).
Tyler, Gus, *Organized Crime in America* (Ann Arbor: University of Michigan Press, 1962).

---

sequestered it, so the mob was not able to reach it. Criminal procedure, however, provides that the jury should be selected with the consent of both parties.

Mirror of Violence: the Social Dimension of Gangster Movies

By Gregory D. Black

At the beginning of the 20th century movies became a popular form of entertainment in America. They quickly transcended ethnic, class, religious, and political lines to become the dominant institution of popular culture. Paradoxically, this tremendous popularity worried many people who believed that instead of reinforcing traditional values, films were promoting sexual promiscuity, corrupting the values of hard work (by glorifying criminals), and mocking the sanctity of home, church and state.

It was the gangster movie more than any other genre which concerned reformers, parents and police. For the first three decades of the 20th century, movies were silent. There were a few gangster films, such as Josef von Sternberg's *Underworld* [1927], but the techniques of silent film did not fit the gangster mold. It was when sound came to the movies in the late 1920s that the gangster became a mainstay on the screen and the protests against the genre rose to new heights. The mass appeal of movies, especially those that glorified gangsters, moral guardians argued, meant that film content had to be controlled. These advocates of censorship quickly succeeded in establishing a number of state and municipal censorship boards, the legality of which the Supreme Court upheld in 1915[1]. It was to prevent a proliferation of these organs of censorship, and to clean up the image of the industry caused by a series of sex scandals in the early 1920s, that the industry created a trade association in 1922, the Motion Picture Producers and Distributors of America (MPPDA), and hired Will Hays, the architect of Warren Harding's 1920 presidential victory, as its spokesman. Hays faced an almost impossible task – how to satisfy industry critics and maintain fan interest. In the early 1930's a series of flashy gangsters – Edward G. Robinson in *Little Caesar* [WB, 1930], James Cagney in *The Public Enemy* [WB, 1931], and Paul Muni in *Scarface* [UA,1932] – murdered their way to the top of the gang world and to the top of the box office charts. Penetrating the dangerous, but seductive, urban underworld, movie gangsters spoke colorfully, their guns barked out their own form of law. They flaunted the traditions of hard work, sacrifice, and respect for institutions of authority. These films generated such interest that fans flocked to see weak imitations such as *Hatchet Man* (1932), *Blonde Crazy* (1931), and *Blondie Johnson* (1933) starring Joan Blondell as a machine-gun toting head of a gang. Despite the

---

1. Garth Jowett, "A Capacity for Evil: The 1915 Supreme Court Mutual Decision," *Historical Journal of Film, Radio and Television* (1989), 59-78. The Court held that films were not protected under the First Amendment protection of "free speech." There was no federal, or national, censorship board in the United States. This was a state responsibility. By 1915 state censorship boards were functioning in New York, Pennsylvania, Ohio, Kansas, Maryland and in some 200 municipalities throughout the United States. While each had a different set of rules all the boards were committed to eliminating portraits of changing moral standards, limiting scenes of crime (which they believed responsible for an increase in juvenile delinquency), and avoiding screen portrayals of civil strife, labor-management discord, or government corruption and injustice. The screen, the censors held, was not a proper forum for presentation of controversial issues.

fact that gangsters were almost always killed in the last reel of the film, concerned citizens worried that gangster movies taught disrespect for the law. Walter Lippmann, an astute observer of American culture, wrote in the early 1930s that in his opinion the damage of gangster movies was done long before the criminal was handcuffed. "The damage is done," he claimed, "when the gangster [is] shown in splendor, wearing magnificent clothes and riding around in great limousines[1]." The warden of Sing Sing agreed. He stated unequivocally that "prisoners have told me that crime pictures started them on their course[2]." In Houston, *The Chronicle* claimed the film industry had infected the public with a plague of "bedroom, liquor, gangster and criminal themes[3]."

In 1930, the Catholic Church offered Hays a movie code which it hoped would limit screen sex and violence. It was written by Father Daniel Lord, a professor of dramatics at St. Louis University and sponsored by Martin Quigley, a staunch lay Catholic. The basic premise behind the code was that "no picture should lower the moral standards of those who see it." Recognizing that evil and sin were a legitimate part of drama, the code stressed that it was acceptable to have both in films but that no film should go so far as to create a feeling of "sympathy" for the criminal, the adulterer, the immoral or the corrupter. No film should be so constructed as to "leave the question of right or wrong in doubt." Films must uphold, not question or challenge, the basic values of society. The sanctity of the home and marriage must be upheld. The concept of basic law must not be "belittled or ridiculed." What Lord wanted films to do was to illustrate clearly to audiences that "evil is wrong" and that "good is right."

But the Production Code was not enforced with any rigor in its first four years. By 1934 the Catholic Church had become disgusted with Hays and Hollywood. It formed a Legion of Decency [LOD] to monitor the movies and threatened a national boycott of all films unless the industry enforced Father Lord's code. Facing a boycott by 20 million Catholics during a national depression, the industry caved in and hired Joseph Breen, a conservative lay Catholic, to head a newly created Production Code Administration [PCA]. For the next three decades Breen and his staff censored every film made in Hollywood and the Legion of Decency rated each film for moral content. The impact of Breen, the PCA and the Legion was felt almost immediately on gangster movies. When Warner Bros. sent Breen a script for *Bullets or Ballots* (1936) he objected because the script suggested "that crime is not only profitable, but that criminals, when they are clever, are immune from punishment." The violence in the film was toned down and a prologue added to remind the audience of their responsibility in making sure the police had public support to apprehend criminals[4].

Another change insisted on by the PCA and the LOD was that the stars like Edward G. Robinson and James Cagney begin enforcing the law instead

---

1. Quoted in Frank Walsh, *Sin and Censorship*, 71.
2. "Protests Against Gangster Movies," 1931, box 43, Hays Papers.
3. Joseph Breen to Jack Warner, "Bullets or Ballots", November 30, 1935, PCA Files, Academy of Motion Picture Arts and Sciences Library, Beverly Hills, Ca.
4. Clayton Koppes and Gregory D. Black, *Hollywood Goes to War*, 125.

of making a mockery of it. Cagney played a tough Federal policeman in *G-Man* (1935) and Robinson a dedicated prosecutor in *I Am the Law* (1938). Criminals were no longer presented as heroes – they were much more likely to be presented a sick, sociopathic murderers. Humphrey Bogart perfected the role in *Dead End* (1937) when he played a washed-up hoodlum, Baby Face Martin, who is killed by his boyhood friend. In a similar fashion *Crime School* (1938) and Angels With Dirty Faces (1938) portrayed criminals as deviant cowards who were only tough when they had a gun. During the era of World War II government propaganda played a role in how gangsters were presented on the screen. The Office of War Information (OWI), the official United States propaganda agency, formed a Hollywood office to guide filmmakers in the proper way to present America on the screen. OWI was especially concerned that films not promote the idea of a nation overrun with gangsters. America's ideological battle between democracy and fascism would not be helped if the gangster image continued to be shown in foreign nations. OWI told Hollywood not to show "pictures of unsavory aspects of American life – gangsters, slums, hopeless poverty, etc."

The gangster made a strong comeback in the post-war era. The film noir era in Hollywood featured a much different America. Noir gangsters inhabited a sleazy world of cheap night clubs, floozy femme fatale women who were as dangerous as their male counterparts, corrupt cops who used torture and murder when it suited their purposes. Blackmail, illegal drugs, prostitution and gambling were as American as apple pie in the world of the noir gangsters. The films took place at night, in dark, wet urban streets where danger lurked around every corner. Thrillers such as *The Killers* (1946), *Brute Force* (1947), *Scene of the Crime* (1949), *The Gangster* (1947) and classics such as *Force of Evil* (1948), *White Heat* (1949), *Key Largo* (1948) flooded the screen. In this same period two of the original screen gangsters, James Cagney and Edward G. Robinson, returned to play roles that launched them into stardom. James Cagney reprised his gangster image in *White Heat*. Directed by veteran Raoul Walsh, Cagney plays Cody Jarrett, a violent, psychopathic killer who is certifiably insane – and even he recognizes his illness when he states: "Maybe I am nuts." He was indeed. He murders without remorse, be it friend or foe. In the end, he is outsmarted by federal agents who place a spy in his gang. *White Heat* was an intensely violent film that was extremely popular at the box office earning over 3 million dollars revenue. Edward G. Robinson returned to his gangster roots in John Huston's *Key Largo* as Johnny Rocco, an aging gangster who has been deported for his past criminal actions. He is trying to sneak back into the United States with a large stash of counterfeit money which he hopes will allow him to rebuild his old gang. But he is trapped in a small Florida hotel by a hurricane. The hero is played by Humphrey Bogart (Frank McCloud), a World War II vet who has come to Key Largo to pay his respects to the family of a buddy killed in the war. Johnny Rocco is no Rico from *Little Caesar*. He is an old man trying to recapture his days of glory. In the end, Bogart exposes Rocco as a coward and kills him.

By the early 1950s the America public was no longer enthralled with the criminal class. Senator Estes Kefauver's 1950-51 investigation of organized crime was televised live to a fascinated nation. Kefauver grilled real mobsters such as Frank Costello and Joe Adonis while millions watched a new era in communications unfold. Hollywood was quick to respond with a spate of organized crime films. *The Enforcer* (1951) starred Humphrey Bogart as a crusading district attorney who not only prosecutes the criminals but guns the leader down as well. *The Mob* (1951) featured tough guy Broderick Crawford as an undercover cop who exposes corruption and mob rule on the waterfront. Waterfront corruption was a theme explored by Elia Kazan in his *On the Waterfront* (1954). Kazan had been called to testify by the infamous House of Un-American Activities Committee (HUAC) in 1952. HUAC which was conducting an investigation of Hollywood communists, demanded that witnesses "name names" of members of the communist party. Kazan did so and then made *On the Waterfront* to justify his actions. In the film, Marlon Brando stars as Terry Malloy, a rather punchy ex-prizefighter whose brother is in tight with a mob of gangsters who run the waterfront union. Slowly, Brando is awakened to the dangers the criminals pose to American society and in the end testifies against his pals. The film won eight Academy Awards and its politically conservative theme pleased critics and public alike. By the late 1950s the gangster film had been regulated to mostly "B" features. *Murder by Contract* (1958), *Machine Gun Kelly* (1958), *The Brothers Ricco* (1957) and many, many others covered the familiar ground of crazed killers, indifferent cops where street justice was meated out in the end.

The decades of the 1960s and 1970s brought new life to the gangster film. After almost four decades of censorship, Hollywood scrapped its Production Code Administration and created a ratings system for films which restricted audiences by age according to the amount of sex and violence in any given film. The Catholic Legion of Decency quietly went out of business just as two attractive folk criminals from the Depression era murdered their way into America's psyche. Arthur Penn's *Bonnie and Clyde* (1967) exploded on the screen with a level of violence that shocked almost everyone who saw the film. Warner Bros. ads for the film set the tone: "They're young. They're in love. And they kill people!" Bonnie and Clyde, starring Warren Beatty as Clyde and Faye Dunaway as Bonnie, was a counter-culture movie that had a direct appeal to the youth movement in the United States that was protesting the war in Vietnam and challenging authority at every level. Penn's film made folk heroes out of two petty Depression era killers. The film was both funny, sexy, hip and extremely violent. The most controversial scene in the film is in the final reel when Bonnie and Clyde are killed in a fire-storm of bullets. Using slow-motion photography to emphasize the violence we see blood exploding across the screen, as the young couple is ripped apart in a barrage of fire. Under Father Lord's code movies were not supposed to create a feeling of sympathy for criminals. However those rules no longer applied, and most of the audiences which saw Bonnie and Clyde left the theater mourning the death of the outlaws. Older, established critics like Bosley Crowther of the *New York Times* were infuriated by Bonnie and Clyde and the increasing violence in American films. Crowther carried on a personal campaign against it in the pages of his paper. But young people disregarded the opinions of traditionalists and flocked to theaters in records numbers. Bonnie and Clyde was Warner Bros. biggest hit of the year generating over twenty-two million dollars at the box office.

Five year later Francis Ford Coppola brought the bloodiest, most violent, yet fascinating study of American mobsters to the screen in his Godfather trilogy. *The Godfather* (1972), *The Godfather, Part II* (1974) and *The Godfather, Part III* (1990) trace the fortunes of a Mafia family – the Corleones. The first film is dominated by the family patriarch Don "Vito" Corleone played masterfully by Marlon Brando – a kindly grandfather, a protective patron and a deadly enemy. The family has connections into every facet of American society, controlling the traditional mob businesses – the numbers racket, prostitution and gambling. However, the Corleone family's reach is far broader than the illegal rackets. They control legitimate businesses, banks, the police and politicians. When a Hollywood producer resists casting a friend of the family in his film, he wakes up covered in blood from the head of his favorite horse in bed beside him. The Don's friend got the part! There were over twenty gory murders in the film but what fascinated audiences was not the violence, but the matter-of-fact way in which the family enforced its will on a corrupt America. The film won Academy Awards for Best Picture, Best Actor (Brando refused to accept the award) and Best screenplay and finished the year at the top of the box office charts earning more than 150 million dollars in worldwide box office revenue.

Paramount rushed a sequel into production. Unlike most sequels, *The Godfather, Part II* was seen by most critics as even better than the original. In this saga, Michael Corleone (Al Pacino) has taken over the reigns of the family. Like his father, Michael cuts down anyone who gets in his way. He has expanded the family business to Cuba and the mob works hand-in-hand with Batista government as equal partners in prostitution, drugs, tourism and communications. In America Michael works with United States Senators while his henchmen carry out his bloody orders. As critic Pauline Kael noted the film was "an epic vision of the corruption of America." A smash hit at the box office, the film won six Academy Awards including Best Picture, Best Actor (Pacino), Best Supporting Actor (Robert DeNiro) and Best Director. In 1990 a third film was released but it created little excitement and was generally panned by the critics.

Perhaps Americans were simply tired of gangster films. Several were released in the 1980s but none really captured the imagination of the public the way the two earlier Godfather films had. Brian DePalma's remake of the *Scarface* (1983) was panned by the critics and shunned by the public. It contained nothing of interest but excessive violence. DePalma followed with *The Untouchables* (1987) another excessively violent film which failed critically and financially. Although it seemed Americans were tired of gangsters, the genre has made a dramatic comeback in the 2000-2001 on Home Box Office (HBO). The most popular cable television program in the past two years has been the Sopranos. The HBO program follows the life of a mobster, Tony Soprano, played by James Gandolfini. Tony is in many ways a traditional mob boss – he runs the rackets, prostitution, illegal gambling, drugs, etc. But it is not his mob life that fascinates viewers – it is his middle-class suburban life style that seems so very normal. He and his wife live in a posh suburban home, send their kids, who are generally uncontrollable, to private schools and have the neighbors in for dinner. Tony is a tough guy, but he sees his shrink every week. He has a mistress, but loves his wife. He's as American as apple pie. The gangster has been and remains a staple of American entertainment. Whether at the movies or on television, Americans continue their fascination with organized crime.

Bibliographie

Black, Gregory D. *Hollywood Censored: Morality Codes, Catholics and the Movies* (Cambridge: Cambridge University Press, 1994).

Gabree, John. *Gangsters: From* Little Caesar *to* The Godfather (New York: Pyramid Books, 1973).

Koppes, Clayton and Gregory Black. *Hollywood Goes to War: How Politics, Profits and Propaganda Shaped Worl War II Movies* (Berkeley: University of California Press, 1990).

Munby, Jonathan. *Public Enemies, Public Heroes: Screening the Gangster From* Little Caesar *to* Touch of Evil (Chicago: University of Chicago Press, 1999).

Naremore, James. *More Than Night: Film Noir in Its Contexts* (Berkeley: University of California Press, 1998).

Parish, James Robert and Pitts, Michael R.. *The Great Gangster Pictures* (Metuchen, N.J.: Scarecrow Press, 1976).

Sklar, Robert. *City Boys: Cagney, Bogart, Garfield* (Princeton: Princeton University Press, 1992).

Warshow, Robert. "The Gangster as Tragic Hero," *Partisan Review* (February, 1958).

De la mafia, ou d'un business à l'américaine
Par Marie-Christine Michaud

Il est courant de faire coïncider le crime organisé aux Etats-Unis avec les activités de la Mafia importée par les immigrants italiens[1]. Cette institution a effectivement joué un rôle significatif dans le développement de la criminalité en Amérique, notamment après l'adoption du XVIIIe amendement et de la loi Volstead en 1919. Mais il serait inexact de considérer que la Mafia a organisé le crime aux Etats-Unis. Le but de cet essai est de montrer pourquoi la Prohibition en particulier a représenté un contexte propice à l'expansion du crime organisé par la Mafia italienne et comment elle s'est avérée une opportunité sans précédent pour quelques membres de la communauté italo-américaine qui ont su profiter de cette occasion pour gravir l'échelle socio-économique et s'affirmer dans la société d'accueil de leurs parents. Mais force est de constater que la Mafia, loin de demeurer une institution italienne typique, s'est tranformée pour devenir un *big business* à l'américaine.

La mafia est une institution sicilienne fondée sur la notion de famille et de protection des membres du clan. En Amérique, elle devient un terme générique pour désigner une fédération de gangs à vocation criminelle dont les responsables sont des Italiens. Cette appellation provient de l'ignorance des Américains qui, par commodité également, ne différencient pas les origines régionales des immigrants qui viennent de la péninsule italienne. Pourtant, sans faire un historique des institutions italiennes, il est important de rappeler que la mafia (sans majuscule, singulier de *mafie*) est un système sicilien tandis que ce genre d'institution est appelé la Camorra à Naples ou encore les sociétés d'honneur (*onorata società*) en Calabre.

Toutes ces organisations ont des points communs. Secrètes, elles s'organisent autour de la *famiglia*, la famille au sens large, c'est-à-dire le clan, afin de défendre les individus contre les forces extérieures qui viendraient mettre en danger la cohésion et l'honneur de la famille. Elles cherchent également à perpétuer la tradition des paysans contre toute domination politique imposée soit par les autorités soit par les classes supérieures, l'aristocratie ou le clergé.

En Calabre, les sociétés d'honneur s'opposent à l'oppression politique et militaire du gouvernement du Nord dont les mesures à partir des années 1860 bouleversent l'équilibre des villages et apportent la misère. Recourant à la violence, ces sociétés organisent une guérilla pour défendre leur région contre les troupes gouvernementales. Elles apparaissent comme un moyen d'auto-défense et sont donc soutenues par la population.

À Naples, la Camorra est une société secrète criminelle, d'abord constituée de repris de justice qui prêtent serment de devenir des « hommes d'honneur », d'où l'analogie avec les sociétés de Calabre. Elle se caractérise par un profond patriotisme et tente par des moyens illégaux, habituels des membres qui la composent, de s'opposer à toute domination venue de

---

1. La commission Kefauver (1950-1951) comme nombre de films noirs de l'après-Seconde Guerre mondiale ont propagé cette image.

l'extérieur. Cependant, après la réunification de l'Italie en 1870/1871, sa vocation politique commence à disparaître pour laisser place à des activités criminelles tels que le chantage, la contrebande ou le vol. Or, c'est à cette époque que l'immigration italienne aux Etats-Unis atteint son paroxysme, d'où l'assimilation que font les Américains des Italiens avec des criminels. En effet, ce sont les individus originaires de la péninsule italienne qui constituent le groupe d'immigrants le plus important. En 1930, près de cinq millions ont déjà immigré en Amérique, dont 80% venus du Mezzogiorno, c'est-à-dire des régions du sud et de Sicile[1]. Au tournant du siècle, toutes régions confondues, ce sont les Siciliens qui sont les plus nombreux à immigrer. Entre 1900 et 1910, plus de 56 000[2] arrivent aux Etats-Unis, ce qui peut expliquer le choix du terme de la Mafia, l'institution sicilienne, pour désigner l'ensemble de ces sociétés secrètes familiales.

Le terme Mafia est un acronyme (Morte alla Francia Italia anela) du cri de guerre, repris en 1800 par la police parallèle du roi de Naples, des Siciliens qui combattaient la France en 1282 et qui voulaient prévenir un éventuel débarquement français. Cette appellation est révélatrice des objectifs de cette société secrète, à savoir lutter contre l'oppression et la tyrannie imposées par les étrangers. La Mafia est donc un appel à l'indépendance, à la rébellion et au maintien des valeurs traditionnelles insulaires. Ainsi, les *mafiosi* combattent les officiers étrangers et le recours à la violence est perçu comme un acte de bravoure pour la sauvegarde des intérêts siciliens, d'où le second sens du terme mafia qui signifie courage, endurance, intelligence. Ainsi, les hommes qui composent ces sociétés sont grandement respectés. Les gangs de *mafiosi*, surtout répandus dans les villages de l'ouest de l'île, peuvent être engagés par les paysans pour défendre leurs intérêts contre les propriétaires terriens ou pour lutter contre les mesures opprimantes du gouvernement. La Mafia se présente donc comme une organisation pour la défense des plus faibles et le combat contre les autorités.

L'appartenance à ces sociétés se caractérise par deux attitudes qui s'apparentent à des vertus nationales : l'honnêteté, l'*onesta*, c'est-à-dire le refus de donner des informations aux autorités, et la vengeance, la *vendetta*, qui amène les familles à régler leurs problèmes elles-mêmes. La Mafia s'organise suivant un mode de vie traditionnel, autour de la *famiglia*, et n'obéit qu'aux ordres du chef du groupe, le parrain, dont le rôle est de veiller au maintien de l'ordre familial et au respect de ses membres. En fait, la Mafia répond aux principes du familisme amoral[3], organisation du système sociétal de l'Italie du sud et de la Sicile. La socialisation des individus comme leur code moral ne suivent pas les commandements de la société dans son ensemble. Ils ne répondent qu'aux exigences de la *famiglia*. Ses principes reposent sur la méfiance envers le monde extérieur au clan et seuls les intérêts de la famille sont pris en considération. La famille est une entité indivisible et unie ; ses membres sont censés satisfaire ses besoins et la Mafia est l'instrument prédominant pour protéger les individus, les

---

1. D'après les chiffres annuels du bureau du recensement, ministère du commerce.
2. D'après l'*Annuario statistico dell'emigrazione italiane dal 1856 al 1956*.
3. Banfield, Edward, *The Moral Basis of a Backward Society*. New York : Free Press, 1958, p. 10-11 et 92.

traditions et la solidarité clanique. Ainsi, les Siciliens qui immigrent aux Etats-Unis apportent-ils avec eux les « codes » du familisme amoral qui dans le contexte américain sont plutôt pris pour des attitudes non civiques voire criminelles d'autant plus que les activités de ces sociétés secrètes sont largement relatées et même amplifiées dans la presse[1], par le gouvernement italien contre lequel la Mafia représente un contre-pouvoir ou encore par les autorités américaines qui craignent son influence politico-criminelle dans les colonies d'immigrants[2]. De fait, les immigrants venant de la péninsule italienne sont précédés d'une image négative lorsqu'ils arrivent aux Etats-Unis. Cette crainte est renforcée au tournant du siècle par deux assassinats qui auraient été perpétrés par des *mafiosi* selon le gouvernement américain qui fait l'amalgame entre anarchistes italiens et membres des sociétés secrètes, et qui conclue que la Mafia s'est implantée aux Etats-Unis.

En 1891, le superintendant de la police de La Nouvelle-Orléans, David Hennessy est assassiné par des Siciliens. Dix-huit sont inculpés. Les Américains considèrent donc que les colonies d'immigrants italiens abritent des criminels. Quelques années plus tard, en 1909, l'inspecteur de police italo-américain Joseph Petrosino qui a pour mission de démasquer les criminels/anarchistes italiens se fait tuer en arrivant en Sicile où il prévoyait de compléter son enquête. Mais on peut se demander si sa mission était double, à savoir de pourchasser les criminels et les anarchistes, ou s'il y avait amalgame entre les uns et les autres.

La population américaine a par conséquent des préjugés à l'encontre de la communauté italienne qui s'installe aux Etats-Unis et des sociétés secrètes qui sont considérées comme des organisations criminelles. Ces idées et la peur qu'elles dégagent sont renforcées lorsque la Prohibition est adoptée au Congrès par le passage du XVIIIe amendement en 1919 et mise en application par la loi Volstead qui prend effet en 1920. Au fur et à mesure que les autorités s'aperçoivent qu'elles ne parviennent pas à faire appliquer la loi, la mauvaise réputation des immigrants italiens s'intensifie. Dès 1921 le *Daily Times* par exemple lance une campagne de sensibilisation au sujet du danger que représentent les colonies d'Italiens aux Etats-Unis. On peut lire : « illegal traffic was due to our foreigners who are allowed to come in here and make their own laws and sell all kinds of intoxicating spirits » ou encore « the most flagrant violators of the Volstead Act are foreigners and naturalized citizens[3] ». La criminalité aux Etats-Unis semble provenir de la présence des étrangers. L'implantation de certaines institutions européennes, telles que les sociétés secrètes italiennes, effraie l'opinion publique.

---

1. En 1875 le *New York Times* écrit : "Our Italian population (...) are frequently guilty of crime of violence. They are extremely ignorant and have been reared in the belief that brigandage is a manly occupation and assassination is the national sequence of the most trivial quarrel." Cité dans : Richard Gambino, *Blood of my Blood*, 282. Discours repris dans diverses campagnes par le journal en 1905, 1909 et par le *South Atlantic Quarterly* en 1905 ou le *Republican* de Denver en 1908.
2. Rapport de la comminssion Dillingham en 1911, par exemple.
3. Cité dans : Bruce McBride, "Prohibition and Ethnicity in Oswego, New York" in *Italians and Irish in America*, AIHA, 1983, 69.

La Prohibition interdit la manufacture et la vente de toute boisson dont le taux d'alcool est supérieur à 0,5% sur l'ensemble du territoire américain. Les termes du XVIIIe amendement, interdisant la vente mais pas la consommation d'alcool, vont inciter le développement de la contrebande ainsi que la commercialisation des boissons illicites dans des bars clandestins, les *speakeasies*. Or, l'organisation comme le fonctionnement de la Mafia semblent être appropriés à la mise en place d'une structure qui réponde à la demande de fournir les boissons interdites. En outre, ce contexte donne aux Italiens l'occasion de développer des activités lucratives conjointes comme le jeu ou la prostitution. Ainsi, ils vont profiter des opportunités qu'offre la Prohibition pour s'enrichir en même temps qu'ils vont imposer une nouvelle forme de crime organisé.

A cause de sa solidarité intrinsèque, de l'*onesta*, de son caractère secret et des habitudes de lutter contre les autorités, la Mafia se révèle un instrument opportun pour satisfaire l'Amérique « wet ». Toutefois, à cause du contexte particulier des années vingt qui poussent les étrangers à acquérir un mode de vie américain (le mouvement d'américanisation battait son plein juste avant la guerre) et de la mythologie nationale qui associe succès et richesse, l'institution italienne va subir des transformations irréversibles. Elle va perdre son identité et le crime organisé aux Etats-Unis ne sera pas italien mais italo-américain à moins qu'il ne devienne totalement américain !

La Mafia, qui, même si elle utilise déjà la violence, le racket, l'intimidation ou le meurtre pour parvenir à ses fins en Italie du Sud, a pour vocation la protection du clan et la lutte contre les autorités. Au contact de l'environnement américain, elle devient une association de malfaiteurs. En fait, les Italiens adaptent leur organisation traditionnelle aux besoins de la Prohibition de telle sorte qu'elle va devenir une structure américaine[1].

Les Italiens n'organisent pas le crime ni la contrebande des produits interdits mais adhèrent plutôt à des gangs déjà établis dans les grands centres urbains par des Irlandais tels que Dion O'Banion et « Big Bill » Dwyer ou « Klondike » O'Donnell puis par des juifs tels que Arnold Rothstein, J. « Gurrah » Shapiro ou Sammie « Purple » Cohen[2]. Les Italiens forment des alliances avec ces patrons de la pègre, ce qui témoigne d'une première modification dans la nature de la Mafia qui s'ouvre vers le monde extérieur. A cause de l'accélération qu'entraîne la Prohibition dans le fonctionnement du crime organisé, les Italiens ne peuvent se permettre de rester replier sur eux-mêmes.

Lorsque les immigrants italiens s'installent en Amérique, les jeunes générations se regroupent en gangs, expressions sociales de leur identité ethnique et instrument de leur socialisation dans un environnement inconnu[3]. Mais ces gangs n'ont qu'une portée locale. Chaque pâté de maison

---

1. Nelli, Humbert, *The Business of Crime*, "The illegal organizations became combinations of the familiar Old World models adapted to the New World needs", p. 137.
2. Ianni, Francis, *A Family Business*, p. 87.
3. Mangione, Jerre et Ben Morreale, *La Storia*. Propos recueillis en 1976 : "Without a gang, you were *niente*, nothing, a loser."

à son gang qui ne sévit que dans le quartier[1]. Ils reposent sur des critères géographiques et claniques puisque l'immigration en chaîne fait se regrouper dans les mêmes quartiers des Italiens originaires des mêmes villages. Ces gangs semblent par conséquent être dans la continuité de l'organisation de la Mafia. Cinq grandes familles[2] se partagent le territoire de New York, c'est-à-dire dirigent les communautés italiennes de la ville. Mais, leurs profits, comparés à ceux qu'une organisation tournée vers l'extérieur peut rapporter, restent limités. En adhérant à des structures qui fonctionnent déjà, les Italiens pensent pouvoir élargir leur champ d'action et bénéficier de l'expérience des gangsters déjà organisés. Ce sont par exemple les Irlandais qui ont le monopole de la distribution en ayant acquis une certaine assise auprès des compagnies de transport et des dockers. Mais ces alliances avec des inconnus rompent avec la tradition du familisme amoral. Elles montrent que les individus sont disposés à obéir à des codes différents.

Ces alliances émanent de deux facteurs déterminants : (1) les immigrants italiens n'ont pas l'intention d'exporter la Mafia hors de leur pays et (2) ils veulent profiter des opportunités que génère la Prohibition même si elles nécessitent d'abandonner la tradition. Lorsque les paysans italiens immigrent massivement aux Etats-Unis à la fin du XIXe siècle jusqu'à la Première Guerre mondiale, les chefs de la Mafia n'ont aucune raison de quitter leur pays où ils bénéficient d'un statut respectable et de revenus substantiels. Les responsables n'immigrant pas, il est difficile pour les individus d'organiser les sociétés secrètes. Ils n'en ont ni l'expérience ni le temps. Il a fallu plus d'un siècle aux Italiens/Siciliens pour mettre en place leur système. On est alors amenés à se demander comment les immigrants pourraient l'établir en Amérique en vingt ou trente ans (période entre la première vague massive d'Italiens aux Etats-Unis et l'adoption de la Prohibition) surtout si l'on tient compte du fait qu'ils ont immigré individuellement et que la Mafia dépend d'une solidarité clanique. C'est seulement à partir de la seconde moitié des années vingt que les *mafiosi* immigrent aux Etats-Unis car Mussolini mène une politique sévère contre la Mafia dont les activités discréditent son pouvoir. Cependant, ces parrains ne jouent guère un rôle important dans l'expansion du crime organisé en Amérique car, lorsqu'ils immigrent, ils rejoignent des colonies en cours d'américanisation. Leur éthique a évolué, elles ne répondent plus aux mêmes principes. En effet, à cette époque, ce sont les immigrants italiens de la seconde génération, c'est-à-dire les individus nés ou élevés aux Etats-Unis, qui dirigent les communautés et les gangs. Le processus d'américanisation des étrangers a été accéléré[3]. La Mafia, comme les autres institutions ethniques telles que l'église ou la famille, s'est altérée. Les jeunes, par mimétisme et par besoin de ne plus se sentir marginalisés dans leur société d'accueil, adoptent le modèle américain et décident de rompre avec le familisme amoral. Constatant que les gangs irlandais et juifs tirent

---

1. Tricarico, Donald, *The Italians of Greenwich Village*. New York : CMS, 1984, p. 63.
2. Les clans de Joseph Bonanno, de Vito Genovese, de Carlo Gambino, de Gaetano Lucchese et de Joseph Colombo.
3. Michaud, Marie-Christine, *Les Italiens aux Etats-Unis – 1918-1929. Progrès et limites d'une assimilation*. Paris : L'Harmattan, 1998.

d'importants bénéfices de la contrebande de produits illicites, ils se mettent à former des alliances avec eux, n'en déplaise aux parents et à la tradition !

L'adoption de la Prohibition est déterminante dans l'évolution de l'organisation sociétale des communautés italiennes aux Etats-Unis car elle force les gangs à travailler ensemble par delà les barrières ethniques et les préjugés nationaux. Au lieu de rester groupés en famille, les nouveaux parrains s'entourent « d'amis » mais cette loyauté est motivée par la recherche du gain et n'est pas aussi fiable que celle construite sur les fondements de la solidarité clanique. Les *mafiosi* italo-américains organisent leurs groupes différemment et surtout se débarrassent des responsables de la Mafia traditionnelle et de ceux des autres groupes, irlandais et juifs, en menant une guerre des gangs dont la victoire leur assure l'omnipotence dans le crime organisé. La période de la Prohibition marque ainsi le début de la domination italienne et l'émergence d'une nouvelle Mafia.

Les Italiens de la seconde génération tels que Lucky Luciano, arrivé aux Etats-Unis à l'âge de dix ans, Franck Costello, immigré à l'âge de neuf ans ou Al Capone, né à New York, ne perpétuent pas la tradition italienne. Ayant grandi aux Etats-Unis, ils ont une mentalité américaine et ne se sentent pas attachés aux principes de leurs aïeux, d'où la propension à établir des alliances inter-ethniques[1]. Comme le répète Al Capone : « I'm no Italian. I was born in Brooklyn[2] ».

Ce sont les préjugés à l'encontre des immigrants italiens ainsi que l'idée que les Américains se font des objectifs de la Mafia italienne qui peuvent amener à penser que le crime a été organisé aux Etats-Unis par la Mafia italienne. Mais, en fait, la Prohibition développe les activités clandestines mises en place par les Irlandais puis par les juifs, et « intronise » les Italiens dans le crime organisé. La contrebande de boissons illicites et le développement de ses corollaires (établissement des *speakeasies*, multiplication des salles de jeu et des maisons closes...) permettent aux gangsters de s'enrichir et d'exercer un pouvoir non-négligeable sur les classes supérieures. Celles-ci cherchent à assurer leur position socio-politique et ne veulent pas se soumettre aux clauses du XVIIIe amendement après les années de restrictions dues à la guerre puis à la dépression économique. La « coopération » entre gangsters et hommes politiques rompt avec l'attitude traditionnelle de la Mafia qui, en Italie du Sud, combat les classes dominantes. Cependant, comme cette collaboration repose sur un système de corruption et d'intimidation, il est tout de même possible de considérer celle-ci comme une compétition entre les deux instances. La Mafia continue de représenter un contre-pouvoir. Or, impatients de s'insérer dans la société américaine, les Italiens voient dans la Prohibition une occasion de s'affirmer, d'où leur acceptation de se conformer au

---

1. Mangione, Jerre et Ben Morreale, *op cit*. Propos de Joseph Bonanno : "No matter how deeply I treasured memories of Sicily, I was Joseph Bonanno of America. I was born in Sicily, but not of that world anymore... Tradition has died in America. The way of life that I and my Sicilian ancestors pursued is dead. What Americans refer to as the 'Mafia' is a degenerate outgrowth of that life-style. Sicilian immigrants who came to America tried to conduct their affairs as they did in Sicily, but we eventually discovered this was impossible." (p. 259)
2. Rolle, Andrew, *The Italian-Americans – Troubled Roots*. New York : Free Press, 1980, p. 94.

système établi par les autres groupes et de former des alliances interethniques, et ceci jusqu'au massacre de la Saint Valentin en février 1929 qui devient le symbole de la prise de pouvoir du crime organisé par les Italiens.

Franck Costello qui a acquis le monopole des machines à sous quand la Prohibition est adoptée n'appartient à aucune famille dans le sens italien du terme. Il se met à travailler avec les Irlandais. En fait, il a pour mentor William M. « Boss » Tweed qui a su corrompre la machine politique newyorkaise et a mis en place une organisation presque militaire pour diriger ses affaires. A l'instar de Tweed, Franck Costello développe une nouvelle forme de criminalité. Il corrompt des gardes côtes et des policiers, impose une discipline très stricte à ses hommes, commence à utiliser les armes à feu et les explosifs. Ses méthodes sont différentes de celles de la Mafia traditionnelle, à savoir le rejet de toute personne extérieure au clan, l'utilisation d'armes blanches...

Lucky Luciano a des amis juifs, Arnold Rothstein et Meyer Lansky qui sont spécialisés dans la contrebande d'alcool et le jeu. Cependant, Lucky Luciano semble loyal envers la Mafia italienne puisqu'il est l'un des lieutenants du clan de l'Italien Joe Masseria, comme Franck Costello et Al Capone. Il travaille ensuite pour le Sicilien Salvatore Maranzano après que celui-ci a éliminé son opposant italien pour garantir à son clan l'hégémonie de la Mafia à New York. C'est l'épisode de la guerre de Castellamare en 1930/1931. Il semble pourtant que Lucky Luciano ait œuvré pour se débarrasser successivement de ces deux hommes, symboles du système traditionnel de la Mafia, afin de devenir le « patron ». Il a trahi les principes de la Mafia en faisant tuer des parrains. Il n'a pas respecté le code d'obéissance et d'honneur qui lie les membres du clan. En outre, ses alliances avec ses amis juifs deviennent de plus en plus formelles, notamment en matière de proxénétisme. Son ascension dans le crime organisé – il devient le chef incontestable du crime organisé à New York à partir des années trente – et la nouvelle structure qu'il développe par ses amitiés extra-claniques marquent la fin de la vieille génération de la Mafia aux Etats-Unis. Son expérience est significative de l'américanisation de la Mafia.

Al Capone également commence par adhérer à des gangs contrôlés par des Irlandais, notamment dans l'organisation de la prostitution à New York avant de s'installer à Chicago. Là, il devient le lieutenant de John Torrio et coopère avec des hommes politiques qui lui garantissent une certaine liberté d'action. Il soutient fortement la campagne électorale de « Big Bill » Thompson qui, grâce à son appui, redevient maire en 1927 et a pour ami personnel le sénateur Daniel A. Serritella.

En 1926, Dion O'Banion collabore avec la police et fait arrêter John Torrio. Malgré l'alliance qui lie les deux groupes, pour montrer la puissance du clan des Italiens et aussi pour châtier l'Irlandais qui n'a pas respecté le code des gangsters, Al Capone lance une guerre des gangs qui se solde par le massacre de la Saint Valentin en 1929 et l'écrasante victoire des Italiens. Al Capone devient le maître du crime organisé de Chicago. La compétition avec les Irlandais dont il continue de se servir pour le transport des boissons illicites avec le Canada jusqu'au massacre de 1929, stimule ses activités. Il s'est fixé un objectif, devenir riche et respecté. D'ailleurs, contrairement aux autres gangsters, il aime apparaître en public, montrer qu'il est devenu en membre influent de la communauté. Il profite donc des opportunités que procurent la prohibition et ses corollaires (proxénétisme, jeu, racket, chantage, usure...) pour s'affirmer dans la société américaine. Pour lui, la loi Volstead représente une occasion de développer des activités, criminelles, qu'il professionnalise. Cette nouvelle organisation lui permet de gravir l'échelle sociale américaine. Comme tous les Italiens de la seconde génération qui dominent le crime organisé à cette époque, Al Capone est disposé à outrepasser les principes de la Mafia traditionnelle pour augmenter ses revenus.

Les méthodes de ces « jeunes parrains » évoluent. Elles se sont américanisées à l'instar des « innovations » de Lucky Luciano. L'emploi d'une violence ostensible qui va de pair avec la guerre des gangs, l'utilisation d'explosifs ou le trafic de narcotiques que lance « Black Tony » Parmagini sont autant de situations qui sont impensables pour les parrains de la vieille génération. D'une part, ceux-ci ne peuvent avoir de contacts avec d'autres groupes à cause des barrières linguistiques qui limitent les échanges et maintiennent le clan soudé, voire isolé, alors que les jeunes chefs, élevés en Amérique, parlent anglais, ce qui autorise l'ouverture sur l'extérieur. D'autre part, la vieille génération suit les principes du familisme amoral *stricto sensu*. Même si en Italie la Mafia fait preuve de violence pour parvenir à ses fins, l'extension des activités illicites en Amérique rompt avec la vocation de la mafia traditionnelle.

Grâce à la Prohibition, la nouvelle génération de gangsters n'est plus, dans une certaine mesure, une génération d'Italiens mais d'Italo-Américains puisque leur mode de travail s'est transformé. Ils ne respectent plus les mêmes valeurs. En fait, ils sont devenus des porte-parole de l'esprit américain de l'entre-deux-guerres. Cette nouvelle Mafia – italo-américaine – s'est fixée des objectifs nouveaux. Elle est fondée sur une organisation moderne et répond à des critères moins conservateurs, ce qui fait d'elle une institution extra-familiale à but lucratif.

C'est dans ce sens que la loi Volstead marque un tournant dans le développement du crime organisé aux Etats-Unis. Celui-ci est alors un produit américain résultant du contexte urbain et du conflit entre la résurgence d'une Amérique puritaine, rurale et « dry », et le désir d'hédonisme des classes aisées des grands centres urbains. Les valeurs traditionnelles et ethniques qui étaient attachées à la Mafia disparaissent. Le crime organisé prend les allures d'une véritable entreprise. En effet, Al Capone affirme que le but de ses activités clandestines est de répondre à une demande, de « rendre un service public (puisque) près de 90% des habitants de Chicago boivent et jouent », comme il le confie à un journaliste en 1927 – en exagérant sûrement. Ainsi, il a la prétention d'apparaître comme « un bienfaiteur pour la population de Chicago[1] ». Il cultive l'image d'un homme populaire, d'un mécène, comme les grands industriels du

---

1. Propos cités dans Humbert Nelli, *Italians in Chicago*, New York : Oxford University Press, 1970, p. 221.

début du siècle, Rockefeller ou Vanderbilt par exemple. La structure de la Mafia doit être modernisée pour satisfaire les demandes. C'est la loi du marché. Al Capone institutionnalise alors la centralisation des ordres, optimise la distribution des produits et améliore leur commercialisation afin d'augmenter ses profits. La Prohibition permet l'ouverture d'un marché plus vaste sur une plus grande échelle[1]. C'est la demande qui régit l'étendue de la contrebande. Ainsi, dans les grandes villes, à New York, Chicago, Détroit, Philadelphie, San Francisco ou Los Angeles..., le crime organisé se développe tandis qu'il y a peu de demande dans les milieux ruraux où la Mafia s'implante à peine[2]. La raison d'être de la Mafia n'est plus de défendre l'honneur du clan familial mais de s'enrichir. Les « nobles » valeurs des sociétés secrètes qui composent la Mafia italienne sont remplacées par une vision pragmatique, presque vénale, de l'efficacité du crime organisé aux Etats-Unis.

Les activités clandestines sont stimulées par les bénéfices personnels et le succès individuel. D'ailleurs, c'est bien individuellement que ces hommes rejoignent leurs gangs et grâce à leurs activités, ils acquièrent richesse et respectabilité. Ainsi, on peut dire que ces gangsters symbolisent l'esprit de la libre entreprise. C'est la notion américaine de succès, qui se mesure au regard des profits et des sommes amassées, qui motive leurs initiatives et leur hâte de gravir l'échelle sociale. Cette perspective, matérialiste, marque une rupture avec la vision traditionnelle de l'honneur, de la *vendetta* et des principes du familisme amoral. La valeur de l'argent est mise en exergue par le contexte américain tandis que l'éthique passe au second plan.

Dans ce sens, on peut admettre que la Prohibition constitue une étape ultime dans l'épanouissement de la Mafia aux Etats-Unis et qu'elle donne naissance à un nouveau crime organisé. Et l'on peut se demander si leur organisation criminelle ne serait pas une façon pour les Italo-Américains de sortir des ghettos ethniques et de réaliser leur rêve américain. En outre, les Italiens ont immigré dans d'autres pays, en France, en Argentine ou au Brésil sans y établir un système semblable. Aussi ne serait-ce pas l'environnement américain qui les a conduit à organiser le crime de la sorte, et la Prohibition ne représenterait-elle pas un exemple type de situation favorable à l'organisation d'une Mafia ? L'Amérique, terre des libertés et des opportunités, s'apparente alors véritablement à un nouvel Eldorado pour les *mafiosi* de la seconde génération.

Le crime organisé permet aux individus de s'insérer socialement et économiquement dans la société américaine puisque c'est grâce à l'argent que la reconnaissance sociale s'opère. C'est une des raisons pour lesquelles la Prohibition transforme le crime organisé en entreprise. A la fin des années vingt, les revenus annuels de Capone s'élèvent à plus de cent millions de dollars alors que les affaires de John Torrio, quand il en hérite, rapportent cinquante millions de dollars par an. Ainsi, Al Capone a étendu

---

1. Propos recueillis dans Mangione, Jerre et Ben Morreale, *op cit*. "This system of ours gives to each and every one of us a great opportunity if we only seize it with our hands and make the most of it." (p. 259)
2. McBride, Bruce, *Prohibition and Ethnicity in Oswego, New York, 1920-1933*. New York : AIHA, 1985 p. 69-70.

son empire et est devenu un homme d'affaires et il agit comme tel. Il sort dans les endroits à la mode, fait parler de lui et donne des interviews. Il agit comme un véritable *businessman*. En entrepreneur avisé, il commence même à investir sa fortune dans des affaires légales, sans aucun lien avec la Mafia, aux Etats-Unis comme en Italie. Il devient producteur de musique de jazz avec l'ouverture du Cotton Club par exemple. Il a acquis l'esprit d'entreprise américain. Le fonctionnement de la nouvelle Mafia met en avant la valeur sociale de l'argent qui confère dignité à l'individu. Cette reconnaissance sociale n'est envisageable qu'au travers de l'acquisition de biens. Le crime organisé qui se développe pendant la Prohibition permet donc aux Italiens de la seconde génération de s'intégrer dans le système capitaliste américain.

Même si l'éthique condamne la stratégie adoptée par les *mafiosi* italo-américains, l'ascension sociale et économique faisant partie du mythe américain, elle pousse ceux-ci à s'américaniser. Ainsi, l'on peut dire que la Prohibition a été un agent d'américanisation et le fait que les *mafiosi* de la seconde génération aient adapté leur institution particulière au contexte américain pour la diriger comme un véritable *business* est révélateur de cette américanisation.

En effet, la Prohibition fait partie intégrante du mouvement d'américanisation de la fin XIXe et début XXe siècles. Elle vise à changer les habitudes des populations étrangères qui sont les plus grands consommateurs et producteurs d'alcool (les Irlandais, Allemands et Italiens) et à leur faire accepter un mode de vie (de pensée et d'alimentation même) américain. Dans une certaine mesure on peut considérer que la réticence à se soumettre à la loi Volstead de la part de la communauté italienne, réticence dont la Mafia est un instrument majeur, révèle le désir de conserver son patrimoine ethnique. Ainsi, paradoxalement, cette Mafia américanisée aurait-elle aidé les Italiens à faire perdurer leur identité ?

Bibliographie

Bardsley, Marilyn. *Al Capone*. www.crimelibrary.com/capone/caponemain.htm
Gambino, Richard. *Blood of my Blood*, 3e edition (Buffalo, NY : Guernica, 1998).
Ianni, Francis. *A Family Business : Kinship and Social Control in Organized Crime* (New York : Russell Sage Foundation, 1972).
« The Mafia and the Web of Kinship », *Public Interest*, hiver 1971, 78-100.
LaGumina, Salvatore. *WOP*, 2e édition (Buffalo : Guernica, 1999).
Lopreato, Joseph. *Italian Americans* (New York : Random House, 1970).
Mangione, Jerre et Ben Morreale. *La Storia* (New York : HarperPerennial, 1993).
Nelli, Humbert. *The Business of Crime* (New York : Oxford University Press, 1976).

The regulation of morals in the United States – a study of State and federal controls of organized crime

By Jean-Eric Branaa

Introduction

In the twentieth century the United States sought by means of statute law to achieve the most thorough oversight of personal behavior in the Western industrial world. Tens of thousands of federal, state and local laws attempted to enforce morality through prohibitions on alcohol, gambling, prostitution and drugs, and through strict censorship and a host of more trivial restrictions. The intention was to end all behavior that a Protestant culture defined as sinful and non productive. Persuasion and education were not enough: Americans had to be coerced by law into a virtuous healthy way of life. These laws failed to make the United States a better nation and, instead, fostered, facilitated and sustained a level of crime and corruption far in excess of more tolerant societies. Corrupt networks, often inclusding police and politicians, ensured that prohibited activities continued. The profits were immense, and often worth killing for. The laws were ignored or selectively enforced, filling prisons with transgressors who had run out of luck or failed to make the right connections. Americans continued to drink, gamble, or take drugs whether or not it was against the law.

The purpose of this study is to show how American society kept fighting this attack against its integrity, despite an apparent federal lethargy, which might lead an observer think to the contrary: At first, lacking the will to enforce the Volstead Act, Congress effectively assigned an entire industry to the underworld. In the early days of Prohibition, groups of young men formed gangs to supply alcoholic beverages to the population of the largest cities in the United States. Their business rapidly developed and turned to illegal gambling and loan sharking. At the same time it is worth noting that they owned a considerable number of legitimate businesses. They went about their business, were able to fix their problems with the local justice system, contributed to political candidates of both sides and lived an apparently ordinary life, without ever being prosecuted for their illegal activities.

Many people believed that fundamental instincts such as gambling and sex could be totally suppressed. In part this was a response to the disruptive processes of rapid industrialization and urbanization, and the influx of millions of migrants and immigrants into the cities. Many reacted to the Catholic attitude towards gambling and liquor by joining or forming anti-vice and temperance societies, and lobbying energetically in state capitals and city halls for more laws and effective enforcement. Those people were not satisfied with more fines and prison sentences for gamblers and prostitutes, however, and their second intention was to enact laws governing other aspects of personal behavior. By 1910 more than 16,000 such laws were on federal, state and local statute books, governing not just gambling and prostitution but cigarette smoking, the length of skirts and size of bathing suits in some states. In 1919 the Volstead Act was passed, providing for the enforcement of the 18th Amendment to the Constitution.

The Amendment prohibited the manufacture, transportation, sale or importation of intoxicating liquor within the United States. At midnight on 16 January 1920 millions of Americans said farewell to legal liquor and prohibitionists rejoiced.

The Prohibition period eroded public respect for the law and turned street thugs into millionaires. By the mid-1920s the gangs, rather than serving politicians as minions, were giving orders to mayors and congressmen. Therefore compromise was out of the question and the only answer was to defeat the menace with more laws and increased law enforcement capacity. But it took time and it was only in the 1960s that the federal government became seriously involved in attempting to enforce morality laws. Thus the very nature of the American institutions may explain this slowness: it is because there is a division of power between states and national government, and because the people are strongly attached to the idea expressed in the 10th Amendment[1] that no real national solution was available before more than 30 years on this particular matter.

Definition

In his book entitled *Organized Crime*, Howard Abadinsky defined organized crime as being "nonideological, hierarchical, limited or exclusive in membership, perpetuitous, organized through specialization or division of labor, monopolistic and governed by rules and regulations[2]."

This definition is useful because the term "organized crime" has come to mean different things to different people, societies or laws. This has been mostly due to the secretive nature of crime syndicates, the consequence being a lack of concrete data available for scholars and organizations to work with. The resulting confusion has led to a muddled policy and criminal law approach which has not diminished the influence of organized crime, but perhaps has even helped it to flourish. This can be understood from the variety of ways in which state and legal agencies and legislation have defined organized crime. Here is a sampling[3]:

California: Organized crime consists of two or more persons who, with continuity of purpose, engage in one or more of the following activities: (1) The supplying of illegal goods and services e.g., vice, loan sharking, etc.; (2) Predatory crime, e.g., theft, assault, etc.

Delaware: A group of individuals working outside the law for economic gain.

Mississippi: Two or more persons conspiring together to commit crimes for profit on a continuing basis.

Missouri: A self-perpetuating criminal conspiracy for power and profit, utilizing fear and corruption and seeking to obtain immunity from the law.

---

1. The 10th Amendment states that "The powers not delegated to the United States by the Constitution, nor prohibited by it to the States, are reserved to the States respectively, or to the people".
2. Abadinsky, Howard, *Organized Crime*. 2nd ed. (Chicago: Nelson-Hall, 1985), p. 31.
3. Derived in most part from National Advisory Committee on Criminal Justice Standards and Goals, *Organized Crime: Report of the Task Force on Organized Crime* (Washington, D.C.: U.S. Department of Justice, 1976), p. 214-215.

New Mexico: The supplying for profit of illegal goods and services, including, but not limited to, gambling, loan sharking, narcotics, and other forms of vice and corruption.

Ohio: Five or more persons collaborating to promote or engage in extortion, prostitution, theft gambling, illegal traffic in drugs, liquors, or weapons, loan sharking, or any other offense for profit.

Tennessee: The unlawful activities of the members or an organized, disciplined association engaged in supplying illegal goods and services, including, but not limited to, gambling, prostitution, loan sharking, narcotics, labor racketeering, and other unlawful activities of members of such organizations.

Federal law[1] defines organized crime as "... those unlawful activities in which a highly organized, disciplined association supplies illegal goods and services." It even acknowledges that organized crime thrives precisely because "... it provides services the public demands..." and that its livelihood "... depends not on victims, but on customers." This explanation illustrates how the law, while acknowledging the power of the market behind the power of organized crime, nevertheless has not implemented this concept in its crime fighting policy.

The most complete and least subjective definition of organized crime is the one provided by Reuter and Rubinstein and will be referred to for the remainder of this paper.

> *Organized crime is viewed as a set of stable, hierarchically organized gangs which, through violence or its credible threat, have acquired monopoly control of certain major illegal markets. This control has produced enormous profits, which have been used to bribe public officials, thus further protecting the monopolies. These funds have also been invested in acquiring legitimate businesses in which the racketeers continue to use extortion and threats to minimize competition*[2].

This definition not only encompasses an implicit economic analysis, but also alludes to public policy issues, which are raised by the inclusion of corruption of police and legislators. In addition, it makes no mention of either the ethnicity of members of crime syndicates or the familial ties which many assume are prevalent in crime "families." While Italian Americans may be among the more prominent and "news worthy" individuals involved with organized crime, they are certainly not the only ones involved. As Dwight Smith points out, "... the historical association with the Italian dominated crime syndicate... was not so much an essential attribute of the enterprise being developed[3]..."

Mark Haller, on this point, remarks that "Organized crime is a product of America". It is not Italian, Sicilian, Jewish, German, Polish or Russian. Its

---

1. For a detailed description of the federal legal interpretation of organized crime see Jeff Atkinson, "Racketeer Influenced and Corrupt Organizations,' 18 U.S.C. 1961-1968: Broadest of the Federal Criminal Statutes", *Journal of Criminal Law and Criminology*, 69, Spring 1978, p. 1-18.
2. Reuter, Peter and Jonathan B. Rubinstein, "Fact, fancy, and organized crime", *The Public Interest* 53 (1978): 45-68. Passas 55-78.
3. Smith Jr., Dwight C., "Some Things that may be More Important to Understand about Organized Crime than Cosa Nostra", *University of Florida Law Review* 26 (1971): 1-30. Passas 25-54.

leaders were American born or socialized, and the context of the American economic and political system effected them[1]".

Elaborating on Reuter and Rubinstein's definition, Haller concurs with the idea of organized crime as being a set of hierarchically organized gangs. This can be expanded upon further by equating the gangs to separate firms in collusion with each other. He views joining a crime syndicate as being similar to joining a college alumni association or the Chamber of Commerce. It is a way for businessmen to network and make contacts that might help them in their future business endeavors, legal or not. Those who are beginners look for more experienced mentors who might pass opportunities on to them while more mature businessmen come to find reliable potential partners and to exchange vital information which can help them in future business decisions. From an economic viewpoint, being a part of this exclusive society minimizes search costs (for partners and possible business deals) and maximizes expected benefits from future market transactions for both the established criminals and for the budding entrepreneur who wishes to be involved in an organized crime syndicate. For the inexperienced, blood and ethnic ties, although beneficial, are no longer requirements.

The Prohibition era: enforcement of the law and its limitations

Crime control became a steadily more prominent issue in national politics during the decades of the 1920s and 1930s. For the first time, presidents of the United States felt it necessary to speak and act on the crime problem. Shortly after taking office in 1929, Herbert Hoover appointed a national crime commission to study and make recommendations about the administration of criminal justice. The expanded role of the federal government, like the return to the death penalty, was an indication of widespread public concern about crime and crime control and there was a greater demand for greater efficiency in apprehending, convicting and punishing criminals. But the question of efficiency of law enforcement, the courts and corrections became a steadily more important theme.

Effective prohibition of alcohol was certainly an impossible dream given the scale of the country. The borders with Canada and Mexico were several thou-sands miles long. There were more than 12,000 miles of Atlantic, Pacific and Gulf shoreline, abounding in inlets. Smugglers won the battle against the customs service and the border patrol without problem. A population of over 100 million inhabited a land mass of around 3 million square miles. Only a huge standing army would have made an impact on distribution. The very true idea of enforcement was mocked. Representative Fiorello La Guardia estimated that it would require a police force of 250,000 men to dry up New York alone, 'and a force of 250,000 to police the police'. Diligent state enforcement in New York, according to Governor Al Smith, would require one-third of the state's citizens to apprehend another third who were violators, while the remaining third would be tied up serving on juries[2].

---

1. Haller, Mark H., "Illegal Enterprise: A Theoretical and Historical Interpretation", *Criminology* 28 (1990): 207-35. Passas 225-54.
2. La Guardia quoted in Herbert Ashbury, *The Great Illusion: An Informal History of Prohibition*, New York, Doubleday & Co, 1950, p. 145-146.

More resentment of liquor law injustice was caused by the disparity in sentencing according to wealth, influence and locality. In most cities, young, affluent and vicious gangsters faced mostly fines for repeated liquor law violations, while the poor in rural areas could face long terms of imprisonment for repeated offences involving mere possession. One victim was Etta May Miller, a mother of four in Lansing, Michigan, who was sentenced to life in 1929 for possessing a single bottle of gin[1].

The one federal government policy, which caused the most controversy, however, was the denaturing of industrial alcohol. Deadly poisons, capable of causing paralysis, blindness and sometimes immediate or lingering death were added to industrial alcohol under government instruction to deter use. By the mid-1920s thousands had died. Some children were even poisoned because their mother had fed them a spoonful of 'whisky' as a cold cure. The historian Richard Hofstadter has made the point that this was just one of the tragic ironies of Prohibition:

> Before Prohibition became law, the prohibitionist decried alcohol as a form of deadly poison. After Prohibition was law, they approved the legal poisoning of industrial alcohol, knowing full well that men would die from drinking it. Excess had this way of turning things into their opposites; an amenity became a crime; the imposition of controls led to a loss of control; the churches created gangsters; reformers became reactionaries; purifiers became poisoners[2].

By passing Prohibition the government was attempting to extend its jurisdiction to every individual and every home in the United States in order to stamp out the long-standing custom of millions of Americans. Some of the methods used in the attempt were necessarily devious and intrusive. To entrap violators dry agents often posed as customers in search of a drink or even persuaded people to buy drinks in order to arrest them. Such entrapment techniques were developed and elaborated and by the middle of the 1920s, Prohibition agents were even setting up phony speakeasies to snare bootleggers. In six months, despite the enormous expense of this operation, only a few bootleggers had been successfully trapped[3].

The practice of tapping into private telephone conversations to gather incriminating evidence also began during Prohibition. Former police-lieutenant Roy Omlstead, who became Seattle's richest bootlegger, was convicted with wiretapping evidence in a case that was fought all the way to the United States Supreme Court. The court upheld the verdict by a five to four decision and declared that wiretapping was not unwarranted search and seizure. In the opinion written by Chief Justice William Taft, the Court ruled that no element of force had been used in obtaining evidence and that the element of force was the essence of unreasonable search and seizure. Two of the four judges who dissented from the majority verdict issued

---

1. Wickersham Commission, *Report on the Enforcement of the Prohibition Laws of the United States*, 71st Congress, 3rd Session, H.D. 722, Vol. 1, p. 149-223; Association Against the Prohibition Amendment, *Reforming America with a Shotgun*, Washington D.C., 1929.
2. Hofstadter, quote from his introduction to Andrew Sinclair, *Prohibition: The Era of Excess*, London, Faber and Faber, 1962, p. 10.
3. Quoted in John Kobler, Ardent Spirits, *Capone*, London, Coronet, 1972, p. 285.

warnings of the inherent dangers involved in undermining constitutional rights. Justice Louis Brandeis took the ground that:

> When the Fourth and Fifth Amendments were adopted, the form that evil had theretofore taken had been necessarily simple. Force and violence were then the only means known to man by which a government could directly effect self-incrimination... Subtler and more far-reaching means of invading privacy have become available to the government. Discovery and invention have made it possible for the government, by means far more effective than stretching upon the rack, to obtain disclosure in court of what is whispered in the closet.

To protect the right to be 'let alone – the most comprehensive of rights and the right most valued by civilized men' Brandeis felt that 'every unjustifiable intrusion by the government upon the privacy of the individual, whatever the means employed, must be deemed a violation of the Fourth Amendment'.

Justice Oliver Wendell Holmes opposed the new police practice even more vehemently:

> It is desirable that criminals should be detected, and to that end that all available evidence should be used. It is also desirable that the government should not itself foster and pay for other crimes, when they are the means by which the evidence is to be obtained... We have to choose, and for my part I think it is a less evil that some criminals should escape that the government should play an ignoble part[1].

The warning of the two Justices was not heeded since the country persevered with the misguided attempt to impose morality even after the war against the liquor was declared lost. The laws prohibiting gambling, prostitution and drugs remained on the statute books and devious and intrusive methods gradually became accepted as necessary to produce the quotas of arrests and convictions in order to create the illusion of success and justify futile and counter-productive policy. Constitutional safeguards could never prevent large-scale abuse and injustice.

The American people showed they accepted the situation in the 1928 presidential elections. Herbert Hoover, the Republican candidate, declared his intention to enforce the 18th Amendment efficiently, and comfortably defeated Al Smith, who wished to repeal it. Hoover proceeded to do everything in his power to enforce the 18th Amendment, strengthening federal enforcement and criminal justice wherever he could. The Prohibition Bureau, in particular, was drastically improved in honesty and efficiency, multiplying the amounts of illegal liquor and apparatus seized or smashed and the number of prison sentences imposed. By the early 1930s most Americans could see that there was no logic left in Prohibition; the remedy for the evils of drink had proved worse than the original problem. Wet pressure finally secured the passage of the repeal of the 18th Amendment on 5 December 1933.

---

1. Wickerman Commission, *op. cit.*, Vol. 5, p. 222-223.

After Prohibition: local justice vs. big business crime

With the noticeable exception of some southern states that preserved anti-liquor laws, bootleggers could not successfully compete once the legal liquor trade was fully established and soon folded up or adapted to the new conditions. Gambling, prostitution and drug taking were flourishing again. Gambling, for example, returned to its pre-Prohibition position as the most lucrative source of income.

Downtown areas supported dozens of illegal gambling houses running roulette, blackjack and dice games. Illegal slot machines were set up in bars, clubs and stores. The most important of illegal gambling from the 1930s was, however, off-track bookmaking. Many states had legalized wagering at horse and dog tracks as a means of raising revenue during the Depression. More races and better long-distance communications enabled bookmakers in virtually every city and state to turn a substantial profit in defiance of the laws against betting. Independents and syndicates, with their political and police protectors, capitalized on the duplicity of the state legislatures[1].

The laws against off-track bookmaking were treated with as much contempt as the laws that prohibited alcohol. The prohibitions of gambling and prostitution were not federal. Instead a myriad of state laws and local ordinances made wagering and commercialized sex subject to criminal sanctions in every state except Nevada which legalized gambling and prostitution in selected areas in 1931. The enforcement of these laws was left to the state and local governments with their limited, conflicting and overlapping jurisdictions and with networks of corruption sometimes inherited from even before the Prohibition era.

To illustrate this idea, three local examples are given here: the cities of New York, Chicago and Los Angeles.

New York

During the 1930s New York made a highly publicized attempt to enforce the laws dealing with morality. Increased police activity against gamblers and prostitutes and the downfall of a succession of gangsters and their political protectors made headlines in newspapers across the nation. The city was held up as an example of what could be achieved if the laws were strictly enforced. It seemed to be a triumph for the forces of law and order against the forces of evil and corruption but this impression was misleading.

A series of investigations headed by jurist Samuel Seabury had revealed much about New York City government in the early 1930s. The system was organized for profit from top to bottom. Top politicians used their influence to make enormous profits in real estate and other business deals or by accepting kickbacks from firms doing business with the city. The criminal justice and law enforcement systems were riddled with corruption, expediency and incompetence.

But in November 1933 the split in the Democratic vote allowed La Guardia to win the election for mayor of New York. He began his term of

---

1. William Moore, *The Kefauver Committee on the Politics of Crime, 1950-1952*, Columbia University of Missouri Press, 1974, p. 18-19.

office on 1 January 1934 with the promise 'The party's over! No more graft', and to the best of his ability kept it[1]. He also did what he could to see that the vice and gambling laws were enforced. La Guardia had no jurisdiction over the district attorneys and minimal influence over the courts, but he literally bullied his police into action.

The new administration's first crusade was against slot machines – a novelty that had become so popular that more than 25,000 stood in the city's stores, bars and restaurants. The fear was they might be a corrupting influence on the young who might become addicted to gambling and steal to finance their play. La Guardia ignored a federal court decision which restrained the police from interfering with slot machines unless it could be proved they were used for gambling and ordered a mass seizure of the devices. Soon afterwards the Supreme Court reversed the previous injunction and the police were free to seize and destroy the machines legally.

Mayor La Guardia continued to try and enforce the unenforceable vice laws until 1945, his final year of office. His crusades to stamp out gambling and prostitution inevitably failed. Slot and gambling machines were successfully barred from stores, restaurants and bars, but New Yorkers could still bet if they wanted and, as the war put more money into their pockets, they bet more. Numbers and bookmaking continued to be lucrative operations, and illegal casinos operated across the river in New Jersey. The courts viewed gambling as a trivial offence and, accordingly, imposed light fines or occasionally short jail sentences.

Chicago

Chicago's attitude towards illegal enterprise was always tolerant. Corrupt alliances between politicians, police and gangsters had been exploiting this immense market for illegal goods and services for decades before Prohibition, but the 18th Amendment provided an important addition to America's second largest city's institutionalized illegal commerce in bootleg liquor.

In 1927 the city's electorate delivered their verdict on the one genuine local attempt to enforce Prohibition. They turned Mayor William Dewer, whose police had been invading private homes in search of liquor, and replaced him with William Thompson, a former mayor who stated categorically 'I'm wetter than the middle of the Atlantic Ocean'. Thompson, in effect, promised and delivered an open city for bootlegging, gambling and prostitution, regulated in a haphazard way by the city's police. Scarcely concealed corruption characterized all aspects of the city's business. Public officials prospered while gangsters killed each other for the privilege of paying off.

Mayor Thompson convincingly demonstrated the limits of Al Capone's power in 1928. Briefly under the illusion that he might be running for the presidency, Thompson decided that harboring the nation's best-known gangster might be an electoral liability. He therefore gave the word to his Chief of Police and a campaign of harassment commenced. Capone's men

---

1. Quoted in Robert Caro, *The Power Broker: Robert Moses and the Fall of New York*, New York, Vintage, 1975, p. 444-445.

were arrested on tenuous charges, breweries, brothels and gambling houses were repeatedly raided, and the boss himself was kept under continuous supervision. Capone left the city but, as soon as Thompson realized the hopelessness of his ambitions, Capone felt safe to return home and resume operations.

By 1931 Capone was finished as a criminal power and jailed for evasion of income tax. His reign at the top of the Chicago rackets had been brief, hard fought, immensely expensive and totally dependent on the sufferance of the local authorities. In 1931 also the Republican administration of Mayor Thompson was defeated at the polls, discredited by years of corruption, gangsterism and financial mismanagement. The newly elected Mayor Anton Cermak's pledge was to purge the city of organized crime and he announced his victory by advising gangsters 'to pack up and leave and prepare for long terms in jail'. But he never had the chance to put his promise into force because he was assassinated on 15 February 1933. With his successor, Edward Kelly, Chicago met a period of stability in organized crime operations unknown since before Prohibition. However, this period of stability was achieved by organizing corruption on a large scale and by enforcing the law on a very selective basis. But Chicago's gang warfare declined to such an extent that in 1942 there were only two gang-connected murders.

Los Angeles

The vice laws were no better enforced in Los Angeles than in other cities. The local newspapers boasted about the city's virtue and proclaimed it the 'white spot of America', free of crime and civic corruption rampant in other cities[1]. In reality gambling and prostitution were openly available in the business district of the city and in segregated districts around Los Angeles County, while, during Prohibition, alcohol was plentiful and cheap. Numerous conflicting and overlapping law enforcement jurisdictions made the laws impossible to enforce consistently in such a sprawling city.

The hypocrisy of Los Angeles in the 1930s was large and it is not until 1938 that the public, at last convinced of Mayor Shaw's corruption, decided to elect Judge Fletcher Bowron, who remained Mayor until 1953. But even Fletcher railed ineffectively against vice, organized crime and police corruption during his long tenure.

Mayor Bowron actively pursued an anti-vice crusade in the early years of his administration. Slot machines were banished from the city, and prostitutes and bookmakers harassed more than usual. Bowron even joined other officials in a crusade against gambling at sea. Gambling ship operators had established floating casinos a few miles off the Los Angeles coast. Bowron's own campaign against the ships was ineffectual, but he traveled up to the state capital of Sacramento and persuaded the State Attorney, Earl Warren, to take steps to eliminate the moral menace. Warren's tactic was to serve the ships with nuisance abatement orders. The ship, the orders read, 'induced people to lead idle and dissolute lives[2]... When the ship owners

---

1. George Mowry, *The Californian Progressives*, Berkeley, University of California Press, 1951.
2. "Gambling Ships", *Life*, 19 August 1946.

ignored the orders, Warren ordered raids. The *Texas*, the *Showboat* and the *Tango* were seized on the afternoon of 2 August 1939. Slots and tables were ripped out, some to be illegally dumped to the sea[1]. Finally, Californian authorities pressured Congress in 1948 to pass a law that prohibited gambling in US coastal waters.

Bowron was re-elected in 1941, 1945 and 1949, exploiting his reputation for honesty and the apathy of the electorate; for example, it took just 16 per cent of the registered voters to return him in 1945[2]. The breaking of inhibitions during wartime and the burgeoning post-war Californian economy made Los Angeles a particular fruitful place to engage in criminal enterprise, while Bowron's only response to organized crime was to issue warnings about an invasion by 'Eastern Gangsters'. In 1948 and 1949, however, a series of scandals came into prominence, embarrassed Bowron's city administration as well as state and county authorities, and showed that electing a reform mayor was no answer to organized crime.

Corruption as a main concern

Organized crime would not have persisted in the United States without the consent of the public. This consent was to be seen in the customers who bet in, borrowed from and bought from gangsters, and in the array of governmental officials who deliberately overlooked or actively promoted gangsters' enterprises. Of course, the strength of criminal organizations and the threats of violence allowed gangsters to behave in ways that occasionally outraged the public. But the usual situation was for gangsters to find acceptance among most levels of the public.

Earlier, it has been mentioned that during Prohibition politicians and police officials were often connected with gangsters, as is evidenced by well-known example of public officials attending gangsters' funerals. Of course, having a 'relationship' or 'communicating' with gangsters doesn't mean necessarily being corrupted. Nevertheless, the web or relationships between well-known criminals and politicians is instructive.

Also interesting is the case of Sidney R. Korshak, reported by Charles H. McCaghy and Stephen A. Cernkovich[3]:

> He graduated from law school in 1930 and his first clients were members of the Capone gang. His history also includes an attempt to blackmail Senator Estes Kefauver during the latter's investigation of organized crime in 1950, payoffs to judges for favorable court decisions, and helping organized criminals infiltrate unions and the entertainment industries. Did this man languish in a dark prison cell? Hardly. Fifteen years later he was a multimillionaire lawyer and highly respected advisor to corporations such as Gulf and Western, Diner's Club, the Hilton hotel chain, and the San Diego Chargers, to

---

1. Bruce Henstell, "Now, Those Really Were 'Floating' Crap Games", *Los Angeles Magazine*, December 1978.
2. Robert Lane, *The Administration of Robert Bowron*, M.A. Thesis, University of Southern California, 1954, p. 41.
3. McCaghy, Charles H. and Cernkovich, Stephen A, *Crime in American Society*, 2nd edition, Macmillan Publishing Company, New York, 1987, p. 287, paraphrasing Bernard A. Gropper, "Probing the Links Between Drugs and Crime", *National Institute of Justice: Research in Brief*, Washington, D.C.: U.S. Department of Justice, 1985.

> name a few. At the same time he was regarded by justice officials as a powerful underworld figure – "the most significant link in the relationship between the crime syndicate, politics, labor, and management."

Korshak's link to persons of power would tend to make us think that the federal level was very often the most important one. Yet, while some senators and governors may have benefited from gangsters' business, organized crime's day-to-day operations took place within the jurisdictions of councilmen or women, judges, mayors and local police[1].

It seems customary always to make police the villains when discussing criminals' immunity to prosecution. According to Donald R. Cressey, honest police are often faced with organizational conditions that make the enforcement of laws against organized crime impractical:

1. Police may be acting under a nonenforcement policy formulated by corrupt supervisors or other officials in the hierarchy. In such cases, honest police usually can do little more than maintain their pride in a difficult situation. Cressey cites the case of one investigation of corruption in which the prosecutor announced that any officer who brought evidence of bribery would not be persecuted for participating in the bribery. Gangsters do not need to corrupt an entire police department; all they need is a few key members within the justice system.

2. Police may be doing the best they can but look corrupt because of insufficient personnel and resources. For example, 24-hour surveillance operations on gangsters may be too expensive and time-consuming. Intelligence work in general often ties up resources for a very long period without producing tangible results. But even if results are forthcoming, any weak link in the justice chain can undo the work. For example, honest but incompetent prosecutors can easily wreck the seemingly best of cases.

3. Police may permit organized crime activity because important community members demand it. This may have nothing to do with corruption; community leaders may honestly feel that police have more important things to do than harass bookies. As long as the gangsters' activities are not flagrant or sensational, the community may be tolerant of or indifferent to them[2].

One of the most thorough research efforts on law enforcement corruption was conducted by John A. Gardiner in the 1960s in Wincanton[3]. Wincanton was a small – just under 100,000 – but corrupt city whose leading gangster, "Irving Stern", controlled gambling and corruption for over thirty years. Stern systematically financed the election campaigns of tolerant candidates running for mayor, city council, and judgeships. He also made weekly payoffs; one mayor received $1,500 and a police chief $100. In addition, there were Christmas turkeys and birthday gifts and other favors for various officials and police.

---

1. For detailed discussion of organized crime and corruption in high places see Michael Dorman, *Payoff: The Role of Organized Crime in American Politics*, New York: David McKay, 1972.
2. List paraphrased from Cressey, *Theft of the Nation: The Structure and Operations of Organized Crime in America*, New York, Harper and Row, 1969, p. 275-281.
3. Gardiner, John A., *The Politics of Corruption: Organized Crime in an American City*, Russel Sage Foundation, New York, 1970.

The citizens of Wincanton were ambivalent about their situation. They did not approve of official corruption, but they did not approve of the gambling laws either. Stern and his bribed officials were simply giving the public the gambling it wanted. For example, many clubs, labor unions, and service organizations – such as the Kiwanis – relied on Stern's slot machines to attract members and to pay the bills. What the citizens failed to see was the relationship between official tolerance of lawbreaking and official corruption. Wincanton went through reform cycles but none lasted long because the honest politicians had little to offer the voters but more honesty and less gambling.

From a local concern to a national one: the alien menace

The Second World War provided an immense boost to illegal businesses. Gambling, in particular, enjoyed a wartime and post-war boom. Despite the fact that practically all the states had passed laws prohibiting gambling an article in *Life* found that:

> In any city where gambling exists... the police department knows that the addresses and owners of every joint own. The reason the joints stay open is always just one thing: graft, paid either to the police, the city officials or the political machines, and in some cases all three. The United States is full of policemen, sheriffs and prosecuting attorneys who have built mansions, bought yachts or loaded their safe deposits boxes to bursting[1].

Despite the hysteria of the popular press, in many ways gambling in post-war America resembled the liquor situation during Prohibition. Gambling was a popular and socially approved pastime. The facts that the gambling laws, like the dry laws, were plainly not being enforced produced some calls for liberalization and regulation, so the tax revenue would replace illegal enrichment. Proposals for the legalization of gambling in various forms were put before the state legislatures of Arizona, California, Florida, Idaho, Illinois, Minnesota, Montana and New York. These proposals failed, mainly because of the Protestant culture which was still dominant in state legislature, but it was a first step in the direction of a federal intervention.

But real assault against organized crime was conducted to defeat a completely different 'crime'. There were numerous theories in the post-war period arguing for an alien conspiracy and more and more people argued that some unknown forces were plotting against the American government. On 5 January 1950, Senator Estes Kefauver of Tennessee introduced Senate Resolution 202, which called for an investigation into crime in inter-state commerce. At the same time Senator Joseph McCarthy of Wisconsin was looking for a dramatic issue on which to bolster his candidacy for re-election in 1952. Initially he wanted crime, making an abortive effort to have the Special Investigation Committee, on which he served, assume principal responsibility for any organized crime investigation. This effort failed and Kefauver was named chairman of the Special Committee to Investigate Organized Crime in Interstate Commerce on 11 May 1950.

---

1. Havemann, Ernest, "Gambling in the United States", *Life*, 19 June 1950.

Kefauver decided to concentrate the work of the committee on gambling because, as he explained, the activity supplied substantial money for corruption of public officials and no federal laws controlled inter-state gambling activity. The conclusions of the committee were no more than an official version of one of the alien theories then so popular. The conclusions were mainly based on assertion, and could not see organized crime as something that had developed inside the United States, and then an internal, domestic problem. The committee's conclusions traced the history of the Sicilian Mafia and its implantation in America:

> The various drives against the Mafia in Sicily, which were made by Italian governments from the 1870s down to Mussolini's time, were... largely ineffective in destroying the Mafia. However, these drives had the effect of causing large numbers of Mafia members to migrate to the New World and many of them came to this country... The Mafia became established in New Orleans and other cities. Moreover, like many underworld organizations, it grew rich and powerful during Prohibition and since that time this organization had entered every racket promising easy money. Narcotics, pinball machines, slot machines, gambling in every form and description are some of its major activities at the present time[1].

To support its case the committee's report then recounted some drug trafficking stories provided by the Narcotics Bureau and made these frequently quoted conclusions:

> 1. There is a nationwide crime syndicate known as the Mafia, whose tentacles are found in many large cities. It has international ramifications which appear most clearly in connection with the narcotics traffic.
>
> 2. Its leaders are usually found in control of the most lucrative rackets of their cities.
>
> 3. There are indications of a centralized direction and control of these rackets, but leadership appears to be in a group rather than in a single individual.
>
> 4. The Mafia is the cement that helps bind the Costello-Adonis-Lansky syndicate of New York and the Accardo-Guzik-Fiscetti syndicate of Chicago as well as smaller criminal gangs and individual criminals throughout the country. These groups have kept in touch with Luciano since his deportation from this country.
>
> 5. The domination of the Mafia is based fundamentally on 'muscle' and 'murder'. The Mafia is a secret conspiracy against law and order which will ruthless eliminate anyone who betrays its secrets. It will use any means available – political influence, bribery, intimidation, etc. – to defeat any attempts on the part of the law enforcement to touch its top figures or to interfere with its operations[2].

But despite a great deal of hopeful effort, no evidence had been produced at the hearings to support this view of a centralized Sicilian organization dominating organized crime in the United States. Nevertheless the Kefauver Committee's hearing were televised and sensationalized between May 1950

---

1. Moore, William, *The Kefauver Committee and the Politics of Crime*, Columbia University of Missouri Press, 1974, p. 32-33.
2. Kefauver Committee, *Third Interim Report*, Crown, New York, p. 147-150.

and May 1951. The committee attracted immense attention and support, but accomplished little in the way of legislative action. But it did a lot against organized crime by creating an anti-crime feeling in the country, which in turn fostered the belief that it was necessary to enact legislation to protect the country's morality from a new sin.

The conception of organized crime as an alien and united entity was vital. The message got across to the people who mattered, the legislators. It was argued that because so much emphasis was placed upon the Constitutional rights of the guilty that it often appeared that the Constitutional rights of the innocent had been forgotten. The result has been an acceleration breakdown in law enforcement, an acceleration of the crime rate, and a developing lack of respect – even actual contempt – on the part of criminals for the law enforcement agencies.

Recognizing this dangerous trend, in 1967 and in 1968 in an effort to combat crime, Congress passed the Omnibus Crime Bill, which established legislation to authorize wiretapping by the Federal Bureau of Investigation and other federal law enforcement agencies.

By the end of the 1960s members of Congress were convinced enough of the Mafia's supposed 'threat to the nation' to enact a series of measures long sought after by the federal law enforcement and intelligence community. Organized crime control provisions in the 1968 and 1970 Omnibus Crime Control Acts included: reluctant testimony; extended sentences for persons convicted in organized crime cases; and the use of wiretapping and eavesdropping evidence in federal cases. They inevitably tipped the balance away from such civil liberties as the right to privacy and protection from unreasonable search and seizure, and towards stronger policing powers. These laws and concurrent anti-drug legislation had a great potential for abuse. However, their potential for genuine and effective organized crime control was minimal because the conditions which fostered endemic crime and corruption in the United States persisted. The new control measures were, as constitutional scholar Leonard Levy put it, 'a salvo of fragmentation grenades that missed their target and exploded against the Bill of Rights'[1].

Conclusion

In 1935, Edgar Hoover wrote:
> The great problem of law-enforcement officers is not that of apprehending the men and women who have offended against the statutes or our country. The difficulty lies in reaching a position from which capture is possible.
>
> It is one thing, for instance, to view the fiction picture of a crime chase. There, capture and punishment are inevitable once the proper clue is found. Real life, unfortunately, presents an entirely different story.
>
> Here, a barbed wire entanglement of various factors confronts the man who would hunt down a criminal. Primarily, there is the maze of politics, ranging from the vote-getting influence of a resort owner, which sometimes encompasses life and death, to the man who controls the election destinies of a crime-ridden city. There is the

---

1. Levy quoted in Sam Pizzigati, "The Perverted Grand Juries", *Nation*, 19 June 1976.

impediment thrown up by well-meaning but non-thinking folk who believe that crime is none of their business, and that it is not their duty to aid those entrusted with the task of law-enforcement. There is the morass of ineffectual laws, many of them created in legislatures by those directly concerned with the fortunes of the criminal.

To all this must be added the codes of the underworld, demanding that each enemy of society gives aid to the other. There is the uncertainty of punishment, once the cases have reached the court, and the definite knowledge that even a supposedly heavy prison sentence in reality may amount to only a trifling time spent behind bars[1].

It took more than 20 years to the U.S. society to take this opinion into consideration. Rather than acknowledge failure and pursue rational policies based on regulation and control, the country persevered with unenforceable, crime breeding and corrupting prohibitions. In the process many civil liberties were undermined to produce arrests and convictions. Unofficial forms of regulation and control were imposed by intimidation and deception by criminals, many of whom had been elected or appointed as public servants. Gambling, which was certainly the framework of organized crime, was never understood as a major criminal behaviour and remained popular in spite of its illegitimate aspects.

The main reason of an apathy from the authorities is the fact that criminal authorities lies on the States, and that they frequently delegated this power to the municipalities.

After the important highlight brought by the Kefauver commission, the only solution was to increase federal involvement in gambling and drug law enforcement. At first it was made clear that drug addiction in the United States was to be a police problem not a medical one. Then draconian sentences would deter both use and sale. Federal legislation was passed in 1951 and sharply increased penalties for drug offenders, both users and suppliers. And in 1956 the peak of federal punitive action against drugs was reached when sentences for some offences were raised to five years on the first conviction, and the death penalty could be imposed for selling heroin to anyone under 18 years old[2]. This is perhaps the starkest indicator of the most important result of the attempt to regulate victimless crimes, namely the enforcement of federal involvement in the area and the recourse to increasingly drastic measures, none of which show any sign of being able to stamp out activities for which there is a large public market.

Bibliographie

Abadinsky, Howard. *Organized Crime.* 2nd ed. (Chicago: Nelson-Hall, 1985).

Adelstein, Richard P. *The Moral Costs of Crime: Prices, Information and Organization.* Charles M. Gray, ed. (Beverly Hills: Sage Publications, 1979) 233-56.

Anderson, Annelise Graebner. *The Business of Organized Crime: A Cosa Nostra Family* (Stanford, Ca.: Hoover University Press, 1979).

Atkinson, Jeff, "Racketeer Influenced and Corrupt Organizations,' 18 U.S.C. 1961-68: Broadest of the Federal Criminal Statutes," *Journal of Criminal Law and Criminology*, 69, Spring 1978.

---

1. Hoover, J. Edgar, "Foreword", in Cooper, Courtney Ryley, *Ten Thousand Public Enemies*, Little, Brown and Company, Boston, 1935, p. VII-IX.
2. Musto, David, *The American Disease: Origins of Narcotics Control*, Newhaven, Conn., Yale University Press, 1973, p. 242.

Block, Alan A. "A Modern Marriage of Convenience: A Collaboration Between Organized Crime and U.S. Intelligence." In Robert J. Kelly 58-77.
Block, Alan A. and William J. Chambliss. *Organizing Crime* (New York: Elsevier, 1982).
Block, Alan A. "Part I: The Historical Perspective." In *Perspectives on Organizing Crime: Essays in Opposition* (The Netherlands: Kluwer Academic Publishers, 1991) 2-32.
Caro, Robert. *The Power Broker: Robert Moses and the Fall of New York* (New York: Vintage Books, 1975).
Clotfelter, Charles F. and Robert D. Seeley. "The Private Costs of Crime." In Gray 213-32.
Cooter, Robert and Thomas Ulen. "An Economic Theory of Crime and Criminal Law." In *Law and Economics* (New York: Harper and Collins, 1988) 506-32.
Cressey, Donald R. "Methodological Problems in the Study of Organized Crime as a Social Problem." *Annals of the American Academy of Political and Social Science* 374 (1967): 101-12.
Theft of the Nation: The Structure and Operations of Organized Crime in America. (New York: Harper and Row, 1969).
Gambetta, Diego. *The Sicilian Mafia* (Cambridge: Harvard University Press, 1993). "Fragments of an Economic Theory of the Mafia." *Archives Européennes de Sociologie*, 29 (1988): 127-45; Passas 171-90.
Gardiner, John A. *The Politics of Corruption: Organized Crime in an American City* (New York: Russel Sage Foundation, 1970).
Charles M. Gray, ed. *The Moral Costs of Crime: Prices, Information and Organization* (Beverly Hills: Sage Publications, 1979). "The Costs of Crime: Review and Overview." In *Ibid*. 13-32.
Haller, Mark H. "Illegal Enterprise: A Theoretical and Historical Interpretation." *Criminology* 28 (1990) 207-35; Passas 225-54.
Havemann, Ernest, 'Gambling in the United States', *Life*, 19 June 1950.
Hoover, J. Edgar, 'Foreword.' In Cooper, Courtney Ryley, *Ten Thousand Public Enemies* (Boston: Little, Brown and Company, 1935).
Kelly, Robert J. ed. *Organized Crime: A Global Perspective* (Lanham, Md.: Rowman & Littlefield, 1986).
"Criminal Worlds: Looking Down on Society from Below." In Kelly 10-31.
Lupsha, Peter A. "Individual Choice, Material Culture and Organized Crime." *Criminology* 19 (1981): 3-24; Passas 105-26.
"Organized Crime in the United States." In Kelly 32-57.
McCaghy, Charles H. and Cernkovich, Stephen A. *Crime in American Society*, 2nd edition (New York: Macmillan Publishing Company, 1987).
Maltz, Michael D. "On Defining 'Organized Crime': The Development of a Definition and a Typology." *Crime and Delinquency* 22 (1976): 338-46; Passas 15-24.
Moore, William. *The Kefauver Committee and the Politics of Crime* (Columbia, Mo: University of Missouri Press, 1974).
Mowry, George. *The Californian Progressives* (Berkeley: University of California Press, 1951).
Musto, David. *The American Disease: Origins of Narcotics Control* (Newhaven, Conn.: Yale University Press, 1973).
Nelli, Humbert S. "Overview." In Kelly 1-9.
Passas, Nikos, ed. *Organized Crime* (London: Dartmouth Publishing Co. Ltd., 1995). 3-14.
Pindyck, Robert S. and Daniel L.Rubinfeld. "Monopolistic Competition and Oligopoly." In *Microeconomics*. (New York: Macmillan Publishing Company, 1992) 423-61.
Pizzigati, Sam. 'The Perverted Grand Juries', *Nation*, 19 June 1976.
Reuter, Peter and Jonathan B. Rubinstein. "Fact, fancy, and organized crime." *The Public Interest* 53 (1978): 45-68; Passas 55-78.
Rizzo, Mario J. "Economic Costs, Moral Costs or Retributive Justice: The Rationale of Criminal Law." In Gray 257-78.
Shelling, Thomas C. "Economics and Criminal Enterprise." In *Choice and Consequences*. (Cambridge: Harvard University Press, 1984) 158-78.
"What is the Business of Organized Crime?" In *Ibid*. 179-94.
Simon, Carl P. and Ann D. Witte. *Beating the System: the Underground Economy* (Boston: Auburn House Publishing Company, 1982).
Smith Jr., Dwight C. "Some Things that may be More Important to Understand about Organized Crime than Cosa Nostra." *University of Florida Law Review* 26 (1971): 1-30; Passas 25-54.
Viviano, Frank. *The New Mafia Order*. Mother Jones, 1994.
Witte, Ann Dryden. "Informal and Underground Economies and the Impact on Ungovernability." *National Strategy Information Center*, Inc. March 12, 1994.

Well-educated, well-dressed and polite? The changing face of the Hollywood gangster in the 1930s

By Ruth Vasey

In the 1930s, the Hollywood cinema produced approximately 400 films per year. The vast majority of these faded completely from public memory almost immediately after their initial period of exhibition, but a small number, though undifferentiable from the motion picture ephemera that surrounded them, have continued to resonate in the public imagination to the present day. Prominent amongst these are the gangster movies of the early 1930s, including *Public Enemy* (Warner Bros., 1931) *Scarface* (Caddo, 1932) and *Little Caesar* (Warner Bros., 1930). When one considers the small number of gangster films that were actually made (no more than twenty-three in the 1930-31 production season, after which their numbers dwindled significantly), it is clear that they have managed to exert a wholly disproportionate influence upon subsequent readings of Hollywood history during the period of their production, and probably upon readings of American social history as well. Why was it that amongst the many cycles of movies produced by Hollywood during the early thirties, the gangster movie provided many of the most enduring images of the era? The reasons probably lie less in any inherently cinematic qualities they may have contained than in the way their themes and content magnified – and continue to magnify – tensions between the American motion picture industry and the society that supported it.

While the movie industry had been an object of celebrity virtually since its inception, the nature of its merchandise as the material of popular culture had simultaneously made it a focus of the anxieties and hostilities aroused by the modern age. There were three areas in which the movies were particularly vulnerable to attacks by conservative forces, including censors, in both the American community and in foreign markets. The first two areas of concern were, of course, the representation of sex and the representation of crime, particularly in "sordid" (read lower-class and/or non-Anglo) situations. The third problematic area was the representation of specific ethnic groups and foreign nationals. All these sensitive areas converged in the gangster film.

The cycle of gangster movies of 1930-31 was part of a broader trend being employed by Hollywood script-writers, in the midst of the Depression, to represent the twenties as a period characterised by the melodramatic rise and fall of moral chaos. The cycle also coincided with the widespread adoption of sound technology, and the introduction of the more gritty, documentarist styles of representation that ambient sound made possible. Ironically, the public relations problems posed by the introduction of sound took considerably longer to solve than the technological challenges they presented. City conservatives, sections of rural American consumers and significant areas of the foreign market, already concerned about the cultural impact of Hollywood, balked at the thought of contemporary social themes being discussed in front of their children. At the same time, the treatment of criminal subjects threatened to become more sordidly realistic. Sound technology provided a new focus for criticism of Hollywood, and called into question its suitability for general consumption.

At base, the probem presented by the gangster pictures was a matter of taste and tone. The American Motion Picture industry in 1930 was still trying to shake off the odium that attached to its origins, in the crowded, lower-class immigrant areas of the largest cities. From its inception in 1922, the movie industry's trade association, the Motion Picture Producers and Distributors of America, Inc. (MPPDA) had seen the solution to the industry's chronic public relations problems to be a matter of the gradual bourgeoisification of motion picture material. MPPDA head Will Hays had expended considerable time and effort trying to convince respectable middle-class organizations, from Daughters of the American Revolution to the Boy Scouts, to run campaigns to boost attendances at high-toned movies, so that box office pressure would persuade producers that their best chance for profits lay in material that was tasteful, moral and middle class. The gangster movies seemed to throw this entire hard-fought process into reverse. The gangster was the antithesis of the upright bourgeois hero: not only was he a criminal, but he was a recent immigrant with appalling taste in suits and ties. Instead of the movies fulfilling their great destiny in Americanizing their own domestic audiences (and thence the world), they threatened to teach their sons to speak in the bastardized Italianesque argot of Muni/Camonte, and push grapefruits in the faces of their sisters at the dinner table; and instead of teaching middle-class girls the virtues of modesty and womanliness, they showed them how to swagger, shimmer and drawl like Jean Harlow. In the underworld settings of the gangster films, the movies returned to the same lower-class urban environments from which they had been trying to free themselves for twenty years.

In the year preceding the gangster cycle, the MPPDA had attempted to confront some of the public relations problems inherent in the sound film by introducing a codified set of standards to regulate aspects of Hollywood's representation, chiefly in the areas of sex and criminality. Titled a "Code to Maintain Social and Community Values in the Production of Synchronized and Talking Motion Pictures," or Production Code, and formulated in consultation with representatives of the Catholic Church, these standards superseded an existing set of guidelines (the "Don'ts and Be Carefuls"), which were themselves based upon analysis of censorship standards; Hollywood had to contend with varying censorship standards in foreign markets, U.S. municipalities and in several U.S. states. The Code was overtly introduced to appease the critics of the industry, but it also helped producers avoid "mutilation" of their products by censors – a much more expensive and difficult issue in the sound era than it had been throughout the twenties. The MPPDA also strengthened earlier efforts to get producers to consult with the Association's own advisory committee, the Studio Relations Committee (later the Production Code Administration) during the preparation of scripts and later during the process of production; after 8 October 1931 the submission of scripts to the Studio Relations Committee was made compulsory. While the movies were still marketed as "sensational," the well publicised regulatory mechanisms of the MPPDA reassured their critics that they would not use their position of cultural centrality to undermine existing social structures. If the movies' appeal was often in their very modernity, this was all the more reason for their narratives to be contained within apparently innocuous frameworks. The themes and issues that preoccupied the MPPDA's regulatory agencies provide a reliable index of the permissable limits of representation in movie narratives of the time, and in turn give an insight into the public anxieties that threatened the movie industry in the form of calls for censorship and legislative intervention. In this context, it is significant that, despite the fact that they were few in number, gangster movies constituted one of the MPPDA's greatest public relations concerns in the early thirties.

The most transparent public relations problem arising from the gangster movies was their tendency to publicize, if not to glorify, the exploits of contemporary gangster figures. *Scarface*, for example, was more or less overtly based upon the career of Al Capone. Although the Production Code dictated that crime in the movies would not pay, and that all criminals would be duly punished by the law by the end of the narrative, there was enormous concern expressed by parents and educators that children and other "impressionable" viewers (who comprised an imperfectly differentiated amalgam of illiterates, "morons" and immigrants) would be so impressed by the personalities on the screen that they would be inspired to imitate them. The motion picture was such a graphic and detailed medium, there was further concern that movies with underworld themes would act as "schools for crime," despite the fact that the Production Code prohibited the detailed representation of action subject to imitation, such as arson, safe-cracking and the "dynamiting of trains," and gambling. In the treatment of *Stolen Heaven* (Paramount, 1931), for example, the Studio Relations Committee advised the studio to shoot a gambling scene "so that the camera is just above the table line, leaving in the hands moving etc.," but excluding any details involving the exchange of money.[1] Such non-specific treatments were encouraged by censorship action: the New York Censor Board, for example, banned any scenes showing roulette wheels or the exchange of money in illegal gambling. Evasive strategies for representing crime were encouraged by the practical methods adopted by censor boards, whose members typically only saw a movie once, marking items for excision as they went along, resulting in a disproportionate emphasis upon concrete visual details.[2] However, while movies could be prevented from

---

1. Lamar Trotti, letter to Fingerlin, 3 Nov. 1930, *Stolen Heaven* file, Production Code Administration Archive, Margaret Herric Library, Academy of Motion Picture Arts and Sciences, Los Angeles (hereafter PCA Archive). Ironically, on a different level of obfuscation, Warner Bros. were advised to *introduce* gambling scenes into *Mandalay* (Warner Bros., 1933), to demonstrate that one of their locations (the Orient Cafe) was "more of a nightclub" than a brothel. James Wingate, letter to Jack Warner, 20 Oct. 1933, *Mandalay* file, PCA Archive.
2. Jason Joy of the Studio Relations Committee had reported on such procedures after visiting censor boards in 1928: "It is the writer's impression that pictures are not judged as a whole but that individual titles and sequences are eliminated often without reference to their relation to the dramatic and moral value of the story. An effort was made to impress the censors with the necessity of judging the picture in its entirety during its first screening and then if necessary to screen it again for the purpose of making eliminations if it contained material which then appeared to be objectionable." Joy, "Resumé of Dinner-Meeting of the Studio Relations Committee," 19 Apr. 1928, Dept of Pub & Ind Rel file, Reel 4, Motion Picture Producers and Distributors of America, Inc. Archive, Flinders University, Adelaide (hereafter MPPDA Archive).

becoming "textbooks of crime" by the removal of the means of literal imitation, the prevention of the *desire* to imitate criminals, as required by the Code, was less straightforward. Stories with irreproachable moral resolutions were susceptible to subversive interpretations on the strength of the performances they contained, and a mandatory punishment for criminal or unconventional behaviour did not necessarily cancel out the appeal of a character's wildness or vitality. James Cagney in *Public Enemy* is the most well-known example of a performance that, despite the character's gruesome end, was celebrated and widely imitated among the young. In the same year, *Are These Our Children?* (RKO, 1931), a story about drink and juvenile delinquency, was approved by the Studio Relations Committee as "a straight, realistic theme, pointing a very strong moral lesson,"[1] but the New York Censor Board subsequently rejected it on the grounds that its scenes of jazz parties and teenage dissipation, and especially its sympathetic teenage lead (Eddie Brand), would prove more attractive than cautionary to its young audiences. By 1932 Jason Joy had become more alert to the wider "educational" potential of motion pictures, especially their capacity to provide role models for youth. Although Tony Camonte was destined to die in a hail of bullets at the end of *Scarface* (Caddo/United Artists, 1932) (or execution, depending upon which version one encounters),[2] Joy advised Caddo to avoid any implication that "the school boys at the scenes of crime and the girls on the streets comment favorably upon Camonte's appearance."[3]

Scarface provided a focus for a number of the anxieties surrounding gangster movies because it was more or less overtly based on the career of Al Capone. Studio Relations head Jason Joy expressed his concerns to producer Howard Hughes:

> *The possibility of an attempt to produce a picture dealing with the life of Al Capone, as such, or even containing incidents and situations universally known as pertaining to Capone and thus serving to identify the character, under whatever name, as Capone, has been the subject of a great deal of thought on our part and it is occasioning us much worry.*
>
> *The motion picture industry has for a long time, in spite of strong denunciation and criticism, maintained its right to produce purely fictional underworld stories, provided certain standards are maintained, but has, on the other hand, admitted the grave danger of portraying on the screen actual contemporary happenings relating to difference in our government, political dishonesty and graft, current crime or antisocial or criminal activities. There is an admitted psychological effect from the exhibition on the screen of such material in giving to those involved a prominence and notoriety inimical to public welfare and in creating in may a desire to imitate, if only to secure the doubtful notoriety apparently reaped by those connected with the incidents so portrayed. There is a real reason why the newsreels produced by the industry never portray criminal happenings. ... [W]e believe it is exceedingly dangerous to make use of*

---

1. Joy, resume, 29 Jun. 1931, *Are These Our Children?* file, PCA Archive.
2. See Richard Maltby, "'Grief in the Limelight': Al Capone, Howard Hughes, the Hays Code and the Politics of the Unstable Text," in James Combs, ed., *Movies and Politics: The Dynamic Relationship* (New York: Garland, 1993), p. 133-182.
3. Joy, letter to E.B. Derr (Caddo), 4 Jun. 1932, Caddo–*Scarface* file, Reel 9, MPPDA Archive.

> *contemporary problems and characters for entertainment purposes. It is impossible to do so without treading on many toes and making the industry the football of opposing forces of public opinion.*[1]

In the event, Scarface was held up in production for nearly two years, while the production company (Caddo) and the Studio Relations Committee struggled to reach a compromise over the nature of the script. By the time it was eventually released it was an anachronism: the arguments of the Studio Relations Committee had largely won the day. While some gangster themes continued to be made, the MPPDA had brought in a special resolution to stagger the release dates of underworld subjects, on the grounds that it was neither good business nor (in this case) good publicity to flood the nation's screens with movies based on a single theme.[2] At the same time, both the Studio Relations Committee and the studios themselves had become more practised at handling criminal themes in ways that did not expose the industry to public disapprobation. The change is illustrated in a 1932 letter from Jason Joy to MPPDA head Will Hays, concerning *The Mouthpiece* (Warner Bros., 1932):

> *Another big question of the week was to do with a Warners story called* The Mouthpiece, *which in its original form was full of dynamite. It dealt with gangsters, a miscarriage of justice which sent the leading character off on the wrong track, and contained doubtful sex situations. First by attacking the theme itself, we were successful in taking the story altogether out of the gangster category and to substitute dramatic motivation which turned it into proper directions. By the time we had the second script we were in such position as to take up the lesser details and by almost casual suggestions even to correct such a policy matter as the character of a crooked banker, changing him into a stock broker. This latter had some significance as you will see in these precarious economic times when faith in banks is strained. This has been an interesting shaping of basic material which the Code makes possible.*[3]

The movie concerned a lawyer who was disillusioned with the legal system, and cynically manipulated it in order to defend underworld characters whom he knew to be guilty. In its final form, the lawyer not only recovered his confidence in American justice and underwent moral regeneration, but also paid for his transgressions by being gunned down in the final sequence by his former underworld contacts.

While Hollywood's principal address was to its domestic customers, its products had to be capable of being distributed internationally, to a foreign market that consistently accounted for approximately 35% of its gross income between the World Wars. The issue of stereotyping of foreign nationals, especially in criminal or comic roles, was taken very seriously by

---

1. Joy to Howard Hughes, 1 May 931, *Scarface* file, PCA Archive.
2. See Will Hays, letter to Robert Cochrane (Universal), 29 Apr. 1931, Prod Code file, Reel 9, MPPDA Archive: Hays reports a meeting with company heads, held on 20 April, at which it was agreed that the release of gangster pictures should henceforth be staggered. In 1932 Joy suggested limiting the release of movies with sexual themes: Report by Joy included in Hays, memo to company heads, 29 Sept. 1932, Reel 10, MPPDA Archive. In 1935 Hays wrote to company heads regarding the "G-man" cycle of pictures, observing that "The quantitative element is a serious factor and it is going to be necessary to stagger the releases": Hays, letter to Ned Depinet (RKO), 6 Sept. 1935, Prod Code file, Reel 11, MPPDA Archive.
3. Joy, letter to Hays, 21 Dec. 1931, *The Man Who Talked Too Much* file, PCA Archive.

customer nations, which were apt to institute boycotts and bans in response to instances of offence. This was of particular relevance to gangster and underworld pictures, which typically depended upon colourful immigrant communities to populate their fictions.

The Italian-American characters in the early thirties gangster movies, including *Scarface*, incensed the vocal and powerful Italian contingent within the United States as well as the Italian government, and led to protests from the Italian Embassy. Italy became so sensitive about representations of gangsters and mafia figures that it banned *Star of Midnight* (RKO, 1935) on the strength of a reference to a Chicago gangster called Moroni, although the studio claimed that the villain was actually an Irishman named Maroney; the point was necessarily moot, since the character never actually appeared on screen.[1]

A solution to the problem of offending customer nations was to occasionally let characters remain foreign, but in an unattributable sense. In 1933 Joy advised that excitable characters in both *As You Desire Me* (MGM, 1932) and *So This is Africa* (Columbia, 1933) be rendered as "not too obviously Italian."[2] His successor, James Wingate, issued the same suggestion in relation to a criminal in *The Headline Shooter* (RKO, 1933);[3] and when advising on *Our Betters* (RKO, 1933) he recommended that, since the character of Pepi was likely to cause objection in South American countries, "it would be wise to avoid difficulties in this regard by omitting any references in the dialogue that label him as anything more definite than a 'foreigner.'"[4]

By the late 1930s the repression of nationality resulted in representational strategies that sometimes challenged the interpretive skill of the viewer. An example is the characterization Nick Brown, a gangster in *The Roaring Twenties* (Warner Bros., 1939). The audience is introduced to him in a sequence placed in a Chicago cafe that begins with a close-up of a plate of spaghetti, which Brown eats throughout the sequence. He does not have an Italian name; he does not look noticeably Italian (he is played by Paul Kelly); he does not speak with an Italian accent; and nobody mentions the Mafia, although we learn that Brown is part of a "syndicate that's running all the high-class [bootleg] merchandise that's being sold in this country." Mr Brown just happens to be eating spaghetti, and Eddie Bartlett (James Cagney) makes reference to this culinary partiality in the only other sequence in which Brown appears.

In 1933, with Hollywood under renewed pressure from moral reformers inclusding the Catholic Legion of Decency, the Production Code was reaffirmed and strengthened, with new financial sanctions available to be used against any instance of non-compliance. The SRC was reconstituted as the

---

1. Breen, letter to Frederick Herron, 12 Feb. 1937, *The Gay Divorce* file, PCA Archive. In the version of the film screened on Britain's Channel 4 in 1990 the character does not appear onscreen at all, and may never have done so, although it is possible that he was eliminated in response to the Italian protest. In any case, character names are not supplied with the cast list, so whether he appeared or not the studio presumably would have been able to issue a denial to either an Italian *or* an Irish protest.
2. Joy, letter to Irving Thalberg, 12 May 1932, *As You Desire Me* file, PCA Archive; Joy, letter to Harry Cohn, 12 Oct. 1932, *So This Is Africa* file, PCA Archive.
3. Wingate, letter to Merian C. Cooper, 19 May 1933, *The Headline Shooter* file, PCA Archive.
4. Wingate, letter to David O. Selznick, 22 Dec. 1932, *Our Betters* file, PCA Archive.

Production Code Administration (PCA) under the direction of Joseph I. Breen. While much was made of Breen's function as a "new broom" to clean up motion picture content, in fact his approach to controversial material was the same as that employed by Joy: to render details of treatment sufficiently obscure for the audience to be responsible for their own conclusions, particularly in relation to sex and crime. For example, Breen issued the following advice to Jack Warner in relation to *G-Men* (Warner Bros., 1935):

> There should be no details of crime shown at any time. The action of the gangsters entering the bank, holding up the clerk and bashing him over the head with the revolver; slapping the girl; getting the money and running away; as well as the use of machine guns either by actual display or by inference from the soundtrack will have to be entirely deleted. We suggest that you indulge yourselves in this connection in a series of Vorkapich shots [i.e., a "Hollywood montage" sequence] merely suggesting the hold-up... There should be no definite details of the hold-up at any time. Not only are the detailed methods of crime forbidden by our Code, but invariably they are deleted by censor boards everywhere – both in this country and abroad.[1]

Breen was overstating the case as was his habit, but the general trend of the treatment towards minimalism is clear. In addition, agents of law enforcement were not allowed to be shown dying at the hands of criminals. These guidelines were introduced in order to avoid setting a bad example to impressionable and criminal elements, although it is possible that, by making violent criminal acts less explicit – and certainly less repulsive – they may have actually lowered public resistance to the spectacle of armed criminality on the streets of America's cities.[2] The guidelines also made it more difficult for the studios to characterize their criminals as utterly murderous, which, from the point of view of the studios, eroded some of the appeal of their criminal subjects. Under these conditions it was comparatively difficult to ensure that criminals would not be viewed sympathetically, especially when they were inevitably doomed to be shot, executed or incarcerated before the end of the picture. The solution the studios arrived at in 1935, in a typically ingenious compromise, was to exploit "G-man" themes, in which an undercover government operative with a cinematic license to kill infiltrated the underworld and, in more ways than one, assumed the role of a mobster.[3]

The G-man movies technically removed the problem of glorifying gangster anti-heroes, while at the same time loudly proclaiming their own worthiness. The G-man movie *Let 'Em Have It* (Reliance/ United Artists, 1935), for example, was praised by Breen on the grounds that "much footage is given over to showing the care with which the Government selects these men, the period of training through which the men are put, and the intelligence with which later they proceed about their work." He

---

1. Joe Breen, letter to Jack Warner, 14 Feb. 1935, *G-Men* file, PCA Archive.
2. This speculation would apply to America's foreign markets as well, although particular historical and constitutional factors tended to make America more susceptible to *armed* criminals than many of its foreign customers. See Richard Hofstadter and Michael Wallace, eds., *American Violence: A Documentary History* (New York: Alfred A. Knopf, 1970).
3. For example, *Bullets or Ballots* (Warner Bros., 1936) and *Gangs of New York* (Republic, 1938).

also noted that, "In all of these pictures there is a fine uplift, and the reaction we got last night after viewing the Reliance picture was most exhilarating."[1] However, problems remained with the iconography that recalled the earlier gangster pictures: Breen frequently complained to Edward Small, the producer of *Let 'Em Have It*, about "details of crime, repeated scenes of vicious brutality, killings and the needless and excessive showing of guns and gunplay."[2] In a tacit admission of the MPPDA's continuing discomfort with the "sordid" lower-class associations of the stereotypical gangster figure, Breen consistently attempted to modify their tone and milieu, and to discourage the appearance of the "hard-looking, foul-speaking" type of gangster. Instead, he tried to promote a new kind of criminal who was "softly spoken and had the appearance of a gentleman": "instead of showing an eagerness to kill, he is eager to avoid killing, preferring to use his wits to gain his ends rather than to use weapons, to resort to scheming rather than violence."[3] In relation to *Bullets or Ballots* (Warner Bros., 1936), for example, Breen wrote to Jack Warner confirming the following strategy for representing racketeers:

> [Producer Lou] Edelman will keep away entirely from those incidents and details which are usually associated with "gangster pictures."... [T]he criminals engaged in the huge and highly profitable "rackets" will be of the suave, well-educated, well-dressed, polite type – more like successful bankers or businessmen than like gangsters. There will be no showing of guns, and no gun battles with police. The two sinister figures in the present synopsis, who are engaged as "killers," will not be shown in the new treatment; and where, for storyline, it is necessary to "bump off" two or three of our racketeers, this will be done either by suggestion or in dialogue, but not in any brutally murderous fashion.[4]

The finished product was not quite so innocuous as Breen's letter suggests, for the viewing public was more in love with the fictional gangster than with the fictional banker. But in this and every other underworld picture of the thirties, one can find evidence of the continuing struggle between sensational and the worthy, and the between rival poles of taste and sensibility, in the mobsters/racketeer/G-men who eventually reached the screen.

Bibliography

Combs, James, ed. *Movies and Politics: The Dynamic Relationship*. (New York: Garland, 1993).
McCann, Sean. *Gumshoe America: Hard-Boiled Crime Fiction and the Rise and Fall of New Deal Liberalism*. (London: Duke University Press, 2000).
Munby, Jonathan. *Public Enemies, Public Heroes: Screening the Gangster from Little Caesar to Touch of Evil*. (Chicago: University of Chicago Press, 1999).
Powers, Richard Gid. *G-Men: Hoover's FBI in American Culture*. (Carbondale: Southern Illinois University Press, 1983).
Ruth, David E. *Inventing the Public Enemy: The Gangster in American Culture, 1918-1934*. (Chicago: University of Chicago Press, 1996).
Shadoian, Jack. *Dreams and Dream Ends: The American Gangster/Crime Film*. (Cambridge, Mass.: The MIT Press, 1979).
Slocum, David J., ed. *Violence and American Cinema*. (New York: Routledge, 2001).

---

1. Breen, letter to Edward Small (Reliance), 1 March 1935, *Bullets or Ballots* file, PCA Archive.
2. Breen, letter to Edward Small (Reliance), 1 March 1935, *Bullets or Ballots* file, PCA Archive.
3. Olga Martin, *Hollywood's Movie Commandments: A Handbook for Motion Picture Writers and Reviewers* (New York: H.W. Wilson, 1937), p. 134.
4. Breen to Jack Warner, 20 Dec. 1935, *Bullets or Ballots* file, PCA Archive.

Le gangstérisme des années trente et la censure à Hollywood

Par Daniel Peltzman

Producteurs et exploitants de salle furent confrontés à la censure dès le début de l'industrie cinématographique aux Etats-Unis. En fait, la censure et ses conséquences sur l'ensemble de la profession pouvaient se résumer en une question à la fois très simple mais essentielle : comment concilier l'opinion publique qui représentait les spectateurs potentiels avec les censeurs et cela sans mettre en péril la stabilité économique de l'industrie naissante ? Force est de constater que cette question n'avait toujours pas été résolue au début des années trente. Les tentatives de négociations avaient pourtant été nombreuses et longues entre producteurs et groupes de pression, qu'ils fussent religieux ou politiques. D'éventuelles législations fédérales ou des états limitant la liberté de création représentaient un péril pour les responsables des studios. Ainsi, au niveau fédéral, il fallait impérativement empêcher le législateur de voter au Congrès des lois qui auraient pu codifier une censure. Le même problème se posait d'ailleurs au niveau de chaque état. Très rapidement, les producteurs comprirent que seul un compromis mettant d'accord toutes les parties pouvait débloquer la situation. Les thèmes des censeurs furent semblables durant les premières années du XXe siècle : la religion, le vice, la violence. Leur justification reposait toujours sur une théorie incontournable : le cinéma constituait une perversion pour la jeunesse. Selon les censeurs, la jeunesse américaine était en danger car il semblait évident que les films avaient une influence directe sur son comportement. Afin de répliquer à une éventuelle offensive des censeurs ou du gouvernement, les producteurs fondèrent en 1922, la Motion Picture Producers and Distribution of America (MPPDA) avec à sa tête William Hays. Les responsables hollywoodiens, conscients des enjeux financiers, n'hésitèrent pas à mettre en place un système d'autocensure dans lequel Hays fut chargé de contrôler le contenu des films à l'aide de son fameux Code.

A ce titre, les années trente présentèrent les mêmes caractéristiques avec, toutefois, une différence notable. Après la Crise de 1929, les mentalités au sein de l'opinion publique changèrent. Plongée en pleine dépression, la population américaine exprima un étrange paradoxe en regard des films de gangsters produits à Hollywood. Des films tels que *Little Caesar*, *The Public Enemy* et *Scarface* furent des succès commerciaux indéniables. Au même moment, l'opinion publique manifesta sa réprobation à l'encontre de ces œuvres, plaçant à nouveau les producteurs et Hays dans une situation délicate. Plusieurs questions découlent de cette conjoncture paradoxale. Pour quelles raisons les films de gangsters provoquèrent-ils une telle réaction du public ? Et surtout, quelles furent les réponses de l'industrie hollywoodienne et de Hays ? Peut-on affirmer que les producteurs, après avoir accepté un contrôle plus strict des films de gangsters, ne pensaient en fait qu'à rester les maîtres de la production en permettant une censure très limitée ? Afin de répondre à ces questions, il sera nécessaire de comprendre l'impact du gangstérisme ainsi que des films qu'il a inspirés sur la société américaine de cette époque et de donner brièvement un historique du fameux Code Hays.

Le Gangstérisme à la fin des années vingt et dans les années trente

A cette époque, le développement du gangstérisme reste indissociable de la Prohibition et de la Crise de 1929. Avec le dix-huitième Amendement qui interdit dès 1919 la fabrication, la vente et le transport des boissons alcooliques, le Congrès offrait une mine d'or aux organisations criminelles. Les politiciens avaient non seulement créé un marché clandestin rentable, mais ils avaient été dans l'incapacité de mettre en place une législation capable de réprimer le trafic ainsi que la corruption. Chicago devenait ainsi la ville symbole de la pègre organisée avec ses fameuses guerres des gangs qui firent plus de 250 victimes en quatre ans. Très rapidement, le nom d'Al Capone symbolisait le monde du crime aussi bien aux Etats-Unis qu'en Europe. En effet, Capone avait connu une ascension rapide au sein du crime organisé. Simple homme de main aux ordres de Johnny Torrio, il lui succéda lorsque ce dernier décida de prendre sa retraite. En quelques mois, Capone édifia un véritable empire grâce à des activités illégales qui lui rapportaient cent millions de dollars par an. Le trafic d'alcool représentait 60% des revenus, les maisons de jeux 20%, les maisons de passe et le racket 10% chacun. Au moment de son arrestation, sa fortune personnelle fut estimée entre 40 et 60 millions de dollars. La corruption était un facteur déterminant qui permettait à Capone de mener à bien ses affaires. Reprenant en compte les méthodes de Torrio, il acheta régulièrement le silence d'une centaine de personnes : policiers, juges et politiciens. La violence, enfin, faisait également partie de l'arsenal de Capone. Lorsqu'il fallait éliminer un concurrent ou tout élément gênant, le meurtre constituait le plus sûr moyen de résoudre le problème[1]. Personnage public, Capone symbolisait à la fois crainte et admiration. Pour les uns, il représentait l'échec des autorités incapables de mettre un terme à ses agissements. Pour les autres, il incarnait la réussite du rêve américain doublée d'une générosité sincère envers les simples citoyens. Tout comme beaucoup d'hommes d'affaires prospères, Capone se substituait à l'Etat. Chaque année, il dépensait une fortune en charbon, vêtements et nourriture pour les pauvres de Chicago. Cette vision schizophrène ne faisait que réaffirmer l'impact de la crise économique subie par des millions d'Américains. Il n'en fallait pas plus pour qu'Hollywood s'empare du personnage afin de produire des œuvres directement inspirées par Capone.

Les films de gangsters au début des années trente

Avec l'arrivée du cinéma parlant, le film de gangsters connaissait un succès populaire indéniable. A ce titre, trois films allaient susciter la colère des censeurs : *Little Caesar* (1930) de Melvyn LeRoy, *The Public Enemy* (1931) de William Wellman et *Scarface* (1932) de Howard Hawks. Si ces trois œuvres avaient pour point commun l'ascension puis la chute de puissants gangsters, *Little Caesar* et *Scarface* s'inspiraient directement de la vie d'Al Capone. Le personnage central de *The Public Enemy*, quant à lui, évoluait

---

1. Asbury (339-374).

dans le milieu américano-irlandais de Chicago. Les raisons du succès furent multiples : d'abord des metteurs en scènes remarquables, une interprétation saisissante de Edward G. Robinson, James Cagney et Paul Muni et enfin des dialogues qui donnaient un aspect réaliste jusqu'alors inconnu du grand public[1].

Ces succès commerciaux n'empêchèrent pas les vives protestations à la fois du public et des groupes de pression. Le contexte socio-économique joua ici un rôle prépondérant. La dépression qui frappait le pays produisit non seulement l'effondrement des valeurs économiques mais aussi des valeurs morales. L'existence d'un gangster tel qu'Al Capone constituait la preuve d'un déclin moral. Le gangstérisme symbolisait ainsi l'incapacité des autorités à résoudre les problèmes liés à la crise. Les attaques contre les films de gangsters étaient révélatrices de cet état d'esprit. Comment Hollywood pouvait-il produire des œuvres qui glorifiaient les gangsters devenus intouchables ? Leur impact ne pouvait qu'avoir un effet catastrophique sur la jeunesse. Les producteurs eurent beau faire remarquer que dans les trois films le personnage central était tué sauvegardant ainsi la morale, que le titre complet du film de Howard Hawks était : *Scarface : Shame of the Nation*, rien n'y fit. Le film de gangsters était menacé par ce paradoxe : succès populaire d'un côté, vague de protestations de l'autre. A preuve cette anecdote rapportée par l'acteur Edward G. Robinson dans un article publié en 1936 : *"The Movies, the Actor, and the Public Morals"*, où il décrivait le comportement du public :

> One day, as I walked out of a picture house [...] I was confronted by an elderly woman who was leading a seven or eight year old boy by the hand. She asked me if I was Edward G. Robinson, I admitted my identity. "So it's you who played 'Little Caesar' and so many other bad men ?" She said more in the form of reproof than seeking information. I pleaded guilty to the accusation.
> "Well, I'm glad I have this opportunity of telling you to your face what a bad influence your pictures have had on our young people."
> "What makes you think so ?" I asked her.
> "I ought to know," she replied quite sure of her ground, "I've taken my grandchild to see 'Little Caesar' eight times[2]".

Al Capone lui-même n'hésita pas à critiquer les films de gangsters. Ce dernier ne reprochait pas à Hollywood de donner une image négative de ses activités mais plutôt d'exercer une influence néfaste sur la jeunesse[3].

Les protestations arrivaient en outre à un mauvais moment. Les studios subissaient également l'effet de la crise économique rendant ainsi les producteurs encore plus vulnérables à une nouvelle offensive des censeurs. Il leur fallait trouver un compromis permettant de maintenir les bénéfices tout en satisfaisant les partisans d'une censure plus rigoureuse.

Censure et films de gangsters

Depuis 1922, donc, la MPPDA avait joué la carte de la concertation devant les revendications des censeurs. Parmi eux, l'église catholique avait

---

1. Schumach (173).
2. Mast (381).
3. Walsh (71).

occupé une place prépondérante. Ce fut par exemple le cardinal Dougherty qui, dès 1927, avait organisé le premier boycottage de salles de cinéma de Philadelphie mettant ainsi les exploitants locaux dans une situation financière grave et les producteurs dans la peur de voir un tel phénomène se développer dans tout le pays[1]. Autre source de préoccupation, le cardinal Mundelein de Chicago était en étroite relation avec les banquiers directement impliqués dans le financement de l'industrie cinématographique. Il était ainsi facile au cardinal de faire pression sur les producteurs[2].

A partir de février 1924 et afin de parer à de telles éventualités, Hays exigea un droit de regard sur tous les synopsis, romans et pièces de théâtre susceptibles d'être adaptés à l'écran. Il fallait avant tout vérifier avant l'adaptation qu'une œuvre ne contenait aucun élément scabreux qui aurait pu soulever des protestations de la part des censeurs. Ce système de contrôle, *The Formula*, fut la première tentative d'autocensure mise en place par l'industrie. La violence ne constituait pas encore le thème prioritaire à rejeter. Hays craignait plus particulièrement les scènes licencieuses qui offusquaient tout d'abord les groupes religieux. *The Formula* offrait plusieurs avantages aux producteurs dans la mesure où ce système d'autocensure ne prenait pas en compte les scénarios originaux écrits directement pour le cinéma. En outre, *The Formula* ne reposait sur aucune base légale, ne constituant qu'un accord entre Hays et l'ensemble des producteurs. Egalement, ces derniers comprirent rapidement qu'un film vérifié par Hays avait toutes ses chances de recevoir une autorisation d'exploitation[3].

Jusqu'ici, les thèmes à problème n'étaient toujours pas clairement définis par la MPPDA. En 1927, Hays et ses collaborateurs établirent une liste de onze sujets totalement interdits et de 26 devant être manipulés avec la plus grande prudence. Cette liste de *Don'ts and Be Carefuls* fixait une fois encore la priorité sur les scènes susceptibles de contenir des messages blasphématoires et licencieux. Parmi les éléments interdits de traitement, le seul ayant un rapport avec la violence, le troisième dans la liste, était le trafic de drogues. L'utilisation dans les films d'armes à feu, de scènes de brutalité ou renvoyant une image positive du criminel devait, quant à elle, être traitée avec la plus grande prudence. Ces derniers thèmes étaient donc exploitables et ne constituaient pas la priorité de Hays. Pourtant, ni *The Formula* ni les *Don'ts and Be Carefuls* ne satisfirent les groupes de pression et les censeurs. Ce fut même le contraire lorsque les critiques envers Hollywood ne firent qu'augmenter vers la fin des années vingt. Parmi les motifs de mécontentement : le film de gangsters. Les studios qui avaient été frappés par la crise économique avaient parié sur ce nouveau genre de films. Les résultats financiers, en effet, étaient loin d'être encourageants. Si, en 1931, certaines compagnies cinématographiques hollywoodiennes réalisaient toujours des bénéfices, la Fox perdait 3 millions de dollars, R.K.O. près de 6 millions et la Warner Bros. près de 8 millions. Deux ans

---

1. Walsh (115-116).
2. Vaughn (52).
3. Jowett (237).

plus tard, le pourcentage de spectateurs par rapport à 1929 était en baisse de 40% et 5 000 salles de cinéma avaient fermé pour cause de faillite[1]. Le film de gangsters représentait donc un espoir pour l'industrie si elle voulait connaître à nouveau une période de prospérité.

Il devenait urgent de mettre en place un système d'autocensure qui rassurerait l'opinion publique et les groupes de pression. Ce fut sous l'impulsion de deux catholiques, le journaliste Martin Quigley et le révérend père Daniel A. Lord, qu'une importante réforme prit place à partir de 1930. Les deux hommes soumirent à Hays et aux producteurs un code, le *Motion Picture Production Code*, qui fut officiellement adopté en mars. Ce document était composé de deux parties : le code proprement dit et les raisons de son élaboration. La description du code permet de comprendre combien l'impact des films de gangsters était devenu un problème essentiel pour l'ensemble des protagonistes. Contrairement aux deux tentatives précédentes, les auteurs du code, après un bref préambule et une déclaration de principes, plaçaient les thèmes chers aux films de gangsters en haut de leur liste. La plus extrême prudence était devenue de rigueur pour les scènes décrivant les meurtres, les méthodes utilisées par les criminels et les trafics en tout genre[2].

Avec ce code, les producteurs espéraient d'une part apaiser les censeurs et éloigner à tout jamais la possibilité d'une loi fédérale. Afin de montrer la bonne volonté de l'industrie, Hays engagea un ancien policier, August Wollmer, afin que celui-ci évalue les films de gangsters. Le choix de Hays n'était pas dû au hasard. En Californie, Wollmer avait été le chef de la police de Berkeley au début du siècle. En 1902, il avait pris la direction de l'*International Association of Chiefs of Police*. Après avoir été l'un des premiers policiers à établir un système de fichier au sein du département de police de Berkeley, il avait obtenu en 1916 la création du *California State Bureau of Identification and Investigation*. Persuadé que les résultats d'une police moderne dépendaient avant tout de la qualité du recrutement, il avait fondé sa propre académie de police et avait convaincu les responsables de l'université de Californie à Berkeley d'ouvrir le premier programme de formation d'officiers de police[3].

Avec Wollner, Hays et les producteurs engageaient un spécialiste connu du public à la personnalité irréprochable. Les studios entendaient ainsi montrer leur bonne foi et prouver aux censeurs leur volonté de réformer le contenu des films de gangsters. A la demande de Hays, Wollner étudia six films dont *The Public Enemy* et émit un avis favorable. Selon lui, James Cagney n'inspirait pas de l'admiration mais bien au contraire, persuadait le public des méfaits du gangstérisme : "It shows clearly that even if the gangster does escape the clutches of the law, [...] death swift and certain is inevitable for all so-called 'big shots[4]'".

Les studios hollywoodiens pensaient alors avoir apaisé les revendications des groupes de pression. En fait, le début des années trente fut marqué par

---

1. Walsh (70).
2. Jowett (466-472).
3. Powers (266-267).
4. Vaughn (61).

une intensification des campagnes en faveur de la censure. Ses partisans étaient soutenus par deux mouvements distincts : d'une part, l'église catholique avec ses vingt millions de fidèles qui ne faisaient toujours pas confiance à Hays et ses assistants, jugés trop proches des producteurs. L'opinion publique, d'autre part, qui était influencée par des études pseudo-scientifiques mettant en garde les parents sur les effets négatifs du cinéma sur les enfants.

Ce fut l'église catholique, une fois encore, qui lança une offensive à partir de 1934 avec la création de la *Legion of Decency*. En quelques semaines, cette organisation redoutable allait constituer un formidable groupe de pression. Avec au départ plus de 1 750 000 adhérents, l'organisation devait compter entre neuf et onze millions de membres quelques années plus tard. Particulièrement bien structurée, la *Legion of Decency* publiait des listes de films jugés immoraux, publiait dans la presse ses avis et développa un système de classification des films par genre. Plus grave encore pour les producteurs, ses activités furent plutôt bien accueillies par certaines églises protestantes[1]. En outre, l'offensive de la *Legion of Decency* arrivait au moment où l'opinion publique avait pu lire les résultats d'études concernant l'impact des films sur la jeunesse. Parmi de nombreux ouvrages, ce fut celui du journaliste Henry James Forman qui produisit le plus d'effets. Bien que ne constituant pas une étude scientifique, *Our Movie Made Children*, publié en 1933, condamna sans appel les producteurs Hollywoodiens. Si l'auteur traitait de tous les genres de films, il insista sur la présence croissante de la violence à l'écran :

> *In 115 pictures taken at random from recent production and analyzed [...] there are 59 in which murders and homicides are either attempted or committed. Seventy-one deaths by violence actually occur in fifty-four of the pictures. The hero, being a hero, is responsible for only twenty-one per cent of them ; forty per cent fall to the villain's share, and the rest are variously distributed*[2].

Devant de telles levées de boucliers et la peur de sanctions économiques, les producteurs furent réduits à mettre en place une nouvelle structure qui cette fois-ci, imposait des pénalités envers les membres de la MPPDA qui auraient refusé de suivre les recommandations de Hays. En juillet 1934, les studios adoptaient le *Production Code Administration Office* (PCA) et plaçaient à sa tête Joseph I. Breen. Désormais, aucun film ne pouvait être exploité sans avoir reçu l'autorisation explicite de ce dernier. Si un studio contrevenait au règlement, une amende de 25 000 dollars lui était infligée. Devant le succès de la *Legion of Decency* et la peur de l'opinion publique, les producteurs n'hésitaient plus à exercer une coercition au sein de l'industrie[3]. Comme il était évident que le PCA aurait un effet direct sur la production des films, leurs contenus changèrent. Les producteurs, toutefois, continuèrent à exploiter la violence à l'écran mais sans offusquer les censeurs. A l'avenir, Hollywood montrerait des films glorifiant la police et plus particulièrement le tout récent F.B.I.. Ainsi, Warner Bros. produisit en

---

1. Jowett (246-253).
2. Mast (349).
3. Walsh (104-110).

1935 *G-Men* dont l'acteur principal n'était autre que James Cagney. Si cette fois-ci il interprétait un policier du F.B.I., son personnage présentait les mêmes facettes que Tommy Powers dans *The Public Enemy* : esprit de commandement, dureté et courage[1]. L'industrie hollywoodienne avait trouvé un nouveau filon populaire remplissant les salles de cinémas. Le film de gangsters avait disparu, la morale sauvée et les producteurs avaient retourné la situation à leur avantage. Il fallut attendre 1945 et la fin de la Seconde Guerre mondiale pour voir les studios produire un film retraçant la carrière de John Dillinger[2].

Les différentes structures relatives à la censure furent mises en place par l'industrie elle-même sous la peur de différents groupes de pression. Ce faisant, les producteurs montrèrent une remarquable capacité d'adaptation au changement à partir de compromis suivis, la plupart du temps, par des concessions envers Hays et les censeurs. En acceptant les négociations et sans jamais entrer en conflit direct avec leurs adversaires, ils surent avant tout maintenir la stabilité économique de l'industrie. Du même coup, ils réussissaient à éloigner le spectre d'une intervention du Congrès américain qui aurait pu bouleverser la structure de l'industrie. Cependant, peut-on dire que les censeurs furent les vainqueurs ? Certes, Hays et Breen allaient, désormais, méticuleusement examiner les films. Quant aux groupes de pression, s'ils obtinrent gain de cause pour les films de gangsters, ils ne firent pas disparaître la violence de l'écran. Plus important, le monde du gangstérisme avait encore de beaux jours devant lui.

Bibliographie

Asbury Herbert, *Gem of the Prairie : An Informal History of the Chicago Underworld*, Dekalb, Illinois, Northern Illinois University Press, 1940, (1986).
Bidaud Anne Marie, *Hollywood et le rêve américain : Cinéma et idéologie aux Etats-Unis*, Paris, Masson, 1994.
Lowett Garth, *Film the Democratic Art*, Boston, Little, Brown and Company, 1976.
Mast Gerald, *The Movies in Our Midst*, Chicago, The University of Chicago Press, 1982.
Powers Richard Gid, "The F.B.I. in American Popular Culture" in Athan Theoharis, ed., *The F.B.I. : A Comprehensive Reference Guide*, New York, Checkmark Books, 2000.
Schumach Murray, *The Face on the Cutting Room Floor : The Story of Movie and Television Censorship*, New York, Da Capo Press, 1975.
Vaughn Steven, "Morality and Entertainment : The Origins of the Motion Picture Code", *The Journal of American History*, June 1990.
Walsh Frank, *Sin and Censorship : The Catholic Church and the Motion Picture Industry*, New Haven, Yale University Press, 1996.

---

1. Powers (272).
2. Schumach (173).

Juvenile Crime and The Kefauver Hearings
By Matthew Guillen

In late 1949, numerous articles in newspapers and magazines warned that a national crime syndicate was gaining control of many American cities by corrupting local government officials. Crime commissions in Chicago and California also reported official corruption under the influence of syndicated crime. Requests for Federal assistance came from the mayors of Los Angeles, New Orleans, Portland, and other cities and finally the American Municipal Association asked the Federal government to investigate efforts of organized national racketeers to gain control of municipal law-enforcement agencies. Federal authorities were ill-equipped to deal with issues which appeared, on the surface, to concern local state governments, how-ever. Thus it was within the scope of Article I, Section 8 – one of Congress' enumerated powers (the so-called "Commerce Clause[1]") – that on January 5, 1950, Estes Kefauver of Tennessee introduced a resolution authorizing the Committee on the Judiciary to investigate interstate gambling and racketeering activities and the use of the facilities of interstate commerce for purposes of organized crime. On May 3, 1950, the Special Committee to Investigate Organized Crime in Interstate Commerce was directed to study and investigate activities, such as narcotics trafficking and syndicated gambling, which could conceivably extend beyond state boundaries. Otherwise, the resolution specifically prohibited the committee from interfering in any way with the rights of the States to regulate gambling within their borders. At first, Kefauver served as chairman, and the committee was sometimes referred to as the Kefauver Committee. On May 1, 1951, Herbert R. O'Conor of Maryland assumed the chairmanship and occupied that position for the final few months until the committee ended on September 1, 1951.

This article proposes to study the growing perception that criminality was gaining acceptance and popularity among youth, seen particularly in the light of children's susceptibility to organized crime depiction in comic books and what appeared to be a corresponding increase in juvenile delinquency and narcotics use[2]. It will be argued that the Kefauver Hearings covering criminality in America were far from over in 1951. In fact, on April 21, 1954, the Senate Committee of the Judiciary to Investigate Juvenile Delinquency, formed in early 1953 under the chairmanship of Robert Hendrickson and aided by Senators Estes Kefauver and Thomas Hennings to look into the causes of juvenile crime, with particular attention to the possible contributing factors in mass culture, began their investigation into the effects of crime comics on children.

The original Special Committee to Investigate Organized Crime in Interstate Commerce was broadly directed to study and investigate

---

1. "The Congress shall have Power [...] To regulate Commerce with foreign Nations, and among the several States".
2. Charles Grutzner "Narcotic Use Rise held 'Tremendous'," *The New York Times*, December 21, 1951.

> whether organized crime utilizes the facilities of interstate commerce or otherwise operates in interstate commerce in furtherance of any transactions which are in violation of the law [...] and, if so, the manner and extent to which, and the identity of the persons, firms, or corporations by which such utilization is being made[1].

The committee's work generated considerable public interest, due to the subject matter and to the fact that it was the first committee to hold televised hearings. Hearings were held in Washington and in cities throughout the country, questioning governors, mayors, sheriffs, policemen, and reputed underworld figures. These efforts led to many citations for contempt of the Senate and a number of local indictments for criminal activities.

The committee also issued four reports concluding that nationwide organized crime syndicates did exist and that they depended on the support or tolerance of public officials. Filed under records relating to crime in general were correspondence, memoranda, investigative files, minutes of executive and public hearings, documents providing tax information, lists of telephone calls furnished to the committee by the phone company, and various other types of documents. There were replies to committee inquiries from public attorneys; police departments; Federal agencies; and stevedore, steamship, and other companies. Various printed materials were among the files, such as copies of committee publications, bills and resolutions, State statutes or legislative proposals regarding organized crime, and press clippings about gamblers and racketeers. Subjects appearing in the records included the committee's investigative program and plans, prostitution, narcotics, gambling, racketeering, homicides, distribution of alcoholic beverages, New York waterfront activities, alien criminals residing in the United States and finally, surprisingly for the era, statistics on juvenile delinquency. By early 1952, in fact, the Narcotics Bureau was able to report that the upward trend in teen-aged addiction "was halted in 1951" with the arrest in New York of Waxey Gordon, the "most notorious of all the hoodlums to fall into the Narcotic Bureau net[2]".

The contours of the notion "juvenile crime" were indistinct in this epoch and in search of establishment recognition and legitimacy. The first Juvenile Court organized in the United States was created in Cook County, Illinois, by an act of Illinois Legislature in April, 1899. Writing in 1934, Dr. Milton E. Kirkpatrick of the Cleveland Juvenile Court expressed regret that

> the movement to treat the juvenile delinquent with more consideration than accorded the adult offender has not made the desired progress[3].

Curiously, in examining the incidence of juvenile crime during the Depression years 1934-1935, his study revealed a significant drop in the number of offenses. Explanations were wanting, however, and the etiology of juvenile offense was itself still a mystery – criminal behavior among

---
1. S. Res. 202, 81st Cong.
2. "Teen-Age Addicts Reported Fewer," *The New York Times*, February 10, 1952.
3. Milton E. Kirkpatrick, M.D., "Delinquency in Cleveland and Cuyahoga County during the Depression Period. Part 1" *American Journal of Orthopsychiatry*, 4 (3) July 1934, 382.

youth remaining a sort of epiphenomenon relegated to the arcana of psychiatric investigation. The best that could be asserted in this era was that the criminality of the adult was the direct continuation of the delinquency of the child, "which fact alone places the delinquent child immediately in the center of the problem of criminality[1]". This and similar notions worked in rather too neatly with a tendency to attribute criminality to the individual's genetic "constitution" as per the work of Cesare Lombroso, a nineteenth-century Italian physician who claimed to have identified the "born" criminal – helpless to do otherwise from their very inception, the concept of environmental or direct adult influence over children never arose[2]. This was all to change, however. In their *Juvenile Delinquency and Urban Areas* (1942), Shaw and McKay examined arrest rates of juveniles throughout the city of Chicago during the years 1900-06, 1917-23, and 1927-33. These were years of high immigration – as the older and more established immigrant groups were pushed along by the arrival of poorer immigrant groups, who took their place in the center of the city. By comparing the average arrest rates from these different time periods, they believed they could show whether delinquency was caused by particular immigrant groups or by the environment in which immigrants lived. Dividing three maps of Chicago into even grids, they recognized that the pattern of delinquency rates remained constant over time and came to the important conclusion that delinquency rates always remained high for a certain region of the city no matter what immigrant group lived there. Therefore, delinquency was not "constitutional" – as Lombroso and his followers had argued – but must somehow be correlated with the particular cultural environment in which it occurs.

By the time of the first Kefauver Hearings, Shaw and McKay's so-called "social disorganization theory" had come to be fairly accepted by the scientific establishment but failed to result in any significant support or application – and would have remained so but for an unexpected turn in the Hearings. Nearing its conclusion, the Kefauver Committee publicly established (many would say "finally acknowledged") the existence of the Italian "Mafia" as a "secret conspiracy against law and order which will ruthlessly eliminate anyone who stands in the way of its success in any criminal enterprise in which it is interested." It would presumably "destroy anyone who betrays its secrets" and will use "any means available political influence, bribery, intimidation, etc.," to defeat any attempt on the part of law enforcement to touch its top figures or to interfere with its operations[3]. More to the point, in tacit acknowledgement of budding culture environmental theories, the link between organized crime and juvenile offenders was stated outright – in this instance, in the context of the peddling of narcotics by organized crime to youngsters:

---

1. Franz Alexander and William Healy, *Roots of Crime*, 1936. 278, cited in Susan Burlingham "Casework With Adolescents Who Have Run Afoul of the Law" *American Journal of Orthopsychiatry*, 7 (4) October 1937, 489.
2. Gina Lombroso-Ferrero, *Criminal Man According to the Classification of Cesare Lombroso*, Montclair, NJ: Patterson-Smith, 1971 (originally published 1911).
3. U.S. Senate Special Committee to Investigate Organized Crime in Interstate Commerce, "Organized Crime in Interstate Commerce," Hearings, Parts 1-19, May 26, 1950, through August 7, 1951 (with composite index). Government Printing Office, Washington. CLCL.

> In the past 24 months, America has been jolted to its foundations by the discovery that youngsters, especially in the larger cities, are using narcotic drugs, many to the point of addiction. New York, Chicago, Baltimore, and Washington, D.C. saw big increases in the number of underaged drug users coming to the attention of the police. In a large number of cases, these young people were engaging in crime for the sole purpose of supporting their drug habit[1].

The Committee recounted tragic stories of a nineteen-year-old boy who threw away a scholarship at an eastern university because of drugs, a Midwestern freshman who dropped out in his first semester and stole money from the mails – "all because of dope," a group of collegians who grew marijuana in their backyard, and girls in their late teens with narcotic habits who admitted resorting to prostitution "rather than endure the horror of going without drugs." From Harlem came reports that 50 per cent of all members of youthful street gangs smoked marijuana, including youths of thirteen; indeed, even some nine-year-olds had reportedly been approached by peddlers attempting to have them take drugs. The most compelling testimony was ultimately to be provided by H. J. Anslinger, United States Commissioner Of Narcotics, and William F. Tompkins, U.S. Attorney for the District of New Jersey and former chairman of the Legislative Commission to Study Narcotics, General Assembly of New Jersey – their report to later be published in book form[2].

As the scope of the hearings broadened, among expert witnesses called in this part of the proceedings was Dr. Frederic Wertham who, testifying as to the possible causes of such youthful behavior, charged that criminal activity illustrated in comic books had a direct influence on the growing incidence of juvenile delinquency nationwide. Wertham's credentials were impressive. He had emigrated from Germany to the United States in 1922, quickly acquiring a position at the Phipps Psychiatric Clinic at Johns Hopkins University. Leaving Phipps in 1932 to become the Senior Psychiatrist for Bellevue Hospital, he continued the writing of books and articles tying together criminal behavior with mental health and environment. During the thirties he advised the City of New York on the first psychiatric hospital for convicted criminals. In 1941, Wertham published "Dark Legend," a work directly connecting popular culture with crime. This was the true story of a 17-year-old New York City teenager who killed his mother in the late thirties. Detailing the boy's life, Wertham noted the boy's interests in movies, radio and comic books, which Wertham believed helped the boy move emotionally into a fantasy world, contributing to the boy's aberrant behavior and finally the crime itself. One judge on the committee was moved to strongly support Wertham's theory, stating he had cases where boys had committed a crime that was patterned after one depicted in a comic book. In response, the Committee sent out questionnaires soliciting a variety of opinions on comic books and their

---

1. U.S. Senate Report 82-307 (third Interim).
2. H.J. Anslinger and William F. Tompkins, *The Traffic in Narcotics*, New York: Funk & Wagnalls, 1953.

possible contribution to crime among youth. The results were indecisive, however, and the Committee then moved on to other issues[1].

Dr. Wertham continued to press his indictment of comic books, meanwhile – through numerous articles in popular family-oriented publications such as *Reader's Digest* and *Ladies' Home Journal*. Thus, by broadening his constituency and gathering support from such influential lobbying groups as the General Federation of Women's Clubs, the American Legion, and the Catholic National Organization for Decent Literature, public pressure began compelling wholesalers to withdraw objectionable comic books from the market[2]. In fact, many states began passing laws prohibiting the distribution of crime comic books to minors[3]. And although some of these statutes were found unconstitutional, the movement was reinvigorated through the publication of Wertham's *Seduction of the Innocent*, a sensational polemic which received widespread publicity and culminated in Wertham's moment of glory before the Senate Subcommittee to Investigate Juvenile Delinquency in 1954. It should be noted that although *Seduction* garnered favorable reviews from Catholic publications like *America* and *Catholic World*, Wertham later complained that the comic book industry had pressured the Book of the Month Club into withdrawing its selection. In *Seduction*, Wertham showed the gruesome covers and pictures of various comics, but the bibliography listing which comic companies produced those pictures was cut out after publication. There are no details as to why this happened, but it is suspected that the comic companies put pressure on *Seduction*'s publisher Rinehart & Co. to delete the bibliography[4].

One thing was certain, however: the comic book industry was quite powerful indeed. The number of comic book publishers had increased with circulation figures rising astonishingly by the time the hearings began. The pattern for comic books (as opposed to comic strips appearing in newspapers) had been set in 1935 when *Now Fun*, a 64-page collection of original material printed in four colors, was put on newsstands. *Action Comics* were put on sale in 1938, and *Superman Quarterly Magazine* appeared in 1939. A conservative estimate is that in 1940 publishers of at least 150 comic-book titles had annual revenues of over 20 million. Ten years later, in 1950 about 300 comic-book titles were being published with annual revenues of nearly 41 million. The upswing in the next 3 years brought the number of titles to over 650 and the gross to about 90 million. Average monthly circulation jumped from close to 17 million copies in 1940 to 68 million in 1953. No accurate figures are available as to the actual number of comic books being published at the time of the Hearings, since apparently many of the newer publishers of comic books had neither reported to the Audit Bureau of Circulations nor to the Controlled Circulation Audits, the two firms that compiled circulation figures. The subcommittee, in making the above estimate, thus assumed that 300,000 copies of each comic-book title were

---

1. U.S. Senate, Special Committee to Investigate Organized Crime in Interstate Commerce, *Juvenile Delinquency*, 81st Cong., 2nd sess., 1950, 6.
2. *New York Times*, December 28, 1953.
3. Kevin W. Saunders, "Media Self-Regulation of Depictions of Violence: A Last Opportunity," 47 *Okla. L. Rev.* (1994), 445, 446-7.
4. Frederic Wertham, Interview, *Inside Comics* 4 (winter 1974-1975), 18.

printed, even though information given to the subcommittee indicated that is a minimum print order and that some print orders were close to the million mark. It was also assumed that one-half of the comic books printed were sold, even though information given was to the effect that the "break-even" point for the average publisher would more likely be closer to 65 percent. And finally it was assumed that one-half of all the comic books were published monthly and that the remainder were published bimonthly, even though information furnished by the publishers themselves indicate that more than one-half of the comic books were published monthly[1].

For these reasons, staff members for the juvenile delinquency subcommittee had already begun conducting an extensive background investigation before the actual hearings began under executive director Richard Clendenen. Chief of the juvenile delinquency branch of the United States Children's Bureau and the bureau's leading expert on delinquency, Clendenen had previously worked as a probation officer in a juvenile court and was an administrator at various institutions for emotionally disturbed children and delinquent children. In 1952, the new director of the Children's Bureau, Martha Eliot, made juvenile delinquency her priority and created a Special Delinquency Project that Clendenen headed. Eliot loaned Clendenen's services to the Senate subcommittee, partly because the subcommittee had insufficient funding to conduct its own investigations and partly to give her agency a voice in the findings; Clendenen joined the staff in August 1953, and began by requesting from the staff of the Library of Congress a summary of all studies published on the effects of comic books on children. He also sent several prominent individuals samples of the comic books under investigation and solicited their opinions on the effects of such material. Extensive work had already been done by the New York Joint Legislative Committee to study comics and by the Cincinatti Committee on Evaluation of Comic Books, and their reports were included in the committee's records[2].

On March 14, 1955, Senator Kefauver, from the Committee on the Judiciary, submitted an Interim Report entitled *Comic Books And Juvenile Delinquency: A Part Of The Investigation Of Juvenile Delinquency In The United States*[3]. Among the more interesting issues raised concerned the advertising of "Weapons and psychomedical nostrums" in comic books designed for children. The illustrations in one advertisement introduced at the New York hearings showed at least 10 dangerous articles that would appeal to a minor, ranging from a powerful hunting crossbow, a throwing dagger and a "fireball" slingshot, to a 22-caliber automatic (not available to New York residents) and an army training rifle. According to the report, "Their descriptions leave little for the imagination" and cited as examples, "Oriental battle knife – designed for long-distance throwing, it is made to split a board at 30 feet and is balanced to stick"; "Commando knife-real

---

1. Roma K McNickle., *Policing the Comics, Editorial Research Reports*, 229-330. See also N. W. Ayer & Son's *Directory of Newspapers and Periodicals for the Years 1945 through 1953*.
2. Amy Kiste Nyberg, *Seal of Approval: The History of the Comics Code (Studies in Popular Culture Series)*, 17.
3. US Congress Senate. Committee on the Judiciary: Juvenile Deliquency. 1955-6. Library of Congress Catalogue Card Number 77-90720 84th Congress 1st Session Report No. 62.

'Commando' weapon. An all-metal, needle-pointed, razor-sharp 12-inch knife that may save your life"; the "'Fireball' slingshot-silent, sweet shooting. Extra powerful – you get that 'feel of accuracy' with your first shots"; "Throwing dagger. An exciting sport that provide fun and thrills – indoors or outdoors. This knife is light in weight and expertly balanced to stick. Tempered steel blade with double bevel edges"; "Arrow sling fun. A new thrill in hunting. Powerful sling fun sends 12-inch metal-tipped arrows through metal-guide barrel to 300 inch range. Swift. Silent. Accurate. Kills all small game. Five arrows included"; or "Finnish hunting knife, handmade in Finland. Richly engraved blade with deep blood grooves. Flashy horse-head handle[1]".

Other questionable aspects of advertising were uncovered. The Post Office Department informed the subcommittee that the mails had been used to advertise and sell a book entitled "The Illustrated Encyclopedia of Sex," by Dr. A. Willy and others; of 297 complaints received over a period dating from April 1951, 93 concerned mailings to minors. Although the book was not considered obscene, the methods of advertising by the publisher included blaring advertisements in numerous magazines, showing pictures of scantily clad young women in sexually provocative poses. Additionally, parents from many States complained to the subcommittee that teen-age sons, daughters, and friends had received advertisements which flagrantly describe obscene material. In the New York investigation it was discovered that Samuel Roth, who for many years had been engaged in "using the mails to advertise lewd and lascivious printed materials," had purchased mailing lists that contained the names of many teen-agers. Roth refused to testify before the subcommittee, claiming his rights under the 5th Amendment to the Constitution. Collaterally, It was found that Roth purchased 136,567 names and addresses from Robert B. Vallon of the Mapleton Service Co. Many of those names were obtained through correspondence with comic-book readers. A sample circular, mailed out by Roth to a 16-year-old high school student, advertised such books as *Wild Passion*, *Wanton by Night*, *Waterfront Hotel*, and *The Shame of Oscar Wilde*, the mailing of which had been proscribed under the postal obscenity law. Roth's advertisements also carried descriptions of "seven books of pleasure and sexual excitement calculated to keep you on blissful heights for days and days[2]".

The sum of which raised still another issue: the misuse of mailing lists compiled through comic-book advertisements. Members of the subcommittee expressed concern that some "purveyors of salacious literature may deliberately seek to secure mailing lists of juveniles" for direct-mail solicitation. One publisher, Alex Segal, testified that "by mistake" one of his trays of addressograph plates "bearing the names of 400 children was routed to the publisher of sex literature. Seagle himself advertises and sells books called How to Hypnotize-A Master Key to Hypnotism." This advertisement appeared in Quality Comics and portrayed a male looking at a young female with the caption "Want the thrill of imposing your will on someone? Stravon Publishers will tell you how." Upon receipt of the book

---

1. *Ibid*, 17.
2. *Ibid*.

on hypnotism, a child also received a list of other purchasable material-including sex literature. It was further established that such advertisements had been received by juveniles as young as 9 years old[1].

The most significant part of the proceedings, of course, was when attention turned to the testimony of Wertham, recognized by the committee as the "leading crusader against comics," and other "experts" on the influence of crime and horror comics on well-adjusted children who normally are not in conflict with society. Majority opinion seemed to coincide with the view that it is unlikely that the reading of crime and horror comics would lead to delinquency in a well-adjusted and normally law-abiding child. But here Wertham differed. He maintained that it is primarily the "normal" child upon whom the comics have their greatest detrimental effects, and thus it is this type of individual who is "tempted" and "seduced" into imitating the crime portrayed in the story. Although admitting he did not adhere to a single factor theory of delinquency causation, he firmly attributed a large portion of juvenile offenses to the comics.

A critique of Wertham's position was uncovered in an article by Prof. Frederic M. Thrasher entitled, "The Comics and Delinquency: Cause or Scapegoat." This article which appeared in 1949, pointed to alleged weakness in Dr. Wertham's approach, the major one being that his propositions were not supported by adequate research data[2]. Professor Thrasher asserted that Wertham's claims rested upon a selected group of extreme cases, and although Wertham had since declared that his conclusions were based upon a study of thousands of children, he never offered the statistical details of his study. He stated that he used control groups, i.e. compared his groups of delinquents with a similar group on nondelinquents, but never established the incidence of comic-book reading as other than a selective process. In conclusion, Professor Thrasher wrote:

> it may be said that no acceptable evidence has been produced by Wertham or anyone else for the conclusion that the reading comic magazines has, or has not, a significant relation to delinquent behavior.

Dr. Harris Peck, director of the bureau of mental health services for the New York City Court of Domestic Relationships, indicated in his testimony that there is a possible relationship of crime and horror comic books to juvenile delinquency through appealing to and thus giving support and sanction to already existing antisocial tendencies[3]. While pointing out that it is unlikely that comic books are a primary cause of juvenile delinquency, he stated that that it should not be overlooked that certain comic books may encourage delinquent behavior which has been set in motion by other forces already operating on the child. Peck also noted the preoccupation with comics of many delinquents with whom he had come in contact.

---

1. *Ibid.*, 18.
2. Frederic M. Thrasher, "The Comics and Delinquency: Cause or Scapegoat", *Journal of Educational Sociology*, December 1949, 195-205.
3. Harris Peck, testimony in hearings before the Subcommittee To Investigate Juvenile Delinquency of the Committee on the Judiciary, U.S. Senate, 83d Cong., 2d sess., Washington: Government Printing Office 1954, 63-69.

Content analysis of crime comics by the subcommittee indicated that in most instances the crimes as portrayed in these books were committed "with little finesse or imagination." Guns were the most frequent weapon for murder. "Holdups," safe blowing and payroll seizures were among the methods employed in robberies. However, there were stories in which utilization was made of the following: lead pipes, kitchen knives, wet rawhide belts (tied around a man's neck to dry in the sun, thereby shrinking and strangling him), whips, hot coffee thrown in a person's face, wrenches, jagged edges of bottles, and acid for "melting a person's face." In a few stories more sophisticated methods of crime were described. For example, it was explained that it is easier to pick pockets in a cafeteria because "a man hesitates to drop a tray of food to see if his pockets have been picked"; and it was suggested that tires can be stolen from one junkyard and sold to another[1].

A number of impressions were obtained from reading how the criminal moves in his cultural pattern as depicted by crime comics. For example, crime may have brought wealth and fame even though it was sometimes temporary. Large monetary rewards from crime were shown through scenes of cash being counted or money being spent on luxurious living. Through committing bizarre crimes, individuals became widely known figures and sometimes became idols, eulogized through the publicity accorded them in the newspapers. Many of the stories included texts describing the sensation experienced by a killer. Killing was described as the means of acquiring "a high degree of self-confidence, giving the individual a feeling of strength and power." A highly pleasing physical sensation was also described as resulting from killing. Finally, some stories in comic books showed membership in the criminal underworld to be dependent upon certain personal characteristics highly valued by experienced criminals. These attributes were mainly physical – criminals being admired for their "toughness," their hatred for "cops" and a willingness to commit any type of crime regardless of the risk involved. In their interpersonal relationships, comic-book criminals never exhibited such human virtues as consideration of others, charity and the like. Furthermore, to reinforce the behavior expected of the potential criminal, names suggestive of toughness were assigned to him. Finally, in some of the stories, murder for revenge was justified under certain conditions. The murderers were not apprehended and there was no suggestion that they would be taken in custody at a future date. The end of the criminal's career came about, if at all, through chance factors or by superhuman beings or other ideal types. As the latter two do not exist in reality, the "obvious interpretation" the committee derived from these stories was that "crime *does* pay if one is ruthless and clever to a sufficient degree[2]".

The comics industry offered little resistance, and it came chiefly from the testimony given by William M. Gaines, claiming to be the "first publisher in these United States to publish horror comics," and who insisted that "delinquency is the product of the real environment in which the child lives

---

1. *Ibid.*, 15.
2. *Ibid.*, 16.

and not of the fiction he reads[1]". The most famous exchange in the Hearings involved questioning Gaines about the cover to the May 22, 1954 issue of *Crime SuspenStories*, published by EC (Entertaining Comics) and featuring the artwork of Johnny Craig, the content of which becomes evident in the following:

"*Senator Kefauver: (holding up the copy)* Here is your May 22 issue. This seems to be a man with a bloody ax holding a woman's head up which has been severed from her body. Do you think that is in good taste?

Gaines: Yes, sir; I do, for the cover of a horror comic. A cover in bad taste, for example, might be defined as holding the head a little higher so that the neck could be seen dripping blood from it and moving the body over a little further so that the neck of the body could be seen to be bloody.

Kefauver: You have blood coming out of her mouth.

Gaines: A little.

Kefauver: Here is blood on the ax. I think most adults are shocked by that.

Senator Hendrickson: Here is another one I want to show him.

Kefauver: This is the July one. It seems to be a man with a woman in a boat and he is choking her to death here with a crowbar. Is that in good taste?

Gaines: I think so.

Chief Counsel Hannoch: How could it be worse?[2] "

This episode was sensationalized in the press, *The New York Times* reporting it in its front-page story on the Hearings. Articles in *Time* and other journals critical of comic books had a field day mocking Gaines' explanation of "good taste[3]". With the incongruous outcome that the Senate committee did not fully endorse Dr. Wertham's theories about the effect of comic books on children after all, since his studies were not done on the "complete environment", but only on juvenile delinquents. But the Senate committee did agree that comic books might have an unhealthy effect on those kids that were already emotionally disturbed or morally delinquent. But because they were uncertain as to whether comics had this effect or not, the committee decided in favor of self-policing by the comic publishers. The industry thus announced the immediate formation of a strict comics code called the Comics Magazine Association of America – the Comics equivalent of the MPAA (the Hays Code) adopted by the film industry two and a half decades earlier. It was to be headed by New York Magistrate Charles E. Murphy who promised the new code would be the strongest ever adopted by the communications medium. The Senate committee's final report also issued a warning to comic companies that if their self-policing didn't work that they would re-visit the issue again, and use whatever means necessary to "prevent our nation's young from being harmed from crime and horror comic books." Ultimately, many publishers of crime comic

---

1. William M. Gaines, Interview, *Comics Journal* 81, May 1983, 97-8.
2. US Senate, Committee on the Judiciary, *Hearings Before the Subcommittee to Investigate Juvenile Delinquency (Comic Books)*, 83rd Cong., 2d sess., April 21, 1954, 103.
3. *The New York Times*, April 22, 1954; "Horror Comics," *Time*, May 31, 1954, 78—and in the same issue Sheerin, "Crime Comics must go!" 162; T.E. Murphy, "The Face of Violence," *Reader's Digest*, November 1954, 56; Rugh A. Inglis, "The Comic Book Problem, "*American Mercury*, August 1955, 119.

books went out of business because wholesalers refused to sell comics without the industry seal[1].

Today, of course, the industry seal is scarcely noticeable on comic book covers, and content is easily as provocative as in the late 40s. And considering the arguable effectiveness of self-censorship in the film medium, and in the context of so many Congressional Hearings in this era (those instigated by Senator Joseph McCarthy receiving the greatest notoriety) the collateral question arises as to why in the 1950s, Congress was so reluctant to pass legislation requiring any level of regulation – either with reference to organized crime as revealed through the 1950 hearings or the later hearings on juvenile crime – choosing instead the questionable "self-monitoring" by interested industry officials. The answer may be found in a political science theory developed in 1964, Murray Edelman's "symbolic politics" theory in which it is posited that politicians engage in symbolic activity rather than substantive activity to manipulate the public into perceiving that they are looking after the public's interests and concerns. Hearings without subsequent legislation, therefore, are examples of symbolic actions taken by members of Congress to *appear* responsive to an issue of some concern to the public without engaging in the time-consuming and complex task of enacting real change. This symbolic action remained the "act of choice" for Congress until the mid-1960s, when legislation was introduced to curb organized crime, racial discrimination, and in the 1980s, crime on television – issues perceived as perhaps far more profound than those addressed by Dr. Wertham who, the questionable aspects of his censorship "crusade" notwithstanding, still contributed largely towards establishing the significance of cultural environment on behavior.

Bibliography

Alexander, Franz and William Healy. *Roots of Crime*, 1936, cited in Susan Burlingham "Casework With Adolescents Who Have Run Afoul of the Law" *American Journal of Orthopsychiatry*, 7(4) October 1937.

Anslinger, H.J. and William F. Tompkins. *The Traffic in Narcotics* (New York: Funk & Wagnalls, 1953).

Blanchard, Margaret A. "The American Urge to Censor: Freedom of Expression versus the Desire to Sanitize Society – From Anthony Comstock to 2 Live Crew," 33 *William and Mary L. Rev.*, (1992).

Edelman, Murray. *The Symbolic Uses of Politics* (Urbana, Ill.: University of Illinois Press, 1970).

Gaines, William M. "An Interview with William M. Gaines," interviewed by Dwight R. Decker and Gary Groth, *Comics Journal* 81, May 1983.

Grutzner, Charles "Narcotic Use Rise held 'Tremendous'," *The New York Times*, December 21, 1951.

Kirkpatrick, Milton E. M.D., "Delinquency in Cleveland and Cuyahoga County during the Depression Period. Part 1" *American Journal of Orthopsychiatry*, 4 (3) July 1934.

Inglis, Rugh A. "The Comic Book Problem", *American Mercury*, August 1955.

Kefauver, Carey Estes, *Crime in America* (Garden City, NY: Doubleday, 1951).

Lombroso-Ferrero, Gina .*Criminal Man According to the Classification of Cesare Lombroso* (Montclair, NJ: Patterson-Smith, 1971), originally published 1911.

McNickle, Roma K, *Policing the Comics, Editorial Research Reports*, 1205 19th street NW, Washington D.C., vol. I, 1952.

Murphy, T.E. "The Face of Violence," *Reader's Digest*, November 1954.

---

1. Margaret A. Blanchard, "The American Urge to Censor: Freedom of Expression versus the Desire to Sanitize Society—From Anthony Comstock to 2 Live Crew," 33 *William and Mary L. Rev.*, (1992), 741, 793.

Nyberg, Amy Kiste *Seal of Approval: The History of the Comics Code* (Jackson, Miss.: University Press of Mississippi, Studies in Popular Culture Series, 1998).
Saunders, Kevin W. "Media Self-Regulation of Depictions of Violence: A Last Opportunity," 47 *Oklahoma Law Review* (1994).
Shaw, Clifford R. & Henry D. McKay. *Juvenile Delinquency in Urban Areas* (Chicago: University of Chicago Press, 1942).
Time, May 31, 1954.
Thrasher, Frederic M. "The Comics and Delinquency: Cause or Scapegoat," *Journal of Educational Sociology*, December 1949.
Wertham, Frederic "Comic Books – Blueprints for Delinquency," *Reader's Digest*, May 1954, 24-29;
"What Parents Don't Know about Comic Books," *Ladies' Home Journal*, November 1953, 214-20;
—Readers Write," *Ladies' Home Journal*, February 1954, 4-6;
—*Seduction of the Innocent*. (New York: Rinehart, 1954);
—Frederic Wertham, interviewed by Ed Summer, June 12, 1974, *Inside Comics* 4 (winter 1974-1975)
U.S. Senate Special Committee to Investigate Organized Crime in Interstate Commerce, "Organized Crime in Interstate Commerce," Hearings, Parts 1-19, May 26, 1950, through August 7, 1951 (with composite index). Government Printing Office, Washington. CLCL.
U.S. Senate Report 82-307 (third Interim).
U.S. Senate, Special Committee to Investigate Organized Crime in Interstate Commerce, *Juvenile Delinquency*, 81st Cong., 2nd sess., 1950.
US Senate, Committee on the Judiciary, *Hearings Before the Subcommittee to Investigate Juvenile Delinquency (Comic Books)*, 83rd Cong., 2d sess., April 21, 1954.
US Congress Senate Committee on the Judiciary: Juvenile Deliquency, Library of Congress Catalogue Card Number 77-90720 84th Congress 1st Session Report No. 62. 1955-6.
Wilson, Theodore, "The Kefauver Committee, 1950" In Schlesinger, Arthur M. and Robert Burns, *Congress Investigates, 1792-1974* (New York: Chelsea House, 1975).

Le crime organisé dans le ghetto afro-américain (1920-1940)

Par Françoise Clary

Etudier le Crime organisé dans le ghetto afro-américain, c'est chercher à mettre à jour diverses entreprises, firmes et affaires, avec leurs stratégies financières propres, en choisissant de s'écarter des perspectives traditionnelles qui tendent à assimiler les activités criminelles à des organisations monolithiques, figées dans le cadre de structures élaborées, n'ayant d'autre but que d'exploiter, en prédatrices, tout marché lucratif. Si, au contraire, on perçoit la façon d'être et de faire des Afro-Américains vivant dans les ghettos de Harlem, Chicago ou Detroit, comme une capacité à recourir à des activités lucratives impliquant le fonctionnement d'un certain nombre de firmes implantées dans leur environnement urbain, le terme « communauté » acquiert alors un sens tout particulier, primant sur l'aspect « criminel » du système établi. Il importe donc de prendre la mesure du paysage urbain dans lequel évoluent les habitants du ghetto dans l'Amérique des années 1920-1930 et des forces sociales extérieures qui ont isolé les communautés afro-américaines – y compris les familles jamaïcaines, antillaises, nigériennes, haïtiennes – en les privant de l'accès aux ressources vitales nécessaires mais, en revanche, en stimulant leur capacité à générer des richesses. Il conviendra, ensuite, de prêter attention à la dynamique d'action et de réaction de la communauté afro-américaine face aux pressions extérieures.

La création de réseaux criminels afro-américains au sein du Crime organisé s'est imposée à la communauté noire, ainsi qu'à tous les groupes ethniques minoritaires, au début du XXe siècle, comme le seul système apte à répondre aux besoins des individus sur le plan social, économique et psychologique ; c'est-à-dire comme un système permettant à des individus défavorisés et marginalisés de survivre et de prospérer. Loin de connaître une croissance anarchique, les ghettos se sont tout de suite démarqués par une organisation et un ordre social qui leur étaient propres, répondant, dans la différence, à des règles normatives qui conféraient stabilité et cohérence à un espace urbain défini par la pauvreté. Le Crime organisé et la délinquance ont rapidement pris pied dans le ghetto où se sont déployés les gangs noirs (Abadinsky, 255). Il importe donc de s'attacher aux diverses activités illégales érigées en système de survie, élaboré par des individus ou des groupes privés des moyens légaux d'accéder à la réussite sociale. Ainsi observe-t-on, dès les années 1920, l'amplification d'un réseau de paris clandestins localisé principalement à Harlem, Détroit et Chicago. Ce type d'activités illégales s'est révélé décisif dans la formation des gangs noirs qui vont affirmer leur position et défendre leurs territoires dans le ghetto au début des années 1940. Constitués sur une base d'alliances entre Afro-Américains, Jamaïcains, Antillais, Nigériens ou Haïtiens, les gangs noirs procédaient à deux types de recrutement, comme le font ressortir les rapports de police archivés au *US Department of Justice, Bureau of Justice Statistics* (Government Printing Office, April 1990). Les gangs noirs cooptaient leurs membres en fonction de filières sociales et culturelles. Prioritaire, la filière familiale était édifiée sur une base patriarcale et s'organisait autour d'une personnalité masculine dominante, entourée de parents proches. Les réseaux associatifs venaient en seconde position, fondés sur des liens d'amitié forgés en prison et des sympathies entre gangs de rue ou chefs de quartier. Il convient, toutefois, de tenir compte du décalage existant, d'une part, entre les années 1920, où le réseau d'activités illégales reposait sur des opérations de paris clandestins conduisant à la mise en place de filières de type familial et, d'autre part, les années 1930 où apparaissaient des gangs noirs de type associatif dont les activités étaient principalement centrées sur le trafic de drogue.

On peut s'interroger sur la position sociale des gangsters noirs face aux gangsters blancs dans le contexte du Crime organisé. En fait, si l'on se reporte à la fin du XIXe siècle et au début du XXe siècle pour juger de la position sociale des membres des gangs, on observe une rupture entre le statut privilégié accordé par les politiciens aux criminels et racketteurs blancs et la marginalisation systématique des gangs noirs. La collusion entre les politiciens et les gangs blancs était un phénomène courant. En échange de la protection accordée aux gangsters, les politiciens attendaient, en retour, un soutien électoral sans faille, les voix de la pègre se révélant décisives lors des campagnes électorales du fait des votes à répétition et du recours aux pratiques d'intimidation destinées à éliminer les autres candidats. Au cours des premières décennies du XXe siècle, qui devaient être marquées par la prise de pouvoir des gangsters blancs et du Syndicat du Crime, les Afro-Américains n'apparaissent pas en position dominante dans les structures du Crime organisé. Au début du siècle, dans la mesure où le système politique les ignorait, les gangsters noirs, privés du soutien crucial que les politiciens accordaient à leurs homologues blancs, ne pouvaient ériger leurs activités en système organisé. Ce n'est qu'à partir des années 1920 avec l'émigration massive des Caribéens et l'exode des Noirs du sud vers les villes du nord-est et du centre des Etats-Unis, que se sont dessinées les structures d'activités clandestines. Bien qu'une controverse se soit développée quant à l'autonomie réelle des racketteurs noirs des ghettos (Maltz, 63), l'existence d'une pègre afro-américaine qui avait la haute main dans les ghettos sur les paris clandestins, les prêts à taux usuraire, la prostitution, le vol et qui devait coopérer pendant un temps à New York, Chicago ou Philadelphie avec des membres du Syndicat du Crime, Meyer Lansky, Lucky Luciano, Frank Costello et Johnny Torrio (Peterson, 24-32), témoigne de la puissance des Afro-Américains dans l'affrontement des gangs et au sein du Crime organisé qu'il importe de définir en évoquant la nature du cadre urbain des communautés noires et leur infrastructure économique afin d'être en mesure d'expliciter la lutte des gangs pour le contrôle du ghetto.

Difficile à cerner avec précision, le Crime organisé a fait l'objet de nombreuses tentatives de définition visant à répertorier la somme d'activités délictueuses érigées en système. La loi fédérale, en référence au racket, au trafic d'influences, aux organisations basées sur la corruption, englobe sous le sigle RICO (*Racketeer Influences and Corrupt Organizations*) les crimes et délits génériques : le meurtre, l'incendie, l'extorsion de fonds, les prêts à taux usuraire, la prostitution, les jeux d'argent. Les paris clandestins s'insèrent dans un schéma d'activités illégales structurées en système d'entreprise dont le code des Etats-Unis propose la définition suivante : « The "enterprise" refers to any individual, partnership, corporation, association or legal entity, and any union or group of individuals associated in fact » (Maltz, 4). Pour mieux comprendre le fonctionnement des gangs noirs et le code d'action qui en découle, il convient d'opposer leurs activités, qui demeurent de type communautaire, au système monolithique mis en œuvre par les organisations criminelles blanches. Foncièrement politique, le Crime organisé repose sur le recours à la violence, aux menaces et à la corruption des fonctionnaires. La Mafia américaine a fait la preuve de sa résistance à la concurrence d'autres figures du Crime organisé, notamment dans la communauté afro-américaine. On retiendra le nom du gangster blanc « Dutch » Schultz qui, en dépit de la vigoureuse opposition de Madame Stephanie St Clair (« the Policy Queen of Harlem »), cette femme noire rendue célèbre par le contrôle qu'elle exerçait sur les paris clandestins de Harlem, parvint à imposer brutalement sa loi dans le ghetto noir au cours de l'année 1931 en prenant la direction des secteurs du jeu, de la vente d'alcool, de la drogue et de la prostitution (McKay,107). On ne peut occulter, non plus, le fait que dans les communautés afro-américaines les night-clubs les plus célèbres étaient aux mains de gangsters blancs, comme le Grand Terrace de Chicago contrôlé par le gang de Capone et le Cotton Club de Harlem par le gang de Owney Madden. Ce fut, d'ailleurs, Madden qui fit venir l'orchestre de Duke Ellington au Cotton Club et ce fut bien l'influence des gangs criminels blancs qui se révéla décisive pour le succès de la carrière de Louis Armstrong. En fait, dans la plupart des communautés noires américaines, le pouvoir était aux mains des gangs blancs devenus maîtres des établissements qui se livraient à des activités illégales. C'est eux qui avaient le pouvoir d'influencer la police et d'imposer leur volonté à des individus privés de la force voulue pour pouvoir les combattre. Faut-il en conclure à l'impuissance des Afro-Américains dans le Crime organisé ?

Lors des paris clandestins organisés par les Afro-Américains, la violence et la corruption étaient présentes dans certains groupes, inexistantes dans d'autres. A Chicago, les responsables des paris avaient constitué un syndicat en mettant leurs ressources en commun et en établissant des contacts avec William Thompson, maire républicain de Chicago de 1915 à 1923 puis, à nouveau, de 1927 à 1931. Ianni souligne, à cet égard, les liens étroits existant à Chicago entre la politique urbaine et le Crime organisé :

> Kickbacks from the policy bankers to Thompson's political machine were estimated at $ 500,000 a year in the early 1930s. Although this was only one source of income for the Thompson machine, and by no means the largest, it was an important one. (Ianni, 112)

On se souviendra, qu'à cette époque, le Syndicat du crime d'Al Capone était l'organisation criminelle la plus puissante de Chicago et des états environnants, vu que dans le secteur des paris clandestins et du trafic d'alcool, le prestige de Capone s'étendait au Wisconsin, à l'Indiana, au Missouri, au Kentucky et au Michigan. Al Capone aurait pu écraser les syndicats du jeu et des paris qui étaient aux mains des Afro-Américains dans le ghetto de Chicago. Pourquoi ne l'a-t-il pas fait ? On constate que le syndicat afro-américain des jeux et des paris est parvenu à maintenir son autonomie en jouant des influences politiques et en luttant pied à pied pour défendre son territoire. En conséquence, comme ce domaine d'activité n'interférait pas avec les entreprises criminelles plus puissantes qui opéraient au sein de la communauté blanche et que le coût de la lutte pour obtenir le contrôle des paris clandestins dans le ghetto s'avérait trop lourd (en terme d'argent à dépenser et de sang à verser) le réseau afro-américain de paris clandestins dans le ghetto de Chicago demeura intact. On ne peut, toutefois, ignorer que le syndicat afro-américain des paris clandestins de Chicago bénéficiait d'une solide organisation politique. Les « banquiers » en charge des paris assuraient le lien entre la machine politique gérée par les Américains de race blanche, et les communautés afro-américaines. Ainsi, lorsque venait le temps des élections, les racketteurs noirs, tout comme leurs homologues blancs, mobilisaient leurs effectifs dans la pègre pour opérer les votes voulus. Ils procédaient à l'enregistrement des électeurs, les dirigeaient vers les bureaux de vote et s'assuraient du bon déroulement du vote. D'autre part, à Detroit, comme à Chicago, les gangsters afro-américains opérèrent un regroupement afin de résister aux violentes menaces de leurs adversaires blancs – tel le célèbre *Purple Gang* – On soulignera, de plus, que dans l'environnement urbain du ghetto, le pouvoir de résistance des entreprises criminelles aux mains des Afro-Américains était essentiellement lié à leur intégration culturelle et économique au sein de la communauté noire.

Si l'on s'attache, donc, à ce cadre urbain et à l'infrastructure économique de la communauté afro-américaine, on note que dans les années 1920, Harlem englobait une foule d'individus issus des classes sociales les plus diverses. Ils allaient des ouvriers agricoles non qualifiés venus du Sud aux immigrants antillais en passant par les élites bourgeoises. Cette période, qui fut celle de la Renaissance de Harlem, a été marquée par les publications de poètes et écrivains noirs, dont James Weldon Johnson, Langston Hughes, Sterling Brown, Claude McKay, Jean Toomer et Countee Cullen. Cette forte activité littéraire fit de Harlem le cœur d'un rayonnement intellectuel afro-américain. Il serait, toutefois, erroné d'évoquer Harlem uniquement en référence à la frange bourgeoise de sa population qui résidait dans les quartiers de Strivers Row ou Sugar Hills. On relève, dans l'ouvrage de Thomas J. Woofter *Negro Problems in Cities* les indications suivantes concernant les conditions de vie des habitants de Harlem :

> Manhattan in 1925 had an African-American population density of 336 persons per acre and a white population density of 223 persons per acre. Although Harlem contained its share of poor housing, many observers would agree that it was the 'home of the best housed Negroes in the world'. Better housing brought social stability by attracting the more affluent to Harlem. And by 1920, 45,2 percent of New-York City's 152,467 African-Americans lived in Harlem. (Woofter, 79)

Limité dans son expansion par les codes sociaux restrictifs de la communauté blanche et un apartheid économique, Harlem devait développer son propre univers ségrégué avec ses églises, ses centres de jeu, sa vie culturelle, imposant ses valeurs originales à la culture dominante de la société blanche. En fait, les relations entre la bourgeoisie naissante et la pègre du ghetto allaient dépasser, dans leur évolution, un simple schéma imitatif, se démarquant de ce qui aurait pu n'être qu'une « réplique noire » de la société américaine. S'identifiant à la bourgeoisie noire, de nombreux Afro-Américains du ghetto s'impliquèrent dans des activités illégales de jeu d'argent, et ce pas uniquement en tant que joueurs. La nature et l'originalité de l'industrie des paris clandestins dans les ghettos noirs, en particulier à Harlem, ne peuvent se comprendre qu'en référence à un arrière-plan culturel. Selon Claude McKay, l'une des figures marquantes de la Renaissance de Harlem, les paris et les jeux d'argent se développèrent à Harlem dans les années 1910-1920 lorsque la communauté afro-américaine commença à s'enrichir de la présence d'un grand nombre de coiffeurs portoricains et cubains qui initièrent leur clientèle noire américaine à un jeu d'argent d'origine latine connu des coiffeurs hispaniques sous le nom de « Bolita » ou « Paquerita » :

> It was introduced to Harlem by a Spaniard from Cataluna, who was nicknamed Catalan by the Spanish speaking Harlemites. Catalan devised his system of playing the numbers from the financial figures of the Stock Exchange. Familiar as he must have been with the method of the Spanish lottery, this could not have been a difficult job. The playing number was deduced from the totals of domestic and foreign sales...
>
> As the financial figures printed in the newspapers are exact, there could be no trickery.
>
> The numbers game has gripped all of Harlem precisely because there is no obvious trickery in it. It is an open, simple and inexpensive game of chance. (McKay, 107)

Autre jeu d'argent illégal, le système de loterie clandestine dénommé *Clearing House Bank Totals Numbers Game* attribué à un certain Casper Holstein, Noir d'origine antillaise, était basé sur la publication, dans les quotidiens, des chiffres officiels transmis par les banques de compensation. Les paris étaient ouverts à des combinaisons de trois chiffres allant de 000 à 999. La combinaison gagnante de trois chiffres se jouait à 800 contre 1 et la combinaison de deux chiffres à 80 contre 1. Les collecteurs de paris recevaient 20% des sommes collectées plus 10% des gains. Le système de pari clandestin devait se développer, évoluant très rapidement en entreprise criminelle structurée comme en témoignaient les reportages du *New York Age*, l'hebdomadaire en vogue à Harlem dans les années 1920. Ainsi pouvait-on lire dans le numéro du 5 mai 1924 que l'on comptait à Harlem 30 « banques » disposant de l'argent des paris ; le terme « banque » désignait les centres de collecte et de paiement qui accordaient des prêts à leurs clients. Les capitaux en argent liquide accumulés dans ces « banques » provenaient des paris quotidiens. Les intermédiaires en charge des paris pouvaient accorder directement des prêts aux joueurs de leur connaissance afin de leur permettre de couvrir leurs paris s'ils étaient désargentés, ou bien avaient toute latitude pour mettre des liquidités à la disposition de leurs clients dans le besoin. L'argent provenant des paris clandestins était donc à la source d'un système de crédit à la consommation. Ces services de crédit accordés aux clients fidèles, aux petites entreprises, ainsi qu'aux commerces de détail, assumaient la fonction d'organismes financiers parallèles du fait de la carence des banques officielles qui, on le rappellera, avaient pour politique de ne pas accorder de prêt aux clients démunis ou aux entreprises endettées (Perucci, 302-311). Parce qu'ils favorisaient la circulation de capitaux au sein de la communauté afro-américaine, les « banquiers » responsables de l'argent des paris clandestins devenaient donc les plus grands investisseurs du ghetto tant dans l'immobilier que dans l'entreprise. Parmi les « banquiers » afro-américains les plus puissants de Harlem dans les années 1920, véritables entrepreneurs au sein du crime organisé, on retiendra les noms de Marcellina Cardena, Joseph Matthias Ison, Wilfred Adolphus Brunder, José Henrique Miro, Masjoe Ison, Alexander Pompez, Stephanie St Clair, John Diamond, Fred Buchanan, Charles Durant, Marshal Flores, Edward et Elmer Maloney, Moe Levy, Hyman et Pauline Kassell. Certains, tel Casper Holstein, l'un des magnats du crime dans le ghetto où il employait une centaine de collecteurs de paris clandestins, assumaient même le rôle de philanthrope, faisant des dons aux églises et accordant des bourses aux étudiants, stimulant, en fait, l'économie locale.

Si l'on s'attache, en conséquence, à la dynamique de réaction des Afro-Américains aux pressions extérieures, on prend conscience de l'importance fondamentale de l'arrière-plan culturel (culture de la pauvreté dans une communauté noire ségréguée) face au Crime organisé. C'est, en effet, une dynamique socio-économique structurelle qui a alimenté le processus de légitimation des entreprises de pari clandestin dont Ivan Light propose l'analyse suivante :

> Banks combine the savings of depositors to create a capital fund for business, mortgage and consumer investments... numbers banks mimic this rhythm, first taking the savings of the poor, then returning capital to the poor community in the form of usurious loans, free loans, philanthropy and direct business investments by racketeers. Therefore, numbers gambling banks are an irregular financial institutions. (Light, 901)

La structure même des loteries et paris clandestins, « légitimés » par la culture afro-américaine des ghettos apparentait le choix et la gestion des activités illégales à une stratégie de survie, se démarquant complètement des activités de la Mafia et ne ressemblant en rien à l'image du Crime organisé associée à La Cosa Nostra. Les loteries et paris clandestins étaient, assurément, des activités illégales mais n'impliquaient ni investissement coûteux, ni racket meurtrier, ni extorsion de fonds par la violence. Elles s'apparentaient, en réalité, davantage à un système de fraude, comme le soulignait la Commission Wickersham désignée par la *National Commission on Law Observance and Enforcement* en 1931 :

> Such criminal schemes shade off by imperceptible degrees into enterprises which are so conducted as to avoid criminal liability although employing unethical or even illegal methods of doing business ; and 'the line between the criminal and non criminal activity is thus frequently a rather arbitrary one'...and the typical criminal of this class is not the bandit or the recidivist, but the business man gone wrong. (Wickersham, 406)

Harlem n'est pas le seul ghetto où ces activités de paris clandestins se soient développées. Une version moins élaborée de ces jeux d'argent illégaux (*the policy wheel*) fut introduite dans les communautés noires de Chicago après celles de la Nouvelle-Orléans au début du XXe siècle. Le système de paris instauré à Chicago (*insurance policy games*) se développa en premier dans les quartiers envahis par le jeu clandestin où se trouvait concentrée la population afro-américaine à laquelle toute intégration immobilière était refusée ; processus qui devait renforcer les préjugés des Blancs comme le souligne John Landesco dans *Organized Crime in Chicago*, étude approfondie sur l'essor du Crime organisé à Chicago, publiée en 1929 :

> The prevalence of vice in the midst of the African-American population (which was virtually trapped by the opposition to integration among the city's real estate brokers and tenants' associations) inevitably linked vice and crime with color in the minds of whites. (Landesco, 38)

On soulignera que dans le ghetto de Chicago, la raison principale du succès des réseaux de jeu clandestins dirigés par les Afro-Américains et du développement rapide du Crime organisé qui lui est associé tient aux liens politiques que les magnats de la communauté noire entretenaient avec le bureau du maire et la machine du parti démocrate qui dominait la vie politique de Chicago; participation au Crime organisé et à la vie politique allant de pair. A Chicago comme à Detroit, New York et Philadelphie où la communauté afro-américaine était importante, deux facteurs ont joué, décisifs pour le développement et la survie des paris clandestins et du Crime organisé dans le ghetto, il s'agit de l'accès aux institutions politiques et du recours à la violence ou à la menace de violence. Mais la puissance essentielle du Crime organisé dans les ghettos, en tant qu'entreprise structurée, tient non seulement aux liens établis avec les élites influentes, mais à une adéquation socio-culturelle avec la communauté afro-américaine. Le fonctionnement et la gestion des paris clandestins étaient propres à une communauté constituée majoritairement d'individus démunis où les parieurs – en très grand nombre – jouaient de faibles sommes d'argent dans l'espoir d'obtenir, très vite, d'importants profits. Le fait qu'à l'origine les criminels professionnels n'aient pas fait partie de l'organisation des loteries, ou même de la gestion des paris, implique que les jeux d'argent introduits dans le ghetto ont bien été une réponse typiquement afro-américaine à l'absence de structures économiques propres à la création d'emplois et qu'ils ont contribué à mettre à la disposition d'une communauté exsangue les capitaux appropriés aux besoins de ses membres et les ressources financières nécessaires à leur survie.

Le Crime organisé dans le ghetto ne recouvre donc pas un ensemble d'activités individuelles déviantes au sein de la communauté afro-américaine. Les réseau de jeux et de paris clandestins constitués par les Afro-Américains représentent une réponse novatrice aux contingences sociales et aux réalités qui régissaient la vie de leur communauté. Le fait que des commerçants – au demeurant respectueux des lois – et des citoyens respectables aient participé à des activités illégales et à des paris clandestins s'inscrit dans une démarche collective, celle d'une communauté marginalisée, stigmatisée par le racisme. Dans le ghetto, les agents chargés de gérer les paris (*policy operators*) n'étaient pas perçus comme des délinquants mais plutôt comme des chefs d'entreprise prêts à saisir les opportunités qui s'offraient à eux. En ce qui concerne l'évolution du Crime organisé, les facteurs culturels ont eu une importance indéniable dans la mise en place d'une structure propre à la communauté afro-américaine avant que les gangsters blancs n'entreprennent de prendre le contrôle du secteur des jeux. Si l'on prend Harlem comme point de référence, on assiste au développement, comme dans le ghetto de Chicago ou de Detroit, de réseaux de prostitution et d'un libre accès aux jeux d'argent, mais contrairement à ce qui se déroule dans le milieu du Crime organisé aux mains de la Mafia, on n'observe pas de guerre des gangs. Le style désordonné, audacieux, individualiste, des souteneurs noirs débouche sur des règlements de compte directs :

> *The black vice industry consisted of streetwalkers and pimps who settled quarrels with fights.(...)Black pimps relied upon their reputation for violent prowess to intimidate workers and rival pimps.(...) On the other hand, the free market organisation of vice in black enclaves permitted individual killings and petty crime, but eliminated gang warfare. (Light, 469)*

La lutte pour la conquête de Harlem, qui a opposé les réseaux afro-américains de type familial ou associatif aux gangs blancs de la Mafia, est au cœur du développement du Crime organisé dans le ghetto. Le jeu, les loteries, les paris clandestins se révélaient des plus lucratifs si l'on en juge d'après les poursuites engagées par l'*Internal Revenue Service*, service des Contributions Directes, contre plusieurs « banquiers » afro-américains qui géraient les fonds provenant des loteries. On retiendra, à cet égard, les noms de deux « banquiers » accusés de fraude fiscale, Wilfred Adolphus Brunder qui disposait de $1,753,342 en « banque » entre 1925 et 1930 et Jose Enrique Miro dont les disponibilités s'élevaient à $1,251,556 de 1927 à 1930. L'importance des profits liés aux paris clandestins devait, on le comprend aisément, attirer la convoitise de la pègre et des gangsters blancs, plus particulièrement de Hyman Kassell et « Dutch » Schultz.

Avant que le gang de « Dutch » Schultz ne s'empare de la majorité des réseaux de jeu à Harlem au tout début des années 1930, les paris clandestins n'étaient ni un monopole du Crime organisé ni une opération de cartel. Le système de jeux clandestins s'apparentait à une entreprise artisanale locale gérée par plusieurs « banquiers » indépendants, Afro-Américains pour la plupart. Perçues du point de vue d'un chef d'entreprise, les loteries clandestines étaient une façon très sûre de s'enrichir. C'est vers le milieu des années 1920 et le début des années 1930 que les gangsters blancs se livrèrent à deux tentatives pour arracher le contrôle des loteries et paris clandestins aux « banquiers » afro-américains. Lors de la première tentative, qui se produisit vers le milieu des années 1920, les « banquiers » afro-américains furent à même de résister à l'intrusion des gangsters blancs dont l'arme majeure était la corruption, notamment celle des fonctionnaires de police. Leur stratégie de prise de contrôle reposait également sur l'infiltration des réseaux de jeu par des bootleggers blancs sous la direction de Hyman Kassell, le magnat des jeux d'argent ; ce qui leur permit de s'emparer d'une grande part du marché en faisant appel aux commerçants blancs de Harlem pour collecter les paris et en utilisant leurs propres saloons pour effectuer les tractations. De plus, pour contraindre les Afro-Américains à céder et à abandonner le secteur de la rue, Hyman Kassell avait fait appel aux policiers corrompus qui harcelaient sans relâche les collecteurs de paris au service des « banquiers » afro-américains. Décrit par *The New-York Age* comme le bootlegger blanc le plus puissant de Harlem, où il dirigeait une douzaine de bars clandestins, les célèbres *speakeasies*, dans les années 1920, Hyman Kassell tenta d'obtenir le monopole des jeux, soudoyant les collecteurs de paris afro-américains afin qu'ils travaillent pour lui.

Si la tentative de prise de contrôle lancée par Hyman Kassell ne se solda pas par un franc succès, il n'en fut pas de même pour le coup de force de « Dutch » Schultz et de son Syndicat. Gangster notoirement connu, semant la terreur dans la pègre new-yorkaise lorsque les gangs s'affrontèrent pour la contrebande de l'alcool, « Dutch » Schultz avait étendu son organisation aux quartiers de Upper Manhattan et du Bronx englobant les secteurs du jeu, les night clubs et se livrant à l'extorsion de fonds. Harlem, avec les énormes profits potentiels des loteries clandestines, était l'objet de la convoitise de « Dutch » Schultz. Bénéficiant d'alliés de poids au sein du parti démocrate et de contacts influents au sein de la police, « Dutch » Schultz dirigeait un gang considérable, composé de tireurs expérimentés et pouvait compter sur l'appui de ses collègues, Lucky Luciano, Frank Costello, Owney Madden, Meyer Lansky et Bugsy Siegel en cas de besoin. Face aux magnats du Crime organisé, la communauté afro-américaine de Harlem était vulnérable car, l'appui politique lui faisant défaut, il ne lui était pas facile de neutraliser la police, les procureurs, les juges, les tribunaux. Bien au contraire, « Dutch » Schultz mobilisait sans peine les officiers de police, les avocats et les juges pour qu'ils le soutiennent dans sa guerre de conquête des paris clandestins de Harlem. Corruption, intimidation policière, violence, appuyées par la puissance de feu des hommes de main du gang de « Dutch » Schultz, eurent finalement raison des « banquiers » afro-américains et les forcèrent à capituler. On note qu'en 1932 « Dutch » Schultz était parvenu à éliminer les « banquiers » afro-américains indépendants de Harlem et à contrôler les loteries et paris clandestins érigés en système centralisé, drainant à son profit des sommes considérables alors que les Afro-Américains avaient toujours réinvesti leurs bénéfices au sein de la communauté. Le Syndicat de « Dutch » Schultz fut dissous après sa mort violente en 1935, mais l'obtention de gains lucratifs et le recours à la violence qui avaient été instaurés par les gangs blancs ne devaient permettre ni de ramener le système de loteries et de paris clandestins à ses origines d'entreprise non criminelle ni de lui rendre son autonomie en le libérant du contrôle exercé par le Crime organisé désormais aux mains des gangsters blancs.

Si l'on adopte, pour conclure, une perspective sociologique et que l'on s'attache à la dynamique des réactions de la communauté afro-américaine aux pressions extérieures, on peut tenter d'expliquer l'engouement de la population des ghettos pour les loteries clandestines ou les paris illégaux à la lumière des théories d'Emile Durkheim, reprises par Robert Merton, comme « un phénomène socio-psychologique d'anomie » (Durkheim, 60).

Obtenir des gains importants, c'est se voir offrir la possibilité d'accéder très rapidement à la richesse. Or, le fait d'obtenir le statut social de « riche » du jour au lendemain, s'inscrit, pour Durkheim et Merton, dans le cadre de la théorie d'anomie selon laquelle tout individu est prêt à s'engager dans des activités illégales et à prendre des risques si les moyens légaux, institutionnalisés, de parvenir à la réussite sociale lui sont refusés.

Pour les habitants des ghettos, parier une petite somme d'argent s'apparentait à un mode d'investissement quasi providentiel. Les motifs qui incitaient les membres d'une communauté à participer quotidiennement à des paris clandestins avaient un fondement culturel et sociologique référentiel. Parce que, dans chaque quartier, les *runners* ou collecteurs de paris circulaient librement dans les lieux les plus fréquentés par tout un chacun (stands de presse, épiceries, bars, salons de coiffure pour hommes ou pour femmes, blanchisseries), parier devenait chose aisée. Qui plus est, la disponibilité des gains et l'importance des rapports étaient une source d'orgueil racial, même si les paris avaient, pour le grand public, valeur d'activité criminelle. Ce qui contribuait, en fait, à la connotation « d'activité criminelle » c'était, ainsi que nous l'avons évoqué plus haut, l'absence d'organisme financier officiel dans la communauté afro-américaine. Activités illégales lucratives sans coût de production, contrairement à la contrebande d'alcool ou à la prostitution, les loteries clandestines – qui avaient acquis l'appellation de « mother racket » – étaient parfaitement désignées pour devenir le fondement du Crime organisé dans la communauté noire en attirant des chefs de gang comme « Dutch » Schultz, Lucky Luciano et Al Capone résolus à prendre le contrôle du Crime organisé dans le ghetto afro-américain.

Bibliographie

Abadinsky, Howard. *Organized Crime* (Chicago: Nelson-Hall, 1985).
Durkheim, Emile. *Suicide* (Glencoe: Free Press, 1951).
Ianni, Francis A.J. *Black Mafia* (New York: Simon & Schuster, 1975).
Landesco, John. *Organized Crime in Chicago* (Chicago: University of Chicago Press, 1929).
Light, Ivan. « Numbers Gambling Among Blacks: A Financial Institution », *American Sociological Review*, 42, December 1977: 892-904.
Maltz, Michael. « Defining Organized Crime » in R.J. Kelly, Schatzberg and K.L. Chin, eds., *Handbook of Organized Crime in the USA* (Westport : Greenwood Publishing Group, 1944).
McKay, Claude. *Harlem: Negro Metropolis* (New York: Dutton & Co, 1940).
Perucci, Robert. « The Neighborhood 'Bookmaster' Entrepreneur and Mobility Model ». In Paul Meadoris and Ephraim Mizurchi, eds. *Urbanism, Urbanization and Change: Comparative Perspective* (Reading: Addison-Wesley Publishers, 1969).
Peterson, Virgil W. *The Mob: 200 Years of Organized Crime in New York* (Ottawa: Green Hill Publishers, 1983).
Wickersham Commission (The), National Commission on Law Observance and Enforcement. *Report on the Cost of Crime* (Washington D.C.: National Institute of Justice, 1931).
Woofter, Thomas J. *Negro Problems in Cities* (New York: Doubleday, Doran & Co, 1928).

2e partie
Cinéma

Introduction
Par Dominique Sipière

Les films et les études sur le crime au cinéma viennent en rafales – avec une accalmie juste avant le regain d'intérêt des toutes dernières années du siècle. Devant l'abondance intimidante des films, il faut d'abord mettre un peu d'ordre, mais je vais surtout ouvrir des rubriques et indiquer quelques pistes (ou plutôt quelques ruelles…). Et, bien sûr, suggérer des lectures.

Autant commencer par la première difficulté, c'est à dire la première raison de s'intéresser à la question : le statut particulier du cinéma dans les études de civilisation[1]. Les films y sont à la fois des *documents* et des *œuvres d'art*, les *instruments* et les *objets* de l'enquête. Le cinéma lui même se trouve au cœur d'une interaction qui en fait le *produit* de la société qu'il représente, tout en étant accusé d'en être un des *acteurs* – soupçonné ici de corrompre la jeunesse. Mais il y a déjà dans le choix heureux du mot « représentation »[2] tout un pan de cette richesse : comme des journalistes, les producteurs hollywoodiens se vantent de *présenter* la réalité du gangstérisme, mais ils en offrent aussi une *représentation* magnifiée – à la fois amplifiée et rendue héroïque – débordant bientôt l'aire réelle des gangsters de quelques grandes villes, pour atteindre plus d'une centaine de millions de spectateurs[3] qui, bien évidemment, n'ont jamais eu le moindre contact avec l'univers du crime organisé.

Il s'agit donc d'étudier « le statut du criminel et des policiers (…) dans l'imaginaire hollywoodien » et le « rôle du cinéma » par rapport au grand banditisme : à la fois une question sur l'*image* (ici du crime) qui, comme le faisait remarquer Boorstin dès 1962, *déborde* la réalité qu'elle est censée désigner, et sur son *influence* en retour sur le monde « réel ». Si on rapproche le travail qui va suivre d'une étude de la presse en civilisation (les producteurs des années trente se comparent volontiers à des journalistes) on comprend mieux la relative nouveauté du sujet par rapport aux trois temps habituels : a) l'étude de la presse utilise les journaux comme documents ; b) elle peut analyser les représentations (plutôt que les « mentalités ») qui s'y lisent en relation avec un ensemble d'autres textes de la même période (systèmes idéologiques) ; c) elle contribue enfin à l'histoire de la presse elle même, en tant qu'objet historique parmi d'autres.

---

1. Voir Francis Bordat, « Pourquoi il faut aimer Hollywood », *Américônes, Etudes sur l'image aux États-Unis*, ENS de Fontenay / Saint Cloud, 1997, et « Cinéma et civilisation », *Revue Française d'Etudes Américaines*, Belin, n° 88, mars 2001, p. 44.
2. Rappelons le début du libellé de la question : « on étudiera le gangstérisme aux États Unis et son évolution jusqu'au début des années cinquante avec le développement de la Mafia. L'exemple de ses représentations dans le cinéma des années trente et quarante (film de gangsters, film noir, film policier semi-documentaire), engagera une réflexion sur le statut du criminel et des policiers qui le combattent dans l'imaginaire hollywoodien….»
3. Voir Andrew Bergman, p. XI, qui rappelle qu'avec l'arrivée du parlant le public atteignait « (an) average one hundred and ten million moviegoers » pour baisser autour de 65 millions de spectateurs par semaine, au plus bas de la dépression.

On retrouve ces trois niveaux d'étude avec les films (faits historiques des États-Unis, représentations, histoire du cinéma), mais le cinéma est un univers qui se pose en rival de la réalité et dont les prétentions à l'autonomie en tant qu'art (fût-ce a posteriori) élargissent considérablement la question : quand il se fait « art » le cinéma vise au delà de la représentation immédiate et datée et il prétend – sans doute à juste titre dans le cas de plusieurs films du corpus – survivre à l'événement qu'il a représenté. La clef de cette difficulté tient peut être dans le respect scrupuleux d'un juste équilibre entre les deux versants de la question posée : il s'agit bien de traiter la réalité du « crime organisé », mais les représentations artistiques que le cinéma nous laisse en héritage font elles-mêmes tout autant partie de la réalité des États-Unis.

Le même genre de prudence permettra d'éviter les pièges habituels où conduisent les grandes affirmations simplificatrices ou globalisantes à propos du cinéma : classement péremptoire des films dans des *genres* en réalité souvent très mouvants ; surévaluation de la rigidité du système des *studios*, des auteurs et des acteurs ; vision manichéenne de la *censure* comme un complot castrateur venu des seuls « puissants » ; théorie du « reflet » réputé inconscient de la part des auteurs du film (on pense à S. Kracauer[1] et à la fascination du complot) dont l'opposé formaliste est aussi infructueux (plus rien ne renvoie à rien…). C'est qu'il n'est pas toujours possible de trancher certains débats : on se dispute encore aujourd'hui pour savoir si la violence visible à l'écran crée la violence des spectateurs. Dès les premiers films (*The Secret Six*, 1931) un enfant de douze ans (Harold Gamble du New Jersey) « imitait » les gangsters en tirant sur un camarade, sans que l'interdiction des films de gangsters qui s'en suivit dans cet État ait eu une influence notable sur la criminalité… Histoire familière.

Les films

Il n'est évidemment pas question de les voir tous et il est d'ailleurs improbable qu'un seul spectateur de l'époque ait vu les quelques 50 films de gangsters produits vers 1931[2]. Une méthode statistique qui choisirait un échantillon représentatif limité à une dizaine de titres est à la fois impossible à appliquer et assez peu utile : les films demeurés disponibles sont aussi ceux que le public de l'époque a majoritairement vus et probablement les meilleurs. Il faudra les classer et les hiérarchiser mais on commencera par une première liste chronologique.

Filmographie chronologique

Films	Sortie	Réalisateurs	Acteurs	Majors
Underworld	1927	Sternberg	G. Bancroft	Paramount
The Racket	1928	Lewis Milestone	Wolheim	Paramount
Little Caesar	1930	Mervyn Leroy	Robinson	Warner
City Streets	1931	Rouben Mamoulian	Cooper	Paramount
The Public Enemy	1931	William Wellman	Cagney	Warner
Quick Millions	1931	Rowland Brown	Tracy ; Raft	Fox

---

1. Siegfried Kracauer, *De Caligari à Hitler*, 1948, Payot.
2. Voir Guérif, p 75. Je n'ai pas vu plus de la moitié des films de la liste ci-dessous.

I Am a Fugitive from a Chain Gang	1932	Mervyn LeRoy	Paul Muni	Warner
Scarface : Shame of a Nation	1932	Howard Hawks	Muni	United Artists
Lady Killer	1933	Roy del Ruth	Cagney	Warner
Manhattan Melodrama	1934	W.S. Van Dyke	Gable	MGM
G. Men	1935	William Keighley	Cagney	Warner
The Glass Key	1935	Frank Tuttle	Raft ; Milland	Paramount
Bullets or Ballots	1936	William Keighley	Robinson	Warner
The Petrified Forest	1936	Archie Mayo	Bogart	Warner
Dead End	1937	William Wyler	Bogart, McRea	Goldwyn
Kid Galahad	1937	Michael Curtiz	Robinson	Warner
The Last Gangster	1937	Edward Ludwig	Robinson	MGM
Marked Woman	1937	Lloyd Bacon	Bogart ; Bette Davis	Warner
Angels With Dirty Faces	1938	Michael Curtiz	Cagney ; Bogart	Warner
Racket Busters	1938	Lloyd Bacon	Bogart	Warner
Each Dawn I die	1939	William Keighley	Cagney ; Raft	Warner
Invisible Stripes	1939	Lloyd Bacon	Bogart	Warner
Kings of the Underworld	1939	Lewis Seiler	Bogart	Warner
The Roaring Twenties	1939	Raoul Walsh	Cagney ; Bogart	Warner
Black Friday	1940	ArthurLubin	Karloff ; Lugosi	Universal
Brother Orchid	1940	Lloyd Bacon	Robinson	Warner
Castle on the Hudson	1940	Anatole Litvak	John Garfield	Warner
Johnny Apollo	1940	Henry Hathaway	Tyrone Power	Fox
High Sierra	1941	Raoul Walsh	Bogart	Warner
Johnny Eager	1941	Mervyn Leroy	R. Taylor	MGM
All Through the Night	1942	Vincent Sherman	Bogart	Warner
The Glass Key	1942	Stuart Heisler	Ladd	Paramount
This Gun For Hire	1942	Frank Tuttle	Ladd	Paramount
Dillinger	1945	Max Nosseck	L. Tierney	Monogram
The Killers	1946	Robert Siodmak	Lancaster	Universal
Body and Soul	1947	Robert Rossen	Garfield	Enterprise
Kiss of Death	1947	Henry Hathaway	Widmark	Fox
Out of the Past	1947	Jacques Tourneur	Mitchum	RKO
T Men	1947	Anthony Mann	Dennis O'Keefe	Eagle
Criss Cross	1948	Robert Siodmak	Lancaster	Universal
Force of Evil	1948	Abraham Polonski	Garfield	Enterprise
Key Largo	1948	John Huston	Robinson ; Bogart	Warner
Thieves' Highway	1948	Jules Dassin	Richard Conte	
The Street With No Name	1948	William Keighley	Widmark	Fox
They Live By Night	1948	Nicholas Ray	Farley Granger	RKO
Night and the City	1948	Jules Dassin	Widmark	Fox UK
Call Northside 777	1948	Henry Hathaway	James Stewart, Conte	Fox US
Caged	1949	John Cromwell	Eleanore Parker	Warner
Gun Crazy	1949	Joseph H. Lewis	John Dall	United Artists
White Heat	1949	Raoul Walsh	Cagney	Warner
Asphalt Jungle	1950	John Huston	Hayden	Warner
The Enforcer	1950	Raoul Walsh	Bogart	United States
Kiss Tomorrow Goodnight	1950	Gordon Douglas	Cagney	Warner
The Racket	1951	J. Cromwell + Nicholas Ray	Mitchum	RKO
Deadline USA	1952	Richard Brooks	Bogart	Warner

On remarquera au passage que certains noms reviennent avec insistance : dans la colonne des Majors (près de la moitié des films sont dus à la Warner), dans celle des réalisateurs (LeRoy, Walsh, Bacon) et, surtout, dans celle des acteurs (Robinson (6 fois), Cagney (8), Bogart (10, mais aussi de petits rôles), Ladd (3), Mitchum (2)...)

Si on veut mettre un peu d'ordre dans cette liste chronologique on doit se rappeler qu'elle est très partielle (les cinquante films de 1931...) et qu'elle couvre une période assez longue au cours de laquelle les États-Unis ont connu de profonds changements : il est donc très naturel que les films changent eux aussi et on s'étonnera plutôt de la récurrence des thèmes et des styles. On s'interrogera donc sur l'articulation entre les constantes, les différences et les effets de cycle.

Genres ?

La notion de *genre* s'impose évidemment comme premier critère de classement[1], mais elle s'avère plus fluctuante qu'il n'y paraît. Ainsi, la moindre histoire du cinéma américain range soigneusement les films de gangsters et le *film noir* dans deux genres distincts que plusieurs chapitres (et une décennie : naissances respectives en 1931 et en 1941) séparent. Or le choix de l'objet « crime organisé » pour ouvrir ce dossier vient heureusement bousculer des habitudes, qui ont eu leur utilité mais qu'il faut maintenant remettre en question. Par exemple, l'« invention » du *film noir* par Borde et Chaumeton flatte encore la critique française qui a su repérer dès les années cinquante la nouveauté d'un sous genre véritablement spécifique aux États-Unis. Le mot d'invention prend ici son double sens de création (d'un concept) et de trouvaille d'un objet que d'autres n'avaient pas su voir, un peu comme le langage administratif parle de l'« inventeur » de fresques néolithiques préservées dans une grotte.

Jonathan Munby[2], sans faire preuve d'hostilité de principe, remet en cause l'autonomie de ce que *nous* avons pris pour un genre cinématographique nouveau. Tout s'explique assez facilement : les cinéphiles français de 1950 retrouvent en bloc, après une absence de plusieurs années due à la guerre en Europe, le meilleur de la production américaine des années quarante. Entre temps, ils ont relu l'Amérique dans les romans de la *Série Noire* dirigée (et souvent traduite) par Marcel Duhamel. Bref, un archipel apparemment autonome leur est offert et ils ont déjà les mots pour le nommer. La plupart des textes de l'époque insistent alors à juste titre sur la spécificité des films noirs, leur atmosphère, leur écriture, leurs anti-héros, leurs femmes fatales et l'*ambivalence* très opportune qu'ils entretiennent à l'égard du pays tel qu'il est perçu – à ce moment précis – depuis les rivages européens.

Ce que Munby refuse plus précisément [3] (sans doute à juste titre) c'est l'idée selon laquelle le film noir serait un joyau *isolé*, un accident extérieur à la continuité de l'histoire du cinéma américain. Bref il faut revenir sur la

---

1. C'est sur une discussion de la notion de « genre » que s'ouvre l'indispensable ouvrage de Jean-Loup Bourget, *Hollywood, la norme et la marge* (Nathan, 1999) dont l'influence sur ces pages est évidente.
2. Jonathan Munby, *Public Enemies, Public Heroes*, Chicago, 1999
3. *idem*, en particulier p. 9-10

notion de genre à Hollywood pour essayer d'organiser le groupe de films qui nous intéresse ici et pour comprendre le mouvement complexe entre le monde représenté et les règles qui régissent sa représentation au cinéma.

Avec les westerns et les films musicaux, les films de gangsters appartiennent aux genres américains les plus fortement identifiés. Au point qu'on glisse insensiblement de l'idée de genre à celle de *formule*, d'attentes réelles ou supposées d'un public réputé captif : de la forme créatrice à la formule mécanique. Cette approche un peu négative résulte d'un malentendu sur la nature et la fonction de l'idée de genre. Comme la reconnaissance d'un éventuel classicisme, l'identité générique est perçue après coup, dans de vastes panoramas rétrospectifs dont l'invention des *films noirs* dix ans après leur réalisation est un exemple canonique. Cela ne veut pas dire que le public et que ceux qui ont fait les films n'avaient pas une conscience nette de ce qu'ils voyaient et de ce qu'ils visaient, mais tout semble alors plus complexe, lié à un ensemble de facteurs extérieurs et à un jeu d'interactions, d'acceptation de règles (écrites ou non) et – surtout – de leur transgression, délibérée ou induite. Le genre se décrit ainsi en deux temps bien distincts : d'abord en étudiant l'*écriture* des films en tant qu'*acte* dans un contexte, selon des contraintes et des attentes à un moment donné ; ensuite en analysant cette même écriture en tant que résultat, comme un *texte* autonome entièrement accessible mais toujours mobile puisqu'il n'existe que dans l'acte de sa lecture.

Si on considère le « crime organisé » comme une rubrique d'ensemble, on peut proposer des sous genres et on constate aussitôt des interactions et des évolutions chronologiques : les genres perdent alors leur caractère intemporel de catégories abstraites pour entrer dans des systèmes à la fois synchroniques et évolutifs :

Genre	Période	Exemples
Gangsters classiques	30-33	Little Caesar, The Public Enemy, Scarface
FBI : le gangster est devenu policier	Années 30	G. Men, Bullets or Ballots
Film Social	Années 30	Angels With Dirty Faces, Dead End
Film noir	Depuis 41	The Maltese Falcon, The Big Sleep
Documentaires policiers	Années 40	House on the 92nd Street
Psychopathes	Fin des 40s	White Heat
Films de « syndicat »	Années 50	Murder Inc., New York Confidential.

On remarquera que ces jeux s'inscrivent eux mêmes dans de plus vastes structures, liées à toute production collective de sens [1] :

– naissance d'un objet filmique alors identifié comme un objet **nouveau** (mais issu de multiples hypotextes = *Little Caesar*) ;

– variations et recompositions à l'intérieur de la même **structure**. Ex. de permutation de fonctions : l'acteur qui jouait les gangsters devient un policier (Robinson dans *Bullets or Ballots*, Cagney dans *G. Men*)

---

1. Il s'agit sans doute d'une constante dans l'évolution des grands récits qu'on retrouve, par exemple, dans l'évolution cyclique des mythes du vingtième siècle comme celui de *Frankenstein* au cinéma.

– variations sur la **forme** et sur les modes d'**énonciation** : lieux, nature du crime (des règlements de compte à la Borgia à la mise en place du hold-up, le « caper »), voix narrative (de la caméra extérieure à la voix off tonitruante du reporter et aux récits autobiographiques qui induisent un flash back...)
– changements de **régime** : comédies, parodies et « spoofs » (Bob Hope gangster, dessins animés de Tex Avery...)
– effets de **nostalgie** (*The Roaring Twenties*).
– prétendus **retours** à l'authenticité initiale...
Bref, les films ont de la mémoire et – comme aujourd'hui – ils sont influencés par les autres productions du même moment : rivalité entre studios, affirmation de leurs identités et paris sur les attentes du public. Mais, au delà de leur inscription dans un système à un moment donné, ils répondent aussi plus ou moins confusément (c'est tout le débat autour de l'idée de « reflet ») et de façon parfois contradictoire aux besoins de distraction (« entertainment ») et aux interrogations de la société. A propos des seuls films de gangsters, Stuart Kaminsky [1] insiste à juste titre sur les aspirations (il parle même de « goals ») des héros, révélatrices de profonds déplacements avec le temps. Je résume son analyse en la commentant :
Little Caesar : le succès professionnel à tout prix. S'affirmer aux yeux des autres.
Bullets or Ballots et *Angels With Dirty Faces* : Kaminsky y voit les efforts du héros pour sauver des membres de sa propre classe.
Roaring Twenties : allusions à la guerre et déception liée au retour dans la société US. J'ajouterais : hommage à des valeurs perdues. (« He used to be a big shot... »)
White Heat : combat ambivalent contre la folie individuelle et affirmation d'un ordre différent.
Il ne faut cependant pas exagérer le poids des contraintes de genre sur l'écriture cinématographique. Le film n'est pas seulement la résultante d'un jeu de forces plus ou moins anonymes et il reste de la place pour une étude mobile et vigilante, entre la croyance un peu naïve en l'*Auteur*[2], source de tout sens, et son envers, l'iconologie extrême, qui évacue l'auteur au profit du seul *texte* (ou du tableau) afin d'y retrouver les pulsions inconscientes d'une époque.

A - Les films comme produit

Après tout, les grandes décisions sont prises par des *producteurs* : les films sont bien des *produits* et l'écriture cinématographique est d'abord une activité industrielle et commerciale. Il convient donc de commencer par essayer de comprendre les phases de cette « production » et de voir leur influence sur le produit : qu'y a-t-il entre les *producers* et les *films makers* (qui fabriquent les œuvres) et peut on déjà parler d'*auteurs* à propos de cette période de production de masse ? Ou encore, au cœur du système des studios, les structures intermédiaires que constituent les genres et le code de

---

1. Stuart M. Kaminsky, *American Film Genres*, Chicago : Nelson-Hall, p. 34-35
2. En français dans les textes américains des années 60-80, en hommage à la « Politique des auteurs » défendue par les *Cahiers du Cinéma*.

censure (deux façons de gérer les attentes du public) ne sont ils pas les vrais « auteurs » des films de la période ?

La liste des réalisateurs ci-dessus suggère tout de même qu'un nombre limité de noms restés connus reviennent avec insistance (LeRoy, Wellman, Hawks, Curtiz, Walsh) comme des *signatures*, mais, dans les salles, ils étaient précédés par les noms des acteurs (Robinson, Cagney, Muni, Bogart...) et par une conscience assez précise de ce que le logo de la « major » (Warner, Paramount, MGM...) promettait. On sait par ailleurs les résistances suscitées par l'idée même que les réalisateurs soient considérés comme des auteurs dans le cas d'Hollywood. Elles sont ici amplifiées par leur relative jeunesse[1] à un moment où le cinéma lui-même semble renaître grâce au parlant, par le pouvoir des producteurs alors à son zénith [2], par la complexité nouvelle des technologies et de leurs très lourdes contraintes [3], par l'aura des nouvelles stars. Pendant le tournage d'un film deux types d'organisations un peu différentes sont à l'œuvre : présence en arrière plan du *groupe* monolithique invisible que constitue la Major, qui dirige parfois encore depuis New York ; travail collectif d'une *équipe* d'individus visibles sur le plateau. Il reste que le réalisateur – qui se compare volontiers au rédacteur en chef d'un journal – trouve parfois sa voix entre ces deux formes de collectivités : mais ce ne sera qu'en analysant le produit, le film, qu'elle pourra être repérée. Et puis, on est frappé par la *plasticité* de ces grands artisans qui passent d'une *major* à l'autre (et épousent parfois leur style[4]) ou d'un genre à l'autre (les filmographies de LeRoy, Wellman et Hawks sont édifiantes de ce point de vue). En tout cas, il serait difficile de trouver un réalisateur qui puisse, par exemple, prétendre être le « Maître du film de gangsters » comme on disait d'Hitchcock qu'il était le « Maître du suspense ».

Dans le triangle fondateur *producteur / réalisateur / acteur*, les biographes renvoient presque automatiquement aux communautés juives pour les premiers (Warner, Zanuck..), américano-irlandaises pour les cinéastes (LeRoy, Wellman, Hawks, Walsh), avant les immigrés de l'Europe du nord (Wyler [5], Lang) et de l'est (Curtiz [6]). Seuls les acteurs affichent alors délibérément une « ethnicité » réelle (Cagney, Irlandais, joue des personnages d'Irlandais) ou traduite (Robinson et Muni, tous deux juifs, jouent des personnages d'Italiens).

Ce brassage et la rencontre avec un public lui même d'immigration récente est au cœur du succès des premiers films de gangsters et il constitue un bon exemple de l'importance des technologies : c'est parce que le cinéma se met à parler qu'il peut se concentrer sur la voix (accent) et sur la parole (argots) des gangsters et c'est parce que le gangster parle qu'il existe avec

---

1. LeRoy, Wellman et Hawks ont moins de trente cinq ans.
2. Douglas Gomery appelle cette période « L'âge d'or des studios ».
3. On pense évidemment au effets comiques obtenus dans *Singing in the Rain*.
4. Bourget cite justement LeRoy comme exemple d'adaptation aux styles très différents de la Warner et de la MGM.. *op. cit.* note p. 94.
5. William Wyler, né en « France » à Mulhouse, parlait un anglais sans défaut...
6. ... au contraire du réalisateur de *Casablanca*, Michael Curtiz, né Kertesz en Hongrie, dont l'anglais problématique alimente plusieurs anecdotes (son impatience devant le retard de figurants habillés en moines alors qu'il criait "send the monkeys, send the monkeys"...)

tant d'intensité. L'importance des technologies est immédiatement l'affaire des producteurs et de choix stratégiques globaux : c'est la Warner qui lance le premier *talkie* et en tire les bénéfices ; ce sera elle qui valorisera le son plutôt que la richesse des décors ; ce sera elle qui « inventera » le gangster-qui-parle.

Les Majors

Toute étude de cette période passe par un minimum de compréhension du phénomène des « majors » tel que le présentent Gomery et Bourget [1]. Huit studios se partagent inégalement l'ensemble de la production et des recettes, mais les grands noms de cette époque ne sont pas tout à fait ceux d'aujourd'hui : à côté des cinq majors (The Big Five : Paramount, Loew's, Warner, Fox et RKO) trois studios peinent un peu à suivre (The Little Three : Universal, Columbia et United Artists). Cette industrie, qui représente 0,5% du PNB et 0,5% des salariés des États-Unis est, selon le mot de Gomery, « modérément rentable » (Bourget, p. 18) même si les bénéfices y sont trois fois supérieurs à ceux de la moyenne des entreprises américaines et si les cadres y sont très bien payés. On remarquera au passage que, jusqu'au début des années trente, les grandes décisions sont prises à New York selon une fabrication décentralisée inspirée du modèle de General Motors. Cet « Age d'Or » ne tient donc pas toutes ses promesses et si 1946 est l'année des meilleurs bénéfices de toute l'histoire des studios on remarque qu'en 1947 ce n'est pas la vente des billets – donc des films eux-mêmes – qui est la plus rentable, mais celle des rafraîchissements et du *pop corn* autour des salles... Les difficultés se succèdent pendant la période qui nous intéresse : baisse du pouvoir d'achat des spectateurs liée à la crise économique (on passe de 90 millions de spectateurs en 1930 à 60 millions en 1932, avec la fermeture de 5000 salles), effets dévastateurs pour les majors des procès anti-trusts sous Roosevelt, guerre mondiale.

On a tout dit sur le despotisme des Moguls et le triste sort réservé aux « créatifs », particulièrement les scénaristes, (on pense à *Barton Fink* et la figure de Faulkner à Hollywood...) et on n'a pas toujours exagéré [2]. Si la question est surtout de mesurer l'effet de ce pouvoir sur les films eux-mêmes, il convient de distinguer entre les interventions ponctuelles – même massives – sur un film (dénouements de films imposés contre la volonté du réalisateur comme pour *Suspicion* de Hitchcock [3] – ou décidés en fonction de

---

1. Douglas Gomery, *L'Age d'Or des studios*, Cahiers du cinéma, 1986 et Jean-Loup Bourget, *Hollywood, la norme et la marge*. On consultera avec profit l'étude très détaillée de David Bordwell, Janet Staiger et Krystin Thomson, *The Classical Hollywood Cinema, Film Style and Mode of Production to 1960*, New-York, Routledge, 1985
2. Anne-Marie Bidaud, dans *Hollywood et le rêve américain*, cite Samuel Goldwyn (p. 48) à propos de *Wuthering Heights* : "I made the movie; William Wyler only directed it". On trouvera page 44 du même ouvrage un utile tableau récapitulatif des majors.
3. On sait que le roman confirme les soupçons de l'héroïne : son mari réussit à la tuer. Mais Selznick, le producteur, ne fait que suivre les attentes du public qui aurait refusé de voir Cary Grant en assassin... La *persona* des acteurs est une composante très forte de l'écriture filmique.

l'air du temps dans *Casablanca*[1]) et la tendance plus générale de chaque studio à affirmer un style, une identité.

Les studios jouaient de leur « image de marque » en exhibant leurs logos et leurs stars maison et les attentes du public ont pu correspondre à de réelles différences de style, de ton et de sujets. Je me bornerai, à titre d'exemple, à une comparaison entre la MGM (proportionnellement la moins présente sur le terrain du crime organisé, malgré *A Manhattan Melodrama*) et la Warner, reine du genre [2]. La MGM, ce sont les deux versions de *Ben Hur*, le « grand style » de la première des grandes majors, les Stars (Valentino, Garbo, Jean Harlow...), la richesse des décors, la gestion des grandes formes (épopées) qu'illustre son goût pour les mouvements de foule, les grands symboles, bref un souffle conservateur qui passe parfois du sublime au pompier[3].

La Warner est toute autre. Rarement au sommet (après l'énorme succès de *The Jazz Singer* en 1927, elle n'est le plus souvent que n° 4 et tout paraît un peu *chiche* dans son mode de gestion...) C'est pourtant elle qu'on a retenu : « aujourd'hui, on considère souvent Warner Bros comme la plus intéressante des major companies... [4]». Au luxe de la MGM elle prétend opposer l'esprit d'invention et l'efficacité du rythme, face au conservatisme elle défend des causes progressistes, au lieu d'une esthétique de l'exotisme et de l'académisme, elle valorise le langage des minorités, leur univers moderne urbain et les décors les plus quotidiens. On aura compris les avantages économiques de tels choix esthétiques : les décors peu éclairés, dans des lieux faciles à reconstituer (et à répéter), filmés en noir et blanc (dès 1925 le premier *Ben Hur* MGM offre des séquences en deux couleurs), l'intérêt porté à des individus ou à des groupes restreints, portant des costumes de ville contemporains – tout contribue à la réduction des budgets. Les films de la Warner étonnent encore par leur énergie, leur rythme impeccable et leurs thèmes. Cette image progressiste et sociale est tout de même assez paradoxale si on se souvient de la personnalité des frères Warner. Leur vrai chef, Harry, par exemple, est présenté par Gomery comme un autocrate en affaires, violemment hostile aux syndicats (omniprésents) et comme un « républicain classique et conservateur » en politique, même s'il sera interventionniste et apportera un soutien énergique à Roosevelt dès 1932.

Les films de la Warner sont des films « engagés » : contre les bagnes, contre les dérives de la justice dans le Sud, contre la répression policière, les milices patronales, racistes ou xénophobes et, bien sûr, contre toute forme de lynchage. On y lit de façon plus diffuse une analyse des causes de la dépression, associée à la première guerre mondiale et une double

---

1. Ici c'est Hal Wallis, de la Warner, qui décide après coup, pour participer à l'engagement des États-Unis en Europe, d'un dénouement laissé ouvert pendant la durée du tournage. Les acteurs ne savent pas comment finira leur récit. Le résultat produit le miracle qu'on sait...
2. Bourget, *op. cit.* p. 95.
3. Bien sûr, comme toujours à Hollywood, les transgressions sont nombreuses, mais révélatrices : *The Merry Widow*, de Lubitsch, film le plus cher de l'année 1934 (trait MGM) étonne encore par son audace sexuelle (anti MGM). C'est aussi la MGM qui produit certains *Tarzan*, Laurel and Hardy et autres Marx Brothers...
4. Gomery, *op. cit.*, p. 104.

ingratitude, de l'Europe envers les États-Unis d'une part, et de la nation à l'égard des soldats américains, d'autre part. Les valeurs de la Warner articulent l'exaltation de l'esprit d'entreprise (individuel) avec le sens de la responsabilité collective et une forme de solidarité. En fin de compte, les films renvoient clairement dos à dos les manifestations américaines du fascisme européen et le syndicalisme révolutionnaire pour proposer une « troisième voie ».

Tous ces éléments ont sans doute convergé pour faire de la Warner le lieu privilégié de la représentation du crime à l'écran, le long du sillon déjà creusé par le cinéma muet depuis Griffith (*The Musketeers of Pig Alley*) et les films de Lon Chaney [1]. Mais c'est la remarquable avance prise sur les autres majors dans le domaine du son qui semble la plus déterminante : achat en 1925 d'une petite station de radio qui utilise le système Western Electric, courts métrages sonores dès décembre 1925 réalisés à New York, ouverture de *Tannhaüser* en 1926 et trois chansons filmées de Al Jonson avant le coup de tonnerre du *Jazz Singer* en août 1927 qui restera son plus beau coup et le plus cher de son histoire... une sorte d'accident si on considère le mode de gestion habituel de cette major. En tout cas, le mariage de la Warner avec le son coïncide très naturellement avec la naissance de Rico – le Petit César – le premier gangster qui parle avec l'"accent italien' [2].

La censure et le Production Code

A côté des studios, le second système qui contraint – et peut être irrigue – la création de films à Hollywood est le code de production, système à la fois brutal et subtil, odieux et risible, imposé et consenti, répressif et défensif, castrateur et productif, bref admirablement paradoxal. Munby s'intéresse d'abord aux films de gangsters parce qu'il veut écrire « a history of the attempts to censor this particular form of production » et « the story of how the concerted efforts to contain the subversive potential of this Hollywood form were resisted and countered [3]». Autrement dit, il pose d'emblée l'hypothèse de l'échec sans cesse renouvelé de la censure et il étaie en historien les intuitions de nombreux spécialistes du cinéma.

La censure est une vieille habitude que les lieux peu recommandables où on voyait les films, la vie privée des acteurs et, surtout, des contenus rendus plus intenses par l'effet des images ne pouvaient manquer de raviver. Elle a traditionnellement deux foyers : les institutions officielles – ici la crainte que la justice des États s'en mêle – et le boycott de certaines communautés. Griffith mène un premier combat assez ambigu pour défendre *Birth of a Nation* qui valorise le racisme affiché du KKK. Quand la Cour Suprême décrète que les films relèvent du « business pure and simple », au lieu d'être protégés par le premier amendement, les censures locales des États et des villes deviennent plus menaçantes. Toute l'histoire du Code retrouve de telles rouéries de l'Histoire : ce sont alors les majors qui préfèrent négocier par avance la faisabilité de leurs produits, selon une sorte de cahier des charges, plutôt que de voir les autorités intervenir ou les ligues appeler au

---

1. Michel Ciment, *Le Crime à l'écran*, donne une image vive et précise de cette tradition p. 14-27.
2. Il s'agit d'une erreur volontaire : le film présente bien un milieu italien, mais Rico – immigré de la seconde génération – est né aux États-Unis et il ne parle pas du tout Italien.
3. Munby, p. 1.

boycott. Et la liste des « Don'ts and Be carefuls » suscite aujourd'hui le rire (on doit présenter les chambres à coucher avec « bon goût ») ou l'indignation (les relations amoureuses interaciales – miscegenation – sont interdites). Mais on comprend aussi deux choses : d'une part, du côté hollywoodien, il s'agit de ne pas choquer des clients potentiels (racistes compris), d'autre part on retrouve un fond de sérieux puritain annonciateur de certains excès de la « political correctness » dans les interdictions concernant les mots qui pourraient blesser les minorités (Frogs, Dagos...) Le prologue de la version la plus répandue du code Hays mérite une attention particulière : ne pas susciter de sympathie pour le crime, s'interdire toute déviation par rapport à un mode de vie « correct »[1] sans nécessité narrative, supprimer toute dérision à l'encontre des lois « naturelles » (mais qui en juge ?) et humaines (c'est à dire instaurées par la démocratie américaine, à ne pas confondre avec les anciennes habitudes ou avec un « ordre établi ».)

La place manque ici pour une histoire détaillée du Code[2]. On retiendra surtout qu'il entre effectivement en vigueur sous l'administration de William Hays (MPPDA) et qu'il a alors un effet rétroactif sur les films déjà réalisés : antérieurs à 1934 (*Little Caesar*...) ils sont simplement interdits après avoir été lourdement coupés et « améliorés » par des scènes ajoutées (*Scarface*). A partir de 1934 l'écriture d'un film devient un fascinant exercice de tractations, de contournements et d'imagination, où l'auto censure et la créativité se livrent à la « circumnavigation » dont parle Munby :

> We should not conclude ipso facto, however, that the films that emerged out of this circumnavigation of code structures in the name of profit were aesthetically lame. (171)

En 1935, les sanctions encourues (sous la forme d'amendes et/ou de refus d'être distribués) amènent une classification des projets soumis à la *Production Code Administration* en trois catégories qui stipulent que :

> Class I : The release of the picture be halted now and that no additional contracts be taken on » (Ainsi Little Caesar, Public Enemy, Doorway to Hell *et bien sûr* Scarface *d'abord « modifiés », ont été interdits après 1934.*)
>
> Class II : « ... permitted to finish ot present contracts, but that no new contracts will be taken » (Cas de A Manhattan Melodrama).
>
> Class III : le film est « acceptable screen entertainment... permitted to continue along without difficulty »   (Munby, 168)

On aura remarqué que le ton n'est guère à la plaisanterie. Pour nous, dans un autre siècle, le Code est d'abord un catéchisme désuet, le « reflet fidèle (et d'autant plus fidèle qu'il est largement inconscient) non seulement des principes, mais aussi des préjugés moraux, sexistes, racistes... d'une société »[3]. Mais il ne faudrait surtout pas croire que tous les censeurs se voient en ennemis du cinéma : c'est parce qu'ils sont convaincus de son succès, de son impact sur la population et de son potentiel moral qu'ils

---

1. Le mot « correct » est bien le même qu'un demi-siècle plus tard.
2. On consultera d'abord Bidaud, Bourget et Munby. Matthew Guillen montre le code en action dans son chapitre, ci-dessous.
3. Bourget, p. 126

affirment agir pour son bien[1]. L'ironie, bien sûr, est qu'ils ne croyaient peut être pas si bien dire. Il y a quelque chose de circulaire dans ces jeux du chat avec la souris : ce sont les films de gangsters qui motivent l'indignation des ligues et déclenchent le mécanisme complexe de l'auto censure d'Hollywood, désireux de continuer à vendre quand même de tels films. Mais ce sont également ces films qui illustrent le mieux la nature particulière de la liberté d'expression et de la créativité dans une période difficile pour elles. La souris courait vraiment plus vite que le chat.

B – Les films comme textes

Allons au plus pressé : en tant que texte (ou document), le groupe de films évoqué plus haut nous renseigne sur trois plans distincts. D'abord par des noyaux de *signifiants formels* (l'exemple plus évident est celui des éclairages) qui reviennent avec régularité, ensuite à travers la reconstruction en amont de quelques '*récits structurants*' comme les histoires d'Horatio Alger, enfin, plus globalement et plus profondément, grâce à la compréhension de la *fonction symbolique collective* du Gangster aux États-Unis (à partir de l'étude fondamentale de Warshow). Il s'agit seulement ici de lancer ces pistes sans les approfondir.

Constantes formelles

C'est en voyant les films eux-mêmes qu'on mettra les motifs et les effets formels en évidence et qu'on pourra repérer des différences ou des évolutions. On aura intérêt à les analyser en séparant plusieurs rubriques qui renvoient à des moments de l'écriture cinématographique :
- choix des sujets et établissement du découpage (*continuity script*), c'est à dire des grandes structures narratives et du remplissage de la tapisserie.
- scénographie : choix des décors, des acteurs, puis organisation de l'espace dans le studio, par rapport au regard de la caméra, éclairages.
- filmage : mouvements de caméra, cadrages et choix des focales (profondeur de champ : on voit à la fois des objets rapprochés et le fond du décor).
- montage : plus ou moins rapide, plus ou moins visible, jouant plus ou moins sur la simultanéité d'événements ou sur des comparaisons...

La majorité des films de notre liste donne une grande impression d'homogénéité avec son absence de films en couleurs (au propre et au figuré) ses éclairages « low key », ses décors liés au seul milieu urbain que fréquente le gangster. On s'intéressera donc successivement à sa *vie publique* : rues, bars, tripots, banquets et bureaux des gangsters ; à sa *vie privée* : maison familiale et chambre d'hôtel de luxe ; et aux *interfaces* avec le monde extérieur : police, presse, usines, église, prison, cimetière, champ de course... Plus quelques images urbaines spécifiques à un film particulier comme celles du salon de coiffure de *Scarface*. Dès la trilogie fondatrice (*Little Caesar*, *Public Enemy* et *Scarface*), les acteurs se démarquent

---

1. D'abord par des *interdits* pour protéger le peuple contre lui même (années 30), ensuite par un jeu d'influences pour que le cinéma donne une *image positive* de la société américaine au quotidien (fin des années 1940) : on passe d'une influence protectrice, plutôt négative, à une pédagogie plus volontariste. Voir Munby et son étude de l'évolution des grilles d'analyse de films.

des attentes de l'époque par rapport à l'image de la star et manifestent un remarquable refus de l'*embellishment*. Robinson n'est plus jeune et, comme Cagney, il ne dissimule ni sa très petite taille (bien d'autres ont beaucoup triché...[1]) ni ses origines (complexes). Celles de Paul Muni sont plus complexes encore puisqu'il est comparé à un singe. Plus tard, Bogart devra attendre que ses tempes grisonnent (*High Sierra* et *The Maltese Falcon*) pour dépasser le statut de comparse ou de *bad guy*. Ce sont des stars à part entière, mais en rupture avec le *glamour* des autres genres. [2]

Il faut revenir sur la rencontre entre l'arrivée du son et celle des gangsters de cinéma. Michel Ciment note très justement qu'au delà de leur voix ethnicisée qui est au cœur des débuts du genre, de nombreux objets du décor semblent naître du *bruit* qu'ils font : « le crépitement des mitraillettes, le crissement des pneus sur l'asphalte, les sirènes de la police, l'explosion des grenades, la sonnerie menaçante du téléphone, la musique du jazz dans les boites de nuit... » et les étranges et brefs moments de silence construisent un univers accéléré dont le mouvement est un peu celui d'une voiture dont les freins auraient lâché. Le montage confirme généralement cette avancée inévitable, ce rythme rapide, mais il frappe aussi par sa capacité à se faire oublier au profit des événements.

Motifs et récits idéologiques

Derrière ces constantes de l'écriture filmique, il est facile de retrouver des récits communs en amont de la plupart des films sur le crime. Le plus parlant d'entre eux – la saga racontée au XIXe siècle par Horatio Alger – est sans doute le moins connu en France. Ancien de Harvard, élève de Longfellow, Alger, asthmatique devenu pasteur faute de pouvoir rejoindre l'armée de l'Union, est l'auteur de plus de cent vingt livres sur le thème de *onward and upward* (« *from-rags-to-riches* ») : l'ascension sociale des Américains méritants. Son héros New Yorkais, Ragged Dick, est brave, généreux, travailleur et persévérant, car la réussite est obtenue grâce aux vertus de « self reliance, self discipline, decency and honesty ». Plus de 250 millions d'exemplaires de ses livres ont été vendus avant 1930.

Edward Mitchell[3] voit dans ces récits une réponse mythique aux contradictions de la vision du monde suggérée par le passage d'un puritanisme diffus au darwinisme social de la fin du siècle. Les héros d'Alger sont, tantôt des orphelins qui retrouveront le vrai statut bourgeois dont un complot familial les avait privés, tantôt de vrais pauvres qui accèdent au même statut à force de courage et détermination. On voit bien ici un utile glissement : l'orphelin déshérité (un anti *Pip*) sait confusément sa vrai nature d'héritier légitime, tandis que le nouveau héros de l'Amérique sent qu'il mérite sa promotion seulement à partir de ce qu'il *est*. Mais dans les deux cas la récompense est l'argent, le succès passe par le « pluck » mais

---

1. On peut sourire des acrobaties techniques (fausses estrades, virtuosité de la caméra..) pour assortir Claude Rains et Ingrid Bergman, dans *Notorious*...
2. La place manque ici pour étudier l'évolution des personnages féminins – molls, mothers et femmes fatales.
3. Edward Mitchell, « Apes and Essences : Some Sources of Significance in the American Gangster Film », in B. K. Grant, *Film Genre Reader*, UP. Austin, 1986, p. 159-168

il ne se produit en fin de compte que *grâce* à un formidable coup de hasard – attendu par le lecteur.

Cette articulation entre deux types de récits reprend donc celle du passage du puritanisme au darwinisme social : le puritanisme, dans la forme très simplifiée qui court dans les récits de l'époque, garde l'idée que l'Homme est né dans le péché et que son destin est écrit d'avance. Seuls certains élus seront sauvés par Dieu mais tout est déjà décidé. Or cette forme extrême de déterminisme comporte un élément de suspense et de lisibilité : les *signes* d'élection sont rares, même si le succès matériel en ce monde – l'argent – est de très bon augure. Le darwinisme importé par Spencer arrive dans une société où les foudres divines paraissent un peu éloignées, et où la jungle des villes remplace avantageusement la Nature (on y reviendra). Son déterminisme – la sélection naturelle, ou « survival of the fittest » – est aussi brutal, mais il laisse la place pour les plus débrouillards qui peuvent espérer passer à travers les mailles du filet. Si le darwinisme peut être lu comme une version sécularisée du déterminisme puritain, il préserve la même valorisation des signes matériels de la réussite et le même sens du destin, de la trajectoire et, cependant, il peine un peu à articuler le poids du déterminisme avec les valeurs individuelles de dynamisme. C'est ici qu'Alger – parmi d'autres – aide à sortir d'un *double bind* familier en associant le sens de l'héritage naturel à celui de l'héritage « ressenti » et à l'intervention du destin narratif attendu.

Si les gangsters suivent les mêmes chemins, ils les prennent à rebours. Mais les temps ne sont pas à l'euphorie et Stuart Kaminsky décrit *Little Caesar*, acte de naissance officiel du genre, comme une des « semi conscious attempts to deal with the depression and the public shaken confidence in American economics, politics, and myths of the self-made man[1] ». Et les spectateurs ont choisi leurs cibles, qui ne sont pas les gangsters punis à la fin du film, mais leurs chefs restés dans l'ombre, comme le Big Boy de *Little Caesar* : « It is these upper – and middle-class – bosses, hiding behind a gang leader of courage, whom we are taught to hate in gangster films »[2]. Pour les gangsters, la *success story* se transforme évidemment en « rise and fall » tragique et dérisoire, selon une trajectoire prévue d'avance : on retrouve bien le monde en noir et blanc (le Bien et le Mal), la volonté d'ascension sociale et l'argent comme signes supérieurs d'identité (re)trouvée, la lutte pour la survie et, surtout, les qualités américaines de dynamisme, de ruse et de courage – *drive, cunning, pluck, toughness* : autant de mots clés d'un univers qui alterne entre le noir et le blanc. Le pire, pour Rico (*Little Caesar*), c'est de devenir « yella », lâche, bien sûr, mais aussi d'une couleur hors système. Le meilleur pour Tony Camonte (*Scarface*), c'est de « Do it first, do it yourself, and keep on doing it ».

On fera peut être observer que ces gangsters italiens, irlandais ou polonais ne sont ni puritains ni darwinistes, mais scrupuleusement catholiques. Ou que leur séduction – car ils plaisent infiniment au public de

---

1. Stuart M. Kaminsky, *op. cit.*, p. 21
2. *idem*, p. 31

l'époque, même dans leur version originale à Chicago ou New York [1] – va bien au delà de leur succès et de leur argent. C'est à cet apparent paradoxe que le texte de Warshow répond dès les années quarante.

Fonction symbolique

Il faut commencer par séparer plusieurs conceptions de la représentation dans des œuvres de fiction pour comprendre certains changements dans les enjeux de la critique. Depuis Shakespeare, les mots de *miroir* ou de *reflet* ont fait fortune dans des directions assez divergentes. Le miroir que Hamlet tend à ses parents vise à imposer (à eux mêmes puis à la cour qui assiste à la scène) une vérité qu'ils essaient de dissimuler ; le « reflet » de la société que Kracauer et la critique marxiste du milieu du XXe siècle cherchaient dans les œuvres était une expression inconsciente, un *symptôme* irrépressible de réalités que le critique prétendait décrypter. Or Raymond Chandler, quand il parle de sa propre écriture de romans noirs en termes de « témoignage impitoyable sur notre temps » (cité dans Guérif p. 23) et quand il ajoute que « le film noir est le reflet le plus fidèle d'une société » (p. 29), en utilisant les mêmes mots, leur donne un sens légèrement différent : il considère le genre comme une structure, ou un lieu, qui lui permet d'*exprimer* consciemment un univers à l'usage de lecteurs qui s'y reconnaissent, mais sans se livrer à une « analyse » méthodique.

Le gangster, lui, offre ouvertement sa visibilité acceptée, presque jubilatoire (*Scarface*), à un public qui le reconnaît immédiatement – non pas comme reflet ou même comme représentation documentaire de son homologue à la ville – mais comme « expérience artistique…commune à tous les Américains »[2]. Warshow réagit au regard européen qui vient de découvrir les gangsters américains : ce ne sont pas les vrais gangsters référentiels de New York ou Chicago qui sont l'enjeu de ces films, mais des gangsters auto-référentiels de film en film, qui sont la vision que chaque Américain se fait de *lui même*. « Il n'y a pour ainsi dire rien que nous comprenions mieux ou à quoi nous réagissions plus spontanément ou plus intelligemment » (p. 142). Personnage du présent (au contraire du héros de western) « le gangster parle en notre nom, exprimant cette partie de l'inconscient américain qui rejette les qualités et les exigences de la vie moderne, qui rejette l'"américanisme" proprement dit » (p. 143).

Pourquoi, donc, une si forte identification ? L'analyse de Warshow est à la fois simple et stimulante : les pays jeunes se construisent autour d'une conception joyeuse de la vie et « le sens du tragique est un luxe réservé aux sociétés aristocratiques » (140). Les sociétés égalitaires (démocratiques ou autoritaires) ont « la prétention de rendre la vie plus heureuse », le bonheur devient un objectif politique et « être heureux devient une obligation civique » qui repose en grande partie sur la culture de masse. Or (dès avant la récession) « à une époque où la condition normale du citoyen est un état d'anxiété, l'euphorie envahit notre culture comme le large sourire d'un idiot » (141). D'où ces fleurs de la différence que sont le jazz, les Marx

---

1. Voir John G. Mitchell, "Al Capone : 'I give the Public What the Public wants'" in Leonard Dinnerstein & Kenneth T. Jackson, *American Vistas, 1877 to the Present*, New York : Oxford U.P., 1997, p. 206
2. Robert Warshow, "The gangster as Tragic Hero", cité in Ciment, *Le Crime à l'écran*, p. 142

Brothers, les feuilletons sentimentaux, la ferveur religieuse et... les gangsters (l'association est volontairement provocatrice).

Le gangster, créature de l'imaginaire, « est ce que nous voulons être et ce que nous redoutons de pouvoir devenir » (p. 143), qui offre aussi la jouissance ambiguë « de participer par procuration au sadisme et de voir ce sadisme se retourner contre son auteur ». J'ajoute qu'en 1929, ce mythe est un des seuls qui n'a pas besoin d'être *ravivé* [1] : la prohibition attise des contradictions spécifiquement américaines et la récession met au centre de la culture populaire « l'intolérable dilemme » des Américains : « que l'échec soit une sorte de mort et que la réussite soit mauvaise et dangereuse ; qu'elle soit en ultime instance, impossible » (p. 145). Les films de gangsters ne sont ni un miroir dénonciateur, ni un symptôme à décrypter : ils sont l'expression à la fois douloureuse et jouissive d'un regard américain sur lui même.

Avant d'étudier cette dynamique à l'œuvre dans les films, il n'est pas inutile d'en rassembler maintenant le contexte et les principales composantes : d'abord elle s'élance entre les rives tortueuses de la négociation avec le Code, ensuite elle s'affirme dans un jeu de comparaisons et d'oppositions avec d'autres genres, enfin son cours principal naît avec le gangster qui parle, c'est à dire qui impose un point de vue et un langage marqués par son « ethnicité »[2]. Mais bien sûr, au delà des satisfactions immédiates qu'ils procurent, ces films n'ont jamais cessé de mettre en question les limites entre le bien et le mal, entre les Américains « légitimes » et les autres... sans parler ici de leur très remarquable représentation de la femme.

Dans ces pages d'ouverture, je m'en tiens aux commencements. Mais les grands mouvements vers la ville (les immigrés viennent d'une *autre campagne* que celle qui fonde les idéaux américains, et ils ne se reconnaissent pas dans l'agrarisme de l'Ouest) reflueront bientôt dans la nostalgie du retour vers l'Américain ordinaire et vers son Kentucky d'origine (Dix, dans *Asphalt Jungle*).

La totale concentration des premiers films de gangsters sur l'univers urbain ne tient peut être pas seulement aux modèles qu'il décrivent (Capone...) mais à un démarquage par rapport aux westerns dont certains récits peuvent ressembler à ceux des films urbains. Après tout, le même roman de W.R. Burnett – *High Sierra* – a été adapté deux fois par le même Raoul Walsh, d'abord comme film noir, puis dans un décor de western (*Colorado Territory*). La force des films du corpus tient d'abord à leur ancrage immédiat dans le présent de leurs spectateurs.

On remarquera, pour conclure avant de se pencher sur des films particuliers, que le gangster de cinéma n'est pas isolé : 1931 voit aussi la naissance d'autres figures de la transgression comme Dracula et Frankenstein. Tous deux viennent d'ailleurs. Le premier parle, mais il a un

---

1. La période sera aussi grande consommatrice de mythes importés (*Frankenstein* et *Dracula*...) mais, surtout, elle s'interrogera sur la régénération de l'esprit contre la lettre, à propos des discours fondateurs de la politique (*Mr Smith Goes To Washington* de Frank Capra) et du sexe (les comédies dites de « remariage » où le couple déjà marié de façon formelle finit par s'aimer vraiment). Voir Stanley Cavell, *A la poursuite du bonheur*, Cahiers du Cinéma.
2. Voir Munby, p. 41 : "No longer simply objects of someone else's story, the poor and the criminal were granted a say in stories narrated from *their* perspective".

fort accent d'Europe de l'est, il ne travaille pas pour vivre et il ne doit son statut privilégié d'aristocrate terrien qu'à ses origines lointaines. Bref, le Dracula importé aux États-Unis impose son altérité sociale mais, contrairement au gangster, il vit en prédateur solitaire et il se situe plutôt du côté des *Big Boys*. Sa fin peu glorieuse ajoute à la satisfaction ambiguë des ravages qu'il a commis et elle ne suscite guère de sympathie. Le premier « Frankenstein » de Boris Karloff est plus « ethnique » encore : son intégration en est au premier stade du grognement, des plaintes et de la colère. Très vite, dès *The Bride of Frankenstein* [1], il apprendra à parler et toute la sympathie se portera sur lui. A la fin du film, la Créature détruit le laboratoire, le mauvais savant Cornelius, la fiancée et lui même, mais il sauve son créateur (Henry) et sa belle : « You... live ! ». Non seulement le récit confie à Karloff la *maîtrise du dénouement* (contrairement aux premiers gangsters) mais il organise la destruction de l'univers qui l'a créé (opposition « us and them » où le capitalisme joue le rôle de « them »), tout en préservant le jeune couple irresponsable qui permettra à l'Amérique de redémarrer.... On voit bien comment les récits importés sont ainsi relus dans un tout autre contexte.

C'est peut être enfin sur l'axe de l'opposition entre ville et nature 'rurale' que les films trouvent leur écho le plus curieux. Le succès des *Tarzan* sert de contrepoint imaginaire à la plongée dans la jungle urbaine. Là bas, dans cette Afrique fantasmée où Burroughs n'est jamais allé, les valeurs américaines et le darwinisme primordial sont à leur zénith. Mais il fallait que cette *jungle* rencontre l'autre et cette épiphanie constitue l'idée initiale de *King Kong* : faire mourir le symbole de la Nature extrême au sommet du symbole de la modernité urbaine (L'Empire State Building). Les ravages new yorkais de *Kong*, ses amours impossibles et sa fin tragique célèbrent et magnifient la même vitalité que celle du gangster.

On trouvera une bibliographie générale à la fin du volume.

---

1. Je feins ici d'oublier son origine très loquace chez Mary Shelley pour me concentrer sur de possibles identifications du public dans les années trente.

American Gangsters in Fact & on Film: the Social Construction of an American Popular Hero

By John Dean

The Circuitry

American gangsters embody a heritage of perceptions, a physical reality, and a state of mind rich with the nation's common personal beliefs and group reactions. They have many significant uses and valid interpretations, often contradictory, but harmonized by a relation to the same original subject. This is as it should be since a culture is a process, interacting circuitry; not a unique list of traits, but a unique pattern of relationships. Plus, truth is an onion. Multi-layered, pungent, delicious when eaten cooked rather than raw. It is the job of the culture to prepare this onion in many ways. One way is to leave life's subjects in the raw, the down and out, pungent, bitter, and ordinary way of the criminal as witnessed on the street, on trial, in prison. Actual crime has its own special reasons for being and modes of expression in America, which I will get into. Plus my additional purposes in this essay are to explain the cultural nature of the systems that get the news and stories out; and to examine the ideal American criminal and the fiction of organized crime as a great national fantasy, legend, truth which is not accepted as mere fact, but as a secular myth of life stories that appear to actually mediate and resolve life's problems in America – however temporary, however artificial and irrational.

As noted by the British cultural historian Robert Lacey, in the United States this popular sense of fantasy is integral to "how organized crime is experienced, perceived, and reported. Many of the criminals themselves are fantasists. It is the character flaw that first drew them to that world." And even "law enforcement officers, often for the best of reasons, tend to exaggerate the problem they are up against", for who "can resist a good story?" Thus, when one examines the fascination in American civilization for the gangster one confronts the "twisted fulfillment" of some of America's "most cherished dreams," one ventures into "systems of almost biblical belief."[1]

Some intellectual readers of American society and culture make the mistake of reading the gangsters who loom large in US life and legends as realistic, mainstream, US role models. Whether it be crime fighters or crime makers, the misreading goes, "popular culture generally helped towards an uncritical public acceptance," of the utterly ruthless ways of outlaws or lawmen in the USA.[2] As if institutional approval by the general public was the issue. In reality, the American public possesses common sense and wry awareness about criminal life and police abilities; they discard the husk but drink the juice. In the assessment of another wily Brit, John le Carré, Americans are characterized by: "A willingness to open themselves to

---

1. Robert Lacey, *Little Man: Meyer Lansky and the Gangster Life* (Boston: Little, Brown and Company, 1991) 312, 444.
2. Michael Woodwiss, *Organized Crime, USA: Changing Perceptions from Prohibition to the Present Day* (Brighton, UK: University of Sussex Printing Unit, 1990) 20; BAAS Pamphlets in American Studies 19.

strangers. A guile that was only there to protect their innocence. A fantasy that fired but never owned them. A capacity to be swayed by everything, while still remaining sovereign."[1]

The criminals and gangsters in the 1920s to early post World War Two period presented in the mass media were dream figures, the mesmeric flames on the walls of the populist, Platonic caves. Seen in the mind's eye in the stories broadcast to living rooms across America and into peoples' heads on the Westinghouse, GE, and RCA radios' new "theater of the mind". Seen on newspapers' front pages in spectacular, photogravure pictures in tabloids like the *New York Evening Graphic* (banner motto, *sic*: "NOTHING But the Truth"; sample headline, *sic*: "I KNOW WHO KILLED My Brother"). And experienced week after week in the light, shadows, music and voices of the movie theater "picture palaces" – with film titles and ads like, *sic*: "ON GUARD, AMERICA! New amazing racket sweeps nation! Told for the first time on the screen... the true story of ILLEGAL TRAFFIC with J. Carroll NASH ('King of Alcatraz') more dangerous, more menacing than ever."[2] Americans had mass produced and popularly meaningful dreams delivered to them with an intimacy, with an abundance and scale, which no civilization had ever before experienced.

The Carriers: American Popular, Mass Culture

The *lingua franca* which carried, distributed, and diffused the systems of almost biblical belief about the gangster in the period under consideration was American popular culture, the grassroots constitution of American democracy. This was the "software" of the time; the set of programs, the fiction, the story, the song, why things related. Since its initial development in Antebellum America, American popular culture had always been one means The People had to address and redress issues. It functioned as a big, imaginary playing field of possibilities. It had ever been fed and maintained by a vast conjoining of the will and whims of popular taste, mass consumption, technological innovations, historical events. Much like the 1787 US Constitution, American popular culture *outlines*, more than it defines, US value structures and powers-that-be. It preserves basic principles, accommodates the promises of the future – specially for the young who live on the front lines of the popular culture. Through the twentieth century American popular culture was multiplied through every possible medium which the written or spoken word, electricity, transistor or satellite could carry. American popular culture has been an often trying but ultimately satisfying expression of democracy cured by more democracy. It became the means by which gangster tales – liberating, invigorating, instructive – responded to popular need.

The popular culture which distributed news and stories about gangsters in our designated period existed in creative tension with American mass culture. This was the "hardware" of the time; the carrying tools, the utensils, how things got done and dominated. The mass culture thrived as a

---

1. John le Carré, *A Perfect Spy* (London: Coronet-Hodder & Stoughton, 1987 [orig:1986] 585-586.
2. Leslie Halliwell, *Mountain of Dreams: The Golden Years of Paramount Pictures* (New York: Stonehill Publishing Co., 1976) 108-118; 116, "The Character Men".

Hobbesian concept applied to everyday cultural practices, that all mankind needed "a common power to keep them in awe" (Hobbes' *Leviathan*, 1651). It has a tactile strength, a physical fixity; there to produce, sell to, and dominate a market. In contrast, American popular culture is a Lockian concept applied to everyday cultural practices, the expression of the unrestrained cultural "liberty of man in society" to be under no restriction save that established by legislative consent and individual desires (John Locke, *Second Treatise of Government*, 1690).

In the twentieth century American popular culture became a new stage of folklore, "the folklore of industrial man" (McLuhan, *The Mechanical Bride*,1951), in which factory age man dreamed aloud and in broad daylight to himself, in which men and women voiced their spontaneous complaints and pleasures. But the mass culture patented and machine-made the popular culture, mass marketed, industrialized, and produced it into economies of scale – till the popular complaints and pleasures became standard fare. The popular and the mass culture exquisitely created and delivered hot messages from the efficient institutions to the hungry audiences. But, as a result, the freshness and visionary quality of the initial generation of gangster movies became just another tired, reliable product.

Period Gives Style

This is why a periodicity for gangster stories in fact and fiction is valid, contiguous from the frenzy of the 20s through the anxiety of the early 50s. First, Prohibition gave American criminals a common reason for getting organized. It was a product every criminal could try to cash in on. Second, the Great Depression, the Second World War, and the onset of the Cold War helped to create a common mood of worry, threat, and unreasoned, irrational need to fight back. It gave a defensive zest to life. Third, both the popular and the mass culture, the messages and the communication systems, were given stylistic uniformity by virtue of the fact that they were created in the localized, condensed, poetry of the people – in their written word (read in tabloids, pulp mags and fiction, heard on the radio) and in the exhibited image (movies, graphics, cartoons, the imagined "theater of the mind" of radio shows). In short: common cause, mood, style. As journalist Jimmy Breslin identified it, back then was not a period like the 1980s and 1990s when people were asked "to live life as it actually is" – but a time, specially the key register of the 20s and 30s, "when people felt the excitement was all about something that only existed when they laughed."[1]

But, as with other genres, eventually a cycle of addressing popular concerns through innovative, engaged entertainment was overshadowed by repetition and dullness; response by tired formulas mismatched with changing times. Till, by the time of stupendously boring gangster films like Warner's *The Rise and Fall of Legs Diamond* (1960), there was nothing left to the gangster genre but zeal (which, as Samuel Johnson wrote, is what wins out when ability falters). Thus the response to the gangster in American popular culture came and went as articulate focus and contemporary rhythm of call and response, audience concern meeting popular and mass

---

1. Jimmy Breslin, *Damon Runyon – A Life* (New York: Dell-Laurel, 1991) 410.

culture reaction. But it had its day beginning in its aftermath start when the urban gangsters themselves first came of age – beginning with Arnold Rothstein (1882-1928) – and when the urban gangster genre in film and fiction was invented as a fresh response to a new America. This is why we can say the period from the 20s to the early 50s was a golden age of the gangster in storytelling and in flamboyant fact. By the 1990s America's *gangster du jour* was John Gotti. But there was nothing effervescent or startling about the man. He was no Arnold Rothstein or Al Capone. By that time, Americans, as *The Economist* recently wrote, simply felt "not exactly safe, but at least familiar with him and his kind."[1] The thrill was gone.

The Means: How the Media Massaged the Gangsters

It was all aided by the means: on the screen with movies, with words by tabloid journalism. To see gangsters on the big movie screen in the 20s, 30s, 40s was a startling experience. City life had become a new experience for most Americans beginning in 1920. With movies about the city many saw a mirror of their own new lives; King Vidor's excellent melodrama *The Crowd* (1928) is probably the single best example of this fact. Also, the gangster movies of the time showed a world far more sensational and dangerous than US cities of the time. For example, in New York City in the "year of the end of the war, 1945, there were 335 homicides, 2,115 assaults and 1,653 armed robberies. You had to ride many times down many streets before coming upon a crime scene" – a couple of decades later, you could have covered double murder by looking out your front window (Breslin, 391).

Events dictate space. Plot and story manipulate space. The gangster story is a tale of close, enclosing space. For example, look at the opening credits of Rouben Mamoulian's *City Streets* (1931). There in the background are the tall, dark, static canyons of the city, leaning inward; traps for the wary, escapes routes for the wily. In either case: from which there appears to be no escape. Unless you can fly away, which, symbolically, is what the good protagonists, played by beefcake Gary Cooper and salacious Sylvia Sidney, did.

The mass medium of the big screen with this intensity and quality conveying a popular culture of new, urban messages to Americans nationwide was a phenomenon with no historical precedence. The size and extent of this dramatic, omnipresent display helped to make the real gangsters themselves larger-than-life. How appropriate that the FBI's staged killing of a look-alike John Dillinger was done outside the Biograph Theater in Chicago – movie lending credence to an invented fact.[2] Not only were gangsters and criminals everywhere in the news. But up on the screen the scale of their faces, their quarrels, their romances were magnified to hundreds of square feet with stentorian voices and draped in Persian rugs of luxurious background music. On the movie screen the images were stronger, with more visual information, sharper contrasts, far more acute sounds than in non-reel life. More powerful images than most people would ever see anywhere else except in their own dream life. The urban gangster and organized crime from the early decades of the twentieth century

---

1. "John Gotti and the American Dream of Crime": *The Economist*, December 7, 1991, 58.
2. Jay Robert Nash, Ron Offen, *Dillinger: Dead or Alive?* (Chicago: Henry Regnery Co., 1970).

onward – but specially from the 20s to the early 50s – lived together in symbiosis with the developing medium of the cinema. Like egret and hippopotamus, one thrived and flew due to the gross, muddy life of the other; while one remained heavy, hurtful, and irrepressibly down-to-earth, the other one soared.

US newspapers intensified the gangsters another way. Gangsters made great news. The US 20s and 30s wave of attention given to gangsters was concomitant with a mass media wave of *tabloid* journalism, which itself was an extension of the blood and guts *penny press* style of the 1890s known as *yellow journalism* (from a popular cartoon feature called "The Yellow Kid" published in a couple of these papers, plus the earliest cartoon used to merchandize products).

Most American popular media is a body of information and images built on the spine of a story. Men adjust to their environment through the medium of stories which reconstruct their common concerns on the logic of a narrative model. American news, like Hollywood movies, is brilliant at story telling, not editorializing or long, slow, intricate speculations on the meaning of meaning (as European news and movies). Things have to *happen*. Journalistic news is neither the raw data of events nor abstract speculations on those events. As they say in the American newspaper business when a reporter returns to his office: "Did you get *the story?*".

America has always had, in addition, straight, respectable reporting that was well sourced and honest. Paradigms of high-toned, journalistic virtue include *The New York Times* and *The Washington Post*. However, by the 1920s the urine of yellow journalism had greatly soiled news reporting; alternately referred to by the literary world and elite society of the time as "Tabloid Poison", "that new black plague", or the "jungle weeds in the journalistic garden."[1] Crime, sex, and scandal were the meat and potatoes of the tabloids. The positive side of this was the creation of a first step, a threshold experience of literate explanations for a first-time, reading audience – the low culture, low-life folk (an early example of which is brilliantly depicted in the John Sloan etching: "The Woman's Page," of 1905.[2] Tabloids were blue collar with a vengeance. Thus when they reported about gangsters and organized crime the tabloids – *New York Daily News, New York World, Daily Mirror*, the *Evening Graphic*, and the old *Chicago Times* – related to city dwellers in their own vernacular, created an order at a level of urgency and danger, yes, but nevertheless put events in places people understood, created a grid of order in the urban chaos which they otherwise would not have had.

On the negative side, in every urban crime area was the risk, and likelihood, of a reporter who was on the take, who collaborated with the crime bosses to get printed what the crime bosses wanted known. The most outstanding case was Alfred "Jake" Lingle, Capone's lackey on the *Chicago Tribune*, assassinated by a rival gang in 1930 – which subsequently led to a

---

1. Jean Folkerts, Dwight L. Teeter, Jr., *Voices of a Nation: A History of Mass Media in the United States*, Second Edition (New York: Macmillan College Publ., Co., 1994) 364.
2. John Sloan, "The Woman's Page,"1905, from the series "New York City Life," available on line at http://nmaa-ryder.si.edu/collections/exhibits/metlives/womanspage.html

national scandal that exposed at least seven other reporters nation-wide who either blackmailed bootleggers, gamblers, and brothel keepers, or who were themselves the paid mouth pieces of organized crime within legitimate newspapers (usually unknown to the newspapers' executive editors).[1]

Thus many forces conspired at the time to create a moment in American history and popular, mass culture which was the time of the gangsters: the demographic urban shift and swift development of urban life, enormous domestic and international immigration to the cities, the crooks who ganged up and profited from the rapid, reckless, rushing development (notably the zealous moralism of Prohibition), and the different forms of mass media that conveyed the story to the general public. The gangsters were the key, the touchstone that tested the dangers and ambitions of the time.

Looking back, US author E. L. Doctorow in his brilliant novel about the New York 30s mobster Dutch Schultz, *Billy Bathgate* (1989), got close to the truth when he extolled the inspiration and energy, the awful thrill at work in these larcenous lives. His protagonist, Billy Bathgate, an all-American boy, would become a man of "a certain renown" because he was privileged to learn in the great school of the American streets, the streets of New York in the golden age of gangsterdom. Billy learned from the lips of the dying Dutch Schultz: "I don't want harmony. I want harmony". He learned that life is a juggling act of temptations, fears, abilities, and that dumb monster chance. Billy saw himself reflected in the actions of the larger-than-life hoodlums, learned about himself through them, but *not to be* them; because: "it is the peculiar power of mirrors to show you what is not otherwise there."[2]

The Gauge

For the student of American gangster movies in their golden age one of the things that must be figured out is why and how they acted as a social barometer. This is a question of the relation between any mass medium and its society. For which a library of possible answers exists. Regarding which I think there are seven fundamental issues and major answers in this case: *cause; consequences; safety valve; the subversive; the outcast hero; the traditional;* and *genre*.

Any mass medium can draw attention to an issue. But if something happens and it is not registered by a mass medium, does it happen? Common sense tells us it *does* – if, at least, any being sees it happen. But contrast an environment of very restricted, regulated mass media, as behind the former Iron Curtain; if crimes were not reported by the police, in the newspaper, then, in effect, in statistics, they did not happen. The case is very different in a nation which converts interesting events into even more interesting entertainments. The guiding rule is exploitation not obfuscation.

So does the mass media *cause* violent incidents? The known details in the shake-his-hands and pump-him-full-of-lead killing of Chicago bootlegger and florist Charles Dion "Deanie" O'Bannion (1892-1924) were repeated in

---

1. Well documented in "A Murder a Day," Chapter 12 in: John Kobler, *Capone – The Life and World of Al Capone* (New York: Fawcett Crest-G. P. Putnam's Sons, 1971) 274-291.
2. E. L. Doctorow, *Billy Bathgate* (New York: Random House, 1989) 321, 309, 300

the stagy *The St. Valentine's Day Massacre* (1967); as was the more humorous, idiotic yet equally lugubrious incident of Louis "Two-Gun" Alterie (1892-1935) going to the stables and assassinating the horse that kicked to death his bootlegger buddy Samuel J. "Nails" Morton – copied in a scene featuring crazed Tom Power (Cagney) and Matt Doyle (Ed Woods) in *The Public Enemy* (1931). The original incidents made the movies happen, not the other way around.

But didn't the media of the time at least create an environment where these bloody things made news, fed murderous egos? And, as we shall see, there is no question that some gangsters liked their pictures in the newspapers. But the best, and most long-lived, gangsters were sharp media managers. One does not find Meyer Lansky (1902-1985) on the cover of a newspaper until he was caught unawares by the tabloid *New York Sun* on June 28, 1949, on his way to Italy; headline, *sic*: "Lansky Sails in Luxury for Italy; Expected to Confer With Luciano – Underworld Big Shot and Wife in Regal Suite." (Lacey, 212). The media was another tool, like a car or a gun, you learned how to use. Or it would use you.

If one accepts that media causes violent incidents, this is the *injection theory* – which means people are puppets of the media, there is little individual choice in human actions since media is midwife, or the flare of media feeds the flame of ego. Or, to put it another way, out of sight is out of mind – "Watch and pray, that ye enter not into temptation: the spirit indeed is willing, but the flesh is weak."(Mark, 26. 41). Conservative, religious organizations of the 1930s, such as the Catholic Legion of Decency, which helped make the Motion Picture Production Codes progressively more restrictive, believed deeply in the injection theory.

A second skin of this onion of the truth of a mass medium as social gauge is the issue of *consequences*. I contend that most American mass media in the twentieth century, the period 1929-1951 being no exception, followed the *law of minimal consequences*. A medium is a mirror. Media reinforce trends, rather than initiate them. The movies no more invented "gangsterism" than designer jeans and hot pants in the 60s and 70s invented tight, buttocks-hugging, crotch-throbbing rear ends. But a new style can draw audience attention in exciting new ways to something that's been around for a long time .

American mass media generally do not rock the boat. They work to accommodate the viewer (a reason why investigative journalism is an exception rather than the rule in the US). *The Public Enemy* (1931) made a gesture toward boat rocking with the final roll-up postscript (after mummified Tom Powers slams back home) which announced that the movie wanted to: "depict honestly an environment that exists today in certain strata of American life, rather than glorify the hoodlum or the criminal." Well: yes and no; mostly no. Because, like Milton with Lucifer in *Paradise Lost*, the antagonist got the best of the story. The way to hell is easy and appeared to demand more humor, agility, and wit than its opposite – as attested by the diabolical brilliance of Cagney in *The Public Enemy*. For all its noble, final fillip, *The Public Enemy* wonderfully illustrated the old proverb about choice: that you can't have your cake and eat it too. A door's either shut or open; in *The Public Enemy*'s case the story was open more to screen swashbucklery than a civic's lesson.

All of which suggests that if the law of minimal consequences is true, then one result is that popular art is *populist art*; a social barometer – that measures a peoples' atmospheric pressure, their social and cultural brew of opinions, beliefs, fears, and hopes. The American public had strong mixed reactions to gangsters in real life and on the screen. One result of this is the burning fact that Fiorello La Guardia was elected Mayor of New York City in 1933 and did an excellent, if imperfect job, of cleaning up gangsterism. But another more uncomfortable fact is that, considering the movies as social barometer, as vast social mirror or treatment of the day's burning issue, mass media served as *safety valve*. A mass medium dealing with a controversial social issue (think of all the so-called pop protest songs that have been written since the 1960s) lets off society's steam: provides vicarious catharsis; safe, sanitary, voyeuristic objections – rather than the real thing.

Not to be paranoid, but one must consider a viewpoint of Noam Chomsky-like realism and manipulation, that one skin of the onion of truth is that gangster movies functioned as a kind of *panem et circenses*, bread and circus games (specially during the time of the Great Depression) that relieved social pressures. Gangster movies functioned as a form of *integration propaganda* at a time when many people were tempted to be gangsters. Much of the American audience who viewed the "early-1930s movie gangsters were poor and stemmed from immigrant stock" – and on the screen saw their kindred become criminals to make a buck. And, once they were successful, their "world impinged on the respectable world," while the "respectable people who wanted to gamble or get a drink during Prohibition entered into theirs" (Sklar, 179). On the dream screen the problem seemed to work itself out. The gangster movies displayed and resolved moral dilemmas – at a safe distance from real life. But as Noam Chomsky said in the documentary *Manufacturing Consent*: "Propaganda is to a democracy, what violence is to a dictatorship. " [1] Did this first great generation of gangster movies function as the social Prozac of their time? And, not to forget, the success of these films also contributed to the common well-being because mass media is a money-making, profitable system – as opposed to genuine, free, social protest, which causes strikes, slow downs, social strife and increases the general discontent.

Yet another layer of skin of the onion of truth is that the mass media is *subversive*. Its objective is to overturn the existing order; to revitalize through change, moral revolution, underground criticism; to tumble down the old in order to build up the new. Though, as one reads about real life gangsters, studies gangster movies, it is hard to see what new *order* is built up. One either sees a grotesque parody of straight American business life or a primitive, law of the jungle, Social Darwinism at work. By the 1930s a layer of organized crime was intrenched in American urban areas because it supplied "what society defined as illegal and what it tolerated as necessary"

---

1. *Manufacturing Consent – Noam Chomsky and the Media* . Necessary Illusions Productions Inc., dir. Mark Achbar and Peter Wintonick, produced by National Film Board of Canada, 1992.

(Lacey, 91) – mainly: gambling, prostitution, drugs, and various kinds of violence.

I think what is truly subversive about American gangsters and the movies that tell their stories is a new *cultural sensibility* presented and observed in the American mainstream. This is altogether appropriate to American civilization, where Thomas Jefferson's famous call for a revolution every twenty years is absolutely valid and true – as long as one accepts that these are cultural, perceptual revolutions that take place in America. Many a gangster in real life or on the screen was seen as a *sympathetic deviant*. Partly because, like Capone in real life, they would be cagey enough with their PR to play the part of social bandit – in the tradition of Railroad Bill or Billy the Kid – and occasionally practice some freehanded generosity by financing a bread line or paying off a poor person's mortgage.[1] But deeper than this was their sympathetic weirdness. Dutch Schultz's dying words as he lay in the Newark City, New Jersey, Hospital filled with bullets from two 38s, words as taken down by police stenographer F. J. Lang and later published, were diabolically eloquent (Nash, 357-362).

Striking for the gangsters is that they follow the characteristic growth and entrance curve for *the outcast hero* in American society and culture, who moves in from the margins; from the bottom up; from darkness to light – the "outcast" being a figure in American society and culture who ranges from the immigrant to the black, from the handicapped person to gay people, to teenager, to troubled veteran. The outcast hero begin *out* and too different to be taken for normal, then gradually the border opens, they are accommodated.[2]

In American cinema over the years just consider the change in presentation of a deranged person from Cagney's character in *White Heat* (1949) to Thornton's character in *Sling Blade* (1996), from Ida Lupinio's character in *They Drive By Night* (1940) to Olivia de Havilland's character in *The Snake Pit* (1948). Other factors intervened: specially the common social traumas of the Great Depression, World War Two, the domestic social unrest at the time of America's Vietnam War (1961-1973). But the gangster and his movie presentation helped to humanize the monsters, laid a foundation of human awareness, human witness, of "Sympathy for the Devil" which simultaneously enriched and created new risks and rewards for modern American society and culture.

That US mass media is also *traditional*, forms a complementary mix and match with the subversive skin of the onion. In the lives and stories of the gangsters the objective is also to support, perpetuate, and preserve the existing order, to maintain a heritage of the conventional, the accepted, the recognized. Don't they all love their mothers? (Though Paul Muni's Scarface loves his sister a little too much.) Marriage is affirmed (when they're at home). Or, when a gangster dies, as in *The Roaring Twenties* (1939) or *Angels With Dirty Faces* (1938), he lugs his bullet-stuffed body to the steps of the

---

1. The breakthrough work on this criminal type was: Eric J. Hobsbawn, *Social Bandits and Primitive Rebels* (Glencoe, 1959); reissued in 2000 as *Bandits* (New Press).
2. See the full outline of America's pantheon of heroes in John Dean, "America's Popular Heroes and Heroines and Their Demise in Modern American Culture," in *La consommation culturelle dans le monde anglophone* (Rennes: Presses Universitaires de Rennes, 1999) 205-234.

holy church or confesses his sins to a tough-minded but condolent priest. Gangsters are bad. But God is good. Here the characteristic growth curve is a culture that moves from the inside out; from the top down; brings the light of forgiveness into the darkness of vengeful hearts.

Finally there is the seventh fundamental cause why the gangster movie acts as a social barometer, it is a *genre*. Genres are the fruits and vegetables, the flavors and styles, of the entertainment industry with something for everybody – e.g., Science Fiction, Western, Musical, Gangster, Horror, Comedy, Adventure, Sword & Sandal. Movie genres are nourished by supply and demand cycles, by audience expectations. For Americans they are a twist on Anthelme Brillat-Savarin's well-known saying: *"Dis-moi ce que tu manges, et je te dirai ce que tu es"* – see what they watch and figure out what they are. "A genre forms a 'set of rules' for narrative construction that both filmmaker and audience knows."[1] Any genre is one in many, "a group of films having recognizably similar plots, character types, settings, filmic techniques, and themes. Such conventions are repeated sufficiently from film to film to make it obvious that all these works belong to a single group and that the filmmaker is relying upon the past use of these conventions and the audience's familiarity with them."[2] Thus: movie genres are: (i) formulaic styles; (ii) trends; (iii) an agreement between maker and consumer; (iv) a contractual narrative between artist and audience.

Genres express taste – and America is a taste culture, rather than a class culture. As Herbert J. Gans brilliantly established back in 1974 in *Popular Culture and High Culture*, Americans choose their style of expression as a matter of identity discovery and affirmation. Until the 1950s, America's dominant taste culture was low culture – mainly "skilled and semiskilled factory and service workers... semi-skilled white collar workers, the people who obtained nonacade – in short, a perfect audience for watching gangster movies on the screen, reading about gangster figures in the tabloids. They knew the neighborhood, the central city, the immediate immigrant background. These were their people, gone bad (or good). And there, America's low-culture folks of the time could say, but for the grace of God, goes I.

The gangster movie shared much with the western or any other male action drama. They were not dumb, but the issues were clear. The hero is sure of his masculinity, and his attempt to save society, or to protect his family or gang. Whether in Western or gangster movie, his independence of mind, resources, character is paramount. As Gans writes: the hero of the male action drama, which was the dominant story form for men and women before the 1950s in America, "works either alone or with 'buddies' of the same sex, depends partly on luck and fate for success, and is distrustful of government and all institutionalized authority."[3] For what it's worth, a well-known man of this generation kept his mind clear and his heart refreshed on the evening before D-Day, 5 June, 1944, by reading a

---

1. David Bordwell, Kristin Thompson, *Film Art – An Introduction* (New York: McGraw Hill, Inc.: 1993) 81.
2. Ira Konigsberg, *The Complete Film Dictionary*, Second Edition (New York: Bloomsbury, 1997) 164.
3. Herbert J. Gans, *Popular and High Culture* (1974) 89-91.

Western novel. He liked his male action dramas. His name was Dwight D. Eisenhower.[1]

Historical Profusion

To try to cut into, unfold, and open up the profusion of meanings at work in the fact and fiction-on-film of American gangsters as popular heroes, anti-heroes, and villains present in everyday American life from the 1920s through the 1950s is, of necessity, a multiple task. To fill out the picture now that we have the frame, one needs to look beyond the carriers of the message itself and its nature as social barometer to the events. To review some history.

America's gangsters, racketeers, and criminals have existed at all times, every level, and in all walks of life: blue collar to white collar, pink collar and dog's collar. Organized crime has followed the historical and political development of America's local and national economy since the early seventeenth century. One can no more say that organized crime did not exist before the twentieth century than one can claim that genocide did not exist before the twentieth century. Modern times rationalized and enhanced productivity, streamlined moral scruples, added diabolically effective leadership, granted unprecedented mass media exploitation.

Organized crime began with Cavalier Thomas Morton and his band at Merry Mount, Massachusetts, in defiance of lawman "Captain Shrimp" Miles Standish and Governor John Winthrop. Along with the gangs of rum runners and contraband merchants before and during the Revolution. Through the illegal groups at work in the internecine range and county wars of the eighteenth and nineteenth century West. With the spreading cankers of bank robbery crews, the frontier's property protection, land claim and water right's thieves, and the vigilante hostility of settlers toward the "drunken Indian" and the "opium-smoking Chinese," cankers that multiplied as railroad lines thickened their net and the towns mushroomed from Pennsylvania to California. Until finally one arrived at America's nineteenth and twentieth century eras of big-city, rationalized, newly innovative organized crime gone effulgent and cancerous with Tommy guns, fast cars, fancy explosives, broadcasts and blankets of tabloid news coverage and gangster movies, with the thick, slimy roots of political and police corruption tendrilled down, out, and across the land as America's national demographic shift underwent a sea change from mainly rural to mainly urban life beginning in the post World War One years.

Organized crime, like the Biblical poor, has always been with America. It is not the mainstream society and culture itself; it is underworld as opposed to upperworld; undercurrent as opposed to main current; place of the disrespected as opposed to the respected. In the 1920s-1950s period it was not new in kind, but original in presentation, representation, and restructuring. First of this new wine in old bottles was Arnold Rothstein (1882-1928), who established himself a decade before Capone.[2] America's

---

1. As documented in: Stephen Ambrose, *Eisenhower: Soldier and President* (New York: Touchstone, 1991).
2. This, of course, is debatable since organized crime's files are not exactly open to public scrutiny. Other contenders for America's first modern organized crime leader: the Brit Owen

organized crime world was there, hidden, in the grey areas, as that intellectual snob Walter Lippman pointed out, because "the underworld performs many services that respectable members of society call for" (Lacey, 91). Organized crime's lower position in America was true in both fact and fiction. Consider the "Top Ten Film" criterion. Not a single US gangster movie was among the top ten films released in cinemas in North America in either the 1920s, 1930s, 1940s, or 1950s.[1]

Defining Crime

Distinctions are necessary. Organized crime is one specific type of US crime. As rightly noted, in the USA organized crime "is best viewed as a set of shifting coalitions, normally local or regional in scope, between groups of gangsters, business people, politicians, and union leaders."[2]
Organized crime itself belongs to a smaller interacting circuitry within the larger, on-going processes of American society and culture. Crime is the illegal business of *city felons* or *farmboy crooks* (such as Charles Arthur "Pretty Boy" Floyd); in the period under consideration those were the only two regions that mattered.

Organized crime is committed in cohort; by a group or band of people joined by ethnicity, religion, old neighborhood allegiances, age or gender associations, or the rites and rituals peculiar to the criminal organization itself. Organized crime is not the lone outlaw or the particular incident (the thief, the rapist, the killer), or the occasional offenders who band together for sudden, illegal profit (American drinkers who decided to smuggle some illegal Scotch whiskey through Detroit customs during Prohibition). Organized crime is a corporate, methodical way of life – a business which both responds to and creates illegal demands, which is a formal, logical extension of American big business; the sharp practices of business "turned murderous," with "tax avoidance made systematic, competition followed to its logical conclusion" of destruction and murder. And thus the "effect, in modern America, of the visible growth of organized crime has been to cast doubt on business as a whole."[3]

The logic of American big business carried to its negative extreme is organized crime – one price Americans' pay for living in a business civilization. This is *not* to say American business is criminal (though a distinct form of this, "white collar" crime, exists). But America became in the twentieth century the world's preeminent business nation. Organized crime is thus appropriately characteristic of a people who find liberty, mobility, and independence in a marketplace mentality of getting bargains,

---

Madden (according to Irishman Breslin); the leader of USA's possiblly earliest Mafia ring which masterminded Police Chief Hennessey's murder in New Orleans in 1890; and whoever lead the 1880s-90s Whyos Irish-American, Five Points, NYCity slum gang. For more, see: Nash, *Bloodletters and Bad Men*.

1. For example, the anti-war hit *The Big Parade* (1925) was the N° 1 film of the US 1920s, and the chick flick *Gone With the Wind* the N° 1 film of the US 1930s. See: Russell Ash, *The Top Ten of Everything 1992* (London: A Queen Anne Press Book-Macdonald & Co Publs., 1991) 141-143.
2. Anon., "Other Models of Criminal Activity – Organized crime," in the *Encyclopaedia Britannica* on CD Rom: EB CD 99.
3. James Oliver Robertson, *America's Business* (New York: Hill and Wang, 1985) 250; James Cook, "The Invisible Enterprise," *Forbes*, September 29, 1980.

keeping up with the Joneses, checking out the goods, keeping up with the competition, getting a better deal, improving their material quality of life, and ceaselessly taking care of themselves in a bootstrap culture where the key mottoes are both "In God We Trust" and "Let the Consumer Beware" – since God helps those who help themselves.

Having said this, the fault line within American business has been the proliferation of "white collar" crime. Professional criminologists distinguish organized crime from what is known as either "corporate crime" or "white collar" crime. Two major differences hold between this kind of crime and organized crime. First, corporate crime in the US means "those illegal actions intended by the perpetrators principally to further the aims of their organizations rather than to make money for themselves personally."[1] That is, when that abstract corporate entity General Motors cheats and makes illegal profits – not when some clerk at GM skims from the office supplies. Second, by the end of the twentieth century it was estimated that the cost, and profit, of corporate crime was *triple* the amount of organized crime. But corporate criminals are far more rarely detected than organized crime offenders. Their "man in the grey flannel suit" demean in dress, voice, and overall manner provides very effective camouflage.[2]

In contrast, the American gangster is a brazen fellow, a trait from which he profits, for which he pays. I, for one, do not believe the gangster's story as told again and again in American culture is one of success or an Adamic, rags to riches, Horatio Alger individualism. The meat is sweeter closer to the bone. Like a fairy tale – "this story has been told before and will be told again" – the gangster films, specially of the late 20s and 30s vintage, were stories of "social pathos. If a disordered society led an individual to lawlessness his strength could not compare with the deviousness and force available to a lawless society."[3]

And, in so many ways with the gangsters real or imagined, there is the issue of visibility. Gangsters customarily draw the most heat and attention within the chain of corrupt business people, politicians, and union leaders to which they belong. Partly because that's their job. Gangsters run point; they function as the lead horse, cut into fresh territories, do the dangerous outriding, and draw enemy fire. This has always been their task amid the mavericks who comprise organized crime in America. The flamboyant character – possessing a range of abilities from great physical, psychological courage to sartorial and firearms display – the character of many in this bastardly breed is another reason why they stand out and become legendary. The American gangsters who live the longest and often reap the greatest profits take the risks but stay discreet, keep their gutsiness inward,

---

1. Britannica, BCD 99: "Crime and Punishment – 'White-collar' crime."
2. Idem, By late twentieth century the estimated cost of corporate crime in the USA was $200,000,000,000 (*two hundred billion dollars*) a year.
3. Robert Sklar, *Movie-Made America – A Cultural History of American Movies* (New York: Random House, 1975) 181. But which fairy tale archetype? Like Grimm's "Robber Bridegroom" tale – wherein a bright and undiluted innocence snares the wicked leader and his gang, or "The Wolf and the Fox" where the gluttonous one in the gang brings about his own downfall? In any case, fairy-tale format is essential since there is archetype of *story* as well as archetype of *character*. See: Linda Degh, *American Folklore and the Mass Media* (Bloomington, Indiana: Indiana University Press, 1994).

to be used judiciously; like Owen Madden (1892-1964) or "Little Man" Meyer Lansky (1902-1985) – their lives "pale copies of the vigor and creativity of the straight world," and who "learn to copy its honesty as well" (Lacey, 444).

At the other extreme are those who needed to be cock of the walk. Chiefly American mobsters like flashy Benjamin "Bugsy" Siegal (1906-1947) amid his fabulous Flamingo Hotel, the "Father of Las Vegas" as he is now known (and brilliantly interpreted by Warren Beatty in the 1991 production *Bugsy*); who dreamed that he and the Flamingo "would rise up so classy and legitimate that his gruesome past would dissolve. "[1] The world knows Al Capone above all American gangsters because he was *the* self-destructive prima donna of the breed, the one with the "brass balls" (as the street phrase goes) who had the guts to do anything. Including accept the decision of one hundred twenty five assembled very corrupt politicians, businessmen, and gangsters in Atlantic City in May of 1929 that he – aka: Big Al, Al Brown, Scarface – become the sacrificial lamb for them all, help take the heat off from government investigators, and accept to go to jail. Which he did. Which would begin an ever downward cycle of incarcerations from which Al Capone would never free himself. Weighed down by his brass balls.

So many American gangsters were gifted performers in the raw and thus prime specimens for the popular culture. They played their life out in public and asked, by dubious virtue of their displays, that their stories be told. Once again, consider Al Capone, who, when journalist Damon Runyon told him that anybody who gets into the newspapers so often as he did "often gets blamed for the nearest traffic accident" – so maybe he should keep his profile low. Runyon told Capone that the "gangsters might try to imitate truly rich women, whose names appear in the paper only at birth, marriage and death. 'What do they do if they want to see their picture in the paper?' Capone wondered. " (Breslin, 287). Big Al never stopped to do a reality check.

Gangsterism & Political Corruption

The occasional American politician, notably New York's mayor "Gentleman" Jimmy J. Walker (mayor: 1926-1932), would give the gangsters stiff competition as darlings of the press, publicity hounds, and targets of corruption scandals. But the corrupt politicians of the time thrived on deceit, not flamboyance. They understood Runyon's warning about staying *out* of the newspapers.

"Vast power and wealth... breed commercial and political corruption and incite public favorites to dangerous ambitions" as Mark Twain said. The gangsters we are mainly looking at were American popular heroes, antiheroes, and villains in the city and on the screen at a time of political corruption in high places. The three greatest periods of widespread political corruption in the USA were during the Grant administration of the 1870s (aka: "The Era of Good Stealings"), the Harding administration of the 1920s, and the Nixon administration of the early 1970s. Americans neither want

---

1. Michael Herr, "F. D. R. / Bugsy Siegel" in: Guy Peellaert, Michael Herr, *The Big Room* (London: Picador-Pan, 1986) 20.

nor expect all politicians to be corrupt; but it happens and, when it happens, it is specially disappointing. Political corruption is different from unethical dealings in other professions. Politicians enjoy the faith, trust, and support of those who voted for them and gave them their jobs. But politicians are people. Some of them cannot rise above their desire for selfish gain.

The 1920s were a period of disillusionment with politicians in general. Political corruption in the 1920s spread from the top down, in the cronyism and profiteering of Harding's Teapot Dome scandal (1921-1922); from the bottom up, in the speakeasy phenomenon that could not have existed without the collusion of police and politicians, the secret agreement for illegal purposes that the public knew about only too well as the 20s progressed to the 30s and US Prohibition finally ended in 1933.

The Gangster, American Crime, American Civilization

But the American gangster is not the child of political corruption. He takes advantage of it if the corruption already exists or nourishes it into existence. As "brain box" Lansky did: "Run a line into the prospective enterprise as quietly as possible... Nurture the line... Attach one end securely and then, without ever touching it personally, never let go."[1]

Plus, the gangster needs be understood as a criminal in the distinctive human context of American civilization and its formative values. Comparatively few Americans have committed crimes or seen the inside of a prison. But one has the peculiar American interaction of liberty, the gun, and great freedom of the press which spreads word and image.

From the beginning, something peculiar happened with law breaking in America. This is a fault line which runs through the nation from the 1600s to the present day. Historical awareness is called for again. The earliest American colonists were impressed by how there were more social irregularities in the New World than in the mother country. This was true of both colonial New England and Virginia. A constant cultural theme was set regarding crime beginning with colonial America.

From the outset, urban and demographic intensity was blamed. As John Winthrop said: "as people increased, so sin abounded."[2] But this was Winthrop's anti-London, anti-King Jamesian prejudice coming out. Winthrop refused to admit that rural folk in America were just as adept at committing crimes as city folk, as witnessed by William Bradford's spectacular catalogue of a farm hand's bestiality and punishment in his *Of Plymouth Plantation* (1631-1651).[3] The key irritant and inspiration in America for crime from the beginning was not the density of the "plantations" – but the new found freedoms, the lack of established, institutionalized restraints in this land.

Various reasons have been given for this, depending upon local customs and temptations, national and local institutions. My guess is that lawlessness in America was encouraged by the expansive, explosive principles of

---

1. Peellaert, Herr, *The Big Room* (1986) 126.
2. John Winthrop (1588-1649), Colonial governor of Massachusetts Bay Colony; as quoted from Winthrop's Journals (1630-1649) in: C. Miller, *The First Frontier: Life in Colonial America* (New York: Laurel-Dell, 1966) 253.
3. William Bradford, *Of Plymouth Plantation* (New York: Paragon Books-G. P. Putnam's Sons, 1962) 202-203; section: Plim: 17. 3. month, 1642.

liberty and equality. Over time, America became an odd, disorderly land by European standards; a king-less land, with the people the sovereign "We". As Thomas Carlyle noted in 1840, in America law and order – such as it existed – was given by the people who declared: "Liberty and Equality; no Authority needed any longer... we have had such *forgeries*, we will now trust nothing."[1] As the British Americanist Geoffrey Gorer underlined in 1955 (four years after Senator Estes Kefauver pioneered the televised Senate investigation with hearings into organized crime): "The typical American attitudes toward authority have remained substantially the same as those manifested by the framers of the American Constitution: authority is inherently bad and dangerous... authority must be circumscribed and limited as legal ingenuity can devise."[2] Gangsters were responding, typically, as anti-authoritarian Americans. And, as we shall see, among the people, in the popular culture, and exemplified by the world of the gangsters and elsewhere, this attitude was enunciated over and again not only as the virtues of liberty and equality and independence, but also of *toughness*.

Convertible Strength

The gangsters. The organized criminals. In fact or in fiction. Open up and smell the perfume of their spiky blossom *tough*. Note, in their ideal presentation, their extreme expectations of themselves and their kind, their hardness, mercilessness, strong-arm tactics, vigorousness, courage, persistence, ability to hang tough, endure hardship, take a difficult course, endure, be tough-minded, hard-boiled, be husky, heavy, be a hard case, even be tough in a certain neat, cheery "tuff" way – in a word, all the ordinary and slang meanings given to *tough* in American English.

Remove this verbal cornucopia and crown of meanings from the gangsters and you eviscerate the wit of Hamlet, the sex appeal of Monroe. *Tough* can be mocked or adored; but not neglected, and not removed. Toughness is the liquid which the tap root of their being drinks from. Sometimes it's unpleasantly cold and dark. The gangster in fact or on film is not always attractive.

In Chicago on May 7, 1929, at the end of a festive banquet at the Hawthorn Hotel in Cicero, Illinois, Al Capone beat three of his top killers to death with baseball bats because he believed they had betrayed him. In the morgue photos taken by Chicago news photographer Tony Berardi the victims' heads look like pulped pumpkins; a Weegee shot blurred. Not just in actions, but in hardball public relations, Capone would also brazen out his life's work with the press – and proclaim for all to hear that he was in a demanding business, supplying a people thirsty for forbidden fruit ("Somebody had to throw some liquor on that thirst. Why not me?" he said), cynically responding to a cynical time ("Lady, he told a *Chicago Tribune* reporter, Nobody's on the legit") (Kobler, 256).

When mobster Myer Lansky was relentlessly hounded and tailed by the FBI in the late 1960s, there was a telling incident when he almost lost his

---

1. Thomas Carlyle, *On Heroes, Hero-Worship and The Heroic in History* (London: Chapman and Hall, Ld., 1872 [orig. 1840] 187.
2. Geoffrey Gorer, *The Americans: A Study in National Character* (London: The Cresset Press, 1955) 20.

temper at one particular agent, Jerry Armstrong, who had breathed down Lansky's neck specially hard. Lansky told him to get off his back, sharply said: "A word to the wise is sufficient. " At which remark the FBI agent asked, "Was that a threat?" In retort, as he turned his back, Lansky said softly: "Jerry, you should read Kipling's poem, *If.*"[1] For Kipling's poem *If* was Lansky's word to the tough and the wise. That is:

> *If you can keep you head when all about you.*
> *Are losing theirs and blaming it on you.*
> *... can meet with Triumph and Disaster.*
> *And treat those two impostors just the same....*
> *Yours is the Earth and everything that's in it,.*
> *And – which is more – you'll be a Man, my son!*[2]

Tales of toughness continue well beyond any one gangster's life story. For the American movie audience of the time and the films which catered to them, the virtue of toughness was more important than the people who embodied it. Toughness was an elixir, a convertible strength, that followed a trajectory which would first be used to glorify the underworld's amoral brutality in Hollywood's initial trio of gangster movie hits: *Little Caesar* (1931), *The Public Enemy* (1931), *Scarface* (1932); then become the fire in the belly of tenacious police officers (often played by the same actors) in *G Men* (1935) or *Bullets or Ballots* (1936); be the grit that got the prisoners through the big house in *Twenty Thousand Years in Sing Sing* (1933) or *Angels With Dirty Faces* (1938); boil out in the stamina and fast-talking language, hard-hitting words of the journalist tough guys – men and women tough guys – in *The Front Page* (1931; 1974), *Front Page Woman* (1935), *His Girl Friday* (1940), *Meet John Doe* (1941), *Objective Burma* (1945); shine out in the sass and stiletto-heels style of the night club singers and the body delicious gun molls from *City Streets* (1931) through *The Racket* (1951).[3]

Toughness was fundamental tensile power in the ongoing story lines. A people adjust to their environment through the medium of stories. American narratives of the period on radio, in the newspapers, on the screen, about gangsters, cops, journalists, soldiers, cowboys or Indians often held out till the sweet or bitter end because the protagonists "had the guts" to hold out. This helped the listener, the reader, the viewer. The American gangster and his story in fact or on film was an expression of a commodious value.

Take the Big Three of Hollywood gangster movies in our designated period: Cagney, Bogart, Robinson. Consider how they comfortably adapted to another American genre of vernacular toughness, the Western – as in (among others) Cagney's *The Oklahoma Kid* (1939), Bogart's *Virginia City* (1940), Robinson's *Silver Dollar* (1932) or *Cheyenne Autumn* (1964). With each man their acting abilities, charisma, and roles undertaken – in combination with their fundamental lack of good looks and lanky height (thus making the most out of their disadvantages) – conspired to make the cocky "little

---

1. Robert Lacey, *Little Man* (1991) 320.
2. Rudyard Kipling (1865-1936), *If.*, circa 1910.
3. Gerald Mast, *A Short History of the Movies* (Indianapolis: Bobbs-Marrill Co., Inc. 1976) 266.

man" a dominating character type in Hollywood movies. As Robinson said: "I remember just before going onto the sound stage. I'd look in my dressing room mirror and I'd stretch myself to my full 5'5" or 5'6" [ab. 1. 65 meters] – whatever it was – to make me appear taller and to make me dominate all the others and to mow them down to my size."[1]

American real life and movie entertainment, the demographics and the celluloid dreams, nurtured this vein of toughness. It has continued for years. In the time with which we are concerned "tough" had many adepts. "F. D. R. and Bugsy Siegel were far from bedfellows, but they weren't complete opposites either," wrote Michael Herr in *The Big Room*. "Each had developed their patented blend of seductiveness and iron, each acquired a legendary stature... and each, in his time and in his way, was a traitor to his class."[2]

A striking newsreel of the 30s shows Franklin Delano Roosevelt being interviewed while standing on the back of a train, while returning to Washington from a fishing expedition in the Caribbean. The reporters asked Roosevelt if he's ready to return to the capital, to all its fights and wrangles, and F. D. R., replied: "Boys, I was fishing for barracuda and shark down there. And I caught them! And you ask me if I'm ready?"[3]

Gun and Country

Finally, added to this turbulent brew of the freedom of the new land, liberty and equality, the value of the hard man – from the outset another component which fostered crime in America was the matter of gun and love of country as a citizen's right. In effect, this was a cultural wedding, a covenant of self-protection. The gun, and therefore violence, was woven into the sinews of the US Constitution in Article Two's declaration that: "A well-regulated militia, being necessary to the security of a free State, the right of the people to keep and bear arms, shall not be infringed. "

This is unlike other cultures, as those of Europe, where a sense of protective violence is the property of the group; properly trained for this purpose or so chosen as an elite. In contrast, the historical pattern of US violence from the beginning "has been mostly anarchic, individualistic, spontaneous. " While the European pattern of violence has a sanctified, institutionalized character, "typified by collective actions" – that is: by armies, sects, crusades, political parties and classes which clash with one another.[4] Thus the fault lines for each nation and the troubling results. Europe fostered cultures of fascism. America nourished cultures of gangsterism.

---

1. James Robert Parish, Alvin H. Marill, *The Cinema of Edward G. Robinson* (New York: A. S. Barnes and Co., 1972) 15. See also the toughness in their *horror movies*: Cagney's *Man of a Thousand Faces* (1957), Bogart's *The return of Dr. X* (1939), Robinson's *Night Has a Thousand Eyes* (1948)
2. Michael Herr, "F. D. R. / Bugsy Siegel" in: Guy Peellaert, Michael Herr, *The Big Room* (London: Picador-Pan, 1986) 16.
3. *Just Around the Corner* [A History of the American 30s], dir. Alexander Scourby, a Stephen F. De Zito-Post Newsweek production, 1976.
4. Stuart Miller, *Understanding Europeans*, 2nd edition (Santa Fe, New Mexico: John Muir Publications, 1996) 7.

Extremist Authoritarian Movements

American gangsters never formed a political party but they invite a political reading. In many ways in the 1920s-1950s period gangs were run as extremist authoritarian movements. They had all the makings. They learned their extremist political habits on the streets (actions echoed by the gangster movies). Organized crime and its followers proclaimed violence their highest value, their ultimate form of arbitration. Violence organized the gang members, marshalled them to war against whatever hit they wanted to profit from. These customs began when they were young. American children through the 1950s regularly played "cops and robbers" in imitation of that larger, stronger adult world. Street games of this kind, specially in the poorer neighborhoods, could be done without the space or material goods demanded by kite-flying, hoop rolling, or bat-and-ball games. With "cops and robbers" power displays of verbal and physical violence, demagogic exploitation of local fears, firm leadership, acts of loyalty, unquestioning obedience, showy generosity developed.

For young city kids in low to lower-middle class neighborhoods in America at this time, their gangs and the tough street games they practiced were their primary, earliest, social and political training. Contemporary witness of this can be seen in the activist, critical, and brilliant documentary *The City* (1939), seen by hundreds of thousands of people at the New York World's Fair (1939-1940), which illustrated the static, stultifying conditions for children in city life at this time.[1] It was only the growth of Levittown suburbs in the USA's post-World War Two years that would help change this situation for lower-income, metropolitan Americans. In the New York area this meant people left the inner city, moved out to the Bronx, along the Sound, to Connecticut and farther.

Gangster movies were far down on a list of real-life influences which nourished gangster life. They displayed the problem much more than they ever caused it. They were a symptom but not the cause. Yet once the Motion Picture Production Code of 1934 kicked in, the US entertainment industry showed they were acutely aware of the lead-and-role-model draw which gangster movie stories had; an awareness clearly evidenced in the teachy, goody-goody, yet charming *Angels with Dirty Faces* (1938). But the street was a free and ruthless place which neither the '34 Code, Joseph Breen, nor the Catholic Legion of Decency controlled. In young Alphonse Capone's generation about 60% of his neighborhood, Italian immigrants, were illiterate and fewer than 1% ever got to high school.[2] Kids entertained themselves in proto-political ways. The story is told of the young boy, ten year old Al Capone, how in his home neighborhood of the Garfield Street district in New York he saw an old woman's wash board stolen. On the spot he organized a gang to get it back, rescued it, personally beat up the kid

---

1. *The City*, dir. Ralph Steiner, Willard Van Dyke, based on outline by Pare Lorentz, American Institute of Planners, 1939.
2. John Kobler, *Capone: The Life and World of Al Capone* (New York: G. P. Putnam-Fawcett, 1971) 16. The myth of criminal instincts for this Italian generation was quite unfounded. While in 1910 they made up about 11% of the total foreign-born population in the USA, the produced only about 7% of the foreign-born convicts and juvenile delinquents. In 1919 a federal study placed Italians 12th among seventeen nationalities in terms of imprisonment rankings.

who stole it, then returned the wash board to the poor old lady. Immediately after which he strode through the neighborhood in parade-like fashion with his new gang behind him whooping and hollering about what a great guy he was. Young Al was a grade "A" student of the street.[1]

As proto-extremist authoritarian political movements, gangs of young and old at the time discriminated against races and creeds – which poured oil on their own fire. Read politically, for a poor neighborhood, a disenfranchised public, gangsters and gangsterism could be an authoritarian temptation – a phenomenon characteristic of democracies when the legitimacy of the elected government is seriously questioned, when there are profound strains of race, religion, and the social order in the world at large.

Additional major ideas put into practice by organized crime were "elitism, racialism, Social Darwinism, irrationalism, the exaltation of violence, the notion that the group has a reality superseding that of the individual, and nationalism."[2] These can be clicked off one by one. For example, American gangster elites: the tough guys themselves, the hierarchy in each mob that went from bookmaking runners and empty-bottle collectors up to The Boss and his praetorian guard. The racialism was there in the self-serving, immigrant-based cult of the Neapolitan, Abruzzian, Sicilian, Irish, Jewish, Polish fellow gang members – that only *your people*, of your blood and religion, could be trusted; anyone else barely human.

Social Darwinism was displayed in the law of the city streets that Edward G. Robinson or Cagney typified when they made their way up their fractured ladders of success in *Little Caesar* or *Public Enemy*. The very name: "Little Caesar" – reeks of extremist authoritarianism, fascism, demagoguery. Or Social Darwinism was evident in the way young Al mastered the crowd of kids in his neighborhood. Irrationalism there in the white, manly heat of anger the gangster displayed in order to keep his friends and enemies guessing. Exaltation of violence? To quote Doctorow again (from a scene where his young hero first fires off): "I will never forget how it felt to hold a loaded gun for the first time and lift it and fire it, the scare of its animate kick up the bone of your arm, you are empowered there is no question about it, it is an investiture, like knighthood, and... the credit is yours because it is in your hand... the credit is all yours, with the slightest squeeze of your finger a hole appears... and how can you not be impressed with yourself, how can you not love this coiled and sprung causation, I was awed, I was thrilled."[3]

Group reality superseded individual: that your gang was your ultimate family – for better or worse, by choice or necessity.[4] Nationalism was

---

1. Anecdote as narrated by Laurence Bergreen, author of *Capone: The Man and the Era* (New York: Touchstone, 1996) and related by him in: *Al Capone – Scarface*, dir. Bill Harris, produced by Tower Productions-A & E Network, 1995.
2. Roy C. Macridis, *Contemporary Political Ideologies: Movements and Regimes*, fifth edition (New York: HarperCollins Publishers, 1992)152.
3. Doctorow, *Billy Bathgate* (1989) 145.
4. Though, important to note, specially strong in opposition to the demagoguery and authoritarianism of gangsters and gang in the American movie and story tradition, has been the American genre of the boxing movie. Specially notable: the plot type with the prizefighter who opposed the mob, the corrupt system – such as Robert Ryan refusing to pull his last fight in

expressed by some gangsters of the time in their outspoken patriotism, as with Myer Lansky who fixed his birth date at July 4th. Or in the outright, self-serving patriotism of Charles "Lucky" Luciano's collusion with the US military – first with the Navy and anti-sabotage work along the New York docks during World War Two, and then by helping to provide vital intelligence information during the US invasion of Sicily in 1943[1]. Was this patriotism as "the last refuge of a scoundrel" or selfless love of country? A muddle of both and something else; actions which Hollywood cashed in on with the movie *All Through the Night* (1942) – in which Humphrey Bogart and his gang chased down fifth columnists in World War Two New York.

Finally, gangster patriotism and nationalism should be considered as expressed by the mob boss who thinks of himself as a nation unto himself, as if he was the father of his own independent, all-American domain (not unlike America's lonely militia men at the end of the late twentieth century). As proof, listen in on what Al Capone said during a telephone interview with journalist-sportswriter Hype Igoe of the *New York American*. Said Capone:

> *'Do they want my old street address? Ninety-five Navy Street. Off of Myrtle Avenue. I'm baptized right around the corner. You want the church? Saint Michael's.'*
> *'That's great,' Igoe said.*
> *'Don't you want to know who my godfather was?' Capone asked.*
> *'Who?'*
> *'No one,' Capone said. 'Since the church was put up I'm the only guy never had a godfather. Do you know why?'*
> *Igoe was silent on the other end of the phone.*
> *'I just axt you to axt me a fucking question!' Capone said.*
> *'Why?' Igoe said.*
> *'Because I'm the godfather of everything.' (Breslin, 289)*

As if he was a one-man, extremist, nationalist, authoritarian political movement in and of himself.

Time After Time

American gangsters in the 1920s and 30s were beautifully, synchronistically, of their time – and yet parallelled by another. In classical echo they functioned like a real and imagined tribe of Greek warriors for the American *demos*; *Iliad* and *Odyssey* parables of war and wandering that alternately and interactively proclaimed: "Give Me What I Want!" and "Protect Me From What I Want!". In echo of medieval times, their stories were American versions of the Inferno and Purgatorio – as interesting as hell and purgation allows. They were strong medicine, a protest reaction expressed in the popular culture. "The tough, uncompromising way in which Robinson, Cagney and Bogart handled any situation was no doubt

---

The Set Up (1949) or John Garfield's fighting integrity, noble looser stance in *Body and Soul* (1947).
1. Nash, 220-221; Lacey,116-124. Luciano in New York used the likes of Joseph "Joe Zocks" Lanza, boss of the Fulton Fish Market, who in turn used the area fishermen; it worked by hierarchy, chain-of-command, pay off, and working-class fear – see. e. g. Breslin, 400-405.

admired by the private citizen, who might have liked to emulate such behavior as a means of lashing out against economic oppression, but who would never have the courage or conviction to do so."[1] They were this, and more.

This violent protest reaction expressed in the language and stories of the popular culture exposed a pattern of relationships, a process of traits, which exhibited itself again in American life in the 1960s, for another time and generation, with the freewheeling, morally reckless rock 'n' roll stars or wandering Neal Cassidy-Dean Moriarty-Easy Rider figures who embodied much this same kind of real and imagined unbridled energy, anarchy, and creativity. Numerous are the musical echoes and bitter-sweet links in the music of this generation with the outlaw, the gangster, and organized crime. Bob Dylan's songs roll through a gamut of sinuously ambiguous gangster heroes, as in: "Highway 61 Revisited," "John Wesley Harding," or the long ballad "Joey" about mobster "Crazy Joe" Gallo murdered in a Little Italy gang war in 1972.[2]

Both the 30s and the 60s yielded political, social, and popular culture responses to public and personal crises in the lives of Americans that lasted well beyond the end of the Great Depression or the anti Vietnam War protest years. In both cases, and stemming mainly from the sympathetic stories in the popular culture which absorbed the political and economic changes in society, the radical innovation of glorifying the outcast, the outsider, the excluded or even the monstrous person became the new orthodoxy of the American consensus. There was consequently a popular, moral deregulation of American life in both the 30s and the 60s. In both periods the range of what was understandable, normal, permissible in mainstream American life became larger than ever before. Another Jeffersonian revolution.

The negative side of this change, as a wide range of critics have repeated (specially in criticism of the 60s) was to neglect the treatment of genuine deviancy in American society, at times aggravated by rationalized shortcuts, such as emptying mental hospitals onto the streets when cities like New York underwent severe debt crises in the 1970s, or to define deviancy upward and create a new witch-hunt, mass-phobia mentality against a range of sex abuse crimes.[3] The positive side was the inclusion and gradual normalization of those who had previously been considered either physically or psychologically crippled, handicapped, perverted. The result was a new risk, and a new generosity of spirit – which began in America's twentieth century popular culture with the sympathetic inclusion of the gangster.

---

1. Robert Bookbinder, *Classic Gangster Films* (New York: Citadel Press Book-Carol Publishing Group, 1985) 7-8.
2. Bob Dylan, *Writings and Drawings* (New York: Panther, 1974) 316-317, 408; "Joey": cut six on the Dylan album *Desire* (1976). See also: "American Rebels and the Quest for Self," in: *Reviews in American History*, 1976, 251-257. CF as well: valid comparison between 60s and Prohibition periods, in that, for a time about as long as Prohibition, the 60s was ripe with the illegal romance of drug dealing, for which an embarrassment of riches in the popular culture exists from the songs of Arlo Guthrie (i. e., "Coming into London" to the films of Barbara Hershey (*Dealing*, 1972). The 60s romance with illegal substances ended when: (i) it went from a populist to a mob activity; (ii) crack cocaine hit the streets.
3. Charles Krauthammer, "Defining Deviancy Up", *The New Republic*, November 22, 1993, 20-25.

Figures of Defiant Sadness

In postscript I would add that American gangsters as presented in fact and fiction incorporate responsibilities with individual achievement; are an ultimate and extreme example of group belonging and self-reliance. They disobey the law to serve their gang and themselves. They are upsetting American proof of the fact that liberty is always achieved against the grain; since there is so much in human life that forbids liberty.

Gangsters are figures of defiance but also great objects of sadness. No Americans in any place or time have had a monopoly on how hard it can be to endure, to get by, let alone to prosper in the New World. It can get pretty depressing. As folk singer Huddie Leadbetter (1888-1949) sang of this roving darkness in American life: "Sometimes I lives in the country. Sometimes I lives in town. Sometimes I haves a great notion to jump into the river and drown." In the context of American society and culture American gangsters at their ideal best – from *Little Caesar* to *The Sopranos* – express a liberating joy; over liberated, sure – but that's the risk. They run the red light.

One may read the gangster in fact and on film as one reason why it is a mistake to overestimate American happiness; as many Americans do. If the American people are so genuinely happy, then why has the nation produced the greatest entertainment industry which has ever existed? They need to *become* happy, not because they *are* happy.[1] The gangster is one way to cope in reality and in the imagination. Specially when private or public times get rough. They are a mediating roadway. Catharsis is not just what happens when the tragic hero dies at the end of a story, the audience feels relieved, goes home to drink a glass of warm milk and goes to bed. Catharsis is listening to the blues again and again and again.

Selected Bibliography

BRESLIN, Jimmy, *Damon Runyon – A Life*, New York, Dell-Laurel, 1991.
DOCTOROW, E. L. *Billy Bathgate*, New York, Random House, 1989.
GRAHAM, Hugh Davis, *Violence in America: Historical and Comparative Perspectives*, Ted Robert Gurr, Editors, Beverly Hills, California: 1979, revised edition, Preface: Milton S. Eisenhower.
JEAN folkerts, Dwight L. Teeter, Jr., *Voices of a Nation: A History of Mass Media in the United States*, Second Edition, New York, Macmillan College Publ., Co., 1994.
KOBLER, John, *Capone – The Life and World of Al Capone*, Fawcett Crest-G. P. New York, Putnam's Sons, 1971.
LACEY, Robert, *Little Man: Meyer Lansky and the Gangster Life*, Boston, Little, Brown and Company, 1991.
MOWRY, George E, Ed., *The Twenties – Fords, Flappers & Fanatics*, Englewood Cliffs, New Jersey: Prentice Hall Inc., 1963, "A Need for Heroes," 75-88.
NASH, Jay Robert, *Bloodletters and Bad Men*, New York, Warner Books, 1987, three volumes.
PEELAERT, Guy, Michael Herr, *The Big Room*, London, Pan-Picador, 1986.
WOODWISS, Michael, *Organized Crime, USA, Changing Perceptions from Prohibition to the Present Day*, University of Sussex Printing Unit, Brighton, UK, 1990, BAAS Pamphlets in American Studies 19.

---

1. Note the common American greeting: "Happy?" Which is like "Hi!", only tinged with a reassuring need for *call* – "Happy?" – and *response* – "Sure." Something is missing. NB: I disagree strongly with Robert Warshow's caveat (in his remarkably quirky & influential "The Gangster as Tragic Hero", 1958): that the gangster type rests on fantasies of irresponsible freedom, is a warning of how city can transform man to monster, exhibits an unhappiness that is a reprobation of his society. See Warshow online at: http://www.mtsu.edu/~slavery/warshow.htm

The Classic Three :
Little Caesar, *The Public Enemy* et *Scarface*
Par Dominique Sipière

Cet incontournable trio est moins homogène qu'il ne semble, même s'il partage assez de traits communs pour fonder un genre incontesté de façon durable. L'unité du groupe, on l'a déjà dit, est facile à identifier : les décors, l'emprunt massif aux personnages « modèles » de New York et de Chicago, le rythme rapide, les dialogues omniprésents dans une langue jusqu'alors réservée à la rue, les éclairages mais, surtout, la structure immuable des récits de type « rise and fall » assurent aux trois films une forte unité de ton, de narration et de style. D'où ce titre de « Classic Three », d'étalon auquel se mesureront les films qui les suivent. Mais on sait aussi que l'unité de façade qui paraît souder les gangs résulte d'un équilibre précaire entre des *individus* bien différents, à la personnalité et aux origines très affirmées.

Leur genèse commune brasse la biographie des vrais gangsters, l'atmosphère des villes dans lesquelles les auteurs des romans ou des scripts ont eux-mêmes vécu, des enquêtes « sociologiques » dont se vantent volontiers W.R. Burnett et H. Hawks ou les souvenirs personnels des auteurs de *Beer and Blood* qui inspirera assez librement *The Public Enemy*. La rencontre entre les gangsters et le cinéma parlant est plus intéressante : Burnett en écrivant *Little Caesar* pense déjà au cinéma. Son Joe Massara est avant tout un Rudolf Valentino qui a mal tourné [1]... Mais les films *de* gangsters ne sont pas seulement des films *avec* des gangsters et les Classic Three sont très différents de leurs prédécesseurs, *The Musketeers of Pig Alley*, de Griffith, ou les films avec Lon Chaney, qui sont des *drames* d'un tout autre style.

D'abord parce que les trois films sont articulés autour de récits antérieurs d'une autre nature : pour *Little Caesar* on pense à l'Agathocles de Machiavel[2] et au « gutter Macbeth[3] » dont parlait lui même Burnett à propos de Rico, pour *Scarface* à l'interview de Hawks qui insiste sur le noyau initial selon lequel les Borgia règnent sur Chicago[4]... Ces récits ont servi de grille au regard porté sur le crime et ils ont anticipé la mise en images et la projection, à partir de l'écran, de la *voix* des gangsters jusqu'alors *inouïe*. On pourrait comparer l'avènement du gangster au cinéma (et sa réussite, car sans succès public il serait oublié) avec l'invention de la photographie au XIXe siècle : tous les éléments de l'invention étaient prêts depuis des siècles – chambre claire, sels d'argent, optique... – mais leur rencontre vers 1830 est née d'un *désir* spécifique, à un certain moment, à l'intérieur d'une certaine

---

1. W.R.Burnett, *Little Caesar*, p. 102
2. Dans un chapitre du *Prince* intitulé « Ceux qui accèdent au pouvoir par le Crime ».
3. Il existe même une version gangstérisée de la pièce de Shakespeare sous le joli titre de *Joe Macbeth* (GB : Ken Hughes, 1955, avec Paul Douglas).
4. Hawks raconte son dialogue avec le scénariste Ben Hecht : « I wanted Ben Hecht to write on (Al Capone) and he said, "Sure, what are you going to make?" I said, "A gangster picture." He said, "Hell, you don't want to make one of those things." I said, "Well, Ben, I've got an idea that the Borgia family is living in Chicago today. See, our Borgia is Al Capone, and his sister does the same incest thing as Lucretia Borgia." And he said, "Well, let's start tomorrow morning." » *Hawks on Hawks*, Joseph McBride, U. of California Press, 1982, p. 45

société. De même, la première rafale de films de gangsters est tirée pour un public qui l'avait pressentie et qui l'attendait déjà.

L'écrivain W.R. Burnett part du pouvoir des *mots* et d'une volonté de rupture dans le langage romanesque alors en vigueur : « I wanted to develop a style of writing based on the way American people spoke – not literary English. Of course, that the Chicago slang was all around me made it easy to pick up[1] ». Comme le récit est livré sur un ton neutre grâce à des phrases précises et très brèves, les dialogues, très abondants, ressortent avec plus de vigueur encore. Munby insiste sur l'ethnicité du film (Burnett dit que c'est « an Italian picture ») et il faudra y revenir, mais seul un personnage (Blackie, p. 35) est encore empêtré dans un mélange italo-anglais, tandis que Rico, né à Youngstown, Ohio, insiste sur le fait qu'il ne sait pas un mot d'Italien... La grammaire est involontairement malmenée (pour confirmer qu'il a vu le Big Boy, Killer Pepi insiste : « Yeah, I brung him ») et la courtoisie limitée (le policier annonce : « I'll get that swell-headed Dago... » (p. 61). Même le discours indirect est contaminé : « Rico was nobody. Just a lonely Youngstown yegg that the bulls wanted » (p. 99) et ses regrets intimes massacrent grammaire et lexique en même temps que Joe : « I ought to plugged him! » (p. 99). Mais le livre ne transcrit aucune trace d'*accent* italien.

Guérif reprend le récit de l'enthousiasme de Mervyn LeRoy quand Jack Warner lui a donné à lire *Little Caesar*. LeRoy revient voir Zanuck et Wallis le soir même : « Ce type, Burnett, il doit avoir écrit ce livre uniquement pour que j'en fasse un film[2] ». Jack Warner doute un peu mais il pressent que le public attend ce genre de film et LeRoy confirme : « Je sentais que le public était plus mûr que nous voulions bien le reconnaître ». On touche ici à une question particulièrement difficile : que savons-nous vraiment du public de l'époque et de ses réactions, une fois acceptée l'idée de sa diversité ? Mathew Guillen[3] met en garde à juste titre contre les projections que nous pourrions faire à partir de nos habitudes d'un autre siècle. Mais nous savons au moins que ces films ont rencontré un immense succès commercial et nous disposons de plusieurs témoignages de l'époque. Je me limiterai ici à trois réactions de la critique contemporaine des trois classiques : le *Harrison's Report* s'adresse aux distributeurs et leur apporte un jugement utilitaire sur les risques encourus avec le public et les censeurs locaux ; le *New York Times* garde ses distances mais son ton très ironique indique que le critique s'est bien amusé et que les lecteurs ne s'inquiètent pas trop ; *Variety* est beaucoup plus intéressé et, somme toute, plus proche d'un regard contemporain qu'on ne pouvait l'imaginer.

Voici, par exemple, comment *Harrison's Report* (1930, p. 195) réagit à la nouveauté que constitue *Little Caesar* :

> *A well produced gangster story, depicting realistically the rise and fall of a gunman (...) But it is unsuitable for the youth and for children, because of its demoralizing nature ; it glorifies a crook. (...) The plot was taken from the well known book by W. R. Burnett...*

---

1. Interview de Burnett citée par Munby, p. 47
2. Guérif, *op. cit.* p. 52
3. Voir chapitre suivant.

La mise en garde s'adresse aux directeurs de salles et elle est très ferme. Les critiques des deux autres « classiques » montrent bien la diversité des réactions :
– *Public Enemy*

> ... it is demoralizing. It is, in fact, much more demoralizing than the others in that the cutthroats are not punished in the end by the authorities, the two gangsters are exterminated by their rivals when they went out to shoot it out with them. It is the type of picture that will bring upon the industry the worst kind of regulation, and the most stringent laws ; so stringent that it will be unlawful even to show a criminal. (...) It is 'poison' as a Sunday show in small towns.
> Harrison's Report, 1931, p. 70 (May 2, 1931)

> There is a prologue apprising the audience that the hoodlums and terrorists of the underworld must be exposed and the glamour ripped from them. There is an epilogue pointing the moral that civilization is on her knees and inquiring loudly as to what to be done.
> The New York Times. April 24, 1931

A l'évidence, le *Times* s'amuse aux dépens des censeurs.

> The audiences yesterday laughed frequently and with gusto as the swaggering Matt and Tom went their paces... The laughter was louder and most deserved when the two put a horse "on the spot", the reason being that the animal had had the temerity to throw Nails Nathan, the gang leader...

Cette fois, le critique ricane ouvertement sans qu'on sache tout à fait de qui il se moque : de la véridique histoire de 'Nails' Morton dont les lieutenants l'ont ainsi vengé, ou de la complaisance du film ? En tout cas, ces rires nous rappellent opportunément une vraie différence de 'sensibilité' entre les époques : la mort d'un cheval ne suscitait guère d'émotion dans un milieu d'origine rurale, transplanté en ville.

Variety, qui évoque également la mort du cheval, semble confirmer à la fois l'indifférence aux animaux et la sympathie pour le gangster : « It's a solid audience whoop ».

> Roughest, toughest and best of the gang films to date. (...) It's so strong that full-throated protests across the country are either apt to smother or enhance its natural box office capabilities. There's no lace in this picture, although there's a nance piece of business included. It's low-brow material given such workmanship as to make it high-brow. This film seems sure of two or three weeks at the Strand. Especially in view of what other gang pictures have done at the same house where this type of film draws a prize fight crowd.
> Variety, April 29, 1931

– *Scarface*. Cette fois, le contraste est encore plus marqué entre les trois critiques :

Harrison's Report, April 23, 1932, est indigné :

> This is the most vicious and demoralizing gangster picture produced. There is no doubt that it will be resented by civic, educational and religious organizations ; and rightly so, for both in action and in talk it is brutal and obscene. If ever an argument was needed by reform bodies in favor of censorship, this picture will furnish it. Even though the hero is killed in the end, there is no moral

> in the story. (...) There is not one character in the picture that arouses sympathy.

The New York Times. May 20, 1932, reste neutre :
> Shakespearian tragedy... "Pictorial recapitulation of the high lights of Chicago's recent history of crime"...

Variety, May 24, 1932, au contraire, dissimule à peine sa jubilation :
> Presumably the last of the gangster films, on a promise, it is going to make sorry that there won't be anymore.(...) It isn't for children. And it's pretty strong even for adults. But to keep people away from the theatre it plays will be about the same as keeping 'em out of speakeasies.
> ... the punch is on the violence, the killings, the motives and the success of the cast in giving the director what he wants. Paul Muni : "He's tough enough here to make Capone his errand boy..."

Je voudrais maintenant insister sur la diversité à l'intérieur même du groupe fondateur : le trio des *Classic Three* forme bien un ensemble homogène, mais il en est de ces films comme des gangsters qu'ils représentent. Les récits ne cessent de proposer des *duos* aux spectateurs, mais pour qu'ils s'opposent bientôt en *duels*, dans un univers où il n'y pas la place pour un pouvoir partagé. La survie n'est possible que par la différenciation des espèces et des individus.

Les récits

On trouvera des résumés très détaillés des trois récits sur le web[1] mais il ne sauraient remplacer les films eux-mêmes, assez facilement disponibles dans de bonnes copies vidéo. Voici une proposition de résumés plus succincts[2] :

Little Caesar (Warner, filmé en été 1930, sorti en janvier 1931)

Ascension

Une voiture s'arrête en pleine nuit devant une station service. Un homme en sort, menace le pompiste, le tue et s'enfuit avec quelques billets : Rico Bandello et son complice Joe Massara vont ensuite dîner dans un petit restaurant au bord de la route. Rico, après avoir retardé l'horloge pour se créer un alibi, dit sa lassitude des petits coups provinciaux et son désir de gagner la ville pour y devenir « quelqu'un », comme ce Pete Montana dont la presse décrit le banquet en son honneur. Joe, au contraire, voudrait en finir avec le banditisme et devenir danseur mondain.

En ville, au *Palermo*, le bar de Sam Vettori, Rico se fait engager comme homme de main. Vettori le présente à son gang et il reçoit le nom de Little Caesar, d'abord perplexe, puis prêt à en assumer le présage. En parallèle, Joe est engagé comme danseur au *Bronze Peacok* où il forme un couple avec Olga Stassof.

---

1. Voir, à partir du site « google » ou de www.filmsite.org/littc.html, les solides résumés de Tim Dirks.
2. Je suggère aux lecteurs de se livrer pour eux-mêmes à l'exercice des résumés : ils offrent une occasion de s'approprier la structure d'ensemble d'un récit à condition, justement, de les contester.

Le gang prépare un hold-up au *Peacok*, le 31 décembre à minuit, avec la complicité de Joe, mais Rico tue McClure, un policier de haut niveau : cette mort sert à la fois de déclencheur de l'ascension de Rico et de faute initiale qui provoquera sa chute.

Gloire

Rico neutralise Vettori et prend le pouvoir sur le gang, tandis que le policier Flaherty remplace McClure. Tony, le chauffeur de la bande, semble prêt à les dénoncer : Rico l'abat sur les marches de l'église où il allait sans doute se confesser. L'enterrement est l'occasion de multiples rencontres formelles entre les protagonistes (Rico, Joe, Flaherty...)

Un banquet est offert en l'honneur du nouveau boss : le discours de Rico, qui ne boit pas, est très bref. Aussitôt parvenu au sommet, Rico est menacé par son rival Little Arnie qui envoie deux tueurs pour l'exécuter. Leur échec permet à Rico de chasser Arnie de la ville avec un certain panache, qui a pour conséquence sa promotion auprès du Big Boy, à la place du Pete Montana que Rico admirait tant au début du film.

La carrière parallèle de Joe comme danseur l'amène à un succès sans crime avec Olga. Quand Rico lui demande de le rejoindre, Joe refuse avec force et Rico – pour la première fois – sort son revolver mais hésite à tuer son (seul) ami. Olga convainc enfin Joe de témoigner auprès de Flaherty que Rico est bien l'assassin de McClure.

Chute

Rico doit fuir, sans argent, puis se cacher dans un hospice où il se met à boire. Quelques mois plus tard, sur une provocation de Flaherty dans le journal (il l'accuse de lâcheté) Rico téléphone au policier, lui donne un rendez-vous et meurt sous ses balles avant de se rendre. Il prononce ses derniers mots (« Is this the end of Rico? ») devant l'immense affiche qui célèbre la réussite de Joe et Olga dans un musical : *Tipsy, Topsy, Turvy*.

Public Enemy (Warner, filmé en février et mars 1931, sorti en mai 1931)

Enfances

Le film débute par une chronique des premières années du siècle à Chicago : en 1909, deux enfants irlandais (Tom et son ami Matt) traînent dans les rues et les bars et ils se jouent des policiers d'un grand magasin. Tom est cruellement battu par son père policier et les deux garçons vendent à bas prix à Putty Nose, leur médiocre Fagin, des objets volés. En 1915 le même Putty leur fournit un revolver pour leur premier hold-up, qui tourne mal : Tom sursaute devant un ours empaillé, son coup de revolver attire un policier qui tue un des garçons et trouve la mort à son tour. L'irréparable a été commis et Putty, le chef de la bande, a pris la fuite. En 1917, Tom et son ami Matt gagnent leur vie en conduisant un camion.

Prohibition

Le patron d'un bar, Paddy Ryan, les embauche pour organiser le marché clandestin de l'alcool : en le détournant, en le faisant fabriquer et, surtout, en obligeant par la violence les patrons de *speakeasy* à se fournir chez lui. Le film montre l'ascension de Tom et Matt, leurs rencontres et leur violence.

Le récit se resserre alors sur la vie privée de Tom : chez lui, d'abord, où Mike le frère modèle est revenu de guerre et proteste contre la bière qui coule à flot : ce n'est pas de la bière, c'est du sang. Puis à l'hôtel avec Kitty, où Tom écrase un demi pamplemousse sur le visage de sa maîtresse qui semblait lui faire la leçon. Dans la rue enfin, où il rencontre Gwen (Jean Harlow). Mais la vengeance – qu'il envisage comme autant d'actes de Justice – l'occupe de plus en plus : exécution de Putty Nose qui avait trahi les jeunes gens ; exécution du cheval rendu responsable de la mort de leur ami Nails Nathan.

Guerre des gangs

Tout s'accélère alors : Paddy doit cacher ses hommes de main mais Tom, qui a refusé les avances de Jane, tente une sortie avec Matt. Le gang adverse les attendait et Matt est abattu. Le thème de la vengeance domine alors : dans une scène comique Tom se procure deux revolvers puis il se livre à un attentat suicidaire contre le repaire de Schemer, le chef du gang adverse. Sous une pluie battante, il s'effondre au bord du caniveau et admet : « I ain't so tough ». Mais le film le retrouve à l'hôpital dans une scène de réconciliation familiale (mère, frère..) avant que la bande adverse ne l'enlève et n'envoie son corps enveloppé de bandelettes sur le seuil de la maison familiale.

Scarface (Atlantic Pictures, filmé au printemps-été 1931, sorti en avril 1932)

Le film débute par sept séquences de mise en place à partir de la mort du boss précédent – Big Louie – que Tony Camonte (Scarface) exécute pour le compte de son nouveau patron, Johnny Lovo. Après l'acte encore anonyme et son annonce dans la presse, on découvre Tony chez le coiffeur où un policier vient le chercher mais qu'un avocat fait aussitôt libérer... Le récit se concentre alors sur Tony, son ami Guino (Raft), sa mère et sa sœur Cesca, qui n'est pas indifférente aux avances de Guino.

Avec Lovo

Les deux parties suivantes décrivent de façon symétrique la double ascension de Tony : d'abord *avec* son patron Lovo, puis *contre* lui. Elles débutent par la vitre brisée du bureau de l'ancien boss (on y inscrit leurs noms) : Lovo prend le pouvoir sur le gang dont la séquence suivante décrit les activités criminelles (racket et vente forcée d'alcool, mitraillage et bombes sur les récalcitrants, exécution de témoins gênants dans un hôpital) ou burlesques (personnage de Dope). Tony prend de l'assurance, s'intéresse à Poppy, la *moll* de son chef et, contre l'avis de celui-ci, veut agrandir le territoire en attaquant des gangs rivaux.

Contre Lovo

Il fait d'abord exécuter O'Hara (le « fleuriste »), puis il s'installe en face de l'enseigne « The World is Yours », intéresse Poppy et découvre avec joie de nouveaux fusils automatiques. Il réchappe avec Poppy à un attentat organisé par les amis de O'hara, dans un restaurant (la scène est inspirée de la vie de Capone). Le carnage de la guerre des gangs s'intensifie, seulement interrompu par des scènes de comic relief (avec Dope, au théâtre...) ou des leçons morales imposées par la censure. La rupture entre Tony et Lovo se concrétise par une tentative de mitraillage de Scarface dans sa voiture, puis par l'exécution de Lovo dans son bureau, dont Tony brise à son tour la porte vitrée.

Le cercle est refermé, Tony devenu *boss* installe Poppy chez lui et part en Floride. Entre temps, Guino a séduit Cesca qui quitte la maison familiale avec lui. A son retour Tony, en frère attentionné, tue Guino son meilleur ami, mais, quand la police encercle son appartement, Cesca se joint quand même à lui dans ce dernier combat. Elle meurt, Tony est touché, puis abattu par la police sous l'enseigne : « *The World is Yours* ».

Little Caesar peut décevoir par la simplicité linéaire de son intrigue, mais c'est peut être de cette sécheresse monothématique, en écho à la monomanie de son personnage, qu'il tire sa force et sa nouveauté au cinéma. Le film ressemble ainsi au personnage : « He had none of the outward signs of greatness.(...) Rico's great strength lay in his single-mindedness, his energy and his self-discipline[1] ».

C'est le seul des trois films pour lequel le passage du roman initial au script modifie profondément le sens de la trajectoire des protagonistes et montre une volonté lisible de symétrie. (Les deux autres romans, même adaptés par leurs auteurs, fournissent un matériau général mais le résultat est trop éloigné pour parler d''adaptation' du roman au film.) LeRoy garde l'essentiel de la carrière de Rico et l'acteur E.G. Robinson (malgré ses trente-sept ans) se superpose parfaitement au personnage. Si tout le début du film est entièrement nouveau, la description du gang de Sam Vettori diffère très peu (Sam est obèse dans le roman) et l'impression dominante commune aux deux versions du récit est la même : ces Italiens évoquent moins les violences de la Renaissance revue par les Elizabethains qu'une simple *meute* de prédateurs témoins des combats incessants de leurs chefs. Cette impression est paradoxalement renforcée par la remarquable densité verbale des conflits, dans un film où la violence physique n'occupe que très peu de temps (mort du pompiste, mort de McClure, mort de Tony... à chaque fois quelques secondes, le bruit d'une arme et un corps qui tombe).

Beaucoup de mots et très peu de psychologie – même pas les pages froidement descriptives du roman, dont on retrouve quand même la trace ironique dans un carton du film [00 : 55 minutes] : « Rico continued to take care of himself, his hair and his gun – with excellent results ». Mais certaines précisions de Burnett passent dans le personnage du film sans avoir besoin d'être explicitées. Ce qui fascine et trouble chez Rico, c'est à la fois son sérieux d'employé modèle et son énergie, deux valeurs américaines : « ... he was never sleepy, never felt the desire to relax, was always keenly alive. » Mais ces vertus présentées de façon clinique deviennent alors inquiétantes : « What distinguished him from his associates was his inability to live in the present. He was like a man on a long train journey to a promised land. To him the present was but a dingy way-station ; he had his eyes on the end of the journey ». Moins que le portrait d'un homme, *Little Caear* est le film d'une passion.

La comparaison entre le roman et le film fait ressortir des structures binaires qui seront reprises dans d'autres films : tout chez LeRoy est construit autour de l'axe qui sépare Joe Massara et Rico. Burnett insistait sur le physique et l'élégance de 'Gentleman Joe', dont les modèles à la ville font partie de l'époque, et il s'en servait de deux façons : d'abord pour offrir un contraste avec les autres membres mal dégrossis du gang, mais surtout pour matérialiser la fonction narrative de l'*hamartia* chez Rico (qui a tiré d'instinct sur un policier). La menace obsédante du personnage de dénonciateur est préparée par la mort de Toni et elle s'effectue avec Joe. Mais le reste est très différent dans le roman : le plus souvent, Joe est absent, maillon indispensable et corrompu dans l'exécution d'un hold-up, Rico le déteste et ne s'en cache même pas. Si Joe finit par parler et par provoquer la chute de Rico, c'est parce qu'il a été reconnu par un témoin et que la police l'enferme, feint de croire qu'il est l'assassin et lui fait subir ce qui ressemble beaucoup à de la torture physique. Enfin, le nom de *Gentleman Joe* devient dérisoire et

---

1. W.R. Burnett, *Little Caesar*, V - 2, p. 62.

amer : on est encore loin de la synthèse du rêve américain qu'offrira *Gentleman Jim* en 1941 (Raoul Walsh) : Errol Flynn, à la fois Irlandais en famille et membre de la bonne société de San Francisco, y est le champion de boxe des États-Unis tout entiers.

Le Joe Massara du film est la moitié d'un duo, ou plutôt, de deux duos (à la fois professionnels et affectifs) successifs et incompatibles : avec Rico, puis avec la danseuse Olga. Le second duo transforme le premier en *duel* et le film entier est le récit de ces dualités. La participation de Massara au hold-up y est minimisée, mais le film insiste (le ton est alors mélodramatique) sur l'impossibilité de quitter le gang. Olga représente clairement la droiture désintéressée et c'est elle qui va éviter à Joe la tache 'jaune' du dénonciateur en le forçant à témoigner contre Rico[1]. Tout conspire alors pour faire de Joe un héros positif racheté par son travail et par l'amour : la symétrie avec Rico, absente du roman, est ici très nette. Les deux hommes sont des professionnels hors pair, tout deux s'accomplissent en arrivant dans la ville américaine, mais l'un suit le mauvais chemin du crime, l'autre retrouve celui de la vertu.

L'image finale de la chute de Rico dans le caniveau n'est pas seulement ironique, elle est aussi quelque peu moralisatrice : « Is this the end of Rico? » s'oppose à la fin heureuse visible sur l'affiche de Joe et Olga, qui en sont tout enivrés de bonheur (leur 'dernier mot' à eux, c'est : *Tipsy, Topsy, Turvy*). On ne fait pas plus moral, car il n'est pas de leçon plus efficace que celle de la conversion difficile du héros qui avait en partie succombé – non pas l'impeccable Abel face au sombre Caïn, mais le *Bad Guy* devenu héros. Bref, on s'étonnerait presque des inquiétudes de la censure à l'époque.

Elle savait sans doute que le public ne se contenterait pas de ces ivresses appartenant à un autre genre cinématographique et que Rico reste le vrai cœur du film. Et puis, le cinéma modifie profondément la sexualité de Rico et, indirectement, ses relations avec Joe. J.R.Burnett, tout à son idée de monomanie, s'amusait des appétits sexuels et de la méfiance de son personnage : « Blondy Belle (...) was big, healthy and lascivious. This exactly suited Rico's tastes ; she excited him, and for that very reason he was on guard against her[2] ». On était souvent dans la comédie, comme à la fin du grand banquet : « Blondy Belle was a little drunk and Rico had to support her as they went down the stairs. As she weighed about twenty pounds more than he did, this was not an easy job. » (p. 51). LeRoy, en la supprimant, suggère une attirance pour Joe, que l'amitié jalouse et les protestations insistantes de virilité de la part de Rico éclairent très différemment, en contribuant à faire de ses relations avec le couple Joe-Olga une véritable *subplot* dans le film.

L'autre différence majeure entre le livre et le film tient dans la scène initiale du meurtre du pompiste. Dans la tradition tragique de *Macbeth* le public est prévenu du destin irrévocable du héros. En 1931, Rico vit dans un monde sécularisé où l'oracle tentateur des sorcières est remplacé par les journaux (on y découvre le *banquet* donné en l'honneur de Pete Montana),

---

1. Pour le gang elle joue le rôle qu'aurait pu jouer le prêtre irlandais auprès de Toni.
2. *Little Caesar*, p. 52

mais où l'acte initial scelle l'irréparable, l'impossibilité narratologique d'une issue heureuse.

The Public Enemy

C'est l'absence de cette certitude de la chute annoncée, liée à l'acte irréparable initial, qui fait de *Public Enemy* un film profondément différent des deux autres, à la fois plus foisonnant, beaucoup plus riche 'psychologiquement' et peut être moins 'nouveau' en son temps. Au lieu d'être mis devant le (mé)fait accompli, le spectateur découvre la chronique d'un lieu, d'un milieu et d'une communauté, avant d'assister à la genèse expliquée du premier crime – cette fois irrévocable. Il s'agit bien de la tradition du récit d'apprentissage issue de Balzac, Dickens et Griffith.

Les auteurs du script ont travaillé à partir de leur propre roman – *Beer and Blood* – en coupant dans les 300 pages et les cinq intrigues de leur chronique touffue basée sur des souvenirs du Chicago d'avant la première guerre. Henry Cohen insiste sur le passage du naturalisme (darwinien) propre au roman, au réalisme plus neutre du film : le livre décrivait « ... a bitterly competitive human environment created by biological and social inheritance (...) treated as deterministic of character, plot[1]... » Dans cet univers, les personnages étaient « powerless playthings of society and nature, they could not be effectively responsible » (p. 15).

Mais Warner engage William Wellman, homme d'action[2] qui s'intéresse à la fois aux causes du mal et au thème de la survie, mais qui est aussi un cinéaste particulièrement efficace. Il veut réaliser « the toughest », « the most vicious », « the most realistic movie yet[3] ». Et le contraste avec *Little Caesar* est saisissant : Tom Powers a une enfance, une famille longuement décrite, un père rendu plus menaçant par son mutisme, une mère et un frère tous étrangers au milieu du crime. Seul, Matt, son meilleur ami, a les mêmes fréquentations que lui. Autrement dit, le film explique le personnage et, surtout, il lui laisse une certain marge d'initiative et de psychologie entre les rails de son destin. Tom n'est pas une entité, l'incarnation d'une passion pure, mais un personnage qui aurait pu être ordinaire. Sauf que le rôle – après quelques hésitations – a été confié à Cagney[4] dont le dynamisme, la présence et l'inventivité gestuelle font merveille.

Les différences, certainement perçues à l'époque, sont nombreuses : insistance sur la vie quotidienne en période de prohibition (que personne à l'évidence ne respecte) et allusions au retour douloureux de ceux qui sont allés se battre en Europe. Présentation quasi documentaire des activités des gangsters, cette fois irlandais, et chronique détaillée des aventures sexuelles de Tom qui, contrairement à Rico (abstinence) ou Tony avec Poppy (ascension sociale), ne sont pas directement liées à sa carrière de gangster. Bref, Tom Powers a une vie à côté de la vie du gang, surtout en famille.

---

1. Henry Cohen, préface du script de *Public Enemy*, Wisconsin-Warner, 1981, p. 14
2. 'Wild Bill' Wellman jouait au hockey, pilotait une moto et avait été pilote de guerre. Cohen le présente comme un « hard-drinking womanizer... the genuine article », p. 23
3. Cité par Cohen p. 13
4. Kaminsky fait justement remarquer que le personnage de Joe Massara et les acteurs Cagney et George Raft (Guino dans *Scarface*) sont tous des danseurs professionnels. Les films de gangsters ont vécu une liaison visuelle avec les musicals.

Mais on retrouve ici une ressemblance plus profonde entre les trois films, liée à la structure narrative des récits. L'histoire de Rico se lisait sur l'axe de son *duo/duel* avec Joe Massara ; Tom est construit grâce à une double comparaison sensiblement plus complexe. Le premier axe Tom/Matt est celui de l'amitié dans le crime, qui montre en quoi Tom n'est pas un gangster comme les autres. Or Matt ne lui sert pas seulement de *foil* – de faire valoir – il sera aussi la victime sacrificielle nécessaire à l'ébauche de sa rédemption et à sa régénération morale – sinon physique – au sein de sa famille.

Le second axe (Tom/Mike) est plus moralisateur et il reprend tout une culture pédagogique basée sur le modèle des deux frères de la Bible, Cain et Abel. Dans la perspective déterministe du film, qui insiste sur l'influence du milieu et des circonstances au lieu de faire du criminel un monstre à part entière, venu d'on ne sait où, le recours aux deux frères élevés dans la même famille laisse l'issue ouverte tant que le frère innocent n'est pas tombé sous les coups de l'autre. Mais, justement, Mike ici n'est ni blanc ni 'jaune' et il n'a rien d'un agneau : c'est l'aîné, il s'est sali les mains contre les Allemands et à chaque affrontement entre les deux frères c'est lui qui garde le dessus. Il ne suffit pourtant pas d'avoir *raison* contre Tom si on n'a pas sa vitalité, sa loyauté paradoxale et son charme et c'est évidemment à contre cœur que le public doit donner raison à celui qui a toujours raison.

Tom Powers plaît aux femmes, qui sont au cœur d'une nouvelle spécificité de ce film plus complexe qu'il n'y paraît. Les scènes que l'on retient ne sont pas tant celles où il les séduit (Kitty dans un dancing, Gwen dans la rue puis en voiture, Jane chez Paddy) mais celles où il leur résiste et celles où il les rejette. Ces scènes ont en commun le même sens de la *fidélité* masculine à autre chose que des femmes : a) fidélité à un ami dans la séquence la plus ambiguë qui est celle où Gwen (Jean Harlow) semble rejouer, sur fond de « *Ain't Misbehavin* » langoureux, une scène de séduction que Cohen trouve ironique et sans doute comique pour le public de l'époque[1]. Tom la quitte dans l'urgence (au moment où il allait céder) parce que son ami 'Nails' Nathan vient d'être tué par son cheval. b) fidélité à sa propre liberté dans la célèbre scène où Tom écrase un demi-pamplemousse sur le visage de Kitty parce qu'elle commençait à lui faire la leçon (ne pas boire dès le matin) bref, à l'embourgeoiser. c) fidélité, surtout, à son chef et aux règles du milieu dans la scène matinale (devenue un peu obscure dans le film) au cours de laquelle Tom gifle Jane. Le script était plus explicite : Tom se souvient que la veille, Jane, qui est aussi la maîtresse de Paddy Ryan, a tenté de le séduire alors qu'il était ivre. Comme Spade, dix ans plus tard dans *The Maltese Falcon*, le héros préfère la loyauté envers un monde (et envers l'image que ce monde renvoie de lui) plutôt que l'amour d'une femme.

On retiendra enfin que les femmes sont présentées comme un frein à l'énergie vitale de Tom et qu'elles le veulent redevenu enfant (sa mère), embourgeoisé (Kitty) ou qu'elles le trahissent (Gwen est partie sans l'attendre à la fin du film). Tant de misogynie mériterait sans doute un chapitre pour en déchiffrer les raisons.

---

1. Il parle même d'une « special sardonic glee », p. 5

Scarface

Il n'y a pas que Hawks ou Hughes pour trouver ce film exceptionnel, au-delà de l'aura que la censure a créée autour de lui en retardant sa rediffusion officielle de près de cinquante ans (de 1934 à 1979). La raison donnée par Hawks peut surprendre, mais elle est très révélatrice : « *Scarface* is my favorite picture, even today, because we were completely alone, Hughes and I ». Ils étaient 'seuls' sans Hollywood, et *Scarface* est un film libre, une sorte de poème furieux qui exprime avant tout une jubilation de la violence pure.

Les emprunts à des crimes réels et à la biographie de Capone sont connus[1]. Ce qui est plus curieux, c'est le plaisir que Capone lui même semble avoir pris en voyant le film. Dans une de ses interviews, Hawks répond à McBride qui lui demande si Capone, avec qui il a passé plusieurs heures[2], a vu *Scarface* :

> *Five or six times. He had his own print of it. He thought it was great. He'd say, 'Jesus Christ, you guys got a lot of stuff in that picture! How'd you know about that?' I said, 'Look – you know how somebody can't testify if he's a lawyer? Well, I'm a lawyer. (p. 49)*

La rencontre entre Howard Hawks et de vrais gangsters et sa méthode d'information très journalistique expliquent en partie le ton différent du film, son apparente neutralité à l'égard des assassins, l'absence totale d'analyses « psychologiques » au delà du simple constat. Je retiens aussi deux autres clefs – en dehors des constantes que l'œuvre révélera chez ce réalisateur : le *professionalisme* des gangsters et leur *immaturité*. Même en 1977, Hawks pense manifestement à Rico quand il dit

> *I get awfully sick and tired of a lot of the gangster stuff that I see where everybody is growling at somebody and being the toughest guy in the world. These fellows were not that way. They were just like kids. When we conceived the idea that these fellows were childish, it helped us do some scenes. (McBride, p. 47)*

D'où les scènes de jubilation enfantine au cours desquelles Tony découvre de nouveaux fusils automatiques. Ce sont à la fois les instruments de son excellence dans l'ascension vers le pouvoir et des jouets. Le voici avec son nouveau fusil dans la salle de billard de Johnny Lovo :

> *Hey Johnny, look what I got! ... Look it, Johnny, you can carry it around like a baby...We don't give 'em time. We go after them. We throw them micks up for grabs...There's only one thing that gets orders and give orders. (He taps the gun) And this is it. That's how I got the South Side for ya and that's how I'm gonna get the North Side for ya. Some little typewriter, eh? I'm gonna write my name all*

---

1. Voici ce qu'en dit Tim Dirks avant son résumé détaillé du film (*web cit.*) : « Capone was already in jail starting 1931, serving an eleven-year sentence in federal prison in Atlanta for tax-evasion (...) In addition to Tony Camonte portraying Al Capone, Johnny Lovo resembles crime figure Johnny Torrio, and "Big Louis" Costillo represents rackets crime czar Big Jim Colosimo. The notorious St. Valentine's Day massacre (the slaughter of seven members of George "Bugs" Moran's gang on February 14, 1929), the hospital murder from the life of Legs Diamond, and the 1920 killing of Capone's Irish, North Side enemy Dion O'Bannion in a flower shop are also recreated. »
2. « We had tea, and he was dressed in a morning coat, striped trousers, a carnation, being a very nice man, saying how much he liked the picture », Mc Bride, p. 48

over this town with it in big letters...Get outta my way, Johnny, I'm gonna spit!

On retrouve la même ambition que celle de Rico, mais dans une atmosphère de fête puérile : « Just this gleeful 'fun' and lack of growling distinguishes *Scarface* from those other, more familiar films of the gangster cycle ». Les autres étaient « more palatable precisely because they took the gangster world seriously, not as a sport[1] ».

Avec les femmes, Tony ressemble aussi un peu à Rico, dans la mesure où Poppy (la maîtresse de son chef Lovo) ne semble le fasciner que comme *signe* du pouvoir et de la réussite sociale, qu'il dispose en miroir devant l'enseigne *The World is Yours*. Contrairement à Tom Powers, toujours en quête de figures paternelles positives, son ambition va de pair avec le mépris du chef. A Poppy qui résiste très mollement à ses avances (« I thought you were Johnny's friend ») il répond : « Sure, I like Johnny, but I like you more ». Mast insiste sur les deux triangles amoureux du récit[2] : le premier (Tony / Poppy / Johnny Lovo) est celui de l'ambition et il finit par la mort du chef ; le second (Tony / Cesca / Guino) est celui des passions incontrôlées, qui finira par un carnage digne des Borgia.

Il n'est donc pas étonnant que le film ait rencontré beaucoup plus de problèmes avec les censeurs que les deux autres. Mast compare utilement le script original avec le film de Hawks pour y repérer la fascination d'une partie de la société de l'époque et de nombreuses attaques contre l'hypocrisie de certains : ainsi, Benson, le State Attorney qui est un ami de Lovo et de Tony Camonte proclame haut et fort dans ses meetings politiques : « the gangs must go. Prohibition must be enforced » (p. 74). La mère de Tony accepte volontiers l'argent de son fils et, pendant le séjour en Floride de Tony, devenu Boss, il reçoit des amis de la société élégante et de l''élite intellectuelle' sur son bateau, qui « find the murderous gangster a perfectly pleasant host and an intriguingly interesting personality ». Scarface est « thoroughly accepted by the very moral, political and cultural life in modern America, which deplores them only in theory » (Mast, p. 75). La fin prévue dans le script faisait de Tony une force de la nature – façon King Kong – dont la résistance surhumaine ne cédait que quand son pistolet était vide, non sans avoir dévasté tout le décor.

Le film tel que nous pouvons maintenant le voir est à mi-chemin entre ces provocations et le sermon moralisateur que les censeurs ont imposé pendant quelques années[3].

Voici quelques extraits encore visibles ajoutées par les censeurs : le Chef de la Police puis le journaliste Garston y sont filmés d'une façon tellement différente du reste du film que la transcription qui suit ne rend pas compte de leur caractère de *corps étrangers*, perceptiblement ironiques. La séquence débute avec le policier qui s'indigne qu'on puisse trouver Camonte « pittoresque » :

Colorful? What color is a crawling louse? Say listen, that's the attitude of too many morons in this country. They think these

---

1. Gerald Mast, *Howard Hawks, Storyteller*, New York, 1982, Oxford U.P p. 86.
2. Mast, p. 82.
3. Voir la fin humiliante de Tony dans le chapitre Matthew Guillen, ci-dessous.

hoodlums are some sort of demagogues. What do they do about a guy like Camonte? They sentimentalize, romance, make jokes about him. They had some excuse for glorifying our old Western badmen. They met in the middle of the street at high noon and waited for each other to draw. But these things sneak up and shoot a guy in the back and then run away...Colorful? Did you read what happened the other day? A car full of 'em chasing another down the street in broad daylight. Three kiddies playing hop-scotch on the sidewalk get lead poured in their little bellies. When I think what goes on in the minds of these lice, I wanna vomit.

Suit Garston, le rédacteur en chef :

> Garston : *Don't blame the police. They can't stop machine guns from being run back and forth across the state lines. They can't enforce laws that don't exist.*
>
> Male Citizen : *Then it's up to the federal government to do something about it.*
>
> Garston : *You're the government – all of you. Instead of trying to hide the facts, get busy and see that laws are passed that'll do some good.*
>
> Male Citizen : *For instance?*
>
> Garston : *Pass a federal law that puts the gun in the same class as drugs and white slavery. Put teeth in the Deportation Act. These gangsters don't belong in this country. Half of them aren't even citizens.*
>
> Third Male Citizen : *(with a heavy ethnic accent) That's-a true. They bring nothing but disgrace to my people.*
>
> Garston : *All right, I'll tell you what to do. MAKE LAWS AND SEE THAT THEY'RE OBEYED – IF WE HAVE TO HAVE MARTIAL LAW TO DO IT...Surely gang rule and wholesale law defiance are more of a menace to the nation than the regulation of oil or a bullfight. The Army will help. So will the American Legion. They offered their services over two years ago and nobody ever called on them. Let's get wise to ourselves. We're fighting organized murder!*

Ces séquences, supprimées ou conservées, semblent appartenir à un autre film, mais elles sont instructives pour étudier l'esprit de l'époque.

Or c'est dans son attention à la *forme* et par son ambition artistique que le film reste une œuvre très originale. On ne s'attardera pas ici sur l'exemple de la prolifération presque maniaque du signe de la mort – le X déjà visible pendant le générique[1] – à la fois jeu enfantin et preuve de maîtrise profes-

---

1. Il s'agit à l'origine des croix censées désigner dans les photos de presse la présence d'un cadavre sur les lieux du crime. Voir, par exemple, Tim Dirks : « Bullets spit from weapons and murder a man as he is thrown from a car – the body lands under a circular spot of light on the sidewalk beneath a sign (UNDERTAKERS) and in the cross-hairs of an "X" shadow. Another murder occurs under a trolly-car X. More crosses signal death. A reconstructed "St. Valentine's Day Massacre" scene is prefaced with a closeup of a trellis of seven X criss-crossed beams in the ceiling above the victims. The camera slowly pans down to black silhouettes of seven of Gaffney's gang members (only Gaffney is absent due to a twist of fate). The outlines of figures are ordered to line up against a wall – where they are "mowed down" and slaughtered with machine gun fire. Clouds of smoke from the firearms billow up and conceal the murders from the gun-shy (and modest) camera. A dog is heard whimpering. (Later when the crime is being investigated, a white cross marks the pile of bodies on the garage floor.) » On pense aussi à la mort de Guino, annoncée par le numéro X au dessus de la porte de son appartement.

sionnelle. Ni sur les jeux avec la caméra (vaste et complexe mouvement de l'incipit) ou la citation de Donizetti sifflée par Tony et utilisée comme un leitmotiv[1]. Bref, *Scarface* demeure un modèle d'écriture cinématographique, d'autant plus remarquable qu'il date des débuts un peu hésitants du cinéma parlant. Gerald Mast développe à juste titre la séparation opérée par Hawks entre les objets, les êtres humains et les humains-comme-objets. Au bout du compte, semble-t-il répéter de film en film, seuls les *objets maîtrisés* (par la perfection technique ou par l'art) survivront à l'homme.

Il reste à proposer quelques pistes de recherches : au niveau des films en tant que récits, il faudrait comparer le traitement du *temps* dans les sous-genres (gangsters, films noirs, chroniques documentaires ou nostalgiques...) et les opposer à d'autres genres policiers, comme le *whodunnit*, ou récit à énigme. Le film de gangsters déverse dans l'immédiateté d'un présent apparent des événements et des dialogues qui courent vers une fin connue à l'avance. Le film noir, plus centré sur un individu 'ordinaire', évite le caractère implacablement mécanique de la tragédie en utilisant le flash back : la fin dérisoire du drame est déjà connue et le chemin qui y conduit peut dès lors être plus tortueux ou plus dérisoire. Ce qui frappe surtout, c'est la grande différence entre les films des débuts (les *Classic Three*) et les *whodunnits* : ces derniers racontent au présent le travail de reconstitution d'un récit perdu et crypté – celui du crime – et ils reposent en grande partie sur les tensions entre deux nappes de temps. Rien de tel dans le film de gangsters : pas d'énigme à déchiffrer, pas de monstre caché. Tout repose sur l'évidence des actes et c'est leur *exhibition* même qui devient un mystère moral.

Mais ce sont les pistes qui associent cinéma et *civilisation* qui seront les plus utiles. Le gangster est d'abord une figure d'*immigré* de la deuxième génération ; il a un rapport direct (*Roaring Twenties*) ou indirect (*Public Enemy*) avec la *guerre* européenne ; il travaille rarement, mais son entourage est confronté au chômage. Les films offrent une typologie articulée de la situation de la *femme* : *mère*, *moll* ('nana' ou prostituée), *jane* (plus 'ordinaire'), ou *femme fatale*...Les héros de ces films s'affirment à côté – ou contre – d'autres figures du pouvoir, *chefs* médiocres (Louis) ou formidables (Gafney), lâches (Putty) ou loyaux (Paddy), peu intégrés (l'accent et la vulgarité de Louis) ou embourgeoisés (le Big Boy). Les *victimes*, à leur tour, sont paradoxalement plus originales : tout conspire à leur neutralisation, tantôt parce qu'elles n'ont que ce qu'elles ont mérité (Big Louis, Putty Nose ou Johnny Lovo), tantôt parce qu'elles restent très anonymes (McClure, dans *Little Caesar*) ou parce que leur mort a lieu hors champ, de façon presque abstraite (Toni dans *Little Caesar*). Le plus souvent, les morts les

---

1. Tony Camonte siffle l'air *Chi mi frena in tal tormento* chanté en trio vers la fin du premier acte de *Lucia de Lammermoor* (1835). Dans cette grande scène de fête tragique Lucia signe, la mort dans l'âme, l'acte de mariage qui la lie à un homme qu'elle n'aime pas. Edgardo, son véritable amour partagé, surgit alors comme la foudre (à laquelle il est comparé) et chante :
Qui me réfrène en un pareil moment ? Qui interromp la course de ma colère ? Sa douleur (Lucia), son effroi sont la preuve de ses remords ! (...) Je suis vaincu, je suis ému... Je t'aime, ingrate, je t'aime encore !
Même si on peut supposer que Tony n'a fait qu'entrevoir l'adéquation entre ce chant, sa violence et ses sentiments confus pour Cesca, le spectateur cultivé (et/ou Italien ?) de l'époque pouvait sans doute les lire.

plus tragiques se lisent dans les yeux des témoins (Cesca voit mourir Guino). Il restera enfin à examiner les représentations de l'ordre, de la *police* et des politiciens, rarement chaleureux, toujours ambigus.

Il ne faudrait pas, enfin, sous prétexte que le sujet concerne d'abord la civilisation américaine, négliger les *analyses de séquences* de ces œuvres souvent habiles et parfois subtiles : les incipit et les fins des trois grands classiques offriront un terrain fructueux pour une étude des signes, de l'ironie et de l'émotion bien réelle dans ces films, même si elle est souvent brouillée et curieusement *retenue*.

"Sanitizing" Little Ceasar & Co.
By Matthew Guillen

> *Culture is not people's most popular set of cognitive classifications, narratives, or images of collectivities [...] Rather culture is the particular one which people feel bound to respect, and are generally prone to obey [...] Culture in its regulative guise is relentless; it never lets people escape[1].*

In the 1930 film *Little Caesar*, Rico's struggle to "get to the top" never veers from its "poverty overcoming all odds" type of demented idealism. Based on a novel written by W.R. Burnett, the incidents arise from events Burnett experienced while living in Chicago during the twenties as well as reports of New York criminal activity available to him at the time. This article suggests that films such as *Little Caesar*, *Public Enemy*, and *Scarface* are certainly commercially and aesthetically significant works which appear to use the particular phenomenon of gangsterism as a means of coping with all the unique political, social, and law enforcement problems that first surfaced with Prohibition and the Great Depression. But there exist presuppositions, bearing on the disparities between these films and the realities on which they are based – as well as on the motivations behind these departures, and possible subsequent effects on audience response – which result in paradox. It is also proposed that the reason lies in a tendency to confuse modern perceptions of audience susceptibility to contemporary media violence with that which informed Depression era America.

That these films stray largely from the truth is incontestable – owing principally to the dictates of The Motion Picture Production Code of 1930 (Hays Code) which inserts, under the heading "Reasons Underlying the General Principles," a somewhat incongruous "Note" – the implications of which could be seized by anyone knowledgeable in the art of cinema storytelling:

> Note: Sympathy with a person who sins is not the same as sympathy with the sin or crime of which he is guilty. We may feel sorry for the plight of the murderer or even understand the circumstances which led him to his crime: we may not feel sympathy with the wrong which he has done.

Roy Bates suggests that the Production Code resulted from public pressure, largely organized through the Roman Catholic Church, to "clean up" movies[2]. One cannot ignore, however, the sensational series of trials in which silent film star Roscoe Conkling "Fatty" Arbuckle was charged with manslaughter issuing from the death (following a possible rape) of film actress Virginia Rappe. The first two trials, November 14-December 4, 1921 and January 11-February 3, 1922, ended in deadlocked juries. The trial lasting from March 13-April 12, 1922 resulted in acquittal. In the course of these proceedings, the Anti-Saloon League, the Moral Efficiency League, and the Women's Vigilant Committee of San Francisco – none of which was a Catholic affiliate – agreed that at the heart of the Arbuckle matter was a

---

1. Richard Merelman "On Culture and Politics in America: A Perspective from Structural Anthropology," *British Journal of Political Science* 19(4): 1989. 480
2. Roy Eugene Bates, "Private Censorship of Movies," 22 *Stanford L. Rev.*, (1970). 618, 619

nationwide lowering of moral standards. As a direct consequence, boards of censors, mayors and film exhibitor associations in countless cities, as well as the states of Missouri, Pennsylvania, and Kansas, banned all Arbuckle movies[1].

Just four days after the first deadlock, 12 of Hollywood's top leaders, including Samuel Goldwyn, Lewis J. Selznick, and Adolph Zukor, asked William Hays, chairman of the Republican National Committee and President Warren G. Harding's postmaster general, to become the czar of the film industry and to insure dignity and respect were accorded the medium – the avoidance of bad publicity, in short – and which resulted ultimately in the self-regulation provided by the Production Code. Like many other media industry codes, the Production Code contained both general provisions and specific affirmative and negative provisions. For example, under the first section, General Principles, it is stated that the "motion picture has special *Moral obligations*[2]". The second section, Working Principles, states that "[n]o picture should lower the moral standards of those who see it." Specific provisions addressed such topics as the portrayal of sin and evil:

> the sympathy of the audience should never be thrown to the side of crime, wrong-doing, evil or sin. This is done: 1. When evil is made to appear attractive and alluring, and good is made to appear unattractive. 2. When the sympathy of the audience is thrown on the side of crime, wrongdoing, evil, sin. The same is true of a film that would throw sympathy against goodness, honor, innocence, purity or honesty.

With the cooperation of the studios, the Code succeeded in circumscribing images of violence so that their function remained instrumental, mostly validating existing values, and never excessively undermining mainstream assumptions. Producers would submit scripts, which would be read by at least two members of the staff to determine whether they met the Code. They would then send written decisions to the producer, including suggestions as to how any problems might be resolved. Finally, completed films were again reviewed by the Code staff. Appeals could be made to a review board, although it appears that most difficulties were worked out by making changes.

Irreproachable principles and strict procedures notwithstanding, possible ulterior motives on the part of the film industry cannot be understated. Case in point: *Little Caesar* was based on a real mobster nicknamed "Little Caesar" or in real life, Salvatore Maranzano – the first and only *Capo di Tutti Capi* ("Boss of Bosses") in the United States. Born and raised in Castellemmare del Golfo in Sicily, Maranzano came to the U.S. originally in 1918 and became involved in the world of Organized Crime. This dapper, Jesuit-educated, ruthless and sadistic man had little in common with the far more sympathetic character played by Edward G. Robinson. Responsible for

---

1. David A. Yallop, *The Day the Laughter Stopped: The True Story of Fatty Arbuckle*, New York: St. Martin's Press, 1976
2. The Motion Picture Code of 1930, reprinted in *Hollywood's America: United States History Through Its Films* 146 (Steven Mintz & Randy Roberts eds., 1993).
http://www.artsreformation.com/a001/hays-code.html

countless killings in the bootleg and other industries, he initiated a battle for power which became known as the Castellemarese Wars and the death total across the country would end up upwards of 50. The film, meanwhile, is suffused with images of pathetic, if not patently sympathetic, human shortcomings which seldom fail to register in the mind of the protagonist himself. It is painfully evident that Rico is a little man (in stature as well as criminal "legitimacy") who has ascended from poverty too quickly and ambitiously. There is a scene in which Rico stands on a table looking into a full-length mirror, as a henchman supervises his boss' fitting of a tuxedo for an upcoming meeting with a major mobster. The henchman praises Rico on his classy appearance: "You look great, boss." To which Rico responds: "Yeah, but it feels terrible." The "sanitizing" influence of the Hays Code thus seems to inadvertently subvert itself by offering the "sympathy with a person, etc." note – an opportunity the film industry could not miss in effectively transforming a gangster into poorly-educated "everyman" incapable of overcoming his tragic and fatal flaws. Later in the film, in the inevitable hubristic aftermath, the viewer is told: "Months passed – Rico's career had been like a skyrocket – starting from the gutter and returning there." Rico ends up in a flophouse where he learns from stories deliberately planted in the newspaper that he has turned cowardly. A derelict reads to him:

> Little Caesar has never been found. According to the statement of Thomas Flaherty of the homicide squad, Little Caesar, the once-swaggering braggart of the underworld wilted in the face of real danger and showed the world his cowardice (Rico makes an animalistic snarling dog sound) Flaherty stated further that Little Caesar has contradicted his oft-repeated boast that he could dish it out and take it too. (Rico snarls again) When a real crisis arose, Rico couldn't take it. Flaherty ended his interview by remarking: "Meteoric was Rico's rise from the gutter. It was inevitable that he should return there."

Insulted, Rico makes a threatening phone call to police detective Flaherty:

> This is Rico speaking. Rico! R-I-C-O! Rico! Little Caesar, that's who! Listen, you crummy, flat-footed copper, I'll show you whether I've lost my nerve and my brains.

Flaherty, as predicted, lures Rico out of hiding: "I knew we'd hear from that guy if I kept giving it to him in the papers... They'll have to build him a special noose to get that swelled head of his through." Rico's last phone call is traced and comes the inevitable shootout and Rico's famous "Mother of Mercy, is this the end of Rico?" The Production Code's specific prohibitions regarding violence were vague: Under the applications concerning "crimes against the law," the overriding concern with depictions of "murder" and "crime" is that specific details or techniques not be presented

> to throw sympathy with the crime as against law and justice or to inspire others with a desire for imitation[1].

Accommodatingly, the shootout is bloodless, and Rico swoons behind a bullet-riddled poster. Little Caesar's demise, however, that of a "villain"

---

1. John Belton, ed. *Movies and Mass Culture*. New Brunswick, NJ: Rutgers University Press, 1996. 139

whose sense of pride is vainly reasserted, elicits a good deal more sympathy than motives justifying the calculating vindictiveness of the police officer. And *Richard III* and *Macbeth* immediately spring to mind for comparison. Burnett described Little Caesar as

> a gutter Macbeth – a composite figure that would indicate how men could rise to prominence or money under the most hazardous conditions, but not much more hazardous than the Renaissance[1].

Then again, this is clearly not Shakespeare – but rather a sort of parody of Shakespeare. An enjoyable one certainly, but only by a stretch in the form of inspiration – although indeed, the purpose of the Code appears to have been radically undercut.

Multiple studies of the morality of film narratives and individual spectacles – shootings, whippings, beatings, stabbings – and their supposed effects on viewers, especially youths and immigrants, appeared after the film's success. The most famous work of the era was the summary of a nine-volume study sponsored by the Payne Fund: Henry James Forman's *Our Movie-Made Children* (1933), which portrayed children as "unmarked slates" (yes, a reprise of Locke's 1690 *Essay Concerning Human(e) Understanding*) requiring protection from the scope and power of motion pictures.[2] This notion was coupled with his concern about the dangers of "movies in a crowded section" – a holdover from earlier, progressive reformers' unease regarding ethnic workers in urban areas.[3] The assumption in either case evoking the possibility of spectator identification with characters portrayed on the screen. These ideas stood in high contrast, however, with a notion of criminality in that era suffusing criminal characterization in varying aspects of culture: that arising from nineteenth-century physician Cesare Lombroso's theory claiming genetic constitutional factors as causative of criminal behavior – the so-called "born" criminal, helplessly spurred down the path of dalliance from infancy, independently of environmental or adult influence.[4] Lombroso's claims relied on physiognomic "evidence" – "stigmata" of sorts – which seemed to characterize criminal types as less than fully evolved human beings. Such cues accommodated perfectly the film medium's reliance on the visual modality and, again, Edward G. Robinson's small, stout figure and bulldog facial characteristics certainly inured to this end.

One may fairly question, thus, the putative "identifiability" and "imitation" issues so urgently pressed by the Code and its supporters. In short, by which process would the viewer come to be enticed into mimicking activity so patently linked to physical deformity? Jonathan Munby's study of the gangster film during the period 1930-1958 provides a response through a dialectical understanding of the complex interactions among film studios and producers, audiences, custodians of public morals, industry agencies for monitoring and regulating film content and theme,

---

1. http://www.filmsite.org/littc2.html
2. Henry James Forman, *Our Movie-Made Children*. New York: MacMillan, 1933. 121-40, 251-72
3. Garth S. Jowett., Ian C. Jarvie, and Kathryn H. Fuller, eds. *Children in the Movies: Media Influence and the Payne Fund Controversy*. New York: Cambridge University Press, 1996.
4. Gina Lombroso-Ferrero, *Criminal Man According to the Classification of Cesare Lombroso*, Montclair, NJ: Patterson-Smith, 1971 (originally published 1911)

and ideological enforcement entities. His approach to the subject leads him to interrogate many of the accepted truths about the meaning, reception, and role of the crime film in popular culture. Rather than a static reading of these films, his thesis raises their historical contexts as illustrative of "a socially volatile formula in flux[1]". Munby maintains gangster films played an active part in shaping and challenging public mores, and had a more complicated relationship to the dominant political and ethical orders, enjoying a "symbiotic relationship with institutional censorship[2]", and providing a subversive challenge to dominant socio-economic values.

In the context of the Depression, in which unemployment crushed hopes of mobility and raised doubts concerning the reigning capitalist/corporate order, Rico in *Little Caesar* thus seems to mock the myth of the self-made man and take on the symbolic attributes of an Italian Horatio Alger. And since Horatio Alger's characters themselves parody through exaggeration the American "rags to riches" formula, Rico's darker tale takes on similar satiric elements. In this vein, David Slocum suggests that the history and recurrence of film violence "represents not only an account of shifting cinematic standards and cultural values regarding the use of force or aggression, but an element in the ongoing negotiation of the place and meaning of cinema itself in society[3] ".

The social function of film is still, in our day, very far from clear. Social scientists have traditionally conceptualized media as serving one of two functions in society: either effecting social change, as in the case of muckraking journalists whose illumination of social ills and inequities contributed to amelioration, or furthering the social control of predominant ideologies and social structures.[4] And in view of the violence latent in "Keystone Cop" comedies of the silent era, film violence in general can be seen as a continuum which expresses the struggles of popular cinema to balance at any given time the forces changing society and those controlling it – the chief purpose of any business, the film industry included, being the generation of profits through appeasement of its clientele. Therefore, one could imagine Hollywood correctly anticipating audience reaction to *Little Caesar* as tantamount to that elicited by depictions of a dark, nevertheless Chaplinesque, striver – at once Code-conformingly sympathetic and ridiculous. Hence, at some distance from reality and, to the chagrin of the Hays Office, immensely and paradoxically entertaining.

And so comes the birth of the Production Code Administration (PCA) in 1934 – a federally-enforced extension of the 1930 Hays Code (perceived by this time as an inadequately self-monitoring film industry ploy) which signals the beginning of far tighter film censorship. This resulted in the declaration of a moratorium on gangster films by Will Hays in July of 1935 – which specifically included a ban on the export of *Public Enemy* and *Little*

---

1. Jonathan Munby, *Public Enemies, Public Heroes: screening the gangster from* Little Caesar *to* Touch of Evil, Chicago and London, U of Chicago Press, 1999. 4
2. Id. at 10
3. David Slocum, "Film Violence and the Institutionalization of the Cinema" Social Research Fall, 2000. 73
4. K. Viswanath and David Demers, eds. *Mass Media, Social Control, and Social Change: A Macrosocial Perspective*. Ames: Iowa State UP, 1999.

Caesar until 1953. Why *Public Enemy* as well? Near climax, a shorter, blonder version of Rico – this time the pug-faced James Cagney – tosses his two guns through a building's windows. From a low-camera angle, he reels into the gutter, coughing and bleeding from a head wound. He utters an epitaph-like set of memorable words and ends up in a drain: "I ain't so tough." Taken to an emergency hospital to recover, Cagney is immobile, bandaged from head to toe on a hospital bed. There, he is reconciled with his brother and mother, apologizing to his brother and making peace with him to renew their friendship: "Just sorry, you know." His mother clasps his hand, "so happy" that the "prodigal son" is penitent, a lost child that will bring the family together again: "You're my baby." Affectionately, he gives her a soft fist tap to her chin. He promises her that he will come home to stay: "Sure, coming home. If I can ever get out of here." The Mother is happy once more that he has apparently decided to go straight: "Both my boys back, all of us together again. I'm almost glad this happened." A tear-jerker, in other words, of the first water, and nothing approximating any reality associated with gangsterism. When the Cagney character is "done in" at the hands of a rival gang, he lives long enough to return to his mother's home before dying. The film's somber message now appears, almost as if to dispel the melodramatic absurdities of the content: "The END of Tom Powers is the end of every hoodlum. 'The Public Enemy' is, not a man, nor is it a character – it is a problem that sooner or later WE, the public, must solve." One is hard-pressed to imagine any credibility being given this by a Depression era audience, meager earnings spent on a few moments' respite from a rude reality on a Saturday matinee screening.

The 1931 version of *Scarface*, on the other hand, was loved by industry regulators. The screenplay for this violent, visually expressionistic film was written by Ben Hecht using his Chicago newspaper experiences, with continuity and dialogue provided by Seton I. Miller, John Lee Mahin, and *Little Caesar*'s W. R. Burnett, and based on the 1930 novel *Scarface* by Armitage Trail (a pseudonym for Maurice Coons). But Trail's novel, although it was inspired by the exploits of Chicago's Depression-Era underworld gangster Alfonso Capone (nicknamed "Scarface"), bears little resemblance to the finished film. Capone was already in jail starting in 1931, serving an eleven-year sentence in federal prison in Atlanta for tax-evasion – he was released early in 1939 and died non-violently of syphilis in 1947.

Tony Camonte, the protagonist, is played by Paul Muni who, true to the Lombrosian recipe, not only sports the telltale scar, but is also made up to look rather simian, with heavy eyebrows and sloping brow – unmistakable signs of inherent criminality and a degenerate nature. The film's opening title credits are presented above a large painted black X, scrawled in the background of the frame. *Scarface* is prefaced with a critical, written statement to indict gangsterism and the public's and government's indifference. Additionally, the audience is blamed for promoting the role of the gangster by its perverse fascination in the phenomenon:

> This picture is an indictment of gang rule in America and of the callous indifference of the government to this constantly increasing menace to our safety and our liberty. Every incident in this picture is the reproduction of an actual occurrence, and the purpose of this

> *picture is to demand of the government: 'What are you going to do about it?' The government is your government. What are YOU going to do about it?*

The film, as originally envisioned by Howard Hawks, climaxes with Tony seeing a way to escape – in the face of death after murdering his best friend and losing his sister – he makes a break for it, but police guns open fire and riddle his body with bullets. He falls into the street's filthy gutter and expires – fulfilling the Chief of Detectives' earlier prophecy of an ignominious death ("And someday you're gonna stumble and fall down in the gutter, right where the horses have been standing, right where you belong"). The camera moves up and away from his sprawled body toward the flashing electric sign that ironically promised Tony the world: "THE WORLD IS YOURS."

At least, this was the intended ending, which was not to be shown in theatres for decades. The studio imposed its own ending, which Hawks refused to direct, and in which Muni is represented by an anonymous, stand-in extra filmed from a distance as a dark, silhouetted figure, who is escorted out of camera range. After a black fade-out, a judge reads his final sentencing (a camera remains on the judge throughout the entire scene), denouncing Tony as a common criminal who deserves to die and atone for his crimes – the simple moral of the tale being: crime doesn't pay:

> *You have been tried by a jury of your peers in this court and the jury has found you guilty without recommendation of murder in the first degree. It is the judgment of the court that you are guilty as found. [The judge stops reading the formal sentence.] Antonio Camonte, I want to go on record as stating that you deserve this verdict more than any criminal who has come before me for sentence. You are convicted of one crime but you're guilty of hundreds. Until now, you've escaped by corruption, perjury, and vicious coercion of witnesses. Since your arrest, they've come forward the first time and told the truth. You've commercialized murder to satisfy your personal greed for power. You've killed innocent women and children with brutal indifference. You are ruthless, immoral, and vicious. There is no place in this country for your type. [The judge resumes the formal sentence.] This court hereby sentences you on the 10th day of December 1931 in the penitentiary of this state to be hanged by the neck until you are dead. [The judge looks up.] And may God have mercy on your soul.*

The gallows hanging mechanism is tested – from a low-angle beneath the trap door of the floorboards. In the vicinity of the jail cell, another statement is read before the execution: "And said Tony Camonte suffer the penalty of death by hanging. Said execution to take place at the state prison on the 10th day of December 1931." It should be noted, meanwhile, that in Illinois in 1922, hanging was replaced by electric chair executions.

In a recent work, Nicole Rafter maintains the Muni character remains attractive despite his disfigurement and primitive violence. She writes

> *[he is] bigger than life, awesome in his greed and boldness, and, accomplishing his aim, he does rise above the dark city's impoverished masses[1].*

He has become then, from our more jaded perspective, a merger of criminal and hero. Robert Warshow was among the first to argue that the criminal hero's traits were first defined by gangster movies, which portrayed him as brutal, individualistic, ambitious, and doomed – hence a "criminal hero," a label that stresses the gangster's break with lawful society as well as his self-acceptance as offender[2]. In this scheme, the gangster must be a failure, not only to absolve viewers for identifying with his earlier successes but also because "the gangster is the 'no' to that great American 'yes' which is stamped so big over our official culture," the pessimistic note at the celebration of success, the dark figure hovering at the edge of one's consciousness[3]. Robert Sklar raises the possibility that the audience identifies with a tragic hero who will inevitably destroy himself literally or figuratively – and thus enjoys the criminal hero's criminality in the knowledge that all sins shall be expiated in the end[4].

Here, Warshow and Sklar seem on the verge of resuscitating the "unmarked slate" hypothesis – suggesting categories of subliminal impressions liable to be submitted to by a compliant if not openly collusive audience. Still, audience malleability implies a certain cognitive receptivity – itself theoretically questionable. In order for recognition and, ultimately, some form of identification to occur, one can reasonably argue that a conceptual groundwork of some sort must exist from which isomorphic correspondences can be made with the object in view. The question remains whether such a basis for comparison could have existed in the mind of a movie spectator a year or so after the first "talkie" and whether the intelligibility of the content of the images was thus apparent. Comparing the initial *un*intelligibility of early cinema with similar difficulties at other points in the history of art, Erwin Panofsky writes:

> *For a Saxon peasant of around 800 it was not easy to understand the meaning of a picture showing a man as he pours water over the head of another man, and even later many people found it difficult to grasp the significance of two ladies standing behind the throne of the emperor. For the public of around 1910 it was no less difficult to understand the meaning of the speechless action in a moving picture[5].*

Similarly, the tacit assumption that censors understood the possible links between screen violence and audience potential for violence, that audiences understood latent "violence messaging" in movie content, and that

---

1. Nicole Rafter, *Shots in the Mirror: Crime Films and Society*, NY: Oxford UP, 2000. 160
2. Robert Warshow, "The Gangster as Tragic Hero," *The Immediate Experience*, Garden City, NY: Anchor Doubleday, 1964.
3. Robert Warshow, "Movie Chronicle: The Westerner," in *The Immediate Experience*. 136
4. Robert Sklar, *Movie-Made America: A Cultural History of American Movies*, rev. and updated ed. New York: Vintage, 1994; 1975.
5. Thomas Y. Levin, "Iconology at the Movies: Panofsky's Film Theory" *The Yale Journal of Criticism* 9,1 (1996) 27-55—the 1947 "final" version of Panofsky's essay was reprinted in quite a few collections, notably that of William S. Heckscher, "Erwin Panofsky: A Curriculum Vitae," Record of the Art Museum, Princeton University 28.1, 1969. 240

Hollywood did more than astutely gauge audience demand for simple entertainment, seems problematic. One can imagine, far more fruitfully, a process over which neither movie makers nor viewers had control – and which overzealous censorship, operating on inadequately tested hypotheses, was bound to render incoherent. As film historian Richard Maltby suggests, contrasting the illegitimacy of violent action with the legitimacy of the government's use of force in Hawks' *Scarface* and throughout the gangster genre, criminal behavior on film became a register for exploring the shifting role of violence and its impact in an age turbulent in and of itself.[1] In this scheme, the issue of audience identification is far more nuanced and questionable. Ruth Vasey maintains, more strongly, that the Code was only part of a broader "Industry Policy" established to regulate and enforce standards of filmmaking that would uphold certain moral and social values and accommodate the interests of big business, political and lobbying groups, and foreign governments[2].

The consensus remains, nevertheless, that public discourse on criminality in film evoked concerns with the legitimacy of violence and the social order in which such behavior was framed. In 1992, Ray Surette expressed these concerns with the benefit of considerable hindsight, and in a cultural milieu where explicit violence was readily available through legitimate news programs and weekly series in the privacy of the family TV room:

> The evidence concerning the media as a criminogenic factor clearly supports the conclusion that the media have a significant short-term effect on some individuals [...] The more heavily the consumer relies on the media for information about the world and the greater his or her predisposition to criminal behavior, the greater the effect [...] Violence-prone children and the mentally unbalanced are especially at risk of emulating media violence[3].

Today, Americans' exposure to television is high – far higher than that of Depression era America's exposure to crime films. There is political content present, and many viewers have positive feelings about the programs and characters they regularly view. If behaviors, and thus values, are reinforced through other experiences, they can become enduring aspects of people's behavior. Structural anthropologists, such as Richard Merelman, hold the view that patterns of behavior recurring in television viewing are replayed throughout the culture in a variety of circumstances and venues. The programs that appear on television, either as entertainment or as public affairs, are the stories people tell about themselves – referred to by Merelman as "collective representations." While they originate with media, governmental, and economic elite, members of society absorb them and they become part of society's consciousness, memories, and collective history. Americans recall the programs, they adopt the language and the behaviors of the media, and their attention is drawn to the issues that are

---

1. Richard Maltby, "The Spectacle of Criminality" in David Slocum, *Violence and American Cinema*, New York: Routledge, 2001
2. Ruth Vasey, "Beyond Sex and Violence: 'Industry Policy' and the Regulation of Hollywood Movies, 1922-1939." *Controlling Hollywood: Censorship and Regulation in the Studio Era*, ed. Matthew Bernstein. New Brunswick, NJ: Rutgers University Press, 1999
3. Ray Surette, *Media, Crimes and Criminal Justice: Images and Realities*, Belmont, Calif.: Wadsworth, 1992.140

the subject of programming. Hence, television, as an agent of socialization, socializes simultaneously with other agents, such as families, peers, schools, and churches[1]. This view echoes that of Gerbner et al., who argue that the patterns visible on television are but one manifestation of common cultural stories or themes. Television viewing, according to the authors, is like a cultural stream:

> The angle and direction of the 'pull' depends on where groups of viewers [...] are in reference to the center of gravity [...] Each group may strain in different directions, but all groups are affected by the same central current[2].

Again, it should be noted that one can too easily confuse contemporary viewer attitudes and social phenomena, "tainted" as it were by a medium similar but far from identical to that of film, with those prevalent during the Depression era. David Ruth far more convincingly argues the more "interactive" aspect 1930s crime films took. Popular cinema was the primary national venue through which concerns of this particular epoch were expressed and debated – all this at a pivotal moment when sound technology was introduced, a variety of film genres were honed, and Hollywood resituated itself in Depression-era America. The Code and its proscriptions, he contends, finally helped to stabilize a new cultural role for sound movies and contributed to a shift by movie-makers from questioning and defying middle-class values to supporting them[3].

Bates suggests that to the extent the Code proved "successful," this was principally because "[f]ilms without the Code Seal of Approval were doomed to failure" since the theaters, which were mostly owned by major studios, would not exhibit films without the MPAA seal. Several factors have been identified as contributing to the success of the Production Code in dictating content during the 1930s and 1940s. First, there was little competition from other forms of entertainment. Second, the oligopolistic structure of the movie industry enabled the MPAA-member companies to enforce the Code. Third, the Code was insulated from constitutional challenge by the position of the Supreme Court that movies were not entitled to First Amendment protection[4]. In its first 30 years, until around the time Jack Valenti assumed the role of president and chief executive officer of the MPAA in 1966, 25,000 films including 12,000 full-length features, were reviewed by the Code Office – and although presently concerned with "Scour" and other forms of film pirating, it is still fairly powerful. In true Hollywood style, therefore, the Production Code may indeed be viewed as a success story. At least, for the movie industry itself.

It is ironic that the characters played by Cagney and Robinson soon after lent themselves so easily to the genre of children's animation comedies (notably Warner Brothers' *Loony Tunes* and *Bugs Bunny* series) and the

---

1. Merelman, 1989
2. George Gerbner, Larry Gross, Michael Morgan, and Nancy Signorelli.. "Living with Television: The Dynamics of the Cultivation Process." In *Perspectives on Media Effects*, ed. Jennings Bryant and Dolf Zillman. Hillsdale, NJ: Laurence Erlbaum Assoc. 1986. 24
3. David Ruth, *Inventing the Public Enemy: The Gangster in American Culture*, 1918-34. Chicago: University of Chicago Press, 1996.
4. Bates, note 243. 619

mimicry of vaudeville and later television standup comedians. The rib-level finger-pointing which punctuates Cagney's hissing "You-u-u dirty rat" and Robinson's cigar-chomping snarl (with a trace of cleft-palate-induced slurring) "I'm the boss. See?" are far more memorable than the somber Muni characterization – attractive indeed, not quite funny at all, and which may explain why the gritty, brutal moralizing of *Scarface* scored far less well at the box office. An even greater irony: this paradigm of self-censorship efficiency was itself to subvert the "principles" of the Code by spawning, in the modern era, a most attractive villainy – brutally sadistic to excess – the incestuous, blood-gorged Al Pacino remake of *Scarface*, lost among myriad *Reservoir Dogs* clones, being but one, relatively inoffensive, example.

Bibliography

Bates, Roy Eugene, "Private Censorship of Movies," 22 *Stanford L. Rev.*, (1970)
Belton, John ed., *Movies and Mass Culture*. New Brunswick, NJ: Rutgers U P, 1996
Forman, Henry James, *Our Movie-Made Children*. New York: MacMillan, 1933
Gerbner, George Larry Gross, Michael Morgan, and Nancy Signorelli, "Living with Television: The Dynamics of the Cultivation Process." In *Perspectives on Media Effects*, ed. Jennings Bryant and Dolf Zillman. Hillsdale, NJ: Laurence Erlbaum Assoc, 1986
Jowett Garth S, Ian C. Jarvie, and Kathryn H. Fuller, eds. *Children in the Movies: Media Influence and the Payne Fund Controversy*. New York: Cambridge University Press, 1996.
Levin, Thomas Y, "Iconology at the Movies: Panofsky's Film Theory" *The Yale Journal of Criticism* 9,1 (1996)
Lombroso-Ferrero, Gina *Criminal Man According to the Classification of Cesare Lombroso*, Montclair, NJ: Patterson-Smith, 1971 (originally published 1911)
Maltby, Richard, "The Spectacle of Criminality" in David Slocum, *Violence and American Cinema*, New York: Routledge, 2001
Merelman Richard, "On Culture and Politics in America: A Perspective from Structural Anthropology," *British Journal of Political Science* 19(4): 1989
Mintz, Steven & Roberts, Randy eds. The Motion Picture Code of 1930, reprinted in *Hollywood's America: United States History Through Its Films* 146, 1993. See also http://www.artsreformation.com/a001/hays-code.html
Munby, Jonathan *Public Enemies, Public Heroes: screening the gangster from Little Caesar to Touch of Evil*, Chicago and London, U of Chicago P, 1999
Rafter, Nicole, *Shots in the Mirror: Crime Films and Society*, NY: Oxford UP, 2000
Ruth, David, *Inventing the Public Enemy: The Gangster in American Culture, 1918-34*, Chicago: U of Chicago P, 1996.
Sklar, Robert *Movie-Made America: A Cultural History of American Movies*, rev. and updated ed. New York: Vintage, 1994; 1975.
Slocum, David "Film Violence and the Institutionalization of the Cinema", *Social Research* Fall, 2000
Surette, Ray *Media, Crimes and Criminal Justice: Images and Realities*, Belmont, Calif.: Wadsworth, 1992
Vasey, Ruth "Beyond Sex and Violence: 'Industry Policy' and the Regulation of Hollywood Movies, 1922-1939." *Controlling Hollywood: Censorship and Regulation in the Studio Era*, ed. Matthew Bernstein. New Brunswick, NJ: Rutgers U P, 1999
Viswanath K. and David Demers, eds. *Mass Media, Social Control, and Social Change: A Macrosocial Perspective*. Ames: Iowa State UP, 1999.
Warshow, Robert "The Gangster as Tragic Hero," *The Immediate Experience*, Garden City, NY: Anchor Doubleday, 1964.
— "Movie Chronicle: The Westerner," in *The Immediate Experience*.
Yallop, David A. *The Day the Laughter Stopped: The True Story of Fatty Arbuckle*, New York: St. Martin's Press, 1976

Cultivating Crime and Criminalizing Culture: Screening Violence from the Depression to the Cold War

By Divina Frau-Meigs

In the United States, cultural and criminal processes tend to weave the same web of marginality, illegality and outbursts of public display and dismay. This chapter tries to explore the common ground between cultural and criminal practices by looking at the intersections between the two through collective behavior, imagery, figures and symbolic meaning, in the context of film and its representation of organized crime, from the 30s to the 50s. The cultural mediation of cinema, both as a media of accommodation and of dissent, seems to appear at pivotal moments, when depression, disorientation and cultural and moral disputes threaten the meaning of the Dream on the Silver Screen. All the more so as the advent of the movies is concomitant with the country's discovery that it had a culture of its own, a distinctive pattern of social and aesthetic organization that it started to document, collect and celebrate, with its own popular brand of nationalism.[1]

In the wake of this cultural interest, the United States started documenting the emergence of all kinds of institutions, habits and even values, and particularly its culture of crime.[2] This culture of crime was localized both in an ancient past, relating to the origins of the nation, and in the contemporary urban scenes, in the cities of Chicago, New York or Philadelphia. Especially under the influence of progressive era reformers, commissions were established to inquire into its causes and the intervention of civil society was called for on several occasions. [3] In the process, the intersecting processes of culture and crime came to be reconsidered: some social groups and events traditionally conceptualized as criminal, appeared as the ordinary operations of a subculture, with its own style and language, as in the case of the gangs or the speakeasies; some social groups and events traditionally conceptualized as cultural became criminalized by legal authorities, civic and moral leaders, and political agencies, as in the case of social drinking (Prohibition) or cinematographic output (the Motion Picture Production Code).

---

1. Lawrence Levine, *Highbrow Lowbrow: The Emergence of Cultural Hierarchy in America* (Cambridge: Harvard UP, 1988); Richard Bushman, *The Refinement of America: Persons, Houses, Cities* (NY: Knopf, 1992); Mark Meigs,*The End of American Emptiness* (forthcoming).
2. A whole body of research deals with "cultural criminology", and considers the relations between crime and culture, with a special focus on the media. Though it deals with very contemporary phenomena, styles and scenes (punk, rave, etc.), I have drawn upon some of its notions, like the "criminalization" of culture, and analyzed its workings during the 30s-50s. See Jeff Ferrell and Clinton R. Sanders, *Cultural Criminology* (Boston: Northwestern UP, 1995) 3-21. See also Lynn Curtis, *Violence, Race and Culture* (Lexington, MA: Heath, 1975) and especially the Chicago situationist school of Edwin Sutherland and Donald Cressey, *Criminology* (Philadelphia: Lippincott, 1978, 10th ed.).
3. See for example *The Report on the Causes of Crime*, vol. 1 and 2 by the National Commission on Law Observance and Enforcement (Washington, DC: US Government Printing Office, 1931).

The American Way of Crime

This cultural presence of violence was not always clearly perceived, though it may be analyzed as both a continuation and a departure from previous traditional tendencies. These trends need to be clarified, as they framed what would be tolerated in the movies about organized crime and what would be renegotiated with Hollywood. The legitimacy of violence as protest or dissent was first established with the traumatic severance from the British rule, with the success of the rebellion and the creation of an armed citizenry (confirmed by the Second Amendment and the right to bear arms). This legitimacy was further engraved in the law with the First Amendment's tenets, encapsulating in the same heading freedom of religion, of expression and of petition for grievances. Life at the frontier produced its own brand of social banditry and found in the cowboy (as cattle rustler or train robber) of the West a native-born Robin Hood-like figure.[1] The "social bandit" label was used to qualify an outlaw whose exploits enjoyed a certain amount of approval in society, especially if he robbed the banks that were oppressing the poor both in rural and urban America.[2]

This was reinforced by the fact that, to a certain extent, criminal careers mirrored the socially approved values of the pursuit of social advancement, autonomy and self-defense. As a result, gamblers and racketeers could be respected members of immigrant and lower class social and ethnic groups, especially before they were described as belonging to highly organized crime institutions.[3] All the more so as the XIXth century had fostered an increasing acceptance of social Darwinism,[4] of the idea that man is a wolf to man and that the survival of the fittest can generate a certain degree of physical violence and lawlessness, and a certain diffidence as to the workings of justice combined with a traditional republican hostility to centralized government. Hence the *modus vivendi* established to make up for the fact that legal norms didn't always cover social beliefs and expectations: some pockets of urban territory could be dedicated to criminal activities (prostitution, drug dealing, drinking), as long as some others were kept crime-free.

More deeply, as often in America, the source for the culture of violence must be found in religion and the specific characteristics of Protestantism as it evolved in Nordic countries. The Manichean order of good and evil, combined with the idea of Predestination, produced the "werewolf complex" and the ambivalent figure of the "evil double" (*le double mauvais*) that may be inside or outside man but can never be gotten rid of, according to Denis Duclos, who specifically looked at cinematographic culture. This figure recurs with metaphors like the beast in man, or the robot out of hand (*le robot détraqué*), with a specific interest in the technology of weapons so

---

1. Richard Slotkin, *Regeneration Through Violence: The Mythology of the American Frontier, 1600-1860* (Middletown, CO: Wesleyan UP, 1973).
2. Paul Kooistra, *Criminals as Heroes: Structure, Power and Identity* (Bowling Green, OH: Bowling Green State UP, 1989) 141-59.
3. Daniel Bell, *The End of Ideology* (NY: Free Press, 1960), especially "Crime As an American Way of Life".
4. Richard Hofstadter, *Social Darwinism and American Thought* (Boston: Beacon, 1992).

characteristic of the iconography of crime in gangster and *film noir* movies.[1] This battle of the evil double can be best exemplified in one of the most formulaic scenes of American cinema, especially gangster movies (but also westerns): the showdown (or the shootout), where two opposing sets of gunfighters (gangsters against policemen, villains against heroes) occupy the street and fire at each other, until the villains lose. The werewolf complex also brings with it the fear of contact with the other. This other, who might be criminal or sinful, spoilt and contagious, can be alternately an alien – with the double-meaning of someone either mad or illegally residing in the United States – or a woman – whose lineage connects her to Eve and the Fall of mankind.[2]

The larger cultural frame also predicates violence around the cluster of values and beliefs of "individualism".[3] According to this complex and yet fundamental creed, the individual is responsible and accountable for his actions; it rejects the idea that people can be influenced by their environment (as exemplified in the Prohibition experiment of "zero tolerance" for drinking). In resonance with the moral fabric of society predicated on religious values, crime then becomes a proof of moral collapse; it is understood primarily as immoral behavior, extenuated sometimes by some structural causes which play a subordinate (though not totally nonexistent) role. Hence the focus on street crime, compared to any other type of crime, which allows the punitive discourse of law and order to take place, as innocent people could be victimized or corrupted. Street crime allows for the depiction of a world in black and white (as in the high-contrast shadows of gangster and *film noir* movies), showing the conflict of the good guys (ordinary citizens, some of them social bandits) and the bad guys (corrupt politicians, bosses, and their cronies in the political machines exploiting the down-trodden citizenry). This depiction can foster the indignation of the civil-minded public against evil machines, especially those thwarting individualism and moral values.

The American way of crime also fosters a special cultural relation to the mass media. This relation refers to "the surveillance function" of the press as exposed by Harold Lasswell, according to which the media exist not only to inform and entertain but also to give clues about the nature of the communities in which people live and their level of safety. In this light, crime becomes a legitimate primary topic of the news and the media in general. The growth of this kind of coverage started with the penny press, as early as the 1830s, when newspapers understood they could increase

---

1. Denis Duclos, *Le complexe du loup-garou. La fascination de la violence dans la culture américaine* (Paris : La Découverte, 1994); Divina Frau-Meigs et Sophie Jeheh, *Les écrans de la violence* (Paris : Economica, 1997).
2. Lea Jacobs, *The Wages of Sin: Censorship and the Fallen Woman Film, 1928-1942* (Berkeley: U of California P, 1997).
3. Robert N. Bellah et al., *Habits of the Heart. Individualism and Commitment in American Life* (Berkeley: U of California P, 1985); Herbert Gans, *Middle Class Individualism* . The Future of Liberal Democracy (NY: Free Press, 1988); Arthur Stinchcombe et al, *Crime and Punishment. Changing Attitudes in America* (San Francisco: Jossey-Bass, 1980).

sales with accounts of crime and sex, rather than politics and finance.[1] Its coverage, amplified by the mass media (especially the dime novels of the turn of the century) in the ever-expanding urban context, conditioned the public to expect representations of a violent society in all sorts of cultural formats. So crime helped shape the definition of news (as the bizarre, the unexpected or the deviant) and the news glamorized crime and made it circulate in the wider society. As a result, crime was (and still is) often used in politics, and especially during elections, as a highly sensitive issue with public opinion.

Crime coverage developed a tendency through time to deal mostly with individual crimes, though this could involve other actors, like victims, prosecutors, witnesses and judges. The journalists tended to use first-hand sources, and counterbalanced their often self-serving accounts by using another witness or policeman's view for objectivity's sake. Only a few hints at the social dimensions of aggression were provided, with very little context. At best the journalists showed a certain populist awareness of class, with hints at a world of privilege contrasted with the world of the many in misery, but without any call for rebellion. No explanations were sought of experts like sociologists, historians or other kinds of scholars.[2] Crime was treated as a "story", as narrative, which meant that the facts could become less important than their imaginary transformation into drama, to serve a specific myth of sin and rejuvenation, around the values of individualism.

Also because of the crime culture of the press, bias and distortion appeared even within the crime descriptions. Though there were many subcategories of crime (property crime, white collar crime, etc.), it was violent crime (murder and rape) that was mostly covered, creating a distortion of nature and frequency in relation to the actual crime statistics and in relation to the actual presence of organized crime. Organized crime was covered through its open and violent murders, such as the famous St Valentine's massacre, not in its covert activities, less newsworthy because less fascinating and repulsive.[3] Less visible activities like liquor trafficking, smuggling, numbers lottery gambling, etc., tended to be covered if they could be associated with a dead body. Press photographs of the period often featured a lonely mobster lying on the pavement, an image which also filled the iconography of gangster movies. By the same token, there wasn't much coverage of how the stories proceeded through the US criminal justice system, in spite of the fact that civil cases, the most common and yet the least covered, were the ones in which the tensions in American society were resolved. Criminal cases like Al Capone's were however extensively covered, because of their sensational nature and because the inquiry unraveled in front of the public eye, not because of Scarface's tax evasions.

The extensive coverage of crime, especially in the 30s and the 40s, created a public backlash, as the press was distrusted partly because of the way it

---

1. Robin Sindall, *Street Violence in the Nineteenth Century: Media Panic or Real Danger?* (NY: Columbia UP, 1990); D. Altheide and R. Snow, *Media Logic* (Newbury Park: Sage, 1979) 63; D. Papke, *Framing the Criminal* (Hamden, CO: Archon books, 1987) 35.
2. This situation would be altered later, especially after the recommendations of the American Bar Association's Reardon Report on Fair Trial and Free Press, in the mid-60s.
3. See for example "Massacre 7 of Moran Gang", *The Chicago Daily News*, Feb 15, 1929.

dealt with crime and partly because of the way it didn't deal with the real issues, most importantly the Depression and the New Deal. The majority of the media of the time did not dwell on the Depression. The Depression didn't present newsworthiness in that it had nothing to show. And those who could have shown it, during the Hoover Administration, the corporations and the written press chose not to do so, in order to contain panic and in hope of bringing back confidence. [1] The press tended to emphasize the fact that nobody was really starving, that relief was efficient; it underplayed the severity of the crisis for the underprivileged. Census data were hard to come by, even under the New Deal and well into the 40s and economic figures were heavily manipulated so as to conceal the reality of the situation. This made Americans very skeptical of their media and their leaders, a divide between the press and public opinion which was exposed in the election of 1936, when Franklin D. Roosevelt won in spite of the opposition of the majority of the press (notably the republican newspapers owned by Hearst in major cities like New York and Los Angeles).

Less of this distrust could go to fiction and especially the new medium of cinema, which can partly explain the people's attraction to it: fiction was freer to tell the truth than news and journalists. It was left to fiction to document the real world. The movie camera was to record the authenticity of what was happening in the depressed world, with an immediacy and a visual truth that was only shared by still photography. The press was perceived as serving the special interests of the newspaper owners, affi-liated to the business community, and could not be trusted. Franklin D. Roosevelt denounced it for creating suspicion of the New Deal, together with instilling fear by its recurrent use of crime stories.[2] And proceeded to counteract it by giving "fireside chats" to the public using radio rather than print. Archibald MacLeish even accused it of using its "printing presses, like machine guns, on the people", [3] metaphorically equating it with organized crime.

The criminalization of alcohol during the Prohibition era and of the mob during the 30s-50s also evinced the strong ties between the mass media and the criminal justice system. Journalists found a lot of their news about violent acts as they worked the police and court beats to get information first hand, in a mix of sensational invention and investigative research. As a result, the press could be used to participate in the public campaigns to create awareness through education and demonstration of evil effects of violence and vice. With its mediated horror stories, the press could thus start "panics" on specific kinds of crime that would have been otherwise tolerated. The cinema could catch those panics in a more ambiguous way, lending its glamour to deviance, presenting it under the garb of dissent and

---

1. "No One Has Starved", *Fortune*, Sept 1932, 19-29, mentioned in William Stott, *Documentary Expression and Thirties America* (Chicago: U of Chicago P, 1986) 70-77 ; Gilbert Seldes, *Years of the Locust : America 1929-32* (Boston: Little Brown, 1933). See also his *Lords of the Press* (NY: J. Messner,1938) in which he demonstrates how the press increased its sensationalist coverage of individual stories and crime to survive the Depression.
2. Roosevelt, *Public Papers and Addresses* VII (NY: Random, 1938) 278-284, mentioned in Stott, *Documentary Expression*, 77.
3. Archibald MacLeish, *The American Cause* (NY: Duell, Sloan and Pearce, 1941) 17, quoted in Stott, *Documentary Expression*, 78.

inarticulate protest (the gangster figure is rather spare of his words). So the processes of information and of entertainment didn't fill the same social purpose, even if they produced similar stories.

In this light, the cultural mediation of cinema about violence dealt mostly with the representation of the gangster and the lifestyle of crime, shown as an aesthetic as it produced ways of presentation of self, symbols and rituals, in which all the members of the organization could participate, in which they found their identity and with which some members of the audience could identify. This aesthetic affected the way the criminal subcultures were caught in the social fabric and the legal relations around them. These criminal subcultures grew out of a certain number of inequalities, (class, gender, age and most important, ethnicity), reproducing social chiasms and the urban lower-class resistance at being integrated and acculturated.

By ironic symmetry, this aesthetic of mediated images – the visible tip of the iceberg of crime, by definition bound to secrecy – made it possible for some of the aesthetic activities of culture to be recast as crime. This happened to Hollywood twice in its golden age, with the rise of censorship and the scandals around some specific gangster movies which became "media events", [1] stories that could not have existed without the cultural mediation of cinema and the press. The pattern of these media events around images of organized crime and of crime control provides an understanding of the interplay between cultural and criminal processes in American society and associates them with moments of deep identity crisis, especially the 30s Depression and the 40s postwar difficult return to normalcy. They tend to show the codependency of crime and culture as they intersect with civil society, with the criminalization of culture and the cultivation of crime. They cast light on the double-edged effects of their interplay in the hands of the various social groups that used the media events: movie producers could use them for promotional purposes; public decency groups and other interest groups could use them for their political agenda, especially to push the passing of law and order legislation; audiences, especially the ethnic groups and the lower classes, could find some vicarious revenge and pleasure.

Within the larger range of society, these media events also had the effect of creating controversy around a relatively new media, talking cinema, whose rise needed to be controlled by the previously established media and society at large. Politically, the media events around crime movies may also have been used to deflect attention from the causes of criminality, like economic inequalities and ethnic racism. The way the controversies evolved tend to show that they aimed at reinforcing the idea that deviant behavior could be treated without touching the structures of the liberal corporate world and its own means of control and authority. Hence the criminalization campaigns were often led against minority groups, ethnic groups, young people who threatened the core values of American individualism

---

1. Daniel Dayan and Elihu Katz, *Media Events. The Live Broadcasting of History* (Cambridge, MA: Harvard UP, 1992); John Fiske, *Media Matters. Race and Gender in US Politics* (Minneapolis: U of Minnesota P, 1996); Divina Frau-Meigs, « Le débat américain entre réforme et censure », *IHESI* 20 2 (1995) : 85-97.

from the margins. All the more so as organized crime dealt in illegal goods and provided services that, though they were illicit, filled a social function of exchange (game, drink, seduction,...), never far from commerce.

Codependency as seen through the gangster movies of the Depression

In the crux of these intersections, gangster movies were perceived as the carriers of the tension between crime and culture throughout the transformations of America from the Depression into the Cold War. They carried with them memories of the repression of Prohibition and of the Wall Street Crash; they materialized the human throes of the transition to an urban industrial world; they were very much anchored in a social realism, that the other lonesome figure of cinema, the cowboy, had ignored. Their social realism was heightened by the arrival of sound, propitious in connection to the representation of crime because of the special effects it allowed: gunfire, sirens, screams of victims, explosions, and the characteristic smart alec hard boiled dialogue of mobsters. It literally gave a voice to a specific community in a specific place. [1]

The cultivation of crime in the entertaining function framed Hollywood's increasing awareness of its role as a forger of the American culture and as a trend setter. Culture seemed to remain one step ahead of the Police, in the sense that Hollywood tried consistently to test the limits of social acceptability and to play within the negotiated terms, avoiding controversy while at the same time titillating the audience's taste. According to Munby, "this maneuvering was driven by commercial rather than ideological imperatives (profit depending on the need to address popular audience desires, even if this contravened the wishes of moral and political watchdogs)."[2] This maneuvering was partly aimed at tapping the desirable young audience of the urban industrial world, who was likely to consume leisure in reality (alcohol, loose women, sports, etc.) and vicariously (via the movies and the novels); this audience could also find in the spectacle of crime a compensation for the deprivations of the modern workplace (alienating factory work, routine white-collar wage labor, etc.), when it did not completely identify with it.

The gangster movies of the Depression era show society's disorder. Mervyn LeRoy's *Little Caesar* (1930) started the controversy over what was perceived as a movie "cycle"[3], the first golden age of Hollywood, where the screen culture found financial interest in crime. The focus was on the gangster himself and on his individual destiny, very much in the individualistic streak of American violence, but with references to the social reality of the mob. Earlier gangster movies like Josef von Sternberg's *Underworld* (1927) and *Thunderbolt* (1929), offered a much more stylized and abstract

---

1. Richard Griffith, "The American Film: 1929-1948", Paul Rotha (ed), *The Film Till Now. A Survey of World Cinema* (London: Vision, 1949); Jonathan Munby, *Public Enemies, Public Heroes. Screening the Gangster From Little Caesar to Touch of Evil* (Chicago: U of Chicago P, 1999) 5.
2. Munby, *Public Enemies, Public Heroes*, 171, note 26.
3. Olga J. Martin, *Hollywood's Movie Commandments* (NY: Arno Press and the New York Times, 1937) 31.

view of crime.[1] The other classic movies of the cycle, *The Public Enemy* (1931), *Smart Money* (1931) and *Scarface* (1932), according to Robert Sklar

> condensed social conflicts and disorders into the ambitions and dreams of their heroes. Society's values and institutions revealed themselves in the way they formed the gangster's life, and in how they reacted to what he had become. (...) their heroes chaotic lives were more than matched by the chaos in society around them (...) the gangster movies were not Depression success stories (...) they were films of social pathos.[2]

For this reason, they were successful with the audience, who identified with the gangster and his temptations. In fact, they denounced public authority and the ruthlessness of a corrupt society as a whole in a vague enough way to cut through all classes. They translated the Americans' disenchantment with the core values of individualism and success, as they turned middle-class Protestant values on their head. The contemporary comic scenes of the Marx Brothers functioned in the same manner. *Monkey Business* (1931) made fun of the world of Protestant society and of gangsters.

On the surface movies delivered the message "crime doesn't pay". *Scarface* and *Public Enemy* both exhibited printed warnings to the viewers about the evil characters that were to be shown, framing them in the rhetoric of a medieval morality play. But if the expected moral message was a kind of cover to pass censorship, the underlying message touched deeper parts of the American psyche and culture and its different transgressions and went against the grain of the moral accommodations expected of society. It explored the inherent violence of the American commercial and corporate system, the corruption and the crushing of the individual that it entailed, when he was not on the winning side of the struggle for life.

The criminalization of culture through censorship can then be seen as a means of masking this crushing power, of making it more or less ideologically invisible. This process implied framing cultural memory into a different mold, forgetful of the inherent pressures of capitalism. Which is why such a seemingly innocuous cultural form as the crime film became the scene of high profile socio-political struggles.

The criminalization of culture took place within some specific groups of the public who put pressure on Hollywood and politicians to change the production of gangster movies. The Legion of Decency campaign against crime movies opposed the depiction of too much flesh and risky language, and saw crime pictures as a betrayal of middle-class values and morality. What scared the people who campaigned for the criminalizing of this movie was the demotion of their own civic values of individualism. Mostly Protestant, they feared that their control over civil society would be undone by the "new" Americans whose demographic expansion might put them in a minority situation; they feared that the cultural transmission of values the media effected would modify their own children's perceptions of violence and punishment.

---

1. Robert Sklar, *Movie-Made America. A Cultural History of American Movies* (NY: Vintage, 1994) 179-181.
2. Sklar, *Movie-Made America*, 181.

So they used the press both to stigmatize the existence of the ghettoes and their un-Americanized mobs and to wage a moral crusade against Hollywood, with threats of economic boycotts of the cinema houses. Their action against cinema was all the more urgent as they knew the messages on the silver screen could cut across class and across ethnicity, in a mass culture that exposed all Americans to the same images. Less extreme in their protests, the Catholics were the ones who brought Hollywood to the negotiation table, probably because of the failure of the Protestant liberal system in the Depression, and because Catholics were urban, organized by their hierarchy, and ready to compromise with Hollywood.[1] They needed to save their own constituencies, and their own Christian values about the family, solidarity and the intercession of religious figures (saints, martyrs, angels, the Virgin Mary, etc) to atone for the sins of mankind, all of which they felt were being defaced by the crime movies.

The compromise reached allowed for the representation of some elements that were immoral provided they were counterbalanced with good elements, i.e. punishment and retribution or regeneration of the bad guy.[2] Crime should be punished, and, characteristically, sin was equated with crime. The Motion Picture Code of 1930 classified them both together:

> In the use of this material, it must be distinguished between sin (crime) which by its very nature repels, and sin which by its nature attracts. (a) In the first class (repellent crimes) come murder, most theft, most legal crimes, lying, hypocrisy, cruelty, etc. (b) In the second class (crimes which attract) come crimes of apparent heroism, such as banditry, daring thefts, leadership in evil, organized crime, revenge, etc.[3]

The reference to the religious meaning of violence in America, in connection to its particular protestant interpretation of Christian values was made as the werewolf complex explicitly took the figure of "The Lone Wolf" in Olga Martin's depiction of him as

> the swindler, the "confidence" man, or other type of offender that may be engaged in shady dealings which place him outside the pale of legitimate business. (...) The offender must be apprehended by the law and punished for any illegal acts he may commit. If he repents of his conduct, relinquishes his criminal activities and seeks to make restitution for any wrong he has done, it is possible to indicate that he is placed on probation. The law itself, however, would have to exonerate him and to free him from the necessity of punishment.[4]

The religious and civic interest groups triumphed with the founding of the Breen Office in 1934, just after the first wave of gangster movies (1930-34). The gangster movies were one of the first victims of the new full and detailed Production Code, with a moratorium declared on all gangster films

---

1. Gregory Black, *Hollywood Censored: Morality Codes, Catholics and the Movies* (Cambridge: Cambridge UP, 1994).
2. Olga J. Martin, *Hollywood's Movie Commandments* (NY: Arno Press and the New York Times, 1937) ; Will H. Hays, *Memoirs* (Garden City, NY: Doubleday, 1955).
3. "Principles of Plot", *The Motion Picture Production Code of 1930*, in Martin, *Hollywood's Movie Commandments*, 276.
4. Martin, *Hollywood's Movie Commandments*, 139.

in 1935.¹ They were thus forever stamped with the mark of the "evil double", which, paradoxically, gave them a certain cultural legitimacy. For, in this light, the figure of the gangster as a social bandit can be interpreted as a transitory character with a cultural necessity: he mediated between culture and crime, between good and evil, order and chaos, law and wilderness. His final death or redemption was a mythic means to ensure that the violence of the frontier and the chaos of wild corporatism lead to the peace of civilized values and accepted capitalism. The social bandit outlaw appealed to the American imagination as much as the positive hero of westerns or detective stories. He gathered to his figure the repulsion that religious groups and established winners felt for disruption and chaos – though a lot of them fed on it legally – and the attraction that dissenters and losers felt for rebels against a system of commercial competition gone awry. The double evil hence mirrored the double standard of morals, politics and economics. These two facets were the double evil of American society at large, caught between its need to harness both power and protest, to maintain its democratic balance.

The gangster as folk outlaw hero can thus be related to two antagonistic forces in the United States: on the one hand, the incorporation of the economy, with the rise of capital, property, the closure and enclosure of the West, and the urban expansion;² on the other hand, forces of resistance and dissent, often outlawed by the associated interests of power and politics, who rebelled against that incorporation. The gangster used for protection values of family, solidarity and clientele that ran against the corporate principles of law, order and rational functionalism, revolving around the individual. The battle was unequal, as the corporations pursued their expansion single-mindedly whereas the dissident outlaws whose views, ideologies and perceptions were not that clear, were a difficult fit in American society, doomed either to disappear or, as happened later, to incorporate. By the 20s, the real battle had been won by the corporations, but the virtual battle in myth and fiction was to be won by the social bandit, and the gangster came to fit into that niche, vindicated by the shock waves of the Wall Street Crash.

The Production Code shifted Hollywood production from sex and violence to the "screwball comedies" of the mid 1930s, and moved Americans away from the depiction of contemporary life. It can be considered as a shift from social responsibility to moral responsibility, a pattern often to be repeated in the American relationship between crime and cinema (and media more generally).³ This shift was supported by the New Deal Administration and its policies to boost the morale and the morals of the people, with national values that were reconstructed around the core values of individualism.

---

1. Richard Maltby, "The Production Code and the Hays Office", Tino Balio (ed), *The Grand Design: Hollywood as a Modern Business Enterprise, 1930-1939* (Berkeley: U of California P, 1995) 37-72.
2. Alan Trachtenberg, *Incorporation of America: Culture and Society in the Gilded Age* (NY: Hill and Wang, 1982).
3. Frau-Meigs, « Le débat américain entre réforme et censure », 85-97.

Codependency as seen through *film noir* movies

The restrictions inflicted by the Production Code also brought about important changes in the formula of the gangster movie (though social changes and Hollywood's attention to audiences had a strong part to play), which can be traced in the *film noir* of the 1940s and 50s. Though it tended to take place in independent production, alongside the studio system, it still met some of the issues at stake in gangster movies of the 30s, issues postponed by the War effort (where the battle between good and evil, democracy and tyranny was eagerly represented by Hollywood propaganda movies).

> Though clearly belonging to an aesthetically distinctive style of cinema, postwar crime films were understood contemporaneously as refinements on a repressed but established formula (...) not only belonging to a tradition but also perpetuating a legacy of dissidence (something made possible in the more permissive realm of B and independent studio production).[1]

In movies like *Dillinger* (1945) or *Key Largo* (1948), the transitory character of the gangster was yet a mutation of the outlaw in the sense that he rejected some of the demands of individualism and of modern urban life. Though he lost his ethnic ghetto gusto, he continued to raise social issues around postwar ideals and politics. With his lack of belief in the American dream of success and inclusion, he symbolized the anti-liberal effects of liberalism and showed an America at odds with its values. In *film noir*, possibly due to external influence of German filmmakers in exile, the gangster belonged to the middle class, not the underclass; he was a part of a secret syndicate, depicted as a kind of anonymous corporation, which could be interpreted as a metaphor for the crushing power of the corporate system, prohibiting the individual from exerting his liberty, as exemplified in Siodmak's *The Killers* (1946).

The cultivation of crime via the *film noir* hero emphasized the increasing alienation of man from a society whose complexity had all the trappings of secrecy to the ordinary person.[2] The heroes of the 40s had moral rectitude but lacked the physical strength to enact it. They were slightly flawed, slightly neurotic, and losers as in *Body and Soul* (1948) or *Asphalt Jungle* (1950). Even if, by convention, moral strength triumphed in the end, the difficulties of their plight and fight that took place before the resolution were what interested the public. Crime then appeared as a defense mechanism, a protection against a corrupt society, with little help to expect from the law or the police. A movie like *Bullets or Ballots* (1936) exemplified the ambiguity in the representation of crime and of the villain, together with establishing a bridge between gangster movies and *film noir*, as the hero denounces the racketeers (as a cop) and expands the numbers racket (as a gangster). The secret bosses who run the syndicate of crime turn out to be a Wall Street banker, an ex-Senator and a young millionaire, – all three

---

1. Munby, *Public Enemies, Public Heroes*, 7.
2. Peter Roffman and Jim Purdy, *The Hollywood Social Problem Film.Madness, Despair and Politics From the Depression to the Fifties* (Bloomington: Indiana UP, 1981), 145-48; see also Joan Copjek (ed), *Shades of Noir: A Reader* (London: Verso, 1993).

members of the Establishment. But as they are very little seen on screen, the ambiguity remains about the cause of their corruption: it is not clear if it is due to the capitalist system or to their own moral decadence.[1]

In *film noir*, the representation of violence and crime was once again showing disillusions and disenchantments with the system and the return of corporate power (facilitated by the war). Themes of alienation and crushed individualism had resonance with the postwar social conditions of America, a period of very numerous strikes as labor was trying to create a new balance with corporations and government. The questioning of the New Deal promises by the corporations and the believers in Republican individualistic values was again creating disenchantment among the lower classes. And disenchantment called for the representation of the disenfranchised individual, once more, as in the 30s, in all his maladjustments, with little solution to the malaise but the realistic representation of everyday life.

Film noir, in its darkness and pessimism, upset the religious and civic-minded interest groups, who had the feeling that there was the return of a cycle with the productions of films like *The Big Sleep* (1946), *The Killers* (1946), *Brute Force* (1947) *Kiss of Death* (1947), *The Gangster* (1947), *Body and Soul* (1947), etc. That movies of the 40s could refer back to those of the 30s clearly showed how the intertextuality[2] of culture and crime worked in the United States: in spite of mutations of aesthetics and history, the codependency remained latent and perceptible to the public, allowing parts of the audience to find some vicarious pleasure and vindication in it and other parts of the audience to be re-mobilized for another cultural war.

So the criminalization of culture took place again, as two movements coalesced: the drive to alter the Production Code and renew the censorship agenda; the arrival of the House Committee on Un-American Activities (HUAC) in Hollywood in 1947 (and until 1953), which led to McCarthyism and its political purge.

Much as in the *Little Caesar* case, the movie *Dillinger* was used as a means of mobilizing the legions and the leagues. It was set against a renewed claim of "an affirmative ideological agenda",[3] which called for positive images of the American Way of Life, as the American Dream was being reframed. Any interest in the gangster that might recall memories of the Depression or bring back interest in the New Deal had to be deflected. Dillinger, the social bandit, represented a real antagonism to the political and economical forces during the Depression as he presented himself as a champion of the poor. His come back in fiction made the moral interest groups fear for a renewed wave of crime glorification. The press and printed letters to editors and to politicians were used to put pressure on the Production Code Administration, and to ask it to resume its watch on movie production. As Munby summarized the episode: "The critical reaction to the film reveals a complex mix of ongoing residual struggles left over from the Depression and the

---

1. Maltby, *Harmless Entertainment. Hollywood and the Ideology of Consensus* (Metuchen, NJ: The Scarecrow Press, 1983) 111-12.
2. This intertextuality was even stronger as most film noir movies were adaptations of highly successful hard boiled crime novels.
3. Munby, *Public Enemies, Public Heroes*, 148.

emerging new demands of presenting a vision of liberal consensus to the world."¹

The *Dillinger* case revealed that the Production Code forged in the 30s needed some updating, especially as it seemed that producers and filmmakers had found ways to circumvent some of its strictures about the representation of criminality and sexuality. The American power class in the 40s, after World War II, didn't want dark political visions to interfere with their domestic situation and their moral order. The passivity of the Production Code Administration (PCA) after the war and its relaxation of self-discipline was seen as having allowed the return of the gangster, via the crime films wave of the late 40s that the French described as *"film noir"* – not in accordance with the cultural American reading of the time which assimilated them to the gangster cycle movies.

These films benefited from the postwar confusion and the reaction only came in 1947. Then it became apparent that the PCA had not been able to censor these films because the reality depicted in them represented changes in society not imagined in the 30s' Code. The PCA had to modify its instrument of censorship and moral control. Its instrument of film analysis was perfected: from one page of general statements and a few pages of "commandments", it was expanded to many more pages, with different sections of items specifically relating the world of fiction to the world of reality (professions, types of actions, types of crimes and victims, values, lessons and messages, etc.). The instrument could be used to check the scripts and expunge any un-American traits in them. It did so less by prohibiting, as it had during the Depression, than by endorsing and advertising the positive aspects of the American liberal world.

The screening of the gangster movies thus became infused with Red Scare paranoia, together with feelings that Hollywood had to be cleansed of its New Deal socio-liberal leanings. Policing film and, in the process criminalizing film culture, became once more acceptable, all the more so if Hollywood could be converted into the police-agency. This was a subtler procedure than the one that was decided by McCarthy who went much farther in his attack against Hollywood, via the HUAC.² The HUAC had the ambition to expunge Communism and anything remotely associated with left-wing politics and it looked with particular care for any broadcasting of leftwing messages to the mass public, in the new climate of the Cold War.³

So it is not so much the PDA as the HUAC that intervened in the checking of *film noir*, a proof that this type of production had some social realism about it, closely related to the 40s. The HUAC exerted its wrath particularly against *Brute Force, Body and Soul* and *Force of Evil*. These movies were perceived as showing criminals with mainstream desires for love, money and power. They tended to cast the forces of control (the police, the prison wardens) as ruthless and cruel, a reversal that could be interpreted as a "communist" criticism of American "bourgeois" values. To the HUAC

---

1. Munby, *idem*, *Public Heroes*, 156.
2. Terence Ball, "The Politics of Social Science in Postwar America", Lary May (ed), *Recasting America : Culture and Politics in the Age of Cold War* (Chicago: U of Chicago P, 1989) 76-82.
3. Stephen J. Whitfield, *The Culture of the Cold War* (Baltimore: Johns Hopkins UP, 1991).

and the interest groups, these movies were a sign of "dysfunctional" Hollywood.[1]

They were also critical of crime per se, as they investigated the nature of greed, acquisition and how it was exploited by society in its institutions and its prohibitions. For instance, the hero in *Force of Evil* (1948) is driven by the villain within himself, which harks back to the image of the werewolf, of the double-edged guilt motif of the pure and the tainted in mankind. The messages of such movies could be interpreted as saying that the American quest for success contaminated the hero, who had to extract the good life at all cost. In the process, he was bound to lose his sense of social and moral responsibility.

Film noir and gangster films became the butt of further criticism as they were often made by political exiles – Europeans of German or Austrian origins –, escaping fascism and having a tendency to criticize all forms of authoritarian regimes. As a result of the HUAC's investigation, some of the producers and writers for *film noir* movies became blacklisted, as a means of intimidation: Jules Dassin, Robert Rossen and Abraham Polonsky, among others, either left the country forever or stopped producing altogether, resulting in the decline of the *film noir* wave and the rise of the light domestic and consensual comedies of the 50s.

Screening the Kefauver Commission

The Hollywood hearings of the HUAC coincided in time with those of the Kefauver Commission (1951-1953). The codependency between crime and culture was thus once more put to the test, as the cultivation of crime was brought to the fore with the Commission. It marked a new campaign for cleaning the streets and getting rid of the mob; partly influenced by the movies, it used itself a new emergent media, television. Fiction met with reality, with gangsters whose life had been made into movies coming to testify and television broadcasting this new media event. The Kefauver Commission's cultural meaning emerged from its interplay of mediated images of organized crime and crime control.

The high point of the Commission took place when the careers of Franck Costello, the racketeer, and William O'Dwyer, the district attorney of Brooklyn and then mayor of New York intersected in reality and in fiction. They met on the witness bench of the Commission, with live coverage by television for 7 days. In a way, fiction deflected the conclusions of the Commission, as it laid the blame on "the mafia" as a threat to civil society, as "an elusive, shadowy, and sinister organization" that had become a "brotherhood", and that came from Sicily. [2] According to Dwight Smith, the Commission used the mafia in a very ambiguous way (it was mostly connected with narcotics, not gambling, in its hearings), in part to deflect public opinion from doubting all its public officials. It used the televised event to mobilize public opinion once more against organized crime, especially the sinister mafia.

---

1. Munby, *op. cit.*, 165.
2. Kefauver, third interim report, conclusions released on May 1, 1951, in Dwight, *The Mafia Mystique*, 134.

The motives behind the probe and the world to which the investigation was broadcast aimed at creating a controlling public response: force the government into a public admission that the mafia existed and then purge itself from it. The fear was that the secret syndicate could subvert the nation and undermine confidence in government. Though the open purpose of the Commission was the control of interstate gambling, its covert purpose turned out to be the creation of a sort of "Puritan board of inquiry".[1] It ended up prosecuting more than investigating, at least in the moral sense, as in the case of New England Senator Tobey, who made several pronouncements against the immorality of gambling. Public opinion organized around the religious and civic groups once more was aroused; it became especially demanding in local politics, starting a series of investigations into mob practices at the local level.

Dwight connects the need of the inquiry with the Puritans' need to public admission of sin (rather than the Catholic private confession or contrition) because public repentance gives more power to the moral standards of the community. So the threat for potential political corruption was less important than the threat of potential sin, to be rejected as a force of evil. The religious groups attached "their minor crusade to a larger public bandwagon (...) From that moment, the law-enforcement community had a conditional, but also highly specific, label for an organizational structure responsible for syndicated crime". [2]

The appraisal of crime as sin was more fictional than realistic, and the report of the Commission made an impact more by its moral tone than by its actual message on crime. The report, with its preference for a mythical secret syndicate with blood pledges and ethnic relations to another country, was characterized by denial: of modern organized crime as a big business; of the fact that the structure of American society could create a natural environment for gangsterism. The answer, according to Bell, was in accordance with America 's capacity "for compromise in politics and extremism in morality".[3]

The Kefauver Commission exhibited the American politics of individualism in screening crime. Sin and corruption had to be ascribed to a secret group or collective, not to the individual. Maltby ascribes it to the American "politics of style", the fact that American ideology refuses to consider the good of society unless it is represented through the good of the individual; as a result it cannot consider the resolution of conflict between opposing groups or forces, it has to show a consensus among individuals.

> The consensus forms not at the level of opinion over issues, but at the level of the manner in which that opinion is presented – the style and rhetoric of political discussion. (...) A consensus over political style thus allows the maintenance of the dual illusion on which American democracy is based. The fiction of the unity of individual and social interest is upheld by the uniformity of political

---

1. Dwight, *The Mafia Mystique*, 141.
2. Dwight, *The Mafia Mystique*, 142.
3. Bell, *The End of Ideology*, 141, quoted in Dwight, *The Mafia Mystique*, 145.

> *style, but that uniformity also permits the man of goodwill to disagree over specific issues.* [1]

This politics of style inevitably called for more investigations in organized crime and its cultivation in the media; they were carried on extensively in the 60s, with television, and are still carried on with the Internet, as the codependent processes of crime and culture keep shaping the tensions within American society.

---

1. Richard Maltby, *Harmless Entertainment*, 182-83.

Clans in *Scarface* and *The Maltese Falcon*. Screening the female

By Eithne O'Neill

Less than a decade divides two classics in the history of the screen representation of the struggle against organised crime in the Thirties and Forties. We speak here of *Scarface*, prototype of the talking gangster movie, set against the backdrop of Prohibition, and *The Maltese Falcon*, Huston's adaptation of Hammett's 1929 novel, shot and released after the outbreak of the Second World War, and brilliantly ushering in *film noir*. In the speakeasies of the Midwest capital, in the hotel-lobbies overlooking the Pacific, the transgressors are brought to bay. Hawks' work is centred on an overreacher, a grass-roots gang-leader, while Huston dismantles the shenanigans of an exotic, motley crew. Heavily armed forces of law and order in hot pursuit of criminals give way to the tracking down of evil by a loner whose main weapon is his constantly whetted cunning. Common to both the ebullient action film and the dramatic thrust of Huston's dialogic fable is the theme of transgressive excess. However, when Scarface whistles "What is there to hold me back", he acknowledges by default the existence of boundaries, unlike Gutman and his partners in crime who ride roughshod over the very concept.

To cover the range of gangland associations, the term "clan" is being introduced in a threefold use. From the Scots and Irish Gaelic for "family", the noun by extension refers to a gathering of people bound by common traits or interests, here to the illegal brotherhood in its singular, localized urban-ghetto form, exemplified by "Scarface and his Merry Men", Rinaldo and Andrew. Clan equally reflects the allusive Italian and Polish ethnic groups pitted against O'Hara's Shamrock "mob", a derogatory, more impersonal term for a gangland set-up. Gutman's bunch or clique, an assortment of merciless crooks, "mobsters" at heart, have seemingly sprung up from nowhere. Although the tagged racism of Hammett's text and the enduring real-life suspicion of immigrants linger, the malicious, fictitious characters belong to an elite, as regards class, appearance and speech. Their variegated plumage notwithstanding, Birdman and Co. are, through a murky bond, kindred spirits. Theirs is the clan clandestine[1].

Little doubt there may have been as to the avowed purpose of organised crime, yet secrecy everywhere binds the initiates. Gaffney gets his comeuppance for spilling the beans; Jacobi, the messenger, in keeping with Greek tragic convention, dies on delivering the goods. By the Golden Gate,

---

1. The definitive "clan" in the history of organised crime in the U.S. is the Mafia with, from 1931 on, its five "cross-American" crime families. For detailed studies of the importance of family structure and blood ties founded, see Francis A.J. Ianni's work *Des Affaires de Famille. La Mafia à New York*, trans. from the 1972 English edition, *A Family Business* by Georges Magnane, Plon,1973. *The Mafia Mystique*, Dwight C. Smith, Jr.,Basic Books, New York, 1975 deals with popular stereotyped conceptions of the "organisation", c.f. especially in the post-war context. C.f. chap. 9 "aka Mafioso: A Case of Mistaken Identity"; Salvatore Lupo's *Histoire de la mafia des origines à nos jours*, trans. from the 1996 Italian work by Jean-Claude Zancarini, and published by Flammarion, 1999, brings the transatlantic story of the Mafia up to date.

mystification is the name of the Bird-Clan's game. By dint of keeping things to themselves, a form of self-defence, they turn against each other, whereby their internal strife becomes an emblem for the gangster dissensions of the recent urban past. In both films, the gang sketches out the design of "three men and a girl[1]". Scarface is flanked by his hard-core band, Angelo, the illiterate *"secretary,* "his loyal, pathetic self, and Rinaldo, the "little boss", his more adult *alter ego*, thus, his rival. Hovering in the wings is the female, embodied by the twinned figures of Poppy and Cesca. Much on their guard against the wiles of their vamp associate, Miss Wonderly, are Gutman, Cairo, Wilmer, beloved "as a son". Out of kilter thanks to the sole acting female, the male swindlers are increasingly bemused by the bird myth they in part fabricate.

Finally, clan includes the notion of blood-ties, which in turn, by the law of nature, entail ancestry and descendants. Woman, as symbol and guarantor of continuity, rears her lovely head. Scarface has a family, of sorts. In addition to Cesca, his flapper-sister, in the humble kitchen, we meet his mother. Old before her time, she sets out his dinner on what can only be a red and white check tablecloth. A caricatural Italian *Mamma*, speaking broken English, broken in spirit, bereft of a hold on her fatherless offspring she may be, yet, in her inarticulate fashion, she hits the nail on the head. Scarface is a bad lot. The handing down of morality will fall to hostile officialdom in the shape of the police.

Calling on "family" to pull the wool over our eyes, Miss Wonderly adds insult to injury. Of the possible effect of the non-existent sister's plight on Mother and Father she says: "It will kill them". *Murder, she said*. Spade's status as a laconic bachelor does not preclude just estimation of what the score is, notably in respect to the fate of his bumped-off partner, "whose wife didn't like him and who had no children". Nor does he lack strong moral and emotional fibre, thanks to which he wins out over the allures of body and heart: "I won't, because all of me wants to". Where ethics, and the value put on human life are at stake, the outcome of his disciplined stance, discomfiture, solitude, were it the dearth of a "clan", are a paltry price to pay.

By dint of their peculiar selectivity, however, Scarface and the "Dingus" hunters are, when it comes to kin, decidedly "clannish". Hell-bent on appropriating persons as much as gold, the gangsters keep "things", sister and knowledge, "to themselves". In vain. Unleashed by his manhandling of Cesca, the final stage in Camonte's sartorial, physical, and psychological disgrace begins with a series of phone-calls to the molls. In their archly courteous fashion, Gutman, Cairo and O'Shaugnessy have as little truck with the niceties of gentlemanly behaviour as with abiding ties, be they with woman or youth. By what methods have they "persuaded" Miss O'Shaugnessy to tell them of the whereabouts of the missing bird? Thrice betrayed by Gutman's unctuous declarations of fatherly love for his "gunsel", Wilmer is elected scapegoat:

---

1. The pattern is already set up in *The Gangsters and the Girl*, 1914, directed by R. Scott Sidney. The story of a private eye who "infiltrates" a gang and wins the heart of a moll seems particularly appropriate for *The Maltese Falcon*.

If you lose a son, you can get another. There's only one Maltese Falcon.

Only when Scarface rips his sister's dress off, kills his rival, her husband(!), does he meet his deserts. At loggerheads, the sexes seize each other by wrist, arm or shoulder. Scarface got his nickname during a war with a blonde in a Brooklyn speakeasy. Through the scratching and clawing between Cairo and a thwarted O'Shaugnessy, the "Eeny-meeny-miny" torture of choosing a fallguy, the crooks of either sex strive, not only to ward off retribution and justice, but to outmanoeuvre the other sex, to sift, phase, or screen "it" out.

The verb "to screen" is therefore being used here in three senses. It conveys the bringing *on screen* of such and such a persona or topos, in the context of the mores which bred them. Secondly, screening, as the phrasal variations *screening in* or *screening out* specify, also means to check, or filter, thereby, to eliminate the unsuitable, in accordance with a fixed rule of conduct. Might it be that, in the films at hand, aspects of screened womankind survive that are all the more captivating as they have escaped the censor's gimlet eye? Did the implementors of the burgeoning Hays Code fail to see the wood for the trees? In 1934, the regulations of self-censorship came fully into effect[1].

Finally, selection will be applied to indicate the process whereby any lasting joint impact of visual image and verbal support, typed though these may be, providing that they are informed by a glimmer of perception, tends to go "against the grain". From the *guise* of stereotypes, we infer a more complex reality, unfolding, as it were, in *disguise*. If a corpus bearing witness to the spirit of a particular period, is, over half a century later, to sustain our attention as *Scarface* and *The Maltese Falcon* have done, screening, as a hermeneutic ploy must be brought into play.

Through this "filter", the viewer is better able to "tell the difference" between how being a female is *presented* within the diegesis of the film, and how this construct may now be *construed*. Similarly, collective hostility to the unfamiliar appears, by latter-day standards, more blatant, but we are dealing with historically defined artefacts and, as such, they should be respected. The aporia between the explicitly shown and the supposedly subdued is subject to further scrutiny. Although Spade and Brigid's sexual encounter is palpable, the fact that in the films under discussion no-one ostensibly goes to bed with anyone, may have blinded the thirties audience, in the first place, to the powerful staging of an erotic relationship that is clandestine (*Scarface*), and subsequently, to a sexual deviation that simmers underneath the apparent plot, veiled by the silver screen (*The Maltese Falcon*). After winnowing, the capacity of a film to arouse our interest should be enhanced. Thanks to the raising of the temporal screen, the individual and the universal join hands.

---

1. C.f. Thomas Doherty's article in *Precode Hollywood Sex, Immortality and Insurrection in American Cinema, 1930-1934*, Columbia University Press, 1999, p. 137-170. The author underlines the fact that it was the physical violence and heroisation that caused a stir and delayed the movie's release. Once again, while O'Doherty underlines the ignominious treatment meted to women in this corpus, the incestuous strain rates a mere mention.

Whether acting as the member of an organisation, or striking out on his own, be he a law-enforcer or denizen of gangland, it seems to be taken for granted that man should rule the roost. Social Wards, precincts, the North and South Sides of Chicago, police headquarters, bowling alleys all belong to the "guys". "While women had been barred from saloons, they were allowed to enter speakeasies[1]". From the rough-and-ready bootleggers' den, to the more sophisticated thieves' hideout on the West Coast, in an era when all citizens have in common an "enemy without", woman is slapped, shouted down, pushed about. In body and soul. Smooth talkers both, do not the illiterate Scarface and Spade, the Shakespeare-reader, alike condone a lopsided, reprehensible, not to say, criminal state of affairs? Since social identity is channelled through the multifarious conventions of a filmic genre, it is in readiness to act out a predetermined role that the female enters our field of vision and gangland. From chorus-girl to gangster's-moll, via *Mamma*, a fellow's cheating wife, kid-sister, childhood sweetheart, or devoted secretary, the female, on the verge of being tempted, finally emerges as the *femme fatale*.

To others and to herself, why is woman fatal? In *Scarface* and *The Maltese Falcon* a subtler picture of womankind is adumbrated. Torn between her two men, as between daylight and the underworld, where does dazzling Cesca belong? In the nether world perhaps? Reaching its highpoint, the rift within the Gutman gang brings out a sight that is sorrier still: that of woman divided against her self.

As Camonte strides into a joint he is taking over, the tracking shot pans behind him along a large oil painting of a Goyaesque Maya, scantily clad in a feathery boa. Is woman as a "bit of fluff" being hinted at? Not so. Mabel wears a furry stole. A mink, "serious stuff", will be draped over Brigid O'Shaugnessy's comely tailored suit as she is introduced to us, and *she* is as tough as nails. Decoding the interaction of audience-expectation and the reception by the informed viewer, the screening mechanism is triggered. Accordingly, when Big Louie Costillo, in his famous last words, boasts of being fulfilled, because he has a house, an automobile and a "nice girl", we begin to wonder: what does he mean exactly? The last of the traditional gangsters, he might parade a respectable "wife", and have a floozie on the side. Before his usurper, Scarface, starts reeling to destruction, the tricky process of re-defining, which is at the core of our problematic, has been, by a minor feat of self-reflexivity, set into motion. To Tony's way of thinking, a "nice girl" rhymes with expensive. Obviously a measure of success, showing off a "nice girl" begs the question as to who, on earth, in the context of America between the wars, she may be? Eve eternal recumbent over the bar is also woman in the Roaring Twenties who deemed she had the right to choose. As Cesca defiantly asserts, she can do "what she likes", and look after herself the while. At how great a cost, we shall see.

---

1. C.f. *Prohibition. The 13 Years that changed America*, Edward Behr, BBC Books, 1997, p. 92-94. Hathaway's *Call Northside 777* (1948) shows Wanda Skutnik's speakeasy with its grocery front in Chicago's Polish district. However, her joint is presented as isolated rather than part of a larger network, although her customers include policemen.

A formal feature of *Scarface* relevant to audience-perception and to the issue of heroisation, is the music accompanying the credits. Romantic, apparently out of synch with the he-man megalomania of the film at large, more characteristic of *film noir* than of the gangster-film proper, the air heralds the "human" interest, said to be the privilege of the female. Livening up the scene are lace underwear, a frilly parasol and females galore, among them, Mabel, Masie, Sadie, heroine of *Rain*, by Somerset Maugham, the play within the play, and Poppy. Speaking to the latter, Scarface himself indulges in screening out:

I know lots of girls, redhaired, blonde, but I'm crazy for you.

Far from going unnoticed, the ellipsis of the brunette category shields a more delicate obfuscation. The exchange encourages the viewer to infer that Mr. Tony has not yet made it to base with Lovo's former mistress. Hence his stepped-up palaver. Contrary to Big Louie, Scarface does not brag that he has what he *would* like. The more numerous his acquisitions, the more wistful his tone of voice, insinuating that he *cannot* have precisely that. Feebly backed up by "what they say", his courtship, in keeping with his mobster discourse, is sheer patter. He feels, but not for the moll.

Regarding Spade's genderized appelations, who would be so foolish as to deduce that his "darlings" and "sweethearts", his "precious" and "own true love" indicate phallocratic contempt rather than hard-boiled realism? Moreover, by a comic twist, they provide the antiphrasis to Gutman's purportedly "plain" speaking. More germane to gender, and our genre, is the sleuth's fondness for "angel", androgynously maintained up to the gallows.

During the Jazz Age, the nice, expensive girl, let us say, the sophisticated moll, fits the bill. As the US enters the fray, it is the "knockout", shooed in/on by Effie, Spade's admiring secretary, who stands for the weaker sex. Miss Wonderly's markedly "feminine" attire, chastely seductive, and more costly than Poppy's to boot, is a "cover-up". She is dressed to kill. In matters of dress, *Scarface* and *The Maltese Falcon* illustrate to perfection a commonplace of the gangster genre: apparel maketh man (and woman) and leadeth to success (and disaster). Women of contrasting backgrounds, playing opposite parts, reveal a propensity for pinching each other's smart ideas. Spade's customer's demure look derives from the white ruffle she has gleaned from Cesca's original, virginal top. In her bewitching widow's weeds, Iva, Spade's (ex-) partner's adulterous wife and about-to-be ex-mistress, pulls out all the stops. Though they both wear fabulous hats, headgear designed to intimidate the enemy, plumage worthy of mythical birds, Iva is no more than a foil to Miss O'Shaugnessy, who outstrips all. Save one.

In a word, good girls and bad girls are usually "bad"/"good" girls, unless, of course, it be the other way around. More to the point, neither sex has the prerogative of garment or ornament. Masculine dress and insignia can, *mutatis mutandis*, be distinctly feminine, and vice versa. Seen in immediate succession, Effie and Mr. Cairo wear fetching neck-and-bowties. Cairo may give off a whiff of perfume; it is Brigid that sports the flower. By the time Spade enters Coronet apartments, Miss Wonderly has donned Johnny Lovo's dressing-gown. Or, could it be Scarface's?

As an upwardly mobile gangster, Scarface casts a lustful eye on his boss' moll's knees, a prelude to exposing his sister's breasts. On the look-out, the viewer has however spotted that Scarface and Poppy are with their own projected images in thrall: "Mirror, mirror on the wall..." "Hot" Poppy, true to type in that she throws in her lot with the best bet, nonetheless detects Camonte's sparklers and says to Camonte:

I see you're going in for jewelry. Isn't it rather effeminate?

And answer there is but one: we are dealing with the partial, unwitting, childish and fetichistic identification with the female.

Cesca is the eighteen-year old, dark-haired sister of the Italian immigrant family. In this respect, today's cinema-goer must "take in" the urban and architectural promiscuity of the ghetto. Kissing on the stairs is a preliminary to the street "hang-out", the embryonic gang-lair[1]. In fits of incestuous rage, Tony parts dancers and kissers; the legitimate and the clandestine reside cheek by jowl. Arms akimbo both: between Poppy, the moll, and Cesca, juggling a self-preserving sense of right and wrong and her urge to do as she pleases, there is a switching of roles. Strutting before Rinaldo, Cesca is the "number" in the Paradise club. Aware of her appeal, "I looked good from two storeys up", the exhibitionist Cesca has a sounder vitality than the narcissistic gangsters. Similarly, in her attempt to pick the right man, she has a sense of fitness as Rinaldo himself has. Echoing her mother's inchoate utterances, Cesca stutters: "You don't treat me like a sister...You treat me like I don't know..." "I'm his sister..." "To him that make no difference. To him you're just another girl", replies her mother. Tony watches the disillusioned Sadie as she hesitates between two suitors, calling to mind Scarface and Cesca at one and the same time. Poppy gleefully takes part in the handling of machine guns, as Cesca will do, nigh to death.

As regards neither genre nor gender does labelling of the female prevail. Yet Cesca, however torn, is also a victim of her environment, of a perverted machismo, of clannishness and clan. O'Shaugnessy, for her part is the culprit and, going against the stereotype, is sent up by her lover. Thanks to him, she will be arrested and tried and hanged or get twenty years in Tahatchapi. The guilty woman takes the rap, there is no miscarriage of justice. Locked in an embrace, the frightened children die. Legitimate family-head and conventional clan have been destroyed. In San Francisco, to begin with, there were none.

Seemingly naive, Effie's professional tasks coincide with those of confidante and caretaker. She falls for Wonderly; the necessity is dramatic. Hers are the indispensable deictic cues, through her "intuition", as to type and gender. Thus she elicits the friendly retort from her boss about Iva: "I wish I'd never let eyes on her." Her cocked head, a playful, meaningful look

---

1. Scarface has a mother and a sister (maybe even two). His gang might be seen as an outgrowth of his childhood background. C.f."The Idle Boy", George K. Turner, McClure's, 1913. In *Organized Crime in America. A book of Readings*, Gus Tyler, Ann Arbor, University of Michigan Press, 1962, p. 373-384. Further reading: "Gang members and the police", Carl Werthman & Irving Piliavin, in *The Police: Six Sociological Essays* Ed. By David J. Bordua, John Wiley&Sons, New York London, Sydny 1967, p. 56-98. In Criss-Cross, Siodmak's 1949 *film noir* set in Los Angeles, family and an *ad hoc* gang of hoods mingle to the extent that the plotting thugs invade the protagonist's parental home and raid the ice-box.

as she hands over Cairo's card pins the newcomer down with a single noun: "gardenia", a highly-scented flower with exotic overtones[1].

Interloper or intruder, Cairo is one of *them*, the member of a special clan, foreigners, to be sure, with a variation on the indices of social and cinematographic typecasting. Over – and – trans-dressed, as we have seen, the Levantine carries a heap of mutually defeating I.D.s, his given name has an amphibological ring. His voice is strikingly high-pitched, underscores O'Shaugnessy's low timbre. Cairo's distaste for Brigid is borne out by the aggressiveness that the bird-clan in general display in her presence. It is a sign of fear and loathing for a female peer who, as her repeated physical onslaughts on Cairo testify, may well outmatch them. Claustrophobic to a degree, almost entirely shot in a handful of bleak interiors, the atmosphere created by the taut *mise en scène* may be called inbred. "Keeping it in the family", and away from the female, points to the possibility of homosexual preference. This explains the underlying tension of the film. Is Hotel Belvedere not a misnomer? In its suites, the gang and O'Shaugnessy make a spectacle of themselves, have it out hammer and tongs. Throughout the film, the churlishness of the gunsel Wilmer corresponds to the stereotype of the brute, embryonic psychopath protégé who is taken under a "bigger" man's wing (as in *D.O.A.*, *Bon pour la Morgue* by Rudolph Maté,1949, or the fully-fledged hideous sadist, Vince, in Lang's *The Big Heat*, 1953).

While in Hammett sexual ambidexterity is rife, and although neither Hammett's Gutman, nor Huston's reworking of him can be described as a conventional *pater familias*, the condensation in the film of the original character of Rhea, Gutman's daughter, and O'Shaugnessy, erasing the clan-head in the literal acceptation, leaves the spectator with... well, O'Shaugnessy. With the result that she is left holding the baby with Spade. Ironically, the centripetal, spatial and verbal dynamics between Spade and Brigid reveal a pattern comparable to the sparring between the vamp and the clan. Identifying with the pearshaped object of his desire, as the unique, low angle camera shots on his bloated belly and bird-head demonstrate, Gutman seems astonishingly light on his pins. Borne aloft by the wings of an inner craving, through coherent hyperbole, the man expresses himself.

Scarface's diction and discourse, emphatic and crude, has been designated as essentially borrowed, when it is not supplanted by a signature-tune. A period-piece representative of the archetypal gangster, firm in his "roots", and his aping of class, Scarface, backed by his clan, mows down his opponents with zest, tries to make up for "lost" time. On

---

1. Hammett's presentation of Cairo makes an excellent introduction to a "Close reading of thumbnail portraits". It begins: "Mr. Joel Cairo was a small-boned man of medium height. His hair was black and smooth and very glossy. His features were Levantine. A square-cut ruby, its sides paralleled by four baguette diamonds, gleamed against the deep green of his cravat. His black coat, cut tight to narrow shoulders, flared a little over slightly plump hips. His trousers fitted his round legs more snugly than was the current fashion. The uppers of his patent-leather shoes were hidden by fawn spats. He held a black derby hat in a chamois-gloved hand and came towards Spade with short mincing steps. The fragrance of *chypre* came with him." *The Maltese Falcon*, first published, Alfred A. Knopf,1929. Vintage Book Ed., 1984, p. 46.
In *G-Men*, Brick Davis' enemy, the gardenia-lover gangster Leggett, appears to be modelled on the real-life Chicago bootlegger Dion O'Banion, gunned down in his own flower-shop. Ironically, in Keighley's film, the buttonhole is a lucky charm.

the other hand, the dogged perseverance of the piratical clan, looming up, so to speak, from another age, a-moral as they are rootless, entails killing with care and no compunction. Has time, for them, stood still? Faced with what he refuses to admit has been a seventeen year-long wild-goose chase, the fat man takes his leave to roam the wide world again. What is experience to the jejune clan? Poor Scarface is not given the chance to repent. Out for grabs, the hot-blooded hood is also a desperado. Ultimately, Camonte is reckless since his forbidden drive spells exclusion and doom. For the coterie, social status is as nought. Their enmity towards woman is concomitant with a frantic desire for control over the bejewelled statue of a bird of prey. Over *what*, did you say? Over the Dingus, he said.

The fat man's attempt to convince Spade of the value of the "bird", by intimating the secret of the clan, occurs halfway through the film, constitutes over two sequences its highpoint, and paves the way for the resolution of the conflict. Rather than falling back on purely marketable terms in his assessment of the artefact, to which O'Shaugnessy may, or may not, have the key, Gutman's passionate loquaciousness, his recourse to superlative, impart to the bird's bedecked, concealed riches a more resonant worth. The strange falcon is "something else" (*Ein Ding*, a thingummy). Unwittingly, the association of woman, as femme fatale, and the bird, which has cost, through the centuries, so many lives, becomes ever clearer.

Initially, Gutman endeavours to make sure of his ground by bringing up the thorny matter of Spade's relationship with Miss O'Shaugnessy and that of his dealings with Joel Cairo. About the lady's sexual practises, we are scarcely in the dark. Cairo's distaste for the woman has likewise been established. The enquiry is phrased as a bilateral choice:

> The question is then, which you represent. It'll be one or the other.

The answer is:

> Neither: there's me.

In other words: I exist and am involved in this bird business, but that does not necessarily hinge on who I sleep with. My gender is not defined by my sex, or my sexual doings. Spade has a sense of self. Utterly self-centred, lacking such inviolate dignity, Gutman misunderstands Spade who, judiciously, lets it pass.

"I dislike a man who says when" echoes Camonte's whistled citing of *Lucia di Lammermoor*. The unbridled quest for domination hinging on the exclusion of a woman 's influence raises the issue of the nature of her prowess. Where is the bird? What is woman? How extensive, how inexhaustible is their sway? Whoever knows the answer to one of these questions may know the answer to all. The fate of the clan may lie in Brigid's hands, a woman's hands, a woman in cahoots with a man who has her trust and who, as it turns out, has a female secretary on whom he can rely.

> If they don't know, I'm the only one in the whole wide sweet world who does.

The world will be his. Exaggeration swells the myth: Like the bird, Spade is "amazing", "astounding"; the wealth of the Order of the Knights was "immeasurable", the precious stones, of the finest. Words fail Gutman. In *Scarface* the blundering *Liebestod* pre-finale is itself an acknowledgement of a vital flaw, a factor that, doubtless, underscores the "glamourisation" of the gangster-figure. *Gutman's dream is made up of being fate's preferred one, favoured over all other mortals.* By linking this hope to the "screening out" of woman, incarnate in Brigid O'Shaugnessy (or so we might imagine), we may be able to solve the Birdgang enigma.

Favourably singled out against all other comers: small wonder that, by their dismay, Gutman and Clan remind us of the aristocrat in *The Merchant of Venice* who falls prey to the sheen of silver (money, lucre!) casing, to find, instead of the resemblance of the beautiful wealthy Portia, his own likeness, "the portrait of a blinking idiot." What is the falcon but a hollow shape covered in lead, that shows us that clever schemers are endlessly gullible. Scarface has dollar-bills pasted over his eyes. Biters bit, from A to Z[1]

"Blinking idiots", (*The Merchant of Venice*, Act 2, Sc.9, 1.54), they are as easily deceived as two of the three suitors for the hand of a noblewoman. It is the symbolism afferent to Bassanio's choice of the lead casket that despite, or because of, the apparent contradiction in the metal, (in Huston, a sign of the factitious, for the Bard, of the genuine) that is, for our purposes, most apt:

> *So may the outward shows be least themselves.*
> *The world is still deceived with ornament...*
> *Gaudy gold, Hard food for Midas*
> *I will none of thee.*
> *Nor none of thee, thou pale and common drudge*
> *Tween man and man.*
> *But thou, meagre lead,*
> *Which rather threatens than it promises.*
> *Thy paleness moves me more than eloquence.*
> The Merchant of Venice, Act 3, Sc.2,l.73.

What's with this paleness? our private eye might ask. Why would any healthy young man, or woman, go for the anaemic? Certainly not Scarface or Cesca. Nor would Spade. Besides, this movie, as distinct from *Scarface* which is about gettings things done, is all talk. It might even be called a treatise on different forms of eloquence: speeches, lies, suave volubility, cross-examination, letting them have it, a Platonic dialogue. It draws closer to the real meaning of things behind appearances, including the lure of easy, stolen words. Is this not the explanation for Spade's taciturnity? He is after the truth and so are we. Bassanio is after the woman of his dreams, to be exact, he hopes to find her living portrait inside. And he does. Why should a lead casket screen the image of woman in all her beauty and wealth and wisdom in? For that matter, why should a lead bird screen the image of woman out?

---

1. Through Bassanio, Cordelia and Freud, we have looked beyond the traditional emblems attached to the falcon in Western culture without in any way wishing to slight such abundant symbolic wealth. The falcon is the sign of royal power. He can also petrify the smaller bird he swoops down upon, or be a sign of victory over the flesh. (*Encyclopédie des symboles*. Trans. From the H. Biedermann's German for Le Livre de poche. Ed. by Michel Cazenave, 1996).

Paradoxically, as Freud demonstrates in his 1913 analysis of Shakespeare's comedy, with the help of his minute study of myths, dreams *and* tragedy, specifically, the greatest in the English renaissance, *King Lear*, it is because lead is associated with pallor, hence with being struck dumb, muteness, and lifelessness. Our "literary critic" conjures up Cordelia's effect on her father as he holds her corpse in his arms, and recalls her erstwhile reserve when summoned to protest her filial love. Raging against his daughter's wise restraint, the paternal hubris is to be ascribed to an inability to admit that he will not reign eternal. As Scarface stumbles to his end, the allegorical sign "The World is Yours" winks at him and us.

Losers, Camonte, Lear and the Birdman differ in that the latter finds his mortality, not difficult to "integrate", but unthinkable. And yet, as Freud so movingly acknowledges, there is no dream that man, *any* man, is more reluctant to give up than that of his destiny as exceptional, to wit, exempt from death, the final form of castration. Whatever our clan, we cling to an illusion of immortality[1]. "We are the stuff that dreams are made on" is Sam Spade's parting shot.

The motivation behind the clan's visceral hostility towards their criminal associate is better understood if we realize why, as woman, she is bad news. Woman is the giver of life, by the same token, the bearer of death. She is the quintessence, philosophically, of ambivalence[2]. However, whereas in *Scarface* women such as Poppy and Cesca enact ambiguous roles, uncertain destinies, they are not viciously destructive. By her own admission to Spade, Brigid O'Shaugnessy can think of nothing "worse than death". But there is. For instance, a woman who, propelled by fear, turns into a death-dealing goddess in flight. It stands then doubly to reason that the clansmen should be under a bondage of fear to woman, infinitely worsened in that she is symbolised by a formidable female, one who is, by the same fear, from her own being alienated. Their partnership derives from their rejection of her difference. In so far as this particular gang seeks to thrive on ignoring the "difference", she is truly in harmony with its members, since she denies her own mythic ambivalence, that is, being two things at once. Her repeated claims to love Spade belie Cordelia's prudence. Bassanio's scroll begins with the address: "You that choose not by the view." That indeed was the cardinal error. Through her verbose spate, O'Shaugnessy is the effacer of truth. Where the seventh art is concerned, through the denial of her self, the original, and most terrifying, of screenworld's *femmes fatales*.

Let there be no quips. Unnatural Bassanio's choice may seem to be, but, as Freud himself has pointed out, it is grist to his mill. The enamoured youth, while "living up to" the sound lesson of the humble accepting of his death-to-come, is simultaneously *exorcising it* through powerful wishful

---

1. Freud's article "Das Motiv der Kästchenwahl", *Gesammelte Werke*, Werke aus 1913-17, vol.10, S.Fischer,46, latest edition 1991, p. 24-37. Freud says: "There is no dream that man relinquishes with greater reluctance than the concept of his destiny as exceptional and thus exempt from death." (Trans.from German by EO'N.)
2. Here not used in its day-to-day meaning of having opposite feelings towards a person, event or incidence, but a phenomenon that is perceived as being at one and the same time, something and its opposite. Ambiguity or ambiguousness denoting the equivocal, will not do. *Ambivalenz* is the term used by Freud.

thinking. *If I choose it, I shall control it*. A mirage of excess, whereby he and the Birdclan meet. Or nearly.

The story of the choice made among three caskets (or three Graces) is a game, whereas Gutman and gang are in deadly earnest. The Falcon is a heavyweight, as the policeman points out. For Scarface and his sister and Rinaldo, we feel sorry. For Gutman, we might have a twinge of sympathy, were he not so silly. Having eclipsed himself, rushing from the scene, he does not even rate a depiction of his fall. On the screen, he cannot be held up as an example to the "nation", Scarface goes down fighting. To the ground, to the gutter, if not quite to Mother Earth, who, as Freud would have us all remember, is the real mother-figure. The O'Shaugnessys of this world will get no quarter[1]. Brigid's screening-out finds a correlative in the criss-cross iron grid of the lift that banishes her from our sight. Spade, in sending her over, is merely carrying out his duty. He does not judge, and he is right. Has the obsessive clutching on to mankind's dream of immortality not borne wonderful fruit? When all is said and done, our heroes, heroines and clans will live forever. On the magic screen.

---

1. While Frank Krutnik's thesis that the "mature" Astor has been intentionally counter type-cast is a stimulating one, it does not necessarily follow that Spade finds it "very easy" to resist her. The entire visual and verbal purport of the film claims that the opposite may well be the case. *In a lonely Street. Film Noir, Genre and Masculinity*, Routledge, 1991, p. 95-96. Dominique Sipière has informed me that there is an O'Shaugnessy Boulevard in San Francisco, bordering Glen Canyon Park. A further hint that Spade is acting in the general interest, for the good of the community, the "clan" we call society.

The Enforcer, La Femme à abattre : un film, des regards
Par Pierre Floquet

Que *The Enforcer* de Raoul Walsh, avec Humphrey Bogart, soit relativement méconnu du grand public, comparé à des *Key Largo*, *Casablanca*, entre autres, tient vraisemblablement à l'absence de romantisme dans le film. Les sentiments amoureux y sont littéralement sacrifiés. Des deux personnages féminins, l'une est abattue par son amant, au nom de la fidélité au Syndicat du Crime ; l'autre est la proie poursuivie par les tueurs et recherchée par la police. Bogart–acteur n'y est pas confronté à une star féminine. Le paramètre de la séduction amoureuse, si omniprésent dans le cinéma hollywoodien classique, est absent de son personnage. Bogart–Assistant District Attorney Ferguson est opposé à la criminalité, une alternative à la « femme fatale » plus insidieuse encore et maléfique (mais tellement moins photogénique) que ne le sont les personnages féminins dans les films noirs de facture plus conventionnelle.

La désincarnation, de l'opposition au représentant de la loi, est telle, que le scénario joue en partie sur l'absence de représentation à l'écran, sur le hors-champ de la criminalité, cette honte de l'Amérique. (Le titre complet de *Scarface* n'est-il pas déjà en 1932 : *Scarface, Shame of a Nation* ?) En 1950, la Warner va la raconter sans trop s'attarder à la montrer. Il s'agira donc ici d'analyser les différents points de vue, les regards, tout autant que leur absence, que *The Enforcer* propose sur le crime organisé à la fin des années 1940.

Les premières séquences du film décrivent la peur panique qui submerge Rico, un prisonnier sur le point de témoigner contre Albert Mendoza, le cerveau du Syndicat du Crime. Rico, semble-t-il, est le seul qui puisse envoyer Mendoza à la chaise électrique, hormis une jeune femme que les assassins ont cru avoir supprimée, et que tueurs et policiers recherchent, respectivement pour l'éliminer et pour la faire témoigner. La terreur de Rico, le criminel, est telle qu'elle le jette dans le vide et la mort, en dépit des efforts de Martin Ferguson et du Capitaine de police Frank Nelson pour le protéger contre lui-même et contre les hommes de main qui ont quatre fois déjà tenté de le réduire au silence. Les heures précédant le matin du procès, qui dès lors doit inévitablement amener la relaxe de Mendoza, sont mises à profit par Ferguson et Nelson pour reprendre le dossier point par point, « en-quête » d'un hypothétique détail qui permettrait malgré tout de faire condamner le suspect.

C'est donc, à la 18ᵉ minute du film, le départ d'un enchaînement complexe mais intelligible de retours en arrière, dont les différentes variations temporelles sont clairement explicitées par autant de procédés cinématographiques. Ainsi, la reprise du dossier est matérialisée par un très gros plan sur la première page dactylographiée du premier volume, qui montre :

The State vs. Albert Mendoza. Case A File 1.

Une main tourne la page, et l'on peut lire :

Bell Street Station.

Le flash-back qui nous entraîne du présent dactylographié et de la réflexion des enquêteurs, vers la narration passée mise en images, apparaît par une onde floue qui balaie l'écran de la gauche vers la droite, accompagnée d'une musique à la fois immatérielle et mystérieuse, un crescendo qui annonce le cliché musical des films de science fiction. Le nom « Bell Street Station » émerge alors du flou filmique, gravé sur le fronton du poste de police. Le spectateur a ainsi pénétré la diégèse de l'enquête policière, à l'intérieur du film. Cette diégèse deuxième va elle-même, par le biais d'interrogatoires et de récits des gangsters arrêtés, engendrer une succession de retours en arrière, comme autant de pans d'une diégèse de troisième niveau. Ces retours en arrière sont tous matérialisés par des fondus enchaînés, en gros plans sur le visage du personnage, passant de son statut de conteur à celui d'acteur dans son récit ; et vice-versa lors de son retour dans le contexte temporel de l'interrogatoire. C'est le cas de Big Babe, dans le commissariat [00:32 et 00:39] ; de O'Hara sur son lit d'agonie [00:42 et 00:45] ; de Philadelphia à l'hôpital psychiatrique [00:51 et 00:55] ; enfin de Rico quand il raconte sa présence lors du premier meurtre commis par Mendoza [01:06 et 01:10]. Enfin, le retour dans la diégèse principale reproduit le procédé du flou ondulant de la gauche vers la droite [01:10], avec toutefois une variante : à ce point du film, Rico est mort. Or, c'est lui que l'on suit dans les derniers instants du flash-back. Aussi passe-t-on d'un gros plan sur son visage et sur ses paroles :

He had nerves like iron

à un très gros plan sur un magnétophone qui tourne ; la continuité diégétique est assurée par la voix enregistrée de Rico, qui, par delà la mort, poursuit son récit sur la fin de Tony Vetto, et sur leurs difficultés à traquer sa fille Angela (tous deux témoins, eux aussi, mais malgré eux, du premier meurtre de Mendoza). L'ironie de sa situation perce à travers ses propres paroles :

Then, I'm the one witness which is left [01:10] ;

ce qui est erroné à double titre, car depuis lors il est mort, et, en outre, ses hommes n'ont pas tué la bonne Angela Vetto.

Ainsi, par paliers successifs, le spectateur suit-il Ferguson dans son immersion au sein de la Société Anonyme du Crime. Celle-ci, ou « Murder Inc. », a bien existé dans les années trente et quarante. *The Enforcer* y fait directement allusion, et s'appuie sur le scandale que la révélation de son existence, à la toute fin des années quarante, a provoqué dans la société américaine. La pseudo découverte, dans la diégèse, de termes tels que « a hit » et « a contract »[1], pourrait laisser croire que le scénariste a eu des intentions documentaristes. D'ailleurs, Borde et Chaumeton considèrent que ce film est

à la limite du genre[2]

---

1. A la 21ᵉ minute du film : Duke Malloy, au policier abasourdi : « She was a hit ; I had a contract ».
2. Raymond Borde, Etienne Chaumeton, *Panorama du film noir américain (1941-1953)*, Les Editions de Minuit, 1955, Flammarion, 1988, p. 16.

du documentaire policier. S'il existe des éléments didactiques dans *The Enforcer*, leur cible est vraisemblablement autre.

Néanmoins, la référence à la réalité dont le film s'inspire est forte. En effet, le titre britannique est demeuré *Murder Inc.*[1], ne laissant planer aucune ambiguïté. Le titre américain est, quant à lui, indicatif du discours que veut avoir le film. La loi et l'autorité détiennent la vérité, et sont les garants de l'intégrité de la société. (Nous verrons plus loin comment le film met en scène ce discours.) Le titre français, en revanche, déplace totalement la problématique vers le point de vue des criminels, faisant en cela un contresens sur le film. Sans doute « La Femme à protéger » aurait-il mieux convenu, mais aurait sûrement été moins vendeur que « *La Femme à abattre* » !

Les femmes occupent une place doublement ambiguë dans *The Enforcer*, en ce sens que, d'une part, elles sont quasiment absentes sur l'écran, alors qu'elles pénètrent dans la diégèse dès la 18ᵉ minute du film :
They made me kill my girl

ne cesse de répéter Duke Malloy. D'autre part, l'action et le suspense rebondissent parce qu'il y a erreur et confusion sur l'identité du personnage féminin clé. En cela, *The Enforcer* serait une œuvre excessivement machiste, dans laquelle les femmes ne seraient que des détails, certes primordiaux, mais dont la spécificité (la couleur de leurs prunelles) ne sauterait aux yeux de Ferguson qu'à la suite de longs mois d'enquête, de milliers de pages de dossier, et accessoirement après une heure et quinze minutes de temps filmique :
La voix de Rico au magnétophone :"(…) And the girl staring at him with her big blue eyes!" (répété deux fois) ;
Ferguson : « Her big blue eyes! »

Alors, Bogart serait la star mâle, confronté à la pieuvre, la criminalité sur laquelle il ne parvient pas à mettre un visage, dans un film d'hommes. Chacun des personnages masculins incarnerait une facette de la représentation hollywoodienne, en 1950, tant de la loi que de la pègre. Auparavant, Bogart a mis son flegme aussi bien au service de rôles de gangsters que de détectives privés, d'officiers de police ou de la loi. Son apparition dans *The Enforcer*, pour ainsi dire, est précédée de son
image de lassitude philosophique et finalement aristocratique[2].

Il cristallise les stéréotypes de droiture, de rigueur et d'autorité que l'on est en droit d'attendre de la loi. Il est « the enforcer », celui qui fait respecter la loi. Il s'appuie non pas sur une violence physique[3], ni sur son revolver, comme le ferait un shérif John Waynien ; il se sert de sa position dans la société, qui l'investit d'une mission ingrate mais noble, dont il s'acquitte à la fois avec tact et lassitude.

---

1. ref ; International Movie Data Base : http : //us.imdb.com/Guides/
2. Jean-Loup Bourget, *Hollywood la norme et la marge*, Nathan Université, Paris, 1998, p. 143.
3. Il use néanmoins de violence morale, en faisant chanter Big Babe et Philadelphia : il met le premier en présence de sa femme et de son enfant, menace l'une de complicité et l'autre d'être envoyé dans une institution ; il promet au second de le renvoyer de l'hôpital psychiatrique où il s'est réfugié s'il ne parle pas.

Le charisme de Bogart, sa personnalité suffisent à expliquer le tact. La lassitude est un paramètre plus ambigu à exprimer à l'écran. Captain Frank Nelson sert alors de faire-valoir à Ferguson. Il est toujours là, et souvent un pas en arrière, pour l'épauler, le seconder. Dans la scène finale, alors que les deux hommes se séparent volontairement pour donner le change aux tueurs qui poursuivent Angela Vetto, le Capitaine, pour compenser son absence aux côtés de Ferguson, lui tend son arme. Celle-ci, accessoirement, lui sauvera la vie, ainsi que celle de la jeune femme :

> *There, you'd better take a friend with you! [01:20]*

Cependant, c'est surtout par les échanges verbaux entre Ferguson et Nelson que Walsh extériorise ces sentiments de doute, d'anxiété et de lassitude. Leurs réflexions interviennent lors de pauses dans la diégèse, qui sont autant de moments où toute issue favorable à leur démarche semble exclue. A la 17e minute, alors qu'une ambulance emporte le corps de Rico, tombé dans le vide en tentant de s'échapper, les deux hommes s'appuient sur les marches et la rambarde d'un escalier extérieur. Puis la caméra glisse sur Bogart et zoome en gros plan sur son visage ; il se tait, l'air soucieux et fatigué (il est trois heures du matin). Nelson, alors hors-champ, rompt le silence, exprimant les pensées de Ferguson :

> *How can that be? What's wrong with the law that we can't touch him (Mendoza)?... I know ! Our kind of laws that're designed to protect the innocent. 'tis not enough that we know a man is guilty. We have to prove it!*

Au milieu de leur enquête, les deux hommes prennent la mesure du système dont ils tentent de démonter les rouages. Ils s'enferment dans le bureau de Ferguson, dans l'attente d'un appel téléphonique :

Ferguson : It is big! Well organised...
Nelson : An organisation of killers; a business built on murders...
Ferguson : Hm, hm; murder for profit[1]... (le téléphone retentit, et les interrompt.)

Ces dialogues sont plus qu'un échange de pensées. Ils sont tout autant destinés à l'information et au conditionnement socio-politique du public. Dans un pays ou la libre entreprise est de droit, des interdits demeurent, que les hommes de loi se doivent de faire respecter. C'est également le sens de leur troisième dialogue sur le même sujet, alors que les deux hommes ont refait le tour du dossier pendant les dernières heures de la nuit. Ferguson enfile sa veste, se tourne vers la fenêtre par laquelle entre le jour qui se lève. Un jour nouveau qui, à ce moment du film, éclabousse de lumière leur impuissance à résoudre leur enquête, à faire triompher le droit sur la criminalité :

Ferguson : A lunatic idea (Murder Inc.), but it worked... Outside is a great big country. Mendoza's robbed it and murdered its citizens... We can't touch him. (Il jette un regard désabusé et découragé vers Nelson ; puis se frotte le visage des deux mains, fatigue, ou aveu d'impuissance ?)... Hm, I guessed it was just a wish I had running through my head...

---

1. A la 50e minute. Les mêmes mots : « Murder for profit » seront répétés par Ferguson à la 58e minute.

Nelson : Yes Sir! That butcher is going out of here a free man [01:11].

A cet instant, leur échec semble inéluctable, puisque Rico, leur témoin, leur a littéralement glissé entre les doigts (suspendu dans le vide à la main dans de Ferguson, il lâche prise petit à petit) :

We protected him against everyhthing but himself [00:16]

Si Nelson est le faire-valoir, et le révélateur des états d'âme de Ferguson, Rico en est le repoussoir, le miroir négatif. Ted de Corsia – Rico incarne, par son physique qui n'est pas sans rappeler le stéréotype du « bad guy » joué par Paul Muni dans *Scarface*, la bestialité et la brutalité du Mal, contre lequel Ferguson se dresse. C'est le gangster hollywoodien typique, qui, ironiquement, nous apparaît d'abord dans un contre-emploi emblématique de ce que, selon la Warner, le syndicat du crime peut faire de ses propres lieutenants. Nelson dit de lui :

He's falling apart [00:04]

Rico est donc déjà mort avant de tomber dans le vide, comme l'annonce, avec ironie dramatique et prémonition la scène [00:09] où deux tueurs le mettent en joue depuis la terrasse d'un immeuble voisin. Ils vont néanmoins le rater, alors que, comme un condamné, il réclame :

Give me a cigarette! ... And a light!...

bien en vue devant une fenêtre.

Lors du récit à l'intérieur de la diégèse, Rico apparaît sous un jour plus classique pour un lieutenant du crime :

Behind the desk, all nerves and all brain (...) [00:35]

Il est brutal, cynique, caricaturalement autoritaire, ne craignant pas d'assassiner Vince, l'un de ses hommes, pour préserver la sécurité de l'organisation, et bien que ce dernier ait été son ami d'enfance [00:55]. Il n'hésite pas à manipuler certains de ses hommes, et à les trahir [01:00] ; puis il tente de négocier son impunité en échange du nom du cerveau de l'organisation, lorsqu'il s'agit de sa propre survie. Tout en lui est mauvais ; c'est du moins l'image qui en est donnée au spectateur. C'est comme si le scénario s'appliquait à nier chaque fragment d'humanité chez Rico, ou chez ses complices. Tom Philadelphia Zaca est fou, une scène le montre même totalement immobilisé dans une camisole de force ; Vince, qui finira dans une malle d'osier avec sa propre victime, a les nerfs malades :

A bundle of nerves with no brain [00:32]

O'Hara est un faible, et un alcoolique ; Big Babe Lazich se décrit comme :

So that's what I was: a nut! I've never been anything but a nut! [00:39]

Ce dernier décrit, comme il l'a découverte, l'arrière-boutique d'Olga Kirshen, qui sert de lieu de rendez-vous aux criminels. C'est une petite pièce sans ouverture, dans laquelle les jeux photographiques sur les gros plans en courte focale, les ombres portées, un éclairage à la fois précis et parcimonieux, ne sont pas sans évoquer une plongée toute hollywoodienne dans une cour des miracles revisitée par la pègre américaine :

Backroom was just like what you'd expect of a back of store [00:33] affirme d'ailleurs Big Babe.

La hiérarchie parmi ces ombres d'hommes est animale et violente, les dressant les uns contre les autres dans une mascarade de cérémonial machiste et agressif : la plèbe de la pègre tassée, écrasée autour du bureau où siège Rico [00:35]. Le silence, qui étouffe cette arrière-boutique, est lourd au point que le spectateur peut ressentir la tension qui y règne. L'organisation ne peut tolérer la moindre des frondes : la structure en est verticale ; il y est interdit de penser. Les tueurs de Kansas City, venus supprimer Rico et ses acolytes pour les empêcher de parler, en font le constat amer :

Le tueur, au sujet de Rico : This is not time to be filling a contract! Has he flipped his lid?

L'homme de Rico : Yeah; that's what I thought;

Le tueur : You... told him? !

L'homme de Rico : Yeah! We told him; didn't we, Shorty?

Le tueur, à son comparse : You see! Everything is coming apart; the country is on fire! [01:03]

Prendre des initiatives sous-entend nier l'autorité, le pouvoir décisionnaire du chef. Une telle société pyramidale ne saurait, ne doit pas exister dans l'Amérique telle qu'elle est souhaitée implicitement dans le film.

Un seul de ces exécutants (dans les deux sens du terme), Duke Malloy, veut asseoir son autorité sur l'un de ses collègues, Big Babe, le nouveau venu. Il est aussitôt rappelé à l'ordre par Rico, qui ne saurait accepter de partager son pouvoir. Malloy s'empresse cependant de reprendre son jeu cruel dès que son supérieur s'est éloigné. Si Malloy agit ainsi, et différemment des autres hommes de main, c'est qu'il se targue d'avoir aussi une tête, et un cœur. C'est lui qui tombe amoureux de sa victime désignée, qui essaie de fuir avec elle, en vain. La maxime de Nietzsche :

> Si froid, si glacial qu'on s'y brûle les doigts ! toute main s'épouvante de le saisir[1] ! (...)

pourrait s'appliquer à lui, comme à Rico. Mais jusqu'à un certain point cependant : Duke Malloy se brûle les ailes en se prenant à son propre jeu. A la différence des autres personnages sacrifiés par le Syndicat, il assumera son crime jusque dans le suicide. Quant à Rico, si, pendant ses années de collaboration avec son chef Mendoza, il a pu croire à sa supériorité sur les autres, alors qu'il reconnaît :

> All that time I was just a crap [01:07]

il ne survivra que peu de temps à l'aveu de sa vanité : on l'entend affirmer sur la bande magnétique :

> Then I'm the one witness which is left. Only me!... And you know why? Because I'm smart! I'm even smarter than Mendoza! [01:11]

Ce à quoi Nelson ajoute laconiquement :

> And he is dead!...

---

1. Nietzsche, *Par-delà bien et mal*, Paris, Folio Gallimard, maxime n° 91, p. 83.

Selon Rico, l'intelligence est donc un facteur de réussite sociale – dans l'organisation – autant qu'une garantie de survie. Ne dit-il pas à Ferguson, alors qu'ils passent leur marché :

> *If you are smart, you can be a hero. If you're dumb, you can be dead!* [01:05]

Ainsi représentés, ces gangsters sont marqués par un manque de discernement et de clairvoyance. Ce sont de caricaturales brutes, en bute à des personnages plus forts qu'eux, parce que plus subtils et sans doute plus intelligents. Ferguson, the Assistant Attorney, est de ceux-là. Pour plagier George Lucas, et schématiser le discours hollywoodien sur la société et sa moralité, Bogart incarne le Bon Côté de la Force. Son pendant, le Mauvais Côté, apparaît sous les traits d'Everett Sloane-Mendoza.

Encore ce dernier n'est-il le plus souvent « présent » que hors-champ. C'est un parti pris, dans *The Enforcer*, que de ne pas montrer Mendoza, le cerveau monstrueux du Syndicat du Crime. Lorsqu'il apparaît enfin à l'écran, à la 65ᵉ minute du film, c'est en tant que victime de racketteurs, comme un petit voyou qui se fait tabasser ; un faible certes, mais d'entrée un habile manipulateur. D'apparence, Mendoza semble très commun, un homme que l'on croiserait sans crainte dans la rue. *The Enforcer* respecte les tendances du genre, comme le rappelle Jean-Loup Bourget[1] :

> *Dans les années quarante, la vague du film noir « naturalise » les monstres qui, perdant leur stigmate fantastique, se répandent partout.*

Mendoza est tellement ordinaire qu'il en devient invisible, dans la diégèse comme dans le film, pour les spectateurs autant que pour ses hommes et ses adversaires. Il est pourtant omniprésent, rôdant dans le hors champ ; dès la 6ᵉ minute, le film montre Rico *voyant* Mendoza, qui reste invisible pour le spectateur.

Les crimes, tout comme Mendoza, restent dans la marge filmique, entre la monstration et la suggestion. Il est juste dit que Smiley est retrouvé mort dans une cheminée. L'exécution de Tony Vetto est annoncée par un gros plan sur le rasoir que le barbier, puis, à sa suite, le meurtrier aiguisent sur une courroie de cuir. Celle de Vince est suggérée par Rico qui lui dit :

> *D'you know Vince, I think there is room for two in this basket* [00:54]

De Duke, pendu dans sa cellule, on n'aperçoit, vaguement et très fugitivement, qu'une partie du corps dans la semi-pénombre, derrière des barreaux. Le hors-champ acquiert ainsi un effet métaphorique, au même titre que des plans imposés au spectateur, tel celui du tas de chaussures repêchées dans les marais, qui suggère l'énormité de l'entreprise criminelle.

Le jeu sur le voir et le non-voir déborde le procédé du hors-champ. Les regards ou leur absence, leur matérialité ou leur présence métaphorique pénètrent l'ensemble du film.

Tout d'abord, la voix de Bogart se fait entendre avant même qu'il apparaisse à l'écran. Le terme « eye witness » est prononcé deux fois [00:11

---

1. Jean-Loup Bourget, *op. cit.*, p. 262.

et 01:16], sans compter les nombreux « witness ». Les personnages ne cessent de voir, ou de refuser de voir :

Ferguson: Do you want to see him? All right! I'll show him to you.
Rico: I don't want to see him!
Ferguson: Yeah, take a look! [00:06]

Un peu plus tard, c'est Ferguson devant un cadavre :

Ferguson: Is that Nina Lombardo?
Big Babe: Don't make me look! [00:38]

Ensuite, c'est toujours Ferguson qui provoque Mendoza, en lui jetant les photos de ses victimes dans les mains :

> Look at their faces, Mendoza! (...) And Angela Vetto, the little girl that you hunted from childhood until you killed her; look at her Mendoza! May be this is the face that'll haunt you! May be these are the eyes that'll drive you crazy! [01:14]

Il ne pense pas alors si bien dire, puisque Mendoza va mesurer sa méprise, et provoquer le dénouement. La dernière réplique de Ferguson, la phrase ultime du film, enfonce le clou :

> I want to see that smile fade on Mendoza's face when he looks into those big blue eyes again

Le refus de voir peut également être involontaire, comme, lorsque dans les dernières minutes du film, Angela Vetto, se sachant en danger, passe inaperçue dans le dos du tueur lancé à sa poursuite. Ce peut être aussi un pur procédé d'ironie dramatique, destinée autant aux spectateurs qu'aux enquêteurs : dans le flash-back, décrivant le meurtre du cafetier Webb par Mendoza, la caméra s'arrête sur les yeux grands ouverts – clairs – du témoin Angela, alors enfant [01:10]. Plus tôt, deux hommes de la police scientifique décrivent le cadavre de Nina Lombardo, la femme que tous prennent à tort pour le témoin capital. Un policier donne les détails, l'autre les note en les répétant. Ferguson et Nelson entrent alors dans le champ de la caméra, au moment où résonne, avec un temps d'arrêt de deux secondes qui rompt le rythme de la description, et par là-même met en relief le mot ainsi isolé :

Le premier policier : Eyes,... brown.
Le second policier : Brown! [00:41]

Cependant, à ce moment du récit, ce détail passe aisément inaperçu. Ce n'est qu'incidemment, à la 70ᵉ minute, que Rico en dévoile malgré lui toute l'importance, alors qu'il décrit l'enfant témoin du premier meurtre :

> That kid! Looking at us with her big blue eyes...

La solution de l'enquête reste, encore un temps, dissimulée, échappant à la clairvoyance de Ferguson.

L'intérêt est, ici, essentiellement dramatique. Il prolonge cependant l'approche rhétorique particulière du film.

Le choix esthétique, du hors-champ et de la métaphore, est sans doute également un choix politique, qui suit, à une époque même ou la censure se relâche, les recommandations du Code Hays. Bourget écrit :

> Il est reproché, comme à la plupart des films de gangsters, à la fois de montrer « les méthodes qu'utilisent les criminels » et, de façon plus générale, de dépeindre le héros criminel comme « riche,

> *courageux et rusé, ce qui n'est pas le cas des représentants de la loi* » : *double risque donc que les gangsters « fassent école[1] ».*

Dans *The Enforcer*, le point de vue des criminels n'est absolument pas partageable.

Le film tend à diaboliser la criminalité. Ce qui est montré, le système criminel, tout est définitivement négativisé. Rico et ses hommes évoluent dans la pénombre, les bas-quartiers, les arrière-salles. Le jugement de valeur est imposé au public par le point de vue du réalisateur, ou du moins du studio.

Ferguson compare la rue, la nuit, à un cimetière [00:08]. Cette remarque s'adresse t'elle aux criminels, ou bien est-ce une allusion à un climat d'insécurité dont souffrirait l'Amérique ? Depuis le début des années trente, la représentation du crime organisé à l'écran fait débat. Le démantèlement de Murder Inc. est l'occasion, pour la Warner, d'en offrir une vision quasi patriotique : le combat de la Nation et du Droit contre le crime. Alors, la mort du tueur, à la fin du film, dans la rue et en plein jour, tendrait à faire comprendre que le cimetière, évoqué par Ferguson tout au début, sera symboliquement celui de la criminalité.

Diaboliser le crime demande de s'attaquer au criminel, comme à ses actes. Ainsi, Rico confesse, dans sa terreur, dès l'introduction du film,

> *I'm afraid. He (Mendoza) will never die! (...) He ain't human!* [00:07]

Les actes, dont Mendoza est responsable, ne sont pas explicitement montrés ; cependant, l'iconographie de leur suggestion approche l'insoutenable. Le tas de chaussures, arrachées à la boue, n'est pas sans évoquer les piles de vêtements et souliers photographiés dans les camps de concentration. Par un raccourci aussi brutal que fugace, Mendoza est assimilé à l'horreur nazie.

En même temps, à trop montrer le mal, on risque de le banaliser, et d'en asseoir l'existence. En limiter la représentation est aussi une manière de le marginaliser.

Cette marginalisation du crime, son ancrage dans une fiction, qui prône son rejet d'une société « propre », sont exprimés également par une théâtralisation de la thématique. C'est pourquoi le générique, qui se déroule en suivant la progression d'un fourgon dans la nuit, cesse quand ce dernier s'arrête. Un plan en courte focale montre une double haie de policiers, se resserrant vers la porte arrière du fourgon. Celle-ci va s'ouvrir, après qu'un policier ait frappé avec sa matraque trois coups distincts sur la carrosserie : code intradiégétique signifiant que la voie est libre ; annonce rhétorique du début du drame. Ce plan a un symétrique quinze minutes plus tard : le corps sans vie de Rico est hissé dans une ambulance dont la porte arrière est ensuite fermée. On entend alors les trois coups de trois heures sonner à une église hors-champ : c'est la sortie du témoin qui est ainsi signifiée, en même temps que le début de la reprise de l'enquête. En surconnotant la mise en scène, on en extrait le contenu de la réalité : le point de vue du criminel

---

1. Jean-Loup Bourget, *op. cit*, p. 127.

disparaît en même temps que lui ; de là à en refuser l'existence, il n'y a plus qu'un pas que le film encourage à faire.

La criminalité ainsi rejetée, vers quoi se tourner, qui puisse conforter le spectateur citoyen ? Bogart-Ferguson offre une solution à la fin du film, lorsque, par haut-parleur, il enjoint Angela Vetto (tout en s'adressant à la foule entière, et donc symboliquement au peuple américain) d'appeler pour son salut le numéro : « temple, 2, 3, 1, 1 ». Il répète plusieurs fois le numéro, si bien que l'on finit par comprendre : « Temple, to free one, won! » Ce temple serait le symbole de la vertu morale préservée, l'un des fondements de la société américaine. Le combat de Ferguson serait une symbolique glorification des institutions, à travers la sauvegarde de l'Etat face au crime organisé.

Si les institutions sont ainsi célébrées, on comprend mieux, a posteriori, l'emphase cinématographique de la représentation des immeubles où logent les serviteurs de l'ordre établi, en opposition à la précarité urbaine dans laquelle les criminels évoluent. L'architecture du bâtiment de police [00:08] est minérale et monumentale, comme érigée à la gloire du corps qu'il abrite. A la 20e minute, dans un plan fixe en contre-plongée, l'entrée du poste de police, au-dessus de laquelle est gravé dans la pierre : « BELL STREET STATION », fait plus penser au fronton d'un temple néo-classique qu'au hall d'un commissariat, avec sa frise et ses amorces de colonnes cannelées. Au premier plan, en bas à droite, une sphère lumineuse : « POLICE » efface toute ambiguïté ; ou plutôt, elle inscrit l'ordre et la loi dans un contexte de célébration, sinon de vénération.

Face à la figure démoniaque, face à l'Autre (Mendoza n'est pas un nom anglo-saxon, au contraire de Ferguson et Nelson), l'Amérique de 1950 cherche à se protéger, et à se rassurer par le biais de productions telles que *The Enforcer*. Plus qu'une évocation documentaire de Murder Inc., ce film va au-delà du genre du film noir, car il rejette toute évocation indulgente de la criminalité. A une époque où la surveillance de la censure se relâche, Raoul Walsh, qui a pris la suite de Bretaigne Windust, se plie à la commande de la Warner, et prend résolument parti pour le discours consensuel de la nation américaine. Est-ce un hasard ? Ce film fut le dernier de la Warner dans lequel Bogart tourna. Ou bien *The Enforcer* ne marque-t-il pas plutôt le décalage définitif entre les idées progressistes de la star, et le virage conservateur et antisyndical que Jack Warner fit prendre à ses studios à la fin des années quarante.

Key Largo : le gangster au miroir du cinéma, réflexivité et mélange des genres

Par Gilles Menegaldo

Key Largo est réalisé par John Huston dans un contexte de crise générée par le Maccarthysme. Le film, adapté d'une pièce de Maxwell Anderson par Huston et Richard Brooks est diffusé en 1948, quelques mois après une première vague d'interrogatoires menés à l'automne 1947 par la commission d'enquête parlementaire mise en place par le sénateur Maccarthy, House Unamerican Activities Comittee (HUAC) dont le but avoué est de purifier le milieu hollywoodien de toute trace d'influence communiste. Des dizaines de scénaristes, réalisateurs, producteurs vont subir des interrogatoires serrés visant à leur faire avouer leurs liens éventuels avec le parti communiste ou des associations proches de celui-ci. La plupart accepteront de répondre aux questions : ce seront les « friendly witnesses », parmi lesquels la majorité des producteurs et des responsables des grands studios, Louis B. Mayer en tête. Un petit groupe composé de huit scénaristes, un metteur en scène, Edward Dmytryk et un producteur de la RKO Adrian Scott, refuse de témoigner. Ils vont constituer les « Hollywood Ten » et seront les premières victimes de la commission présidée par J. Parnell Thomas et à laquelle collabore Richard Nixon.

John Huston et Humprey Bogart (ainsi que Lauren Bacall), font partie de ceux qui mettent en cause la légitimité de la commission et dénoncent ses méthodes inquisitoriales qui violent les droits du citoyen définis dans la constitution américaine, en particulier le premier amendement. Après avoir rédigé une pétition, ils se rendent, avec d'autres contestataires, à Washington, dans un avion affrété par Howard Hughes et tentent de convaincre l'opinion du bien fondé de leurs idées en tenant une série de meetings.

En dehors de cette implication personnelle et de ses prises de position courageuses, Huston fournit avec *Key Largo* une autre forme de réponse au Maccarthysme, dénonçant implicitement, à travers la figure du gangster Johnny Rocco et de ses agissements, une dérive idéologique fascisante du gouvernement des Etats-Unis. Il est en effet possible de voir, à travers cette histoire d'un groupe de citoyens honnêtes séquestrés et maltraités par une bande de malfrats, la métaphore d'un autre type de rapports de force, celui qui s'instaure entre les professionnels du cinéma et les membres de la commission.

Outre ses résonances politiques implicites, le film présente plusieurs intérêts par rapport à la question de la représentation du crime organisé à l'écran. Le film revisite le cinéma de gangster des années trente, en particulier ceux produits par la Warner. L'intertexte principal est constitué par *Little Caesar*, réalisé par Mervyn LeRoy en 1930 où le rôle principal est tenu par Edward G. Robinson qui incarne Rico Bandello, petit gangster à l'ascension fulgurante. Dans *Key Largo*, le même acteur incarne, dix huit ans plus tard, Johnny Rocco, un ex-roi de la pègre qui évoque, avec nostalgie, son passé glorieux. La présence de Humphrey Bogart invite à établir d'autre liens avec des films antérieurs, mais elle incite également à nous interroger sur le caractère « hybride » du film qui associe les conventions du film de gangster (en les replaçant dans un contexte distancié) et celles du film noir. Huston se livre ausssi à une série de déplacements, d'inversions et de subtile subversion des deux genres, notamment par l'utilisation dramatique et symbolique de la Nature et les modes de caractérisation de certains personnages.

> *At the southernmost point of the United States are the Florida Keys, a sring of small islands held together by a concrete causeway. Largest of these remote coral islands is Key Largo.*

Ce carton initial s'inscrit sur un plan général de l'archipel où la ligne de la route partage l'écran en deux parties. Il explicite ce que l'on peut déjà déduire de l'image et constitue une première manière de se démarquer du cadre traditionnel du genre où l'action se déroule souvent dans une grande métropole. Le lieu de l'intrigue est périphérique et non central (il s'agit de l'extrême pointe du continent américain). La proximité de la mer suggère la possibilité d'une échappée vers un ailleurs géographique ou, à l'inverse, l'intrusion d'un groupe extérieur, ce qui sera confirmé par la suite. Les gangsters installés dans l'hôtel Largo sont venus de Cuba par voie de mer. Cependant, le début du film exprime aussi l'idée que ces îles font malgré tout partie du territoire américain, et sont, de ce fait, soumises au contrôle des autorités représentées ici par le shérif Ben Wade et son adjoint. La route rectiligne constitue une sorte de cordon ombilical entre l'archipel et le continent.

Ce contrôle est d'emblée affirmé. Un plan général en forte plongée montre un autocar pris en chasse par une voiture de police et contraint de s'arrêter sur le bas-côté. Cette scène est accompagnée par une musique dramatisée, mimétique de l'action. Deux policiers, à la recherche de deux indiens évadés de prison, perquisitionnent à l'intérieur de l'autocar où se trouve Frank McCloud (Bogart), soldat qui revient de la guerre et dont le visage fatigué se reflète dans le rétroviseur. Cette courte scène semble affirmer la présence et l'autorité de la police. Les tous premiers plans introduisent cependant une ambiguïté. La voiture qui poursuit puis dépasse l'autocar n'est pas identifiée d'emblée dans la mesure où elle est filmée de loin (il pourrait tout aussi bien s'agir d'une voiture de gangsters). C'est seulement au moment où l'on entend la sirène que l'ambiguïté est levée. Un parallèle implicite est donc établi entre les autorités légales et les gangsters. La recherche de deux indiens échappés se révèle en fait une quête dérisoire même si elle détermine certaines péripéties de l'intrigue. L'idée sous-jacente est bien que les policiers se trompent de cible et de méthode. Ils ne semblent d'ailleurs jamais en mesure d'inquiéter sérieusement les gangsters. Huston se livre ici à une critique implicite de l'institution policière et met en cause aussi une certaine forme de racisme exercée ici à l'encontre des indiens Séminoles : les deux fuyards étant qualifiés par le shérif de « young bucks with fancy shirts ».

Key Largo se fonde en partie sur la notion de retour. Le premier est celui du vétéran qui, après une campagne d'Italie meurtrière, vient rendre visite au père et à l'épouse d'un de ses compagnons, George Temple, mort au combat. L'autre est celui de Johnny Rocco, chef de gang exilé à Cuba, qui s'introduit clandestinement en territoire Américain pour effectuer une transaction avec d'autres gangsters venus de Miami. Les circonstances amènent Rocco et sa bande à se réfugier dans un hôtel isolé et manifestement peu fréquenté en dehors de la saison touristique, et à séquestrer le propriétaire James Temple, un invalide confiné dans son fauteuil roulant et sa fille Nora, belle et séduisante veuve de guerre.

Le film est structuré en trois parties. La première concerne l'arrivée de Frank à l'hôtel Largo et la relation qu'il établit avec les personnages déjà installés dans l'hôtel (dont il ignore qu'il s'agit de gangsters). Le tournant du film se produit au moment où les gangsters jettent le masque et révèlent leurs véritables intentions. Ceci donne lieu à diverses péripéties où s'affrontent le chef des gangsters et le vétéran, d'abord désabusé et passablement cynique mais qui retrouve graduellement une stature héroïque, remise en cause momentanément en raison d'un comportement qui peut sembler ambigu. Après la fin de l'ouragan qui contraint les personnages à rester à l'intérieur de l'hôtel, l'affrontement final se déroule à bord du bateau de James Temple, le *Santana*[1] que les gangsters ont réquisitionné après la disparition de leur propre yacht afin de regagner Cuba.

La première phase narrative laisse le spectateur dans l'expectative en se focalisant essentiellement sur l'évocation du fils disparu et l'ébauche d'une relation affective entre Frank, soldat désabusé et Nora qui vit encore dans le souvenir de son mari que le tmoignage idéalisé (voire mensonger) de Frank contribue à ériger en figure héroïque. Différentes scènes contribuent à suggérer une complicité grandissante, sinon une idylle naissante entre Frank et Nora, d'autant plus attendue par le spectateur en raison du caractère déjà mythique du couple Bogart/Bacall et qui apparaît ici pour la dernière fois à l'écran après avoir figuré dans plusieurs films au milieu des années quarante : *To Have and Have Not* et *The Big Sleep* de Howard Hawks et *Dark Passage* de Delmer Daves. Ici, une « affinité élective » est suggérée en particulier lors de la scène de l'amarrage du bateau. Alors qu'ils se dirigent vers le hangar à bateaux, suite à l'avis de tempête, la caméra suit leur parcours côte à côte en une série de brefs travellings avant ou latéraux, précédant ou suivant le couple. Ils sont souvent filmés dans le même cadre, en « two shot ». Le fait d'être associés dans une action commune, l'amarrage du bateau (ils se lancent les cordages en échangeant des sourires) accentue ce sentiment d'harmonie. Leur conversation prend parfois un tour intimiste notamment quand Nora évoque les conditions de sa rencontre non seulement avec son mari, mais aussi avec ce paysage particulier de l'archipel qui a contribué à lui donner un ancrage. Elle se compare aux palétuviers qui ont pris racine dans cette terre : « Now I am like one of these mangroves ».

Parallèlement cependant, l'intrigue criminelle s'ébauche, mais le film joue clairement sur un décalage de savoir entre le spectateur et les personnages. En effet, ceux ci sont censés ignorer l'identité véritable des clients qui ont loué l'hôtel pour une semaine et semblent se laisser convaicre par le discours en dépit d'un comportement pour le moins suspect. Par contre, le spectateur, nourri d'images de films de gangster, ne se laisse pas abuser aussi facilement et peut décrypter différent signaux. Ainsi, quand McCloud pénètre dans le hall de l'hôtel, il voit d'abord un jeune homme qui lui déclare que l'établissement est fermé, mais l'homme est surtout habillé (et il

---

1. Nom du propre yacht de Bogart amoureux de la mer et des bateaux comme son personnage.

se comporte) comme un personnage stéréotypé de film de gangster, le « gunman » : costume voyant, bretelles blanches, cravate et chapeau. Plus tard, c'est ce même personnage (Toots) qui se comporte de manière sadique avec le policier blessé, encourage son chef à brutaliser Nora qui vient de lui cracher au visage et plus tard se prépare à torturer Frank pour le convaincre de les conduire en bateau. C'est aussi lui qui rit stupidement en lisant les blagues du journal et s'extasie naïvement au cours de l'exposé des exploits passés de son chef. Ce personnage ne peut manquer d'évoquer d'autres « petites frappes » du cinéma hollywoodien : le jeune tueur stupide et maladroit incarné par Elisha Cook Jr. (habitué des seconds rôles) qui se fait ridiculiser par Spade (Bogart) dans *Le Faucon maltais* également réalisé par Huston et souvent considéré comme le premier[1] film noir, ou encore le tueur plus inquiétant et non moins sadique incarné par Richard Widmark dans *Kiss of Death* de Henry Hathaway. Les trois autres « clients » renvoient à autant de stéréotypes : Curley (Thomas Gomez), gros truand plus jovial et communicatif ; Ralph, sombre, impassible et peu loquace ; Angel, débraillé, mâchonnant un cigarillo et à l'allure sexuellement ambiguë. La femme, Gaye Dawn (Claire Trevor), accoudée au bar, écoutant fébrilement le résultat des courses de chevaux, et manifestement ivre, incarne un autre stéréotype, celui de la « moll » (ici vieillisssante), en apparence totalement soumise aux désirs du chef de gang, et rejoint aussi une autre figure emblématique, la « fallen woman ». C'est le seul personnage qui manifeste quelque sympathie au visiteur en exigeant qu'on lui serve à boire. Le chef de gang reste hors champ et n'est évoqué que dans le dialogue. Il est, à ce moment du récit, identifié comme le mystérieux Mr Brown, « a rich ladykiller » qui ne sort de sa chambre que la nuit.

Le récit reste un temps indécis, même si la tension monte graduellement, en particulier quand Curley brutalise Gaye Dawn et l'enferme dans sa chambre insinuant qu'elle est sujette à des crises de *delirium tremens*. McCloud refuse par ailleurs à plusieurs reprises de trinquer avec Curley ce qui déclenche la colère de celui-ci. L'espace même semble graduellement investi par les « visiteurs ». Ainsi, chaque fois que Nora se déplace dans le hall, elle se heurte à l'un des hommes et doit faire un détour pour les contourner. C'est cependant en raison d'une péripétie ignorée du spectateur, la présence dans une des chambres, d'un policier (Sawyer) blessé par les truands alors qu'il était à la recherche des deux indiens, les frères Osceola, que la situation change.

A l'occasion d'un appel téléphonique du shériff à la recherche de son adjoint, Curley empêche Nora de répondre, affirmant que Temple, le propriétaire et Nora sont absents. Un rapide mouvement d'appareil serre le cadre sur le visage soudain dur et figé du gangster. Nora qui s'approche pour saisir le combiné est repoussée brutalement. McCloud tente d'intervenir et se fait encadrer par les deux truands qui sortent leur revolver, montrant ainsi leur vrai visage. A partir de ce moment, le

---

1. En fait ce film relève du film noir à certains égards, mais il n'a pas la dimension déterministe, voire fataliste de certains films ultérieurs. Son intrigue linéaire est relativement simple et le traitement de l'image reste sobre, assez éloigné de l'esthétique expressioniste et de la stylisation formelle qui caractérisent souvent le film noir.

mystérieux Mr Brown rentre en scène, mais d'abord seulement à l'intention du spectateur. On passe, par un fondu enchaîné, à un plan rapproché de Edward G. Robinson, prenant son bain en lisant le journal, un gros cigare entre les lèvres. Le visage est en partie masqué par un énorme ventilateur. La musique qui accompagne ce plan crée un climat presque sinistre avec des cuivres qui se prolongent sur une note unique. Un panoramique latéral droite gauche nous révèle le visage d'un gangster vieillissant avachi dans son bain, son torse puissant à demi émergé, la main ornée d'une lourde bague posée sur le rebord de la baignoire.

Cette première image du chef de gang est particulièrement saisissante. Elle nous le fait découvrir dans une situation d'intimité, mais de plus dépouillé de ce qui fait traditionnellement son image (cinématographique), en particulier ses vêtements et son révolver (« rod »), littéralement sans son armure (ou sa parure), dans une situation de vulnérabilité. Pourtant cette image dégage une grande impression de force et elle nous signale que, dès cet instant, c'est lui qui prend le pouvoir et occupe le devant de la scène. Le plan se prolonge par un panoramique latéral qui accompagne le mouvement du gangster qui sort de l'eau, enfile une luxueuse robe de chambre et vient se placer devant un miroir. Le plan est construit en profondeur grâce à l'emploi d'une courte focale qui permet l'emboîtement de différents cadres. Dans le premier, on voit le reflet de Robinson filmé en plan épaules, s'admirant dans la glace. Un second cadre est constitué par la porte de la chambre où vient s'inscrire le corps d'Angel venu rendre compte des évènements. Au moment où les deux hommes sont filmés ensemble en plan serré, le buste (réel) de Robinson apparaît en amorce droite. Le reflet vu dans le miroir ressemble à un plan d'un film dont le spectateur serait le gangster lui même. Cet effet de distanciation métadiégétique signale l'une des problématiques du film qui confronte Robinson, grand acteur du cinéma de gangster des années trente, avec sa propre image, dix huit ans plus tard, dans un rôle analogue, mais décalé.

Dans la suite du film, cette évocation, en partie nostalgique, d'une époque révolue, celle de la prohibition, est vécue sur un double mode. Dans l'univers diégétique du film, les gangsters, Johnny Rocco, mais aussi ses acolytes, font référence à l'époque bénie de la prohibition et évoquent les fastes passés et le pouvoir qui était le leur. Pour le spectateur de cinéma, cette époque est celle des grands films de gangsters de la Warner, *Public Enemy* et surtout *Little Caesar* qui constitue l'un des intertextes explicites du film de Huston. La simple présence de Robinson suffit à reconvoquer le film de LeRoy, l'un des premiers grands films de gangster parlants[1] où l'acteur incarnait une figure emblématique du gangster très vaguement inspirée de la vie et des exploits d'Al Capone.

Little Caesar est adapté assez librement d'un roman de W. R. Burnett, écrivain qui participe également au scénario du *Scarface* de Howard Hawks. Une caractéristique du film consiste à considérer la violence et l'agressivité du gangster comme quelque chose de donné en soi sans trop tenir compte des conditions sociales qui pourraient justifier ces comportements. Pour Rico Bandello, petit truand provincial d'origine italienne, prototype de

---

1. Le premier film de gangster parlant est *Lights of New York* produit en 1928 par la Warner.

« l'ethnic gangster », il est seulement nécessaire, à un moment donné, de passer à un stade supérieur et d'abandonner les holds up minables de stations service pour se faire un nom dans une grande ville. La première séquence est programmatique. Lisant un journal dans un *diner* miteux après un braquage expéditif, Rico s'extasie sur le compte rendu d'une fête donnée en l'honneur d'un roi de la pègre, Diamond Pete Montana et décide avec son ami Joe Massara de changer de vie, d'aller à l'Est : « East! Where things break big ». Rico s'intègre au gang de Vettori, un truand assez lâche qui reste derrière son bureau et passe son temps à faire des réussites pendant que les autres font le travail. Graduellement Rico affirme son pouvoir et monte dans la hiérarchie : il contraint Vettori à lui céder la place, fait partir un autre gangster, Arnie Lorch[1], qui a tenté de le faire assassiner et finit par remplacer Diamond Pete Montana, son modèle initial, auprès du « Big Boy », le chef de la pègre. Son ascension sociale est marquée par des changements vestimentaires et un intérêt grandissant pour son apparence physique et les signes extérieurs de sa réussite, en particulier l'appartement et les bijoux. Le gangster ne fait, en fin de compte que prendre au pied de la lettre l'idéal américain de l'individualisme forcené, du capitalisme sauvage et de la mobilité sociale. La chute de Rico est cependant encore plus foudroyante que son ascension. Ayant refusé – c'est la faille tragique qui le rend vulnérable et lui fait transgresser son code de conduite habituel – de tuer son ami Joe Massara qui a quitté le gang pour faire carrière dans la danse, il tombe rapidement dans la déchéance. Victime d'une provocation orchestrée par l'inspecteur de police qui le traque depuis le début, il est abattu d'une rafale de mitraillette en pleine rue, au pied d'un immense panneau publicitaire qui présente le nouveau spectacle de Joe, devenu vedette de music hall avec sa femme Olga Stassoff qui l'a poussé à dénoncer Rico. Cette fin met clairement en parallèle les deux destins, les deux « success stories » : la carrière criminelle vouée à l'échec et la réussite professionnelle légitime et reconnue par la société.

Ce bref aperçu du film permet de comprendre le lien avec la représentation du gangster dans *Key Largo*. Les références sont multiples. Johnny Rocco représente l'avatar cynique et rusé d'un Rico qui aurait eu le temps de vieillir et de parvenir au sommet d'une hiérarchie ici clairement marquée, chaque gangster ayant une fonction spécifique. On retrouve aussi dans *Key Largo* certaines des phrases emblématiques de *Little Caesar*. Dans ce film, à chaque fois que Rico élimine un rival, il énonce le même constat d'un ton méprisant : « You can dish it out all right, but you can't take it anymore ». Ici Rocco utilise la même expression (en partie), mais à l'adresse du policier blessé par Toots le tueur : « you sure can take it ». Un autre rappel évident concerne l'intérêt manifesté par Rocco envers sa propre apparence. L'image au miroir étudiée plus haut évoque celle où Rico juché sur un lit en raison de sa petite taille, se contemple dans la glace (qui constitue un surcadrage) alors qu'il vient de revêtir son premier smoking. Tout comme Rico, Johnny Rocco prend soin de ses cheveux, porte des

---

1. Dans le roman de Burnett, ce personnage d'origine juive est qualifié de « youpin ». Le film gomme ces connotations anti-sémites masquant le fait que nombre de gangsters sont d'origine juive : Arnold Rothstein, Meyer Lansky et bien d'autres.

vêtements coûteux, une épingle à cravate et une bague et se fait raser de près. Les deux personnages sont passablement irritables et prompts à sortir leur revolver. Ils sont également avides de pouvoir et rêvent de revanche. Rico déchu, réduit à vivre dans un asile de nuit (« flop house ») cherche encore, contre toute attente, à se venger du policier qui l'a présenté comme un lâche dans un article de journal. C'est ce sursaut d'orgueil qui lui fait oublier sa situation réelle et cause sa perte. Rocco, humilié par son expulsion en tant que « undesirable alien » alors qu'il a passé trente ans de sa vie aux USA ne pense qu'à son retour et à sa reconquête du pouvoir perdu. Lui aussi échoue et meurt abattu par McCloud sur le bateau qui le ramène à Cuba.

Outre la référence spécifique à *Little Caesar*, *Key Largo* met en relief des traits essentiels du monde de la pègre tel qu'il est représenté au cinéma. Le film nous donne d'abord un portrait de Rocco vu par Frank qui l'identifie tout de suite et évoque ses activités criminelles : « His rule extended over beer, slot machines, the numbers racket[1] [...] He was a master of the fix, when he couldn't corrupt, he terrified, when he couldn't terrify he murdered ». Ce portrait est complété par Rocco lui même lors de la scène centrale du rasage où il évoque ses méthodes, en particulier la manière dont il « fait » un homme politique :

> *I take a nobody, teach him what to say, get his name in the papers, pay for his campaign expenses, get my boys to bring the voters out and then count the votes over and over again and he is elected*

Pendant toute la scène, Rocco est filmé en plan rapproché, en contre-plongée. Alors qu'il exprime sa rancœur à l'égard des politiciens qui l'ont « lâché » et fait de lui un « public enemy », son visage couvert de mousse lui donne l'air d'un clown grotesque, mais effrayant, masque grimaçant aux traits déformés par l'emploi de la courte focale.

Une autre scène révélatrice est celle de la rencontre entre Rocco et Ziggy venu de Miami pour acheter des faux billets. En apparence, il s'agit de retrouvailles joyeuses entre deux vieux complices, mais la méfiance règne. Ziggy a emmené avec lui un « expert » pour vérifier la qualité de la marchandise. Pendant l'examen, les visages sont figés et les tueurs de chaque camp s'observent. Le climat ne se détend qu'après le diagnostic favorable. Cette scène contredit la vision « idéaliste » exprimée par Curley, puis Ziggy, d'un retour de la prohibition mais sans guerre des gangs.

Compte tenu de ces mutiples références au gangstérisme, il n'est pas surprenant que *Key Largo* ait connu quelques problèmes avec la censure. Jerry Wald, le producteur et John Huston ont dû beaucoup argumenter face aux critiques formulées par le PCA à un moment où le film de gangster a été largement remplacé par les films noirs moins clairement liés au contexte historique. Selon Jonathan Munby[2], la différence majeure entre ces films et *Key Largo* est que le personnage de Rocco (en partie inspiré de Lucky Luciano[3]), peut être directement associé à une figure de gangster (réel ou

---

1. Le film d'Abraham Polonsky, *Force of Evil*, traite ce sujet.
2. Voir son ouvrage *Public Enemies, Public Heroes*, The University of Chicago Press, Chicago and London, 1999.
3. Comme Rocco, Luciano a été expulsé des Etats-Unis et exilé à Cuba. Il ira ensuite en Italie.

fictionnel). Par ailleurs la présence de Robinson contribue à faire de *Key Largo* un « produit » immédiatement identifiable.

La présence de Humphrey Bogart induit d'autres rapprochements et permet, en outre, de faire la liaison entre le film de gangster et le film noir. D'abord, l'acteur figure beaucoup dans les films des années trente où il joue des rôles secondaires de gangsters ou criminels plus ou moins psychopathes qui meurent souvent avant la fin du film. Dans certains de ces films, *Bullets or Ballots*, *The Amazing Dr Clitterhouse*, *Brother Orchid*, il est déjà confronté à Robinson qui reste le personnage principal du film. Bogart participe aussi au renouvellement du genre à partir de 1937, avec *Dead End* de William Wyler où le propos moral est clairement affirmé et *The Roaring Twenties* de Raoul Walsh qui adopte une approche historique et distanciée (avec un commentaire off pseudo-documentaire) de la période de la Prohibition. Dans *Angels with Dirty Faces* de Michael Curtiz, le comédien incarne un avocat corrompu et manipulateur qui de nouveau meurt sous les balles avant la fin du film et la rédemption du gangster héros incarné par James Cagney. Cependant, le rôle le plus marquant de Bogart pendant cette période demeure celui de Duke Mantee dans *The Petrified Forest* d'Archie Mayo (1936). Ce film illustre un autre mode, plus archaïque, de représentation du gangster en tant qu'aventurier associé à la nature[1], (le désert de l'Arizona) et confronté à la police qui représente le monde urbain. *Key Largo* constitue une sorte de reprise inversée de ce film où le gangster traqué séquestre, avec sa bande, à l'intérieur d'un bar perdu, un groupe assez composite d'individus : une jeune femme (Bette Davis) et son grand-père, un poète[2] vagabond suicidaire (Trevor Howard) et un couple de bourgeois accompagné de leur chauffeur noir. Dans *The Petrified Forest*, Bogart incarne un tueur farouche, taciturne et mal rasé, prêt à tout pour survivre. *Key Largo* reprend le dispositif du huis clos mais le rôle du « méchant » est dévolu à Robinson, gangster urbain beaucoup plus sophistiqué (mais plus sadique) alors que Bogart se voit attribuer celui du héros positif et victorieux. Les deux films ont aussi en commun l'importance du cadre naturel même si la fonction symbolique de celui-ci (et surtout de l'ouragan) est plus marquée dans *Key Largo*.

En 1948, Bogart a aussi derrière lui toute une série de rôles où il incarne des personnages bien différents, non plus des tueurs, mais des détectives privés, dans des œuvres qui marquent l'avènement d'un genre nouveau, tels *The Maltese Falcon* (1941) déjà dirigé par Huston ou plus tard *The Big Sleep* (1946) et *Dead Reckoning* (1947). Dans ces films, Bogart tient le rôle principal et il ne meurt plus à la fin, obtenant même parfois la femme désirée. Le spectateur de *Key Largo* retrouve en partie l'ambiance de ces films non pas tant en raison de l'intrigue assez simple, mais plutôt en raison de la tension dramatique générée par la confrontation de deux mondes, et de la mise en scène qui joue beaucoup sur la construction en profondeur dans le plan et

---

1. Bogart tient un rôle un peu semblable, mais plus tragique dans *High Sierra* de Raoul Walsh.
2. Pour le poète, Mantee est un personnage dépassé, condamné par l'évolution de la société, mais il représente : « the last great apostle of rugged individualism [...] He ain't a gangster, he's a real old-time desperado. Gangsters is foreign. He is an American."

un éclairage jouant sur de forts contrastes, parfois quasi expressionnistes, entre ombre et lumière.

Le fait que Bogart incarne un vétéran de la deuxième guerre mondiale introduit un autre lien avec le film noir où figurent des personnages de soldats déboussolés, parfois amnésiques, comme dans *Somewhere in the Night* (1946) ou *Ride the Pink Horse* (1947) et incapables de se réinsérer dans une société qu'ils ne reconnaissent plus.

D'autres personnages de *Key Largo* évoquent le film noir. En premier lieu, celui de James Temple (Lionel Barrymore) qui représente une figure de patriarche bienveillant et moralement juste, mais dépassé par les évènements et, finalement, impuissant, comme en témoigne son infirmité. Celle-ci nous rappelle le personnage du Général Sternwood, également confiné dans un fauteuil roulant et victime d'un chantage dans *The Big Sleep* où Lauren Bacall incarnait le rôle de sa fille Vivian qui séduit le détective Philip Marlow (Bogart). L'autre personnage féminin, la chanteuse déchue Gaye Dawn est incarné par Claire Trevor, célèbre pour son rôle de femme fatale, manipulatrice et criminelle dans *Murder My Sweet* (1944) de Edward Dmytryk où elle est confrontée à un autre avatar (Dick Powell) du héros de Chandler.

Cependant, Huston ne se contente pas de recycler des personnages vus ailleurs. Il instaure une série de décalages dans les rôles des principaux protagonistes. Johnny Rocco est certes un avatar vieilli de Rico Bandello, mais son comportement est assez différent. Rocco est un gangster expérimenté, voire blasé, aux antipodes de la relative naïveté et immaturité de Rico. Les deux personnages se distinguent aussi en ce que l'un respecte encore un certain code de conduite et protège ses amis, mettant sa propre vie en danger, alors que l'autre tue froidement Angel qui refuse d'affronter McCloud. Huston insiste aussi sur la roublardise et le caractère manipulateur de Rocco, notamment dans la scène où le gangster propose à Frank de le tuer alors que son revolver est vide. Plus tard, sur le bateau, il fait encore semblant d'être désarmé afin de tromper Frank. A l'inverse de Rico qui n'a peur de rien, Rocco est aussi présenté comme un lâche terrifié par l'ouragan qu'il ne prenait d'abord pas au sérieux. Il s'attire ainsi la remarque cinglante de Frank : « You don't like it, do you, Rocco? If it doesn't stop, why don't you show it your gun? ». Le montage alterné de plans de Rocco en légère contre plongée, le visage en sueur, marchant de long en large et de plans de Frank, un léger sourire aux lèvres, met en évidence cette faille du personnage. Enfin Huston met en relief la cruauté, voire le sadisme de Rocco qui n'hésite pas à persécuter son amie alcoolique. Il la persuade de chanter en lui promettant à boire, et, alors qu'elle se ridiculise, refuse de tenir sa promesse. Frank brave l'interdit et lui sert un verre d'alcool, provoquant la fureur du gangster qui cherche à l'humilier en le giflant à toute volée. Dans ces différentes scènes, Huston joue sur un filmage en plan serré et un montage en champ contre champ valorisant l'expressivité des comédiens, mais il a également recours à des plans larges où l'ensemble des personnages figurent dans le cadre. Une dernière différence entre Rico et Rocco concerne la relation aux femmes. Alors que Rico leur témoigne une indifférence[1] totale et ne souhaite pas s'embarasser d'une « moll », Rocco est manifestement attiré par Nora qu'il qualifie de « wild cat » et qui lui rappelle Gaye du temps de sa splendeur. Il l'embrasse par surprise sur la bouche alors qu'elle tente de le frapper (il vient de provoquer et d'humilier son père), lui chuchote des propos, sans doute de nature obscène, à l'oreille et, au moment de quitter l'hôtel, lui offre encore de l'accompagner, sans succès.

Bogart compose également un personnage assez différent de ses rôles habituels de « dur ». Il exprime une certaine forme de cynisme désabusé et son attitude semble confiner à la lâcheté quand il refuse de tirer sur Rocco ou encore quand il reste sans réaction face aux diverses provocations de Rocco et de ses acolytes. Son attitude prudente provoque la colère de Nora et l'apparente résignation du père. Dans ces moments, Huston filme Bogart en gros plan pour capter l'expression fugitive de son désarroi ou de sa douleur morale, en particulier quand Nora lui signifie son désaccord et son mépris, ou quand il apprend la mort absurde des deux frères Osceola. Le vétéran finit par accepter son destin de héros et son savoir faire lui permet de se débarasser de tous les gangsters au cours d'une scène inspirée directement du roman de Hemingway, *To Have and Have Not* déjà adapté par Hawks.

Le personnage de Nora est aussi éloigné de la « moll » (cf. Mae Clarke ou Jean Harlow dans *Public Enemy*) que de la femme fatale du film noir emblématisée par Phyllis Dietrichson (Barbara Stanwick) dans *Double Indemnity* de Billy Wilder ou encore Kitty Collins (Ava Gardner) dans *The Killers* de Robert Siodmak. Victime et héroïque à la fois, en butte à la convoitise de Rocco, elle prend des risques quand elle manifeste sa répulsion à l'égard du gangster et lui crache à la figure. Elle exprime aussi ouvertement son désaccord avec Frank en dépit de la complicité qui les lie.

De même le personnage de Gaye s'écarte du stéréotype. Prenant conscience de la malignité de Rocco après la scène humiliante où elle s'efforce de chanter en état d'ivresse, elle prend fait et cause pour Frank et lui fournit le révolver qu'elle subtilise adroitement à Rocco lors d'une scène faussement pathétique ou elle fait semblant de le supplier. Les deux femmes incarnant des personnages antinomiques sont finalement réunies dans le même plan, observant anxieusement le départ de Frank.

La fin du film est, à certains égards, plus conforme à la convention. Les gangsters sont éliminés et le héros revient triomphant. L'un des derniers plans montre le *Santana* qui sort de la brume et Bogart debout, aux commandes, stoïque face à la douleur (il a reçu une balle dans le ventre). Au plan suivant, le cadre se resserre et sa posture est magnifiée par le surcadrage constitué par la fenêtre de la cabine. Juste avant cette scène, Nora ouvre les volets de la maison et la lumière s'engouffre à flots, irradiant la pièce alors qu'on entend le motif mi-héroïque, mi-romantique (violons et harpe) associé au couple tout au long du film et qui se prolonge et s'amplifie sur les images de Bogart. On peut cependant se demander si Huston ne prend pas ses distances vis à vis de ce « happy end » (par ailleurs assez peu courant dans les films noirs). De plus, une certaine ambiguïté plane car on

---

1. Dans le roman, Rico méprise tout autant les femmes, mais il manifeste un certain appétit sexuel.

ne sait si Frank va survivre à ses blessures ou succomber comme Harry Morgan le « skipper » manchot d'Hemingway.

En se servant de différentes conventions, John Huston rend hommage à un classique du cinéma et convoque, par l'image et le discours, une époque révolue et déjà mythifiée par le cinéma – la prohibition et l'âge d'or du gangstérisme – qu'il confronte avec un moment de crise correspondant au contexte de production de son film, ce qui peut permettre une lecture métaphorique de celui-ci. Il se livre également à une réflexion sur l'évolution des genres, émaillée de citations filmiques. En concentrant l'intrigue grâce au dispositif du huis-clos, il propose l'hybridation réussie du film de gangster et du film noir par le biais d'une confrontation stimulante de deux acteurs qui, à eux seuls, incarnent l'histoire des deux genres. Le film porte cependant la marque du réalisateur et on y retrouve la plupart de ses thèmes privilégiés, notamment la confrontation de l'homme avec les éléments naturels et la tension entre destin et volonté individuelle.

"Investigators, undercover men and the F.B.I.: from gangsterism to Communism and back again"

Par Reynold Humphries

This chapter is concerned with four films: *The Enforcer* (Bretaigne Windust and Raoul Walsh, 1950), *The Street with no Name* (William Keighley, 1948), *The Woman on Pier 13* (Robert Stevenson, 1949) and *I was a Communist for the FBI* (Gordon Douglas, 1951)[1]. I shall be dealing not only with the representation of crime but with what was considered to be a crime, particularly in the case of the last two films, made as Hollywood's "contribution" to the ongoing "Red scare". We shall see, not only that Communism (never defined, except in the speech made by the hero at the end of *I was a Communist for the FBI*) was looked upon as a crime, but that spectators had been conditioned by years of Hollywood film-making to a stereotyped and profoundly ideological view of characters and events and, hence, their representation. This is particularly striking in *The Street with no Name* which deals with the FBI and undercover agents and where it will be necessary to draw attention to certain narrative devices whose purpose is to represent the FBI and Hollywood as "natural allies", the political ramifications of which are considerable, given the anti-Communist climate of the country from 1946 on. It is a remark in *The Enforcer*, however, that will enable us to approach the question of organized crime, those who fought it and how Hollywood tackled the various issues at stake.

At one point towards the end of the film Martin Ferguson (Humphrey Bogart) – a state official investigating a series of seemingly unlinked murders in an attempt to convict the "brain" behind them all, a certain Mendoza – finds himself in a quandary. A suspect who has moved to an adjacent state is now outside his jurisdiction and Ferguson must appeal to the local police to make the arrest. It is generally accepted that Ferguson's fight against organized crime refers to the ongoing investigation into the subject by the Senate Committee set up in 1950 and headed by Senator Estes Kefauver, but the topic – who had jurisdiction to combat crime? – was in fact an old one. In August 1933 Homer Cummings, the Attorney-General, made a speech to the Daughters of the American Revolution where he stated:

> We are now engaged in a war that threatens the safety of our country – a war with the organized forces of crime (Theoharis, 154).

The word "crime" was to be replaced by "Communism" after the war in a variety of discourses, including that of J. Edgar Hoover, director since 1924 of the Federal Bureau of Investigation (a post he held until his death in 1972). A newspaper summed up the situation as Cummings saw it

---

1. Only Windust is credited with the direction of *The Enforcer*, but all references to the film insist on the fact that Walsh replaced him for most of the shooting. Certainly the quality and style of the film bear the mark of the director of two of the most remarkable gangster movies in the history of the cinema: *The Roaring Twenties* (1939) and *White Heat* (1949).

> *Crime, which was increasing to vast proportions, was no longer a local phenomenon but was conducted by interstate gangs who operated across State lines... (Theoharis, 155).*

thus justifying in Cummings' eyes his call for a federal police, one that could operate nation-wide. Already, as a result of the kidnapping and murder in 1932 of the baby of Charles Lindbergh (the killer was never apprehended), kidnapping was now a federal affair: the FBI no longer had to call on the police of the State involved to make an arrest, but could step in directly. Both conservatives and liberals were dubious about any extension of the powers of the FBI, the former because of their hostility to centralized government, the latter because of their commitment to civil liberties (Theoharis, 125). As organized crime took on new forms and burgeoned along with unemployment, the powers of the FBI were reinforced by a vote of Congress in 1934, the year that saw the shooting down of such figures as Bonnie and Clyde, Dillinger, Baby Face Nelson and Pretty Boy Floyd.

The ambiguity of *The Enforcer* lies in the fact that, despite the success of Ferguson (he finds the one witness whose testimony will send Mendoza to the electric chair), the status of this victory is not clear: one crime has been solved – thanks to a combination of luck and Ferguson's keen powers of observation – but nothing suggests that organized crime is over. This leaves intact the suggestion that certain laws must be modified in order to help the crusade, a notion made explicit by Ferguson's collaborator who says early in the film about Mendoza

> *What's wrong with our laws that we can't touch him ?*

The Street with no Name and *I was a Communist for the FBI* make it quite clear that Hoover's power should be extended, but another aspect of *The Enforcer* needs to be elucidated as it is one that ties in with the representation of gangsterism as a form of business enterprise, a notion that had precise subversive and anti-capitalist implications that are clearly highlighted in a number of contemporary films[1].

Ferguson himself refers to "a business built on murder: murder for profit" and in one long and remarkable sequence Mendoza's henchman Rico is seen sitting behind a desk, taking notes and interviewing professional killers as to their suitability for the elimination of citizens whose murder is paid for by person or persons unknown to the killers. The word "contract" is used to describe what must surely be called a "business deal", with Rico acting as intermediary[2]. This creates an intriguing parallel between organized crime and capitalism. In the case of the latter we have the capitalist, the middle-man and the worker. In the case of the former, the person who pays, the intermediary (Rico), with the killer in the place of the person selling his labour. The fact that the person paying/the capitalist remains behind the scenes corresponds to what is now called "the invisible hand of the market" that is said by neoliberals to determine our lives. The strings are meant to be pulled by "economic forces", a discourse which

---

1. Key examples of this are Abraham Polonsky's *Force of Evil* (1948) and Jules Dassin's *Thieves' Highway* (1949).
2. The very name at once refers back to the central character of *Little Caesar* and evokes the role of the Mafia in organized crime.

conceals those responsible: bankers, speculators, insurance companies and gangsters, not to mention the politicians who allow them to flourish. Moreover, the film's use of flashbacks breaks up the narrative in a way that perfectly represents the fragmented and alienated nature of our everyday lives and the paranoia this can cause. Certainly paranoia, fear of discovery and betrayal sum up the general climate of *The Enforcer*.

If the film does not make explicit the precise status of its investigator Ferguson, this cannot be said of *The Street with no Name*, a veritable paean of praise to the FBI. The Bureau's plaque, to the accompaniment of military music (to which we shall return when discussing the ending of *I was a Communist for the FBI*), forms the opening shot of the film, followed by a crane movement past the American flag and down to the main entrance of an imposing edifice (also one of the opening shots of *I was a Communist for the FBI*) bearing the inscription "Federal Bureau of Investigation". We are then assured of the factual nature of what we are about to see by the written statement that the film is "adapted from the files of the FBI" and that "wherever possible it was photographed in the original locale and played by the actual FBI personnel involved". Shortly after we accompany the FBI official in charge of the investigation (a crucial example of imaginary audience identification) and are introduced to the undercover man (Eugene Cordell) who is to be the film's hero. The scene takes place at the Bureau's training centre. Clearly Cordell is not only someone to be reckoned with, but also a man of scruples when it comes to using his firearm. Presented with visual representations of classic situations an agent has to face, he shoots only in self-defense; to shoot a man who wants to surrender would be "to shoot in cold blood". This, of course, is how the gangsters behave, not hesitating to shoot down an unarmed woman in a restaurant, thus leaving a widower and children. Moreover, the gangster Alex Stiles beats up his wife, yet another sign of his being "un-American". I shall argue presently that this is part of a particularly insidious sub-text of the film, but for the moment let us turn briefly to the film's plot.

Agent Cordell has a phony identity manufactured for him by the FBI so that he can infiltrate the gang by frequenting the sort of sordid venues they apparently operate out of. He is thus able to accumulate enough evidence not only to confound Stiles but also to unmask the senior police official who is taking huge bribes in order to inform the gangster about all attempts to unmask him. By juxtaposing the authentic and the artificial and binding them together into a supposedly homogeneous narrative, the film reveals the implications of its rhetorical and discursive devices. One critic has pointed out that

> most of the film's exteriors were shot at night on Main Street in Los Angeles' Skid Row (Christopher, 166).

The *Encyclopédie du Film Noir* places the film firmly in the semi-documentary tradition inaugurated by 20th. Century Fox, adding

> ... la photographie de Joe MacDonald, très liée au style semi-documentaire de l'époque... impose la vision d'une ville corrompue et des images pleines d'ombres menaçantes peu différentes des films tournés en studio... (Silver and Ward, 109).

J.P. Telotte has this to say on films belonging to this sub-group of *film noir*:

> ... the documentary techniques themselves gradually began to function less as tools for revealing and attesting to truth than as part of a formal rhetoric of belief that might be applied in reassuring ways (Telotte, 156).

Later he takes up this crucial insight, stating that such techniques,

> particularly the form-conscious prologues, newsreel footage, and voice-of-god narration, invoked their own share of obscurantism, rooted in other conventions of belief viewers had been conditioned to bring to the film experience (175).

The repetition of the word "belief", the use of the formula "voice-of-god narration" and the way audiences are "conditioned" by the social activity called "cinema-going" to interpret other, apparently quite different films, in similar fashion – or, to be more precise, in a fashion carefully constructed to impose a particular world view – merit closer attention.

After the film's tribute to the role played by the FBI in making the film comes a little homily on crime and security by none other than Hoover himself who warns that, if unchecked, gangsterism will affect the lives of "three out of four Americans". The country must remain "alert and vigilant". We are given no indication of the time and place of this remark, whether he wrote it at the request of the film's producers or had already made the statement in public. The film thus renders it impossible to judge objectively the veracity of the remark concerning the return of gangsterism on a grand scale. At the same time the remark naturalises both the film's rhetoric – noble agent and vicious gangster, FBI Headquarters as the seat of security, Center City as the embodiment of filth and corruption – and Hoover's own strident prose. Moreover, his words do not come to us in the form of a voice-over but appear on the screen on a teletype in FBI Headquarters, thus giving them an extra dimension of "truth". Discussing *Call Northside 777* (Henry Hathaway, 1947), Christopher refers to

> the early fax-machine prototype... which becomes the principal "character" in the film's climax..., transmitting between two cities an enlarged portion of a newspaper photo in order to save an innocent man from a life sentence in the penitentiary (91).

Towards the end of *The Street with no Name* a teletype appears again, also with a message from Hoover. This time, however, it is not addressed *urbi et orbi* to the spectators but to the film's characters: they receive orders from Hoover himself and the final operation against Stiles and his gang is put in motion.

What is happening here? Just as the time, place and circumstances of the enunciation were carefully elided in the first use of a Hoover message on a teletype, here the Director of the FBI is literally inscribed into the diegesis, transformed into a character having the same function as his representative Briggs and the assorted agents and police working under him, such as Cordell. Thus do Hollywood and the FBI merge, each representing the other, in the name of the war against crime. Hollywood believes in Hoover and Hoover counts on Hollywood. The film's "documentary" style, already forgotten except in brief shots of ballistic experts going about their business – with an efficacity that is a way of simultaneously reassuring and intimidating the audience – is nothing more nor less than propaganda, a particular vision not only of what film "is" but what America should be.

Let us now return to Hoover's call to be "alert and vigilant" and place it in its historical context, as it provides us with an essential clue as to the subtext of *The Street with no Name* and the different meanings to be given to that all-purpose word "crime". With the benefit of hindsight today we can move forward from 1948 to 1951 and to the horror/science-fiction film *The Thing from Another World* (Christian Nyby, 1951) which finishes with a journalist telling the world to "keep watching the skies" to spot future alien landings. 1951 was also the year the Red scare and witch-hunting started in earnest, the year that saw the production of *I was a Communist for the FBI*, directed by Gordon Douglas, soon to direct (in 1954) the film *Them!* which, among other things, is an anti-Communist tract[1]. I would suggest Stiles' desire to "run an organisation along scientific lines", with a police informant helping him to undermine the noble edifice of American society from both within and without, is the Hollywood Right's version of Marxism, with the Hollywood Left cast in the role of fellow-travellers ready to turn to gangsterism and other un-American activites to help Communists obtain their nefarious goal. We must not forget that witch-hunts were based on the premise that a "Commie" was in the pay of the Soviet Union. That Stiles should ask, rather incongruently, "What's the use of having a war if you don't learn something?" must not be taken as a simple character trait – megalomania – but a hint: Stiles may have been on America's side during the hostilities, but alliances have changed. It is also revealing that there is no reason why Cordell should start his investigation as an undercover man in the most rundown and poverty-stricken part of Center City, nor that he should blend in so easily. Once we interpret this rhetorically and therefore ideologically, and not simply as one way among many of opening a movie, the situation becomes clearer:

> ... like Stiles and his men, Cordell grew up in the slums; like so many cops in film noir, he arrived early in his life at that fork in the well-travelled highway that cuts through the heart of the noir city... (Christopher, 167).

In other words, being poor is an accident you can overcome if you are inherently honest and pro-American; gangsters are simply corrupt individuals who refuse to earn a living honestly. Just what that can imply in post-war society in general and Hollywood in particular can be teased out of *The Woman on Pier 13* and *I was a Communist for the FBI*, although many detours will have to be made along that particular highway.

Stiles' reference to "an organisation run on scientific lines" corresponds to another common fantasy: the Communist-influenced trade union. It is composed either of obstreperous workers who keep on asking unreasonably

---

1. It is also a justification of martial law in the name of national security and an unthinking acceptance of authority, both government and military. One of the film's heroes is an FBI agent.

for more money from financially hard-pressed bosses, or of deluded workers who allow themselves to be led up the garden path by what the late and unlamented British Prime Minister Harold Wilson once notoriously referred to at the time of the seaman's strike of 1967 as "a tightly-knit group of politically motivated men". In other words: Reds. This, as is well known, was an obsession of Hoover's since the Bolshevik Revolution and the American miners' strikes of 1919. The convictions of "the Boss" are neatly encapsulated by Theoharis:

> That he should have found 'Communism' the greatest evil in the world is not surprising when one considers that it advocated violent expropriation from the owners of the means of production and rejected religion as the opiate of the masses. This, to one who reportedly said grace at the dining table both morning and night and who, according to one longtime acquaintance, had a 'wealth reverence' was clearly intolerable. ... Convinced that radicalism was a monstrous threat to America, Hoover, who saw himself as in some way the savior chosen to carry the light to the gentiles, could act with conviction (75).

Hoover's missionary zeal went from the conviction and deportation of hundreds of alien radicals in 1920[1] via the arrest of anti-Franco activists in 1940 (as America was not at war, Hoover doubtless saw himself as justified in persecuting anti-Fascists) to his infamous "educational campaign", which meant illegally leaking documents to those likely to make the best use of them: Joseph McCarthy, Richard Nixon (who started his illustrious career as a lawyer working for the House Committee on Un-American Activities, hereafter referred to as the HUAC) and John Rankin, a Southern Democrat, of whom more presently (Theoharis, 79, 195, 322).

I am well aware of the risk of over-simplification in what follows, but it is a risk I am willing to take, given the nature of *The Woman on Pier 13* and *I was a Communist for the FBI*. The basic ploy of both films is to present Communism as a crime and to portray Communists as constantly in the act of instigating criminal activities. As such the films involve a shift from gangsterism to Communism where the latter is indistinguishable from the former, down to the using of the panoply of *film noir* codes where dress, looks and behaviour overdetermine the acts the characters perpetrate to the point of making it impossible for uninformed audiences to do anything but acquiesce in the blatant and mendacious propaganda purveyed by the films. Such generalisations, however, are insufficient. We need to place the films in a precise historical context.

Both films proceed by attributing certain crimes to Communists as if such accusations went without saying (literally, as we shall see); and by inverting the real historical events represented – sometimes made explicit in *I was a Communist for the FBI* – so as to lay at the door of Communists the actual crimes or complicity in crimes of the witch-hunters or the various interests

---

1. The most celebrated "alien radical" to be deported was, of course, Chaplin: in 1952, with McCarthyism in full swing. Chaplin's "scandalous" sex life, his vaguely left-wing sympathies and, especially, his anti-Fascist *The Great Dictator* (1940) had made him a prime target for assorted witch-hunters since the 30s.

they represented[1]. Smearing trade-union leaders as Communists had been a popular tactic since the aftermath of World War I, so it is not surprising to find that the sympathetic union leader in *The Woman on Pier 13* is anti-Communist. It is generally accepted that Vanning, the vicious Communist leader who orders murders (he becomes thus a condensation of Rico and Mendoza in *The Enforcer*) and provokes a waterfront strike on the part of the stevedores, is the trade-union leader Harry Bridges who was a Communist sympathizer. As the film is set in San Francisco where Bridges led a successful maritime and general strike in 1934, this is hardly objective and innocent, especially as Bridges acted at the time against the wishes of trade-union leaders who had lost the confidence of rank-and-file members (Lipsitz, 105). What is ironic about the situation is that, during the war and as part of the war effort, Bridges and CP unionists worked tirelessly to avoid strikes, seeing this as a patriotic duty: "The communist commitment to wartime labor peace assumed concrete form in the everyday affairs of unions, much to the delight of employers and much to the dismay of rank and file" (Lipsitz, 195). The author goes on to quote the journal *Business Week* in 1944 to the effect that "unions identified as communist-dominated have the best no-strike record, are the most vigorous proponents of labor-management cooperation..." (195). The position after World War II, however, was dramatic for workers, as the author notes:

> By the winter of 1945-6, one quarter of all war workers had lost their jobs. Nearly 2 million workers found themselves unemployed by October 1, and real income for workers fell by an average of 15 percent in three months. Prospects for the future offered little hope for improvement, as 10 million servicemen and women returned to civilian life to join the competition for jobs (99).

From the wealth of material Lipsitz provides in his essential book, I would like to choose two items of information: the importance of wildcat strikes in favour of working conditions or in defense of workers unfairly treated or dismissed; and the role played by Communist union leaders who devoted their energy to defending wages and working conditions, rather than applying the Party line and exploiting militancy over genuine grievances for propaganda purposes. It was clearly this that led the Hollywood Right to exploit the equally genuine Red scares of the post-war period, transformed into something akin to panic when the Soviet Union exploded its first Atom bomb in 1949 (the year the Communists took power in China). For the success of such union militancy was much closer to home than the waterfront, oil refineries and coal mines: Hollywood had already gone through the strikes of screen writers throughout the 30s and was involved after the war in a prolonged strike on the part of technicians that lasted from 1945 to 1947. That CP members were involved in creating an independent union that would represent writers' interests as a protest against the "house union" which bent the knee to the studios was instrumental in the creation by the Hollywood Right of the Motion Picture

---

1. Attacks on Roosevelt and the New Deal on the part of the most reactionary elements within the Republican Party and their objective allies, the Southern Democrats, had been under way since the 30s.

Alliance for the Preservation of American Ideals. And the links between the official union representing technicians and the world of organized crime, in the shape of union leader W. Bioff, have been well documented (Nielsen and Mailes)[1]. The transformation of real-life unionists who worked hand in glove with studios bosses on the one hand and known gangsters on the other into trouble-making and murderous Communists is, however, only one of the tactics used by the films. Far more was at stake than dressing the Communist enemy in one's own clothes.

Let us turn to a specific case, the representation of workers and strikers in *The Woman on Pier 13*. The Communists, according to the film, foment discontent where only brotherly love and mutual understanding through dialogue should normally prevail. However, this has to be shown to convince audiences that workers were only interested in working and Communists in preventing them from doing so (for reasons never made clear in the film: a Communist is a trouble-maker seemingly for the pleasure of it). There is a fascinating montage sequence showing the anti-Communist union leader clearly losing control as Communist-inspired workers get up to speak. The problem for the film is that nothing must be communicated to the audience, except that the trouble-makers are winning the day. For the film cannot use arguments that workers might resort to in order to justify a strike: to do so runs the risk of placing sections of the audience on the "wrong" side, that of the strikers. The film comes up with a disarmingly simple solution: appropriate "atmospheric" music is played but no speeches are heard! It is at this juncture that Hollywood know-how and the codes of the *film noir* prove crucial: the leading trouble-maker is not a Communist, but someone who has been "misled" by falling in love with an unscrupulous "femme fatale" who, not surprisingly, is a Red! Furthermore, he has been subjected to "indoctrination" at a party where the Party faithful have referred to "anti-labor legislation". Prominent here is the smooth discourse of a well-dressed man with a "posh" accent and horn-rimmed spectacles: clearly an "intellectual" and arguably a reference to such leading Hollywood Communists as Dalton Trumbo and John Howard Lawton. As a result the young man, who had never given the matter any thought, is all "mixed up" (his own expression). Thus the film contrives to present as the ideal worker one who asks no questions and goes about his business unthinkingly: once he starts to reflect he no longer thinks straight. Here it is as a result of meeting Communists without knowing who they are, but the implications are clear: let the bosses and trade-union leaders like Bioff do the thinking. This contempt for the intelligence of workers is nothing, however, to the tactics of inversion indulged in by both films.

The film cannot possibly limit its anti-Communist stance to denouncing militant unionists: despite the "Red scare", 1946 was embarrassingly close

---

1. This intimate link between corrupt unions and gangsterism was taken notice of only when it could be transformed discursively into a "natural" link between unions and the CP. This was then translated into legal terms by the passing of the Taft-Hartley Act in 1948 whose purpose was to "restreindre le pouvoir des syndicats. Entre autres dispositions, il était interdit à ceux-ci de financer un parti politique et leurs dirigeants devaient déclarer sous serment qu'ils n'étaient pas membres du Parti communiste" (Navasky, 201). There is no better way to create in the public mind a link that was ideologically determined.

and certain spectators might have good memories. Something stronger is called for: a crime that is immediately recognizable as such. So two henchmen of Vanning truss up like a fowl a Party member who is accused of going to the FBI and throw his body into the water, watching with amusement as it sinks. I am not concerned here with whether the American CP actually behaved this way as nothing in the film invites a reading on the grounds of verisimilitude or historical accuracy. What we witness does, however, have a long and hideous tradition in the States: lynching. Which brings us back to John Rankin.

A notorious anti-Semite who denounced the presence of Jews in Hollywood – he gave the original names of such well-known liberals as Danny Kaye and Edward G. Robinson on the floor of Congress and was applauded – Rankin also distinguished himself by systematically and successfully blocking all federal attempts to outlaw lynching. Obviously anyone opposed to such a pastime as mutilating and murdering negroes could only be un-American! In his autobiography Alvah Bessie, one of the Hollywood Ten sentenced to prison for contempt of Congress in 1947 for refusing to state whether they were members of the CP (Lawton and Trumbo were others), quotes from the transcript of the hearings of the HUAC on Communist infiltration of the film industry. Rankin put the following question to a "friendly" witness (i.e., one whose anti-Communism was known in advance):

> You said before that sixty percent of the Communist Party here are aliens. Now what percentage of these aliens are Jews?... Is it true, Mr. Bullitt, that the Communists went into the Southern states and picked up niggers and sent them to Moscow to study revolution? (Bessie, 225).

When we learn that the HUAC was of the opinion that the Ku Klux Klan was "an acceptable American institution" (Bessie, 232) and hear the Communist boss in *I was a Communist for the FBI* refer to black workers as "niggers" (he is immediately taken to task by the FBI undercover man passing himself off as a Communist), then it becomes clear that for the makers of these films "anything goes". This, however, is only the tip of the iceberg.

Why so much venom and hatred? This is the moment to clarify matters. My concern here is to show, by recourse to History and various documents, that the assimilation of Communists to gangsters is without proof in the films in question, indeed: that the crimes shown can be imputed to the extreme Right rather than to factions of the Left. The word "Communism" goes back to Marx and its use and abuse since has and will always be a subject of bitter controversy. Enforced collectivization, purges and the persecution of artists under Stalin had provoked hostility to the Soviet system in Europe and the States from the extreme Left, liberals and the Right[1] but what we are faced with in *I was a Communist for the FBI* has

---

1. The question of the role and function of works of art triggered off heated debates and confrontations within the Hollywood CP. Dogmatic members tended to champion the Stalinist notion of "Socialist Realism", whereas writer Albert Maltz insisted on the question of form,

nothing to do with this. At the risk of simplifying once again, I would argue that those who showed clear pro-Fascist and pro-Nazi sympathies throughout the 30s, whether the Hollywood hierarchy or various business interests, needed a smokescreen to make citizens forget their earlier support for the enemy[1]. Thus studio boss Harry Cohn was a great admirer of Mussolini – nothing like a Fascist dictatorship to keep unruly workers in their place, hence the notion of a "house union" in Hollywood! – and kept a photo of *Il Duce* in his office until his death in 1958. Celebrated director Howard Hawks made anti-Semitic statements to Lauren Bacall on their first meeting (Friedrich, 241) and was a leading member of the Motion Picture Alliance for the Preservation of American Ideals which contacted the HUAC and asked it to investigate Communism in Hollywood before the war was even over. Congressman Martin Dies of Texas, Chairman of the HUAC in 1938, attributed what he saw as widespread Communist propaganda in Hollywood to the fact that "most of the producers are Jews" (Friedrich, 52) and, notoriously, referred that year to "premature anti-Fascism". Bessie gives some eloquent information on one Edward F. Sullivan, HUAC's chief investigator in 1938:

> In 1934 he addressed a meeting of German-American Bund members and uniformed American storm troopers in New York City. In 1936 he was a featured speaker at a meeting in Asheville, North Carolina, which was attended by leading anti-Semitic and pro-Nazi propagandists and at which the Roosevelt Administration was denounced as a "Jewish Communist plot"[2]. Sullivan also had a long police record, involving everything from public drunkenness to larceny, and the Senate Civil Liberties Committee later brought out the fact that he had been employed for a time as a labor spy by a "strikebreaking, labor espionage agency" (185-6).

It is revealing at this juncture to refer to the career of Orson Welles who plays an anti-fascist sailor in *The Lady from Shanghai* (1947) and a corrupt, fascistic cop in *Touch of Evil* (1957)[3]. Welles was a condensation, in his opinions and in the causes he espoused, of everything the fascist and anti-union elements in Hollywood detested. His thinly-veiled attack, via the character of Charles Foster Kane, on newspaper magnate William Randolph Hearst resulted in his being tracked by the FBI as from 1941 (Denning, 364). Hearst's sympathies were public knowledge:

> His public statements supporting Hitler and Mussolini were notorious, and his newspapers were rabidly anti-labor. He had led

---

arguing for the elaboration of a Marxist aesthetic. This seems to have been perceived as "bourgeois" by many. Unfortunately, this complex subject is beyond the scope of this study.

1. It must not be forgotten either that, as a result of the Wall Street crash and the economic slump of the ensuing years, Hollywood was to come increasingly under the control of Banks and other economic institutions located in New York. The interest of such people in art and their concern for the welfare of the underprivileged is well known.
2. Leading liberal Edward G. Robinson was not only denounced as a Jew by Rankin in Congress. As a result of lending his home for a meeting of those fighting the 1947 investigations of Communism in Hollywood, he received anonymous phone calls denouncing him as "a filthy Communist Jew".
3. For a detailed account of the links between Welles' artistic and political activities from the mid 30s to the late 50s, see Denning, pp. 362-402.

> the attack on the 1934 San Francisco general strike and continued to hound the ILWU leader Harry Bridges (Denning, 385).

Hearst's supporters in Hollywood took over that task in *The Woman on Pier 13*, but it is in *I was a Communist for the FBI* that we find, both in the dialogue and in entire sequences, references to celebrated occurrences that highlighted the climate of the country, particularly on racial matters and the crimes racism precipitated.

The first of these was the Scottsboro case of 1931 where 9 blacks were arrested and sentenced to death for rape: the victim, of course, was white. The convictions were later quashed. Of more immediate importance was the Sleepy Lagoon affair which mobilised Welles and much of Hollywood, not to mention the CP and civil liberties associations:

> The Sleepy Lagoon case began when seventeen young Chicanos were arrested in August 1942 for the murder of Jose Diaz. Two of the defendants were severely beaten by the police, and their trial took place in a lynch-mob atmosphere whipped up by Hearst headlines about a Mexican American "crime wave" (Denning, 399).

There is every likelihood that this occurrence inspired the film *The Sound of Fury* (1950), whose director Cy Endfield was to be blacklisted soon after[1]. A year later came the "zoot suit" riots in Los Angeles, so called because of the tight-fitting trousers worn by young Mexicans, which turned into a systematic "search and destroy" operation against Mexicans by American sailors, with the police complacently looking on. The local and national racial climate at the time has been summed up thus:

> These were the pachuco or zoot suit riots that roiled downtown Los Angeles throughout the first week of June 1943. They are largely forgotten now, partly because much worse rioting broke out between blacks and whites in Detroit two weeks later. Thirty-four people died there, and about seven hundred were injured, before the national guard restored order. To anyone who is young enough to think that American race riots involve gangs of black marauders attacking frightened whites, let it be recalled that in the race riots of the 1940's (Harlem and St. Louis suffered major outbreaks too), blacks fled for their lives from pursuing gangs of whites. In Los Angeles, though, where there were still very few blacks, just beginning to immigrate to work in the arms factories and to occupy the abandoned tenements of Little Tokyo, the victims were the Mexicans, and the attackers were the United States armed forces (Friedrich 141-2).

The upshot of all this (un-)American activity was predictable: zoot suits were banned by the Los Angeles City Council.

Senator Jack Tenney of California announced he was investigating "a possible connection between the juvenile gangsters and Axis agents"

---

1. It was common practice in post-war Hollywood to offer roles in anti-Communist movies to actors who had been "compromised" by appearing in "Communist" films or because of their support for such subversive organisations as the Anti-Nazi League and the National Association for the Advancement of Colored People and to ask directors suspected of Communist sympathies to direct certain films. Thus liberal Robert Ryan played the former CP member who finds himself trapped by Vanning in *The Woman on Pier 13*; and Frank Lovejoy, the central character of *The Sound of Fury*, played the undercover agent Matt Cvetic in *I was a Communist for the FBI*.

(Friedrich, 144). Note that the blame is put on the victims who are assimilated to gangsters. After the war Tenney was to use the same tactics against Communists, but it is interesting to note how the "zoot suit" riots percolate into *The Street with no Name* (not an explicit anti-Communist movie): we are told that "the juvenile gangsters of yesterday" have become "the gangsters of today". This is hardly a coincidence, but more to the point is the situation described in *I was a Communist for the FBI* where the son of the undercover agent Matt Cvetic, who knows nothing of his father's real identity, is in danger of being turned into a "juvenile gangster" because of fights at school whenever chums call his father a "Commie". Significantly the film avoids the possible accusation that delinquency might be due to Cold War anxiety and paranoia by making the boy's teacher a member of the CP: she and the other CP teachers are only interested in indoctrination, and as it is the teacher herself who says it, then this becomes CP "policy". Central to the film's "argument", however, are the questions of strikes and racism.

These are cunningly condensed in a sequence where workers opposed to a strike and to the picket line try to cross it and are beaten up by CP thugs brought in from outside, using lead pipes wrapped in Jewish newspapers[1]. The idea is to set the community against the Jews, then against Catholics, then Jews against Catholics, and so on. Readers will, I hope, see the purpose of my references to anti-Semitism in Hollywood and elsewhere and to various forms of racist activity throughout the 30s and 40s. Friedrich's remarks quoted above about black victims of white race riots is a precious antidote to the accusation formulated in *I was a Communist for the FBI* to the effect that the Detroit riots of 1943, which resulted in the deaths of several negros, were Communist inspired: "their death sentences were signed in Moscow", as one character says darkly. Needless to say, the CP members have stirred up local blacks and Brandon, their leader, hopes a black will pick a fight with a white, a perfect instance of ideology representing reality in an inverted form. Brandon, of course, has nothing but contempt for "niggers" whom it is so easy to fool, but the film encounters a problem here with its own codes of representation. There is a sequence where the Communists incite black workers to – do what? Strike? Attack whites on the street? It is not clear as the film resorts to the same "silent" tactic as *The Woman on Pier 13*: we see a sea of black faces with a commentary over by Cvetic, just to make sure audiences adopt the right attitude. Impossible to determine if the blacks are hesitant, perplexed or just plain ignorant. It is certainly significant that one black, better dressed, reacts negatively to what he is being told and is shouted down: the film therefore, unconsciously, exhibits its anti-working-class prejudices, overdetermined by a "belief" in the inherent inferiority of blacks.

It is perhaps fitting to conclude discussion of this repugnant and properly scurrilous film with information on its noble, patriotic, clear-cut hero Matt Cvetic. In real life – for this film, we are assured, is based on fact – he was

---

1. One striker, a woman, hurls abuse at "scabs" and the police and talks as if Moscow were already running the States. Her hairstyle makes her look like a refugee from a Nazi film or, more to the point, from a Hollywood anti-Nazi film, thus making the usual link between Communism and Nazism. One must not lose sight of the fact that the Nazi-Soviet pact of 1939 was badly perceived on both Left and Right and many people left the CP. See also note 7.

somewhat different. Hospitalized several times for chronic alcoholism and mental illness, he claimed Communists had infiltrated both major parties and were planning to assassinate one third of the population after organizing an invasion via Alaska. He could boast of having deprived nearly one hundred people of their jobs in Pennsylvania through his testimony (Sayre, 86). At the end of the film, the fictional Cvetic makes a similar claim: the Soviet Union is planning to transform the States into a "slave colony". This is followed by a shot of the bust of none other than Abraham Lincoln, to the accompaniment of "John Brown's body". When one remembers that Hoover harrassed anti-fascists for recruiting people to fight against Franco in the Abraham Lincoln Brigade (in which "Hollywood Ten" victim Alvah Bessie fought); that Rankin was a professional racist who supported lynching; that the Ku Klux Klan was never investigated; that blacklisted director Polonsky's Christian names were Abraham Lincoln; then one cannot but find obscene this appeal to the spirit of the man who helped abolish slavery. By representing Communists systematically as gangsters and having them commit crimes that can frequently be laid at the door of those whose interests such films serve, it is hardly surprising that *I was a Communist for the FBI* can eat its discursive cake and make us choke on it. Appearing before the HUAC in Washington, Brandon and the other CP members are informed that "it is not a crime to belong to the American CP", and are then asked: "Are you a Communist? Yes or no!" Unfortunately, this open violation of constitutional rights – if freedom of thought is guaranteed, what right does Congress have to demand someone make public his or her political or religious beliefs? – had already been upheld by the Supreme Court which thus sided with a highly ideological view of "crime" and "gangsterism".

Bibliography

BESSIE, Alvah, *Inquisition in Eden*, Seven Seas Books, Berlin, 1967.
CHRISTOPHER, Nicholas, *Somewhere in the Night, Film Noir and the American City*, Henry Holt and Company, New York, 1997.
DENNING, Michael, The Cultural Front. The Labouring of American Culture in the Twentieth Century, Verso, London and New York, 1997.
FRIEDRICH, Otto, *City of Nets. A Portrait of Hollywood in the 1940s*, Headline Book Publishing, London, 1987.
LIPSITZ, George, *Rainbow at Midnight. Labor and Culture in the 1940s*, University of Illinois Press, Urbana and Chicago, 1994.
NAVASKY, Victor, *Les Délateurs. Le cinéma américain et la chasse aux sorcières*, Balland, Paris, 1982 (originally published in 1980 as *Naming Names*).
NIELSEN, Mike and MAILES, Gene, *Hollywood's other Blacklist. Union Struggles in the Studio System*, British Film Institute, London, 1995.
SAYRE, Nora, *Running Time. Films of the Cold War*, the Dial Press, New York, 1982.
SILVER, Alain and WARD, Elizabeth, *Encyclopédie du Film Noir*, Rivages, Paris, 1987 (originally published in 1979 as *Film Noir*).
TELOTTE, J.P., *Voices in the Dark. The Narrative Patterns of Film Noir*, University of Illinois Press, Urbana and Chicago.
THEOHARIS, Athan G. and STUART COX John, *The Boss. J. Edgar Hoover and the Great American Inquisition*, Virgin Books, London, 1993 (1988).

Sergio Leone's *Once Upon a Time in America* looks back at the roaring twenties

By Zeenat Saleh

> *I'm fascinated with America – more fascinated than with American Myths or fables.* (Sergio Leone)

Once upon a time, there were "angels with dirty faces" in the "city streets"

Leone's film (1983) is what he affectionately called "a fairy tale for adults". The 228 minute epic made by the maestro of the "Spaghetti Western" is the third film of his trilogy (*Once Upon a Time in the West* and *Once Upon a Time a Revolution*). The choice of using Leone's film as the framework to this paper may seem somewhat paradoxical because it is, as critic Richard Combs puts it, "a most unlikely gangster film". Leone's intention was never really that of actually making a "gangster movie" but the register and the genre of the film transcend various cinematic genres. The very use of the phrase "once upon a time" transports the reader/viewer to a period in American cinema which has been vilified by some, glorified by others, and yet continues, decades later, to fascinate movie buffs and filmmakers. Moreover, even though some of the events in the film seem totally out of context, when not incomprehensible, the reader should keep in mind the idea of it being cinema, in its purest form – self-reflexive – and yet one is drawn to the story due to Leone's ingenious craftsmanship. The revival of the gangster movie, despite its different transformations, emerged in the 1970s with Francis Ford Coppola's *The Godfather*, and the genre was continued by such directors as Brian De Palma, Barry Levinson, or Martin Scorsese, even though the Prohibition period only lasted for thirteen years and despite the fact that the gangster movie, as a genre, was a phenomenon of the 1930s.

As many critics have noted, the Prohibition was perhaps the most stupid mistake made in American history as it had a totally adverse effect to the very purpose of the Volstead Act. Volstead had proudly declared to journalists, once the law was passed: "la loi règle la morale depuis les Dix Commandements."(J-P Martin, 1993: 62). The phrase: "The Roaring Twenties" is of course a direct reference to this era, but to experienced viewers, it is a nod to Raoul Walsh's eponymous film, made in 1934[1] in a more or less semi-documentary fashion, with a voice-over which cannot help but remind the viewer of the technique which Orson Welles would later use in *Citizen Kane* (1941).

---

1. Walsh's film had made such an impact on film audiences that a television series ran very successfully in the 1960s. In the series, the atmosphere is one of an exciting time during Prohibition. The characters were glamorous, and little crime was shown. It was, in fact, an enchanting moment for viewers who imagined that the 1920s meant beautiful women dancing the Charleston and enjoying their drinks in speakeasies which were very thinly disguised fashionable nightclubs compared to those shown in feature films of the kind.

The presentation of Walsh's film is fairly similar to that used in *Little Caesar* and *The Public Enemy*, as the cinema seemed a convenient vector, at the time, to convey a message of the evils of the crime and violence prevalent during the Twenties. Walsh's film is an adaptation of an original story by Mark Hellinger who signs his name at the end of the foreword which follows the opening credits:

> It may come to pass that, at some distant date, we will be confronted with another period similar to the one depicted in this photoplay (sic). If that happens, I pray that the events, as dramatized here, will be remembered. In this film, the characters are composites of people I know, and the situations are those that actually occurred. Bitter or sweet, most memories become precious as the years move on. This film is a memory – and I am grateful for it.

Yesterday

Hellinger's foreword seems all the more appropriate when one analyses Leone's film. The two main characters, in *The Roaring Twenties*, Eddie (James Cagney) and George (Humphrey Bogart), share similar traits with Leone's protagonists (David Aaranson alias Noodles (Robert De Niro) and Max (James Woods). Walsh's film is linear and chronological, beginning with the end of World War I, and following the decade during which everything and anything was possible in the underworld. Leone, however, uses the time structure as the main narrative process since he shifts from one period to another, with the idea that the viewer will put the pieces of the time puzzle in order. "Time," as Chris Peachment points out, "is rarely chronological for any of us; things from the past advance or recede according to their significance." (Peachment, 1984: 301). The shifts in time used by Leone in his film could possibly be comparable to those used by directors from the 1970s onwards. Although they themselves did not experience this particular era in American history, their fascination brings out the childlike fantasy which captivates every movie-goer: a pervading sense of nostalgia and a fairy-tale world in which "ordinary" people do not exist. How else could Benjamin "Bugsy" Siegel, Jimmy Hoffa, Al Capone, Meyer Lansky, Lucky Luciano, and all the other legendary, notorious characters live on in our memories? For Jean-Loup Bourget

> Le film criminel exprime la fascination de l'Amérique (le plus souvent contemporaine et urbaine) pour la violence, même si cette fascination s'accompagne, au moins pendant la période classique, d'une réprobation sincère ou feinte. (Bourget, 1998 : 61)

The "fascination" referred to above becomes all the more significant as gangster movies, especially those dealing with organised crime, tend to make the "baddies" almost endearing to viewers, despite the reprehensible acts for which they always find some justification. Although it is difficult to condone the acts of the gangsters, in *The Roaring Twenties*, for example, Eddie Bartlett (James Cagney) is a victim of the Depression: unemployment is rife, and after having fought for his country in the war, Eddie finds himself unemployed. Circumstances almost force him to enter the world of bootleggers, whereas he had hoped to get back his job as a mechanic and have enough savings to open a garage of his own. Eddie is one of those endearing gangsters, against the idea of killing for money, sincere and a romantic (a trait he has in common with Noodles in *Once Upon a Time in America*). His partnership in crime with the ruthless George (Humphrey Bogart) ends tragically with Eddie sacrificing his life to save the woman he had loved. The final shot where Eddie is lying dead, in the snow, in Panama's arms, on the steps of the church (the analogy with the Pietà is inevitable), remains fixed in the history of the cinema. There seem to be, however, two notable exceptions to these "endearing" gangsters: Tony Montana (Al Pacino) and Rico Bandello/Little Caesar (Edward G.Robinson) are both heinous and devoid of any redeeming features and can, in no way, be considered to be victims of the system.

Mervyn LeRoy's *Little Caesar* (1931), and William Wellman's *The Public Enemy* (1931), Rouben Mamoulian's *City Streets* (1931), Howard Hawk's *Scarface* (1932), or Michael Curtiz's *Angels with Dirty Faces* (1938), mirror the attitude of those battling to stop criminal activities, and there was a growing resentment against the cinema which was held responsible for glorifying the criminals and putting them on a pedestal so that the American youth would identify with the monsters, rather than condemn them. Henry Hill's (Ray Liotta) childhood dream had always been the same:

> As far as I can remember, I always wanted to be a gangster. To me, being a gangster was better than being President of the United States. (GoodFellas by Martin Scorsese, 1990)

Increasing publicity given to gangs resulted in an overall control of marked-out territories which each mob would try and rule in accordance with the tacit agreements made between different "families". Gang wars were common in cities like Chicago and New York, thanks to the availability of the "Tommy Gun". In Richard Thorpe's *Black Hand* (1950), one notes the presence of these *contadini* who control the entire neighbourhood of the city to ensure that all the citizens pay for their protection. There was much at stake for politicians, union leaders and the police force, since anybody could be easily bought off: "don't you know everybody's a crook? Everbody's illegit?" a lesson in morals given by Noodles to his gang in *Once Upon a Time in America*. (Grey,1997:17). The Volstead Act only made it easier for disorganised crime to get better organised. As Jean-Pierre Martin puts it: "la Prohibition universalise la délinquance individuelle mais a pour effet majeur d'offrir un Eldorado au crime organisé [et] le Milieu devient le cinquième pouvoir national." (J-P Martin, 1993: 74-82). Big cities in the east were where all the action was during Prohibition:

> *(Close shot. Headlines of story in newspaper)*
>
> Rico: 'Diamond Pete Montana'. He doesn't have to waste his time on cheap gas stations (...). He's in the Big Town, doin' things in a big way (...) I could do all the things that fellow does. More! When I get in a tight spot, I shoot my way out of it (...) Shoot first, argue afterwards (...) This game ain't for guys that's soft! (...) Yes, I'll show'em. This was our last stand in this burg, Joe. We're pullin' out.
>
> Joe: Where we going?

Rico: *Oh...east...That's it, east! Where things break big!*

(Scenes 5 & 7: Little Caesar*)*

Similarly to Rico, for whom the Big Cities in the east mean money and power, Sergio Leone, a European, looks upon the America of that era through a very personal and affective vision: through writers (Chandler, Dos Passos, Hammett, Hemingway, and Fitzgerald) who were a part of his childhood memory bank. His epic is, by definition, "a masculine universe":

> My America is that of a European attracted to a country of dreams. My standpoint is one of looking at, examining, scrutinising while remaining attracted, involved, frightened, repelled and enchanted. The America of Kennedy and Martin Luther King, of Lucky Luciano and Jimmy Hoffa, racism, industrial waste and energy research, 'No Nukes' and Steinbeck, *Playboy*, Griffith and Spielberg, exploitation and idealism, the West, the war, the musicals, the jazz and the criminals, and an infinity of other violent and explosive contradictions which make it a unique nation. (Mitchell, 1983)

Leone was adamantly against the notion of being a critic or a moralist towards America as he was neither American nor Jewish, and "no more of a gangster than most of my colleagues"! Leone deliberately chose his mob from the Jewish community of the Lower East Side in New York, as the Jewish Mafia were more dangerous. "In reality," as he tells *Time Out* critic Chris Peachment, "the Italians simply exported a load of *contadini* (peasants) and later re-imported the Mafia gangsters. But the Jews were more subtle. They sat behind desks. They made telephone calls. And, as we all know, a telephone call can be more deadly than a gun." (Peachment, 1984: 22). (In Leone's film the telephone becomes the instrument of betrayal: when Noodles is first seen in the opium den, he is jolted out of his drugged state by the piercing unceasing telephone rings. There are thirty four rings over a three minute scene; the rings persist, even when the receiver has been picked up, and also continue when Noodles is dialling the number of the police precinct.).

Leone had cherished the project of shooting *Once Upon a Time in America* for over sixteen years, during which he had already made his name with *Once Upon a Time in the West* (1968). The obsessive idea of obtaining the rights to the book and finding the money to direct the film haunted him to the extent that he even turned down the offer to direct *The Godfather*. *Once Upon a Time in America* is adapted from a book, *The Hoods*, written in 1952, by Harry Grey, a pseudonym for David Aaronson[1]. It is the autobiography of a gangster who had spent a long prison sentence in Sing-Sing. Similarly to Mark Hellinger (*The Roaring Twenties*), Grey had wished to leave some trace after his death. The challenge to sell the rights to Leone was extremely tempting, especially after he had met with the latter. In an interview in *Time Out* (April-May 1984: 151), Leone explained why he wanted to make *Once Upon a Time in America*: his determination to make the film was further boosted by the idea of Time and the way in which an epic of this nature

---

1. In his book, Grey, who was actually called David Aaranson, was nicknamed "Noodles" as he was the one who knew everything and was the thinker of the gang. Leone keeps both names but it is Noodles whom the viewer is familiar with.

could be turned into a tale. As he told critic Brian Case, after the release of the film, in May 1984, he needed to leave behind some legacy of *his* America, its tenements, brothels and speakeasies – all of which were an "operatic experience". Leone, moreover, strongly identified with Grey: for him, both men had lost time – one in prison and the young Leone under fascist censorship. "Neither of us wanted to depart in oblivion. I wanted to mix my own souvenirs and memories with his, and to make a film about my lost time and his, and perhaps we would both find it again in this film." Grey/Aaranson wanted to depict an era which, according to him, had been wrongly mythified by Hollywood and was responsible for idolising the gangster. However, Leone's film adaptation, like Grey's autobiography had a totally opposite effect. Presumably, this results from both narratives which are personal and subjective.

Noodles and his gang of teenage street friends, start off by working for Bugsy, the leader of the Lower East side in New York's Jewish neighbourhood. The very name used by Leone for this vicious thug seems a passing reference to Bugsy Siegel. It transpires that the character of Max was inspired by Meyer Lansky (one of the Luciano trio). Leone kept the main characters in Grey's book, but changed a few names, cut out certain events, and his adaptation results in a totally different "text", which simply cannot be "read" in the same manner as the written account given by Grey. Leone's story time spans from 1923 to 1968, with no linear, chronological order due to the numerous flashbacks and flash forwards: the film begins and ends in 1933. It becomes the viewer's task to put the pieces back into the jigsaw puzzle. Stuart Kaminsky, Leone's close collaborator on the screenplay, divides the time structure into three specific periods: 1923, 1934 and 1968[1]. Leone had specifically indicated to Kaminsky the importance of the fantasy/fairy-tale nature of the story and that of Time as both a theme of the dialogue and an element in the presentation. "It was in [Leone's] view, to be a film dealing with the ephemeral nature of time and human interaction[2]".

In order not to confuse the reader with too many superfluous details, it seems preferable to use Kaminsky's precise and coherent summary from the final version of the script, which the screenwriter entitles *The Tale*[3].

> *Gangsters looking for Noodles Aaranson, a Jewish gangster in New York in 1933, kill Eve, the woman with whom he has been living, beat his friend Moe. Noodles barely escapes from them by hiding in a Chinese opium den. He then flees New York.*
>
> *At this point, we leap forward to 1968 and Noodles' return to New York City. Through various leaps from 1968 to 1933-34 and 1922-24 and back, we discover that Noodles was once the co-leader of a small gang on the Lower East Side. As a child he went to jail for killing another gang leader [Bugsy]. Out of prison, Noodles and his partner Max have a disagreement about which direction to take the gang after the end of Prohibition. Noodles wants to stay*

---

1. Stuart Kaminsky, "*Once Upon a Time in America* as Narrative Model", *American Film Genres*, p. 48
2. *ibid* p. 48
3. *ibid*, p. 48-49

small; Max wants to align with the "syndicate". The gang does a few syndicate jobs, particularly backing a union organizer named Jimmy in his bid to move up union leadership.

When Max appears to go mad and insists that the gang tackle a federal bank, Noodles turns himself and the gang in to the police to keep them from getting killed in what is sure to be a disastrous robbery. However, there is a shootout as the police close in; and all the gang members, except for Noodles, are killed. It is at this point in 1934 that the syndicate comes after Noodles to punish him for his betrayal of the gang.

Noodles' 1968 return to New York is the result of having been lured from his hiding place by a cryptic message. Various events take place that force Noodles to deal with the memory of his old friends and the woman whom he loved and lost.

Near the end of the tale, Noodles discovers that Max was not killed in the shootout, that the entire event had been staged with syndicate help, and that Max, who has summoned Noodles back to New York, is a high-ranking government official [Secretary of Commerce] under congressional investigation. Max's purpose in summoning Noodles is to give his old friend the opportunity to even scores and execute him, since the syndicate and Jimmy have now decided Max must go to prevent scandal. Noodles refuses and, apparently, the mob does kill Max.

The penultimate scene of the film is more than enigmatic. The viewer has to find his own interpretation for Max's death/suicide. Noodles leaves Max's luxurious Long Island Gatsby-like mansion. An enormous garbage truck with two flashing red lights appears from nowhere, and as Noodles is walking away alone in the dark, he sees the back of the truck churning what *may* be Max's body. Some old automobiles, dating back to the 1930s flash past, loaded with party-goers and, similarly to the opening credits sequence, *God Bless America* can be faintly heard in the background. The final scene shows a younger Noodles back in the opium den and the camera freezes on the frame where Noodles' wide, almost cretinous grin continues to fill the screen as the final credits roll.

Technically, one cannot omit two important details. Firstly, the editing process which shows the ingeniously done shifts in time. Of the many scenes worth describing in detail, the following is an interesting example: when Noodles buys a one-way bus ticket to leave New York, he is seen in a long shot facing a wall which is decorated in pastel colours, advertising Coney Island. The centre of this hoarding is meticulously cut by a door which says "entrance", but which, in fact, Noodles uses as an exit. The set clearly shows the time: 1930s. Noodles emerges from the same entrance, in a jump cut, but it is now 1968; the Coney Island board has been replaced by a bright red Big Apple, with the Manhattan buildings in the background. This is the first shot of an old Noodles, who is first seen looking at himself through the mirrored glass pane, with the strains of Lennon/McCartney's *Yesterday* playing in the background.

Secondly, the opening credits sequence produces a completely puzzling effect on the viewer who is sure that s/he has come to see a gangster movie.

The screen is totally black with the credits rolling, line after line, in white: Arnold Milchan presents: A Film by Sergio Leone. The credits continue to roll, without a single sound, until the Art Director's name (Carlo Simi) appears. It is at this point – the screen is still black – that a faint version of *God Bless America* is heard on a crackling radio, followed by distinct footsteps which stop and, in total darkness, someone can be heard trying to switch on a light. The first shot appears: a close up on a woman's hand fiddling with the light switch on the bedside table lamp. The camera zooms on a silver-framed photograph (this is how Noodles is presented). The camera shows a medium shot of the horrified woman who discovers the outline of a man's body made on the bed, with bullet holes. The first gun shot is fired, aimed at the photograph. The film has been criticised for its excessive violence in some scenes, but the opening credits sequence tends to give the opposite effect to the viewer who is totally unsure of the genre at this point, until the shot of the bullet-made outline on the bed. On Leone's part, it can be viewed as a deliberate strategy to confuse the viewer, and perhaps soften the blows in the ensuing scenes.

Where were you, noodles?

Leone wanted to make his film with Time as the main protagonist, but as in many fairy tales, there are numerous unfilled gaps in time. Noodles spent over six years in jail but very little is known of this period, other than him reading the Bible every night and thinking about Deborah, the only person he had loved but who betrayed him, just as Max did. The latter has stolen the money made by the gang, become Deborah's lover and even has a son with her (ironically named David, after Noodles). The idea of time is conveyed very early in the film, when Max and Noodles first meet. Max outdoes Noodles and his friends trying to steal a pocket watch from a drunk. Max's domination of Noodles is clear from the first long shot where Max is perched on top of a cart. Once he is a successful "businessman", he sits on a XVIIth century papal throne which he bought for 800 dollars. His paranoid tendencies and megalomania will not deter him from stopping even once he and his gang have made a million dollars and can utilise the money to finance "legit" ventures. His ambition drives him to the point of madness as he plans to rob the Federal Reserve bank.

Both Max and Noodles are aware that they will soon be "unemployed", due to the repeal of Prohibition. It is a known fact that the prohibition era was responsible for ever-increasing criminal activities. When Noodles is released from jail, he gradually discovers that Max has been organising the gang into big-time business with the police and politicians as accomplices, and the syndicate to back them. The funeral parlour and undertaking venture is a mere cover-up for "the hottest spot in town": Fat Moe's speakeasy, where the best Scotch flows through the water pipes! Noodles, who has been totally cut off from the events, realises that it may be wiser to be part of the affluent class, although he is strongly opposed to Max's arrangement with the Mafia.. After carrying out one of his first major jewellery heists, which, unbeknownst to him, ends in taking Joe, a gangster, "for a ride". Once Joe is brutally murdered, Noodles begins to discover what his friend and partner is really like. His somewhat idealistic view of the business does not involve betrayal or elimination. He angrily tells Max: "today they ask us to get rid of Joe. Tomorrow they ask me to get rid of you? Is that ok with you, cause it's not ok with me." As Adrian Martin notes:

> Betrayal – especially betrayal between brothers, or lifelong buddies – has always been a prime motor of gangster movies. Leone's film superimposes two stories of betrayal, of two very different shades. Noodles betrays Max out of love, out of a desire to save him from himself. (...) In his complete and utter act of misrecognition, Noodles becomes a dupe. (...) In the gangster genre, the theme of betrayal has often found its privileged from in such an eviction: the hero's loss of control over his own story. For Leone this theft of life is made even more bitter-sweet by the fact that it is stage-managed by the hero's veritable 'double' or doppelgänger – his beloved brother, his mirror, his killer.   (A.Martin, 1998: 40,41)

After the fiasco which ends in the killing of his three friends, Noodles spends thirty five years in hiding, wracked with guilt at the thought of having turned his "family"[1] in to the police. Upon his return to New York, he immediately comes back to his old neighbourhood, back to faithful Fat Moe who asks him what Noodles had been doing all these years. The only laconic answer an old, tired, guilt-ridden and embittered Noodles can give: "went to bed early." Another long time span (thirty five years) is totally eclipsed. Nobody will ever know what happened to Noodles during that period. However, events turn out very differently in the case of Max and Deborah. It is only when he comes back to New York, intrigued, as "they" seemed to have found him and want him for another contract, that he begins to piece together each clue which will reveal Max's and Deborah's life. Max has reached the top by becoming a senator, and Deborah, as ambitious as Max, has become a very successful actress. (One wonders whether Leone is hankering after some childhood memory of treasure hunts, especially as Noodles's past is effaced, but it is Noodles who plays the game and only ends up as the loser).

It is a mysterious summons which brings him back to New York, but he cannot escape the memories of his youth, the past begins to catch up with him through beautifully shot flashbacks; an excellent example of which is "innocent" eroticism: Noodles finds the slit in the wall, above the toilet seat, and as he peers through the slit in the store room behind Moe's father's restaurant, the young, lithe body of a narcissistic Deborah is ready to give the performance of a lifetime, knowing Noodles is spying on her[2]. This

---

1. "Family" in the literal sense has absolutely no significance for the four members of the gang, including Cockeye and Patsy. But, as Noodles bitterly tells the latter, "what the hell should [Noodles] go home for" when his mother is weeping, his father continuously praying, and there is no money for electricity, so, he would rather take refuge in "the john", where he can, at least, read in peace. In the scene in the toilet, he picks up a copy of Jack London's *Eden Martin*, carefully hidden on the window sill, and settles down comfortably to enjoy this moment of escapism, further enhanced by a brief zoom on the drawing of a couple in a pastoral setting.
2. During the entire film, the synchronisation between the three distinct musical themes which allow immediate identification of the characters, is the result of a long-time close collaboration between Sergio Leone and composer Ennio Morricone. The musical score is a blend of haunting melodies which, in several scenes, would otherwise make dialogue intrusive and

flashback transports Noodles fifty years in time to a period when everything, from sexual curiosity and experience to "rolling a drunk", or even the gang's first experience of "real business" (recovering crates of booze for bootleggers) was a thrill which would fade away once they had "made it" in the business. Sadly enough, almost all Noodles' flashbacks are linked with death in some form or other: the "fancy cemetery in Riversdale", where the bodies of his three buddies are buried, his old neighbourhood, without a trace of "Jewishness" – unrecognisable – the first image Noodles is confronted with is the unearthing of the Jewish graves in the area. The only remnant of his past is Fat Moe's – now reconverted into an eatery – with the Star of David painted on the glass front, at intervals. (When Moe first receives a phone call from Noodles, who is in the phone booth across the street, the camera films Moe, dumbfounded, standing exactly under one of the Stars of David). Moe and his place are the only two familiar elements in Noodles' life at this point. Noodles seems to have lost all his bearings. Despite various transformations in the setting, Fat Moe's is the only stable location throughout the film.

On his final voyage to recapture the past, a word, an image on the television set at Moe's, trigger off memories of his heyday. Despite the change in identities, the characters are somehow still bound to their past, but it is undoubtedly Noodles who has been scarred. He ends up not only a loser, but the pessimistic end of the film makes the viewer wonder what Noodles still has to live for. In all these flashbacks, a very clear image of the anti-hero comes out in Noodles. He is the atypical gangster as opposed to Max, whose weasel-like features and crafty look immediately reveal him to be *the* boss. Noodles is a dreamer, a romantic, a thinker, a man of few words, and shows an extraordinary sense of loyalty. While Max does not lift a finger in the gang war against Bugsy, Noodles rushes to avenge Dominic, the youngest member of the gang, by stabbing Bugsy to death. Noodles loses his youth, in prison, and his adulthood is wasted away. Max exploits Noodles to the hilt. He had even staged his own "death", with the help of the police, and when Noodles discovers the three corpses of his friends lying on the ground, he cannot recognise Max's because it is so charred; but as Max/Senator Bailey sarcastically tells him, "your eyes were so full of tears that you didn't even see that it wasn't me lying there." Max brings Noodles out of hiding and leaves him "payment for [his] next contract" to pay back Noodles for everything he had taken from him.

The contract

As it was mentioned earlier, Leone's film was not intentionally a gangster movie. The director was much more interested in the psychology of the protagonists, male bonding, betrayal and loss. However, by situating his film at a very specific time in American history, he could not have omitted the reconstruction of historical events without resorting to very minute

---

redundant. The only intra-diegetic piece of music, *Amapola*, by Joseph M. La Calle, both binds and separates Noodles and Deborah. Leone often said that in his films, music was part of the dialogue and was an expression in itself. It must also be stressed that great importance has been given to the role played by the gaze, whether it is interpersonal or in a POV (point of view) shot.

details, thus, bringing out certain authentic characteristics of the era in the film. His meticulous eye was not content with filming in a studio: the restaurant scene where Noodles invites Deborah was filmed on location in a palace hotel in Venice; the Grand Central Station, where Deborah leaves New York for Hollywood was filmed in the Gare du Nord in Paris, to give the "Orient Express" effect. Hence, the atmosphere of the speakeasy, the negotiations held in the plush office behind, the jazz musical hits of the 1930s, the costumes, among other elements. The demise of Prohibition is celebrated in style: a huge chocolate cake in the shape of a coffin ("so long to Prohibition" in icing) is carried by sad-eyed "pallbearers" with four bottles of Cordon Rouge champagne, "decorating" the four corners, each holding a candle, with the accompanying melancholic jazz tune as the coffin is placed on the table. This demise is an ominous warning to the future of the gang, whose lives will also end soon after, due to one of the contracts which Max binds the others to sign.

Since the gang has the protection of the syndicate, they can honour the various important contracts signed with politicians and especially with the Unions leader, Jimmy Conway O'Donnell (Treat Williams)[1], who, despite his initial scruples in being involved with the mob, is helped by Max's gang who grant him the necessary protection so that his workers are no longer threatened by scabs. The latter are forced to get the factories working again, with the cooperation of the chief of Police Aiello, who refers to the scabs as "unemployed workers". Aeillo is backed by a politician, Crowning, whose mob plans to eliminate Jimmy Conway, the "socialist asshole". Aeillo obviously does not refuse the shares which are given to him for his loyal services. Other than various rigged contracts signed with dirty politicians, Max's gang can now also make a cut by the illegal use of the Transport Union funds. Jimmy learns to "cooperate" with the gang, thereby becoming the "hottest newcomer in American unions" which are naturally backed by various politicians. When the gang arrives just in time to save Jimmy from a gruesome death, he maintains his principles in fighting for equality for the workers; as he tells Max, "our fight has nothing to do with liquor, dope and prostitution". Although he is indebted to the gang, he calls them "the plague." Max simply retorts: "Better get used to the idea. This country is still growing up. Certain diseases, it's better to have when you're still young." Jimmy understands soon enough that the gang had managed to achieve more in one night than he could have in two years of talking. Thus, the solution is *compromise* so that, in time, Jimmy can make his way up the political ladder.

When Noodles sees Jimmy on television denying the rumours and allegations directed against his organisation, he realises that Jimmy "Clean Hands" is as crooked as those whom he was fighting against in the 1930s:

> *Our hands have always been and will continue to remain clean.*
> *My entire life I've fought to keep the American labour Movement*
> *clear of any collusion, forced speculation, criminal elements or*

---

1. Leone has kept Jimmy Hoffa's first name as the character was obviously inspired by the leader of the Teamsters. But, is it purely coincidental to find that Martin Scorsese has used the same name, Jimmy Conway, for the big boss of the Mob, played by Robert De Niro in *GoodFellas*?

corrupt politicians. (...) If any guilt at all exists in this situation, it is elsewhere.

Noodles refuses to honour the final contract Max wants him to carry out: "if you've been betrayed by a friend, you hit back. Do it." Max can only accept Noodles as his executioner. Due to a major political scandal in which Max is involved, he is going to face charges and he knows that if Noodles does not kill him, the syndicate, including Jimmy Conway, will eliminate him. The two main witnesses – a politician and a D.A. – who were to have testified against Max, meet with a sudden death within a month. Noodles finds a suitcase in the Grand Central Station locker; it contains "advance payment for [his] next contract".

Noodles will solve the mystery in his final confrontation with Max. He has discovered all the sordid details, and Max admits his guilt for having stolen Noodles' life. "I took everything away from you. I lived in your place," he confesses to Noodles. The latter pretends not to know Max and addresses him as "Mr. Secretary", "Mr. Bailey". His last words are poignant because he realises that he had been framed by the only friend he *thought* he had ever had. The absence of music and dialogue, at certain crucial moments, is significant because the close ups on the two men's faces suffice. Max is in the dominated position for the first time. The last blow he receives from Noodles is when the latter leaves him, through the secret exit, with the final message: "Good night, Mr. Bailey. I hope that the investigation turns out to be nothing. It would be a shame to see a lifetime of work go to waste." His revenge against Max is suave: his calm voice and impassive face make up the mask behind which he controls his innermost feelings. It is a clear gesture of refusal to honour *this* contract. The camera pans and zooms to Max – from a medium shot to the following close up, with the background music, shows a totally "finished" man. The roles are finally reversed. Although Leone's film is a mixture of genres, the classic gangster theme is present: the contract, the money, betrayal and revenge, all of which Max hands to Noodles on a platter, only to see his offer declined.

To conclude, Noodles has failed as a gangster; he is the tragic hero, *the* victim of manipulation and ambition. There is a hint to Hawks' *Scarface* in that both Max and Deborah are alike ("the world is yours"): they stop at nothing to get to the top. But in this long saga of friendship, and betrayal, Leone leaves us with a very open ending: Noodles' wasted life amounts to nothing[1]. Is it not the best way to end the film by taking Noodles back to the opium den in 1933? The closing scene of the film with Noodles settling down and frantically sucking the pipe could be a return to a dream world which is far better than what reality had offered Noodles. It is perhaps a strategy to remind the viewer that s/he is not expected to believe what s/he has been watching for over three hours. The fantasy world of Sergio Leone's America is a magical and haunting moment but filled with bitter-sweet nostalgia. Leone's fairy tale does not have the classical "and they lived

---

1. Noodles' loneliness, in a number of scenes, as an old man is reminiscent of Ethan Hawks riding away at the end of John Ford's *The Searchers*. To pursue the vein in which Leone had thought about his film, a fairy tale, Noodles' fate then becomes somewhat similar to that of Hans Christian Andersen's Little Mermaid: a tragic end for a sacrifice whereby she is abandoned and betrayed.

happily ever after" end. Leone deliberately reverses the situation and this antithetical ending could perhaps be interpreted as a European's vision of the gradual disintegration of the American Dream because, as he says in an interview:

> America is a dream mixed with reality. The most beautiful thing is that in America, without any notice, suddenly, dream becomes reality, reality becomes dream. (Lomenzo, 1984: 21)

Bibliography

BOURGET, Jean-Loup, *Hollywood, la norme et la marge*, Nathan, Paris, 1998

CIMENT, Michel, *Le crime à l'écran. Une histoire de l'Amérique*, Gallimard, Paris, 1992

GREY, Harry, *Once Upon a Time in America*, Bloomsbury Film Classics, London, 1997. (First published in the USA in 1953 as *The Hoods*)

KAMINSKY, Stuart, "*Once Upon a Time in America* as Narrative Model", *American Film Genres*, Nelson Hall, Chicago, 1985

MARTIN, Adrian, *Once Upon a Time in America*, BFI Modern Classics, London, 1998

MARTIN, Jean-Piere, *La vertu par la loi. La Prohibition aux Etats-Unis: 1920-1933*, Editions universitaires de Dijon, 1993

SCORSESE, Martin & PILEGGI, Nicholas, *GoodFellas*, (Screenplay), Faber and Faber, London, 1990

Film Reviews

CASE, Brian, "Brian Case on 'Once Upon a Time in America'", *Time Out*, April-May 1984

LOMENZO, Elaine, "A Fable for Adults", *Film Comment*, July-August 1984

MITCHELL, Tony, "Leone's America. A gangsters' fairy tale with Max and Noodles", *Sight and Sound*, Summer 1983

PEACHMENT, Chris, "The world was yours", *Sight and Sound*, August 1984

Bibliographie sur le crime à l'écran

Pour commencer

- *Sur Hollywood et l'histoire du cinéma*

BOURGET Jean-Loup, *La Norme et la marge*, Nathan, 1999. Déjà un classique.
GOMERY Douglas, *Hollywood, l'âge d'or des studios* (en anglais : BFI, 1986), VF : Cahiers du cinéma, 1987.
NACACHE Jacqueline, *Le Film hollywoodien classique*, Nathan, 1995, Coll. 128. Propose une bonne bibliographie de base.

- *Sur le crime à l'écran*

CIMENT Michel, *Le Crime à l'écran, une histoire de l'Amérique*, Gallimard, 1992. On y trouvera la traduction du chapitre essentiel de Robert WARSHOW : « Le Gangster, héros tragique », p. 140.
MUNBY Jonathan, *Public Enemies, Public Heroes : Screening the Gangster*, Chicago UP, 1999. Indispensable, au cœur de la question.

Autres ouvrages

Les ouvrages consultables à la BIFI, 100, rue du Faubourg Saint Antoine, 75012, métro Ledru Rollin, sont signalés.

- *Sur le cinéma*

Revue Française d'Etudes Américaines : Cinéma américain et théories françaises : images critiques croisées, N° 88, Belin, Mars 2001. Voir, en particulier, Francis BORDAT, « Cinéma et civilisation », p. 44 et la bibliographie sur la théorie du cinéma.
ALLEN R. & GOMERY D., *Faire l'histoire du cinéma, les modèles américains*, Nathan, 1993 (Ed. USA : McGraw, 1985)
BERGMAN Andrew, *We're in the Money, Depression America and its Films*, Harper, New-York, 1972. Essentiel. Sous-estime peut être la capacité de transgression ou de contournement hollywoodienne. BIFI
BAXTER John, *The Gangster Film*, NYC, Barnes, 1970 BIFI
BLACK David, *Law in Film*, Illinois, 1994
BORDE R. & CHAUMETON E., *Panorama du film noir américain*, Minuit, 1955. Repris en poche chez Flammarion. Livre fondateur. BIFI
CAMERON Ian, *The Movie Book of Film Noir*, Studio Vista, 1992 BIFI
CLARENS Carlos, *Crime Movies : from Griffith to The Godfater and Beyond*, Norton, 1980
COPJEC Joan, Ed., *Shades of Noir*, London, 1993, Verso. Recueil d'articles. BIFI
EVERSON William, *The Detective in Film*, New Jersey, 1972, Citadel Press.
GUERIF François, *Le Film noir américain*, Paris, Denoël, 1999. Très utile et particulièrement bien illustré. BIFI
HARDY Phil, *The Aurum Film Encyclopaedia : Gangsters*, London, 1998, Aurum Press. Impressionnant, probablement le plus complet. BIFI
KAPLAN Ann E., Ed., *Women in Film Noir*, London, BFI, 1978. Articles. BIFI
KRUTNIK Frank, *In a Lonely Street : Film Noir, Genre, Masculinity*, NewYork, Routledge, 1991. On consultera l'annexe concernant les films de gangsters, p. 197-208.
McARTHUR Colin, *Underworld USA*, New York, Secker & Warburg, 1972. BIFI
McCABE John, *Cagney*, New York, Knopf, 1997
McCARTY John, *Hollywood Gangland : The Movie's Love Affair with the Mob*, New York, St Martin's, 1993
NAREMORE James, *More than Night*, Berkeley U.C Press, 1998. Articles. BIFI
RAFTER Nicole, *Shots in the Mirror, Crime films and Society*, Oxford, 2000.
ROFFMAN Peter & PURDY Jim, *The Hollywood Social Problem Film*, Bloomington, 1981
ROSOW Eugene, *Born to Lose, the Gangster Film in America*, Oxford UP, 1978
RUTH David, *Inventing the Public Enemy : the Gangster in American Culture, 1918-1934*, Chicago, 1996
SHADOIAN Jack, *Dreams and Deadends : the American Gangster Crime Film* : Cambridge, MIT Press, 1977
SILVER Alain & URBINI James, *Film Noir Reader*, New York, Limelight, 1994. Traduction chez Rivages. Dictionnaire encyclopédique. BIFI.

- *Sur quelques films*

MAST Gerald, Howard Hawks, Storyteller, Oxford, 1982. A propos de Scarface, p. 71-102

On trouvera les scripts de Little Caesar (Ed. Sight and Sound, 2001), Public Enemy (Warner Wisconsin) ou White Heat...(idem). BIFI

W.R. BURNETT : Four Novels, Little Caesar, The Asphalt Jungle, High Sierra, Vanity Row, London, Zomba Books, 1984

Les auteurs

Gregory D. Black is Director of American Studies at the University of Missouri-Kansas and author of *Hollywood Censored* (New York, 1994) and *The Catholic Crusade Against Hollywood, 1945-1975* (New York, 1998). He is co-author of *Hollywood Goes to War* (New York, 1987) and is currently writing a history of the American film industry.

Jean-Éric Branaa est maître de conférences à l'université René Descartes (Paris V). Il a publié *La Constitution américaine et les institutions*, Ellipses, 1999, dans la collection « Les essentiels de civilisation anglo-saxonne ».

Françoise Clary, agrégée, docteur en littérature américaine, est professeur à l'université de Rouen où elle enseigne la littérature et la civilisation américaines. Traductrice littéraire (Chester Himes, Langston Hughes), elle s'est spécialisée dans la littérature américaine du XXe siècle et a publié *L'espoir de vivre*, une étude du roman afro-américain contemporain, Peter Lang, 1988 (Prix de l'Académie des Sciences d'Outre Mer) et *Black American Stories*, Hatier, 1991.

John Dean, maître de conférences à l'université de Versailles, spécialiste de civilisation américaine contemporaine. Auteur de nombreux articles et ouvrages, il a publié entre autres, *American Popular Culture* (1992), *European Readings of American Popular Culture* (1996, avec J-P Gabilliet), *Les Médias et l'information aux Etats-Unis depuis 1945* (1997), *Regards croisés sur New York/New York in the Crosshairs* (2001).

Pierre Floquet, responsable du département de langues, ENSEIRB, Université de Bordeaux I. Doctorat en 1996 sur le langage comique de Tex Avery. Domaines de recherche : cinéma anglo-saxon après 1960 ; cinéma d'animation. Mise en place de rétrospectives / conférences Tex Avery lors du Festival International du Film d'Animation d'Annecy (1998), ainsi qu'à divers festivals en Italie (1998 ; 1999) et Norvège (2001). Publications en 2000 : « L'Eau, la terre, l'air... d'être et la télévision : L'alchimie du discours altmanien dans *Short Cuts* », in *Image et Texte Robert Altman / Raymond Carver Short Cuts*, P U P, Aix-en-P., 2000.

« Y a-t-il un acteur dans le cartoon ? », in *Bulletin du Ciclaho* n° 2, Paris X. « Tex and Tales : Recurring theme and Evolving Style », in *The Japanese Journal of Animation Studies*, 2000, vol 2.

Divina Frau-Meigs, normalienne, agrégée d'anglais, est Professeur à l'université d'Orléans et co-rédactrice en chef de la *Revue Française d'Études Américaines*. Diplômée de l'université de Stanford et de l'Annenberg School for Communications, elle est sociologue des médias, et spécialiste en matière de violence, domaine dans lequel elle a publié de nombreux articles et un ouvrage, *Les écrans de la violence*, en collaboration avec Sophie Jehel (Paris, Economica, 1997). Son autre domaine d'expertise concerne les technologies de la communication visuelle, à propos desquelles elle a publié *Médias et technologies : l'exemple des Etats-Unis*, avec Francis Bordat et John Dean (Paris, Ellipses, 2001), et *Les médiamorphoses américaines* (Paris, Economica, à paraître). Reconnue au niveau international, elle est vice-présidente du European Consortium for Communications Research, et secrétaire-générale adjointe de l'International Association for Media and Communications Research (IAMCR).

C. Matthew Guillen, maître de conférences à l'université de Nantes, Juris Doctor – Faculté de droit, Columbia University, admis au barreau de l'Etat de New York, auteur de nombreux articles apparus dans *La Revue Française d'études américaines*, notamment « Media Type and Content Regulation », « Unanswered Questions in American Bilingual Education Legislation », et « Thomas Pynchon's Social Aesthetics : Politicized Postmodern American Writing », en attente de la publication de deux livres : *Reading America : Law, Literature and Civilization* et *Manuel de droit américain*.

Armand Hage est professeur à l'université de Nouvelle-Calédonie, auteur notamment des articles suivants dans des ouvrages collectifs sous la direction de Serge Dunis : « Le Rêve californien est-il brisé ? », 1996, « Les Etats-Unis et leurs îles du Pacifique », 1999, « La Récupération de l'espace avec le temps, ou Le Retour des Mexicains en

Californie », à paraître. Auteur également des ouvrages : *Le Système judiciaire américain*, Ellipses, 2000, *Le Capitalisme américain*, Ellipses, 2001, *Censure et libertés aux Etats-Unis*, à paraître.

Reynold Humphries est agrégé d'anglais et Professeur d'Etudes Cinématographiques à l'université Charles de Gaulle-Lille III. Il s'intéresse tout particulièrement au film noir et au cinéma d'épouvante.

Pierre Lagayette, Professeur à l'université de Paris IV-Sorbonne, Directeur du Centre de recherches sur « L'Ouest américain et l'Asie/Pacifique anglophone », a publié de nombreux ouvrages sur la civilisation et la littérature américaines, dont *Les Grandes dates de l'histoire américaine* (Hachette 2001), *L'Ouest américain, réalités et mythes* (Ellipses, 1997), *Histoire de la littérature américaine* (Hachette, 2001). *Strategies of Difference in Modern Poetry: Case Studies in Poetic Composition*, (editor) Cranbury, N.J.: Fairleigh Dickinson University Press, 1998.

Gilles Menegaldo, agrégé d'anglais et Docteur ès Lettres, est Professeur à l'université de Poitiers où il dirige le département Arts du Spectacle. Vice-président de la SERCIA, il est membre du comité de rédaction de La Licorne. Nombreuses publications sur la littérature et le cinéma fantastique, Orson Welles et Woody Allen.

Marie-Christine Michaud est maître de conférences à l'université Bretagne-Sud de Lorient où elle enseigne la civilisation américaine. Elle est spécialiste de la communauté italo-américaine. Parmi ses articles en cours de publication : « A la découverte des Amériques – Les correspondances des immigrants italiens au début du siècle », « Frontières identitaires chez les Italo-Américains (1880-1930) », « *A Bronx Tale* et l'image de l'Italien ».

Eithne O'Neill enseigne à l'université de Paris XIII. Elle est l'auteur de *Stephen Frears* (Rivages, Cinéma, 1994), ainsi que le co-auteur de *Lubitsch, ou la Satire romanesque* (Éd. Stock, 1987, avec Jean-Loup Bourget, réédition chez Flammarion, 1990). Elle publie régulièrement dans la revue *Positif*, dont elle est membre du comité de rédaction, et signe des articles sur la littérature et les arts visuels dans *L'Hypothétique Revue*, Rambouillet.

Daniel Peltzman a été maître assistant à l'université de Davis, Californie, où il a enseigné l'histoire des Etats-Unis. Il a soutenu en 1991, à l'université Paris VII, une thèse sur le syndicalisme hollywoodien dans les années quarante. Il a enseigné à l'université Paris X-Nanterre et est actuellement maître de conférences en civilisation américaine à Besançon, université de Franche-Comté.

Zeenat Saleh est maître de conférences d'anglais à l'université de Franche-Comté Besançon. Elle travaille sur le cinéma anglophone depuis 1989 : britannique (Frears, Greenaway et Laughton) et américain (Altman, Scorsese, Disney et Demme). Elle est Secrétaire de la SERCIA (Société d'Etudes et de Recherches sur le Cinéma Anglophone) depuis sa fondation en 1993 et organisatrice du deuxième colloque international de la SERCIA dont elle a préfacé les Actes. Articles à paraître dans *CinémAction*: "La Justice à l'écran" et "Les cinéastes à table". Axes de recherches: intertextualité dans les œuvres de Greenaway et les cinéastes européens ; la femme fatale dans le "néo-noir" hollywoodien.

Dominique Sipière, agrégé d'anglais et Docteur ès Lettres HDR, est Professeur des Universités (Université du Littoral) et Président de la SERCIA (Société d'études et de recherche sur le cinéma anglophone). Il a publié en 1999 le recueil *Récits Policiers au Cinéma*, La Licorne, Poitiers. Récents colloques de la SERCIA : Londres (1998) Urbino, Italie (1999), Bordeaux (2000) et Paris X (Nanterre 2001). Coordination d'un numéro de la *Revue Française d'Etudes Américaines* sur les influences réciproques entre les critiques américaine et française sur le cinéma (n° 88, 2001).

Ruth Vasey is a lecturer in Screen Studies at Flinders University, South Australia. Her book *The World According to Hollywood, 1918-1939* won the Kraszna-Krausz Moving Image Book Award for culture and history in 1999.